Practical Web Inclusion and Accessibility

A Comprehensive Guide to Access Needs

Ashley Firth

Practical Web Inclusion and Accessibility

Ashley Firth
London, UK

ISBN-13 (pbk): 978-1-4842-5451-6   ISBN-13 (electronic): 978-1-4842-5452-3
https://doi.org/10.1007/978-1-4842-5452-3

Managing Director, Apress Media LLC: Welmoed Spahr
Acquisitions Editor: Louise Corrigan
Development Editor: James Markham
Coordinating Editor: Nancy Chen

Cover designed by Pete Miller

Distributed to the book trade worldwide by Springer Science+Business Media New York, 233 Spring Street, 6th Floor, New York, NY 10013. Phone 1-800-SPRINGER, fax (201) 348-4505, e-mail orders-ny@springer-sbm.com, or visit www.springeronline.com. Apress Media, LLC is a California LLC and the sole member (owner) is Springer Science + Business Media Finance Inc (SSBM Finance Inc). SSBM Finance Inc is a **Delaware** corporation.

For information on translations, please e-mail rights@apress.com, or visit http://www.apress.com/rights-permissions.

Apress titles may be purchased in bulk for academic, corporate, or promotional use. eBook versions and licenses are also available for most titles. For more information, reference our Print and eBook Bulk Sales web page at http://www.apress.com/bulk-sales.

Any source code or other supplementary material referenced by the author in this book is available to readers on GitHub via the book's product page, located at www.apress.com/9781484254516. For more detailed information, please visit http://www.apress.com/source-code.

Printed on acid-free paper

For my mum.

Table of Contents

About the Author

Ashley Firth is head of Front-end Development and Accessibility at award-winning energy supplier Octopus Energy. Since the company's formation, he has worked together with customers to understand their needs and use new technology to make an online experience, and energy supplier, that is as inclusive as possible. Ashley and Octopus Energy have won numerous customer and digital experience awards for their products, and their approach to web accessibility has been described as "best in class" by the Royal National Institute of Blind People. Ashley was shortlisted for the 2018 Young Energy Professional of the Year award for customer service, spoke at the Festival of Marketing on the importance of web accessibility, and was part of eConsultancy's first ever Neurodiversity report. He is a published writer for *Web Designer* magazine on accessibility and acts as a consultant to other companies to help them improve their approach to accessibility. Before Octopus Energy, Ashley ran the front-end development team at Digital and CRM agency, Tangent, helping to build sites for clients such as Walkers, Carlsberg, SAP, and the Labour Party, and before that, at experiential start-up, Fishrod Interactive, helping to make interactive installations for WWE, Sky, and Budweiser. You can find him on Twitter and Instagram @MrFirthy.

About the Technical Reviewer

Katherine Joyce is a passionate designer and developer with over 7 years of experience having worked across the financial and government sectors. She creates innovative, intuitive customer experiences and is an advocate of accessible design. As lead UX/UI designer at Alt Labs, she is leading the UX vision and crafting beautiful solutions driven by user needs. In her previous role, she worked as a senior UX/UI designer for Accenture, promoting accessible design in government services and helping automate legacy processes to improve the customer journey. She has also spent over 5 years with AXA Insurance as an application support software developer where she fixed bugs in legacy financial systems, debugged issues with browser compatibility, and suggested improvements to customer facing journeys. She is passionate about advocating accessible design and mentoring those who would like to have a career in design or development.

Acknowledgments

I've always seen this part of a book as similar to the credits of a film, because far more than one person makes something like this a reality and it's important to recognise that. Credits can also be long and cumbersome but, as you can rarely be sure that you'll get the chance to publish a book again, it feels important to give thanks properly.

My first thanks go to Louise Corrigan, Nancy Chen, and James Markham at Apress for their constant support and advice throughout the writing process and for answering my many, many questions. I'd also like to thank my technical reviewer Katherine Joyce for her insight and fantastic suggestions that helped sharpen my words, and the whole team at Apress that gave me a chance to write for them – it's a dream come true.

Secondly to my incredible research and editorial assistant Jackson Howarth. "I couldn't have done it without you" is a cliché but in this instance, it's true. Thank you for engaging in the world of accessibility with such enthusiasm, entertaining every chat and random idea, and for keeping me sane. Time for a celebratory junior spesh.

Next, to some wonderful people within the world of accessibility, who sacrificed their time to allow me to talk to them: My thanks to James Buller, head of the Access Needs team at the Home Office; Áine Jackson, research and policy advisor at the British Deaf Association (now policy advisor at the Ministry of Justice); Merlyn Holkar, research officer at Money and Mental Health; and Robert McDowell, author of Econsultancy's Neurodiversity and Digital Inclusion report.

Then there are those amazing few that, although didn't help me write the book directly, certainly helped me become capable of doing so. This book is dedicated to my mum Tracey, who is the strongest woman I know.

ACKNOWLEDGMENTS

Her level of care in teaching those with learning disabilities, and now her tireless work in fostering, is no doubt what motivates me to apply the same care and inclusiveness to my work.

Next to my brother Hayden for *constantly* reminding me of the power in being silly and taking a break, teaching me to fish, carrying me in Fortnite, and always visiting (even if it's only for the burgers and cookies). His humor makes me laugh when I don't want to laugh, and I'm proud of the man he's become.

My dad Michael is the only person that will go to the snooker with me and be happy about it, which for me is a big deal. He has taught me to be composed and pragmatic and how to destroy stud walling with a large sledgehammer. His ability to reinvent his career helped give me the confidence to do the same.

My stepdad Richard was actually the first person I spoke to about leaving the study of law to pursue coding, and without his calm words and reassurance, I may not have done so. He's been a great teacher when he didn't have to be, and a strong (albeit biased) football companion.

Turbo-thanks go to my wonderful partner Charlotte for her endless support, love, and unbreakable spirit. Her contagious happiness and craziness have pulled me from bad moods more times than I'd care to admit. I'm lucky to have found her, and for all of the above, she has my thanks and my heart.

Octopus Energy has supported me in my pursuit of an inclusive Web ever since it was founded, and it is quite frankly the best place I can think of to work. To everyone in the octo-family, thank you for making it fun, accepting, and inspiring to work there every day. Love and power.

We're not a company that likes to single people out because we achieve as a team, so I hope they forgive me for making a few exceptions on this occasion. Firstly, I'd like to thank Greg Jackson for giving up the 15 minutes of his time that it took to convince me to join Octopus and for the numerous weeks at the start of the company's life he gave me to build accessible standards, simply because I told him it was "the right thing to do." I believe he's the type of leader all modern companies need.

Secondly to my two mentors/enablers:

Pete Miller, who has put his faith in me twice now to do his front-end bidding and has never mentioned in earshot of me that he regrets that. He designed the cover for this book and asked only for Skittles in return. He's one of those awful work friends that becomes your real-life friend without asking. I'm very lucky.

Rebecca Dibb-Simkin has helped me navigate management, business, public speaking, and about a hundred other things. How she does what she does around long train journeys and endless kickboxing injuries is beyond me. She's a truly inspiring woman.

Lastly to my front-end development team, who wholeheartedly uphold (and improve) my initial standards of accessibility and operate as an incredible hive mind. There's never a day when I don't learn something from them, and that's the very best you can ask for in a team.

To wrap this up, it seems wrong not to mention these amazing humans who have helped and supported me in so many ways, but I also know that the acknowledgments can't be longer than the book itself, so as a compromise, I'll just say thank you to Chris, Natalia, Harrison, Ronan, Sarah, Robin (finish your album), Austin, Louise, and Kat – I'm hugely thankful for all of you.

And a small shout-out to my fish, who had to listen to many read-throughs of this book and never once complained.

Introduction

Welcome to the book! Let's start by clearing one thing up – this is not just a book aimed at developers. It is written for anyone involved in the design, build, or maintenance of a site, or for anyone generally interested in understanding an area that so many people are now talking about.

Accessibility guidelines, which we'll get to in a moment, state that even if a page is accessible, but is part of a wider online process or journey that isn't (like the checkout process of a shopping website),[1] then the whole journey fails, including that page. For the same reason, if one person in a team or organisation is considering accessibility in their work but nobody else is, you'll make positive gains, but run the risk of encountering a similar problem.

In fact, if you are working as a part of a large team, many people have argued that the project manager, and not developers or designers, are in the best place to make sure everyone involved is working with accessibility in mind, as they have oversight on the whole project. My point is that the more people are thinking about this issue, the better, and this idea is the crux of why this book isn't written for any one discipline.

As we'll see, due to the growing trend of lawsuits and media coverage, it's also important for project stakeholders to understand the importance and repercussions of exclusionary design. The more people that are aware, the more likely that accessibility will become the norm in a company.

This book is therefore aimed at all levels and disciplines, written simply to allow everyone to explore the avenues of web accessibility, understand it and its importance, and to apply what they've learned to the sites they're involved with. As you'll see, there will be practical examples throughout the chapters to help you, and they're designed for all levels of expertise. For those interested, the code used in each example will be available on Github (Github is an easy-to-use site where you can share code and track changes) at `https://github.com/Apress/practical-web-inclusion-and-accessibility` – each folder will correspond to the chapter it's used in. Alternatively, in each chapter there will also be a link to a website that you can visit that will show that feature in action without you having to touch any code. I'll make these links short, and easy to type, but you can also find links to every practical example in this book at `https://inclusive.guide/examples`.

These chapters will also sometimes include code snippets, but feel free to skip them and keep reading if you're not a developer – I've ensured that you'll still get value out of what I've written. Alongside these examples will be design principles, user and customer experience examples, relevant case studies, and some other expert opinions from people who care about accessibility as much as I do. Equally, you're also free to steal the project code here and implement it in your sites. It's all here for you to use as you'd like, and if you find any of the examples difficult, you can contact me directly using the details in this book.

An explanation of the book format

Over the course of this book I'd like to share with you, on a chapter-by-chapter basis, a wide range of different disabilities and access needs – some you may have heard of (and even designed for) before and some will be less well known. Through understanding the barriers that different people encounter online, we can identify practical ways in which you can alter your site's build, design, and user experience to cater for these users. After discussing specific impairments, we will move on to areas of websites and user journeys that have, or hold the potential to have, an effect on many access needs.

Here is a quick overview of what we'll be looking at:

Blindness (Chapter 2)

Here, we'll explore the role of screen readers and how to optimise them using a range of features, from alt text to ARIA tags. We'll then look at how to make navigating and interacting with content easier for blind users by adjusting layout, structure, and functionality.

Low vision and colour blindness (Chapter 3)

In this chapter, we'll cover several different types of ocular impairment and the impact they have on how users interact with a design. We'll look at how you can avoid pitfalls that exclude those with vision issues, for example, taking some time to cover the importance of avoiding a reliance on colour to convey meaning (using it as a compliment not a crutch), before turning our attention to user preferences that provide catered accessibility.

Motor disabilities (Chapter 4)

Those who navigate the Web using a keyboard-only setup or other special apparatus commonly encounter several major barriers. This chapter will provide an overview of these challenges, as well as some simple design and experience wins that can drastically improve their experience.

Deafness and hard of hearing (Chapter 5)

Audio and video can be a great way to provide different kinds of content, but it can also inadvertently exclude deaf users. This chapter introduces WebVTT: a new technology to help with subtitles and closed captioning. We'll also look at the importance of servicing customers without a telephone, and the empowering world of deaf-friendly language.

Cognitive impairments (Chapter 6)

Cognitive disabilities impact a large percentage of the population and can take many forms. This chapter will look at making the Web more inclusive for those with impaired language, visual, and visual-spatial comprehension, as well as those with inhibited executive function, focus, and memory. We'll look at the importance of language and word choice, the positives (and pitfalls) or using iconography to convey meaning, mastering self-contained actions, and how sites like Reddit have made life easier for those with heightened sensory awareness.

Mental health (Chapter 7)

This subject has seen a massive increase in exposure over the last few years. In this chapter, we will take a comprehensive look into the causes of anxiety online and how to quell them. We also consider disabilities ranging from dementia to schizophrenia, as well as how to reach and support users with mental health issues, both on your site and away from it.

Imagery (Chapter 8)

This chapter is among the biggest "quick wins" you will be able to make using this book. Imagery is a major part of nearly every site, and we'll assess the pros and cons of images, videos, icon fonts, and SVGs, as well as how to make these accessible for sites both old and new.

Communication (Chapter 9)

A website is only part of your user's online journey with you. This chapter explores the importance of using a range of communicative channels, the power of accessible emails, and how you can make communication easier by reducing the amount of necessary interaction.

New technologies (Chapter 10)

There are some fascinating new technologies emerging right now. As the wave of in-home "smart tech" continues to rise, we'll look at some interesting new ways these can be used to solve accessibility problems, how new tech can be accessible even when the user doesn't have an Internet connection, and delve into the fascinating world of artificial intelligence.

Tools and QA (Chapter 11)

Building an accessible site and journey is great, but ensuring it remains accessible is paramount. We'll discuss how to make sure accessibility is considered during the development process, neat approaches to auditing an existing site, and some key tools to test and improve your site with.

Practical examples

As I mentioned, where relevant, I have built a practical example to demonstrate the use of a feature or change to improve accessibility. Storing these on Github allows developers to access and alter the source code of the examples, but every chapter also includes a website link that you can access on your browser – to view the example and understand its purpose. These could even act as useful examples to share with developers and designers in your company to advocate their inclusion in your sites.

Depending on the purpose of your site, some of these examples may not be the perfect fit for you. However, you are welcome to use each and every one, or adapt them for your needs (I encourage you to – it'll make the Web a better place).

Note

1. *Web Content Accessibility Guidelines 2.1 (WCAG),* W3C, (05/06/2018), <https://www.w3.org/TR/ WCAG21/> [accessed 01/03/2019].

CHAPTER 1

The Accessibility Problem

Accessibility is a difficult subject to approach and it's often tough to know where to start. This is why I have decided to write this book. My aim is to help you understand accessibility and build it into your sites, so that together, we can make the Internet the inclusive, empowering place it has the potential to be. To begin with, we'll take a moment to explore the merits of a "disability-driven" approach, and then we'll turn to look at why the timing has never been more important.

Facing accessibility head on

> *The Internet is for everyone – but it won't be until it can be accessed without limitation.*[1]
>
> —Vinton Cerf

Vinton Cerf is recognised as one of the "fathers of the Internet" for his work in co-inventing Internet protocols, a breakthrough that formed the foundation of the Web. He was also instrumental in the creation of the first ever commercial email system. It's fair to say that Internet and email, as we know them, would not exist without him.

© Ashley Firth 2019
A. Firth, *Practical Web Inclusion and Accessibility*,
https://doi.org/10.1007/978-1-4842-5452-3_1

Cerf's work is well documented, but more attention is paid to his accomplishments, and less to the man himself: the fact that he has a hearing disability is often overlooked.

Vint saw, perhaps before anyone, the power that the Web held for creating a platform that was truly inclusive – allowing absolutely anyone, regardless of their disability or needs, to engage with content. At its very origin, commercial email was an assistive device that allowed deaf users to receive messages. In fact, part of Vint's motivation was to allow him to communicate with his wife Sigrid, who is deaf, while he was at work. Some 20 years after Vint helped to develop his email service, Sigrid was using the Web to research cochlear implants that would improve her hearing. After nobody returned her calls (via relay service) to John Hopkins University, "she sent an email to the doctor and got a response the next day."[2] Thanks to Vint, she had an alternate way of communicating, specifically designed with her access needs in mind. Indeed, this piece of inclusive design was so successful that her doctor was now using it too.

Cerf described email to the New York Times as "the great equalizer in that everyone, hearing and deaf, uses the same technology."[3] This is the essence of accessibility. It means removing barriers that might prevent someone from using something, regardless of their access needs (an access need is anything a person requires to communicate, learn, or take part in an activity). Email has become so useful to the world because it caters for different access needs, and the fact that everyone, from Sigrid to her doctor – from me to you – still uses it shows how considering the needs of a diverse range of people helps us design better, more inclusive services.

Unfortunately, if we fast-forward to today, the landscape doesn't quite match Cerf's expectations.

In an interview just 2 years ago, he lamented:

It's a crime that the most versatile device on the planet, the computer, has not adapted well to people who need help, who need assistive technology... It's almost criminal that programmers have not had their feet held to the fire to build interfaces that are accommodating for people with vision problems or hearing problems or motor problems.[4]

His frustration is clear and understandable, especially given his original vision.

The state of accessibility today

Despite the Web's current shortcomings, there are groups that have been working for decades to make it a more accessible place. There are guidelines that outline how sites can be technically accessible, built over several years by the World Wide Web consortium (W3C), who are headed by one of Cerf's former colleagues, Tim Berners Lee – the inventor of the Internet. W3C's purpose is to work together in the development of standards for the Web and Tim clearly shares Vint's ideals:

> *The power of the Web is in its universality. Access by everyone regardless of disability is an essential aspect.*[5]

> —Tim Berners Lee

With this in mind, the group created the Web Content Accessibility Guidelines (WCAG) – a comprehensive list of requirements that when met, improve a site's web accessibility. It has three levels: "A," "AA," and the strictest "AAA," with "AA" being widely considered as an acceptable legal standard. This, at the very least, offers a consistent way to achieve measurable accessibility.

It's a good resource and a great idea; however, there are a few issues. The first is just how big it is. The latest WCAG release (2.1) has a page entitled "Understanding WCAG" which is nearly as long as the update itself.[6] Each point in WCAG is accompanied by a long page to help the reader actually understand the rule, and a separate page describing how to meet the requirement. This can get in the way of understanding and adopting accessibility, as the solutions are almost always too dense to digest.

Another issue is oversight, as WCAG do not enforce these rules themselves. Although (as we shall see) the threat of litigation is growing, the fact is that you can, with a server and a basic understanding of code, publish your own website without anyone or anything stopping you from doing so on the grounds that your content is inaccessible.

There is also the issue of relevancy; prior to last year, the last full version of WCAG (2.0) was released nearly a decade ago.[7] As technology has evolved at a rapid rate, regulation often struggles to keep pace.

And after all of this, you're faced with the final boss: being WCAG compliant doesn't guarantee that you're fully solving access issues. James Buller, head of the access needs team at the British Home Office encountered this when he undertook some research into how users apply for a passport:

> *We did some testing with deaf people. Initially the query was why would you do that, there's no audio involved in the service? But the researchers were soon vindicated... [The subject] was going through the form, and there had been no big problems until she got to the most boring page on the site – the contact page. It asked her to "provide a phone number" and she did, but also wanted to write "I'm deaf please don't call me". In this case, it wouldn't let her submit an answer with both numbers and text in it. When we tested this page against WCAG it passed, but on human terms, it was not accessible because we did not provide her with that option.[8]*

This is why you need to go beyond being compliant and "ticking boxes." You need to be proactive and check where you may well find nothing wrong.

There was, however, something interesting in the latest version of WCAG: a slight change of approach. This new format addresses accessibility from a "disability-driven mindset."[9]

This approach encourages you to imagine a user with a specific access need, the problem they're facing, and then, using the regulation WCAG have created, consider an appropriate solution. Here's an example of one of the new additions, which states that your site should give a user feedback when an action is initiated:

Accountant who is blind and uses a screen reader:

Problem: *I selected a class for the conference, but I can't tell if it got added to my schedule.*

Works well: *When I add a meeting to my calendar, I hear a confirmation.*[10]

It's simple, and it feels like a return to Cerf's idea of designing and developing to address access needs, in the same way he considered deafness while he developed commercial email. This is important, because a few things happen when you consider accessibility in this way.

First, by approaching your site from a perspective other than your own, you learn to make other access needs a part of your everyday thought process. This practice helps you begin to see potential constraints and design for them from the outset, rather than coming back to them once the site has been built. Cerf said that accessibility shouldn't be "pixie dust" that designers and developers sprinkle on as an afterthought – it needs to be consciously considered.[11] This is what makes disability-driven accessibility a practical solution.

You also see that "accessibility" needs are often also in fact "user" needs. By designing for disabilities, you start solving issues for everybody, accounting for requirements you might not have even considered.[12]

This reflects the World Health Organisation's most recent definition of disabilities, referring to a disability not as a "personal attribute" – as they were described in 1980 – but as "context dependent... reflecting the interaction between features of a person's body and features of the society in which he or she lives."[13] Their point was that disabilities happen during interactions between a person and the world around them on a physical and cognitive level, and this plays out regularly on the Web. The needs of the user are not always reflected in the design or function of a page, and these conflicts prevent a person from engaging, or even interacting, with the content of a site.

Using this definition, everyone has access needs, and anyone could develop new ones at any time. You see this everywhere, in interactions with content in a language that isn't your first, with short-term injuries or illnesses, or even when trying to hold a child in one arm and a tablet in the other. As we get older, our eyesight, hearing, dexterity, or mental capacity may well get worse (one of the new examples in WCAG is focused on correct sizes for buttons to cater for elderly users with hand tremors). These all create needs that can be met by accessible features. Video captions, for example, help those with hearing loss, but also those who want to engage with the content without sound in a quiet room.

It is therefore our job, as designers, developers, and anyone involved in building a site, to factor in these cases and create inclusive web experiences that work for the largest number of people possible.

It's not just about which device has market share right now or what a user's browser of choice is. It's about somebody's experiences of their surroundings. It's about whether someone sees a site or hears it. It's about whether they see your design in a hundred colours or several shades. It's about whether they only use a keyboard to navigate everything on their computer.

The increased awareness of accessibility's ethical importance, and the recent updates to guidelines, makes this the perfect time to explore disability-driven accessibility in more depth.

Why is it important now?

As we have seen, the very people who helped create the Internet knew the moral importance of being inclusive on the Web from the start. An inclusive Web should give users the ability to access information, services, and entertainment independently, regardless of how they choose to do so. For this reason, not only does the UN now consider Internet access to be a basic human right, but the United Kingdom Equality Act (2010) states that companies are obliged to ensure that their websites are accessible to users with disabilities; it's not enough to be able to get online – everyone should be able to navigate the Web with ease and feel like sites acknowledge the way they do that. Ethics aside, however, there are a plethora of other practical reasons why now is the right time to start thinking about accessibility.

Accessibility is receiving more mainstream attention than ever before

A big reason why now is a good time to begin considering accessibility is because the world is beginning to understand its importance. In one of the most widespread accessibility-based news story in recent years, in January 2019, multi-platinum singer/songwriter Beyoncé's official website was hit by a class action lawsuit. Violating the 1990 Americans with Disabilities Act, her company was sued to make the site accessible and seek damages for those who have been subject to unlawful discrimination.

The lawsuit contains a lengthy list of access failings, including but not limited to "lack of alt-text on graphics" (which allows screen readers to describe images), "inaccessible drop-down menus" (for keyboard-only or blind users), "lack of navigation links," "lack of adequate prompting and labeling" (for those with cognitive or mental health issues), "denial of keyboard access," "empty links that contain no text," and "the requirement that transactions be performed solely with a mouse."[14]

This may well be the most mainstream case, but Beyoncé is far from the only person to be hit with these allegations. US lawyer Caren Dexter has described an "onslaught of these lawsuits" in recent years, with cases numbering in the "thousands" after a landmark ruling in 2017 brought against American supermarket chain Winn Dixie.[15] The majority of these cases settle early, with remedial action to fix the inaccessible parts of the site always being part of the settlement. What's more, as there are no official US web accessibility guidelines, courts generally recognise WCAG as the standard for determining if a site is accessible.[16] This is the case in many other countries including the United Kingdom and Australia, the latter having officially adopted WCAG as their benchmark test.

How likely is legal action in the United Kingdom?

It is worth noting that the threat of legal action is slightly lower in the United Kingdom, but Britain is moving in the same direction. There have been no landmark rulings yet, but the Royal National Institute of Blind People (RNIB) has brought two cases against companies for inaccessible websites that were settled, and "It has long been anticipated that a higher-profile test case will be launched against a non-compliant website."[17] Legal actions in the United Kingdom that address areas of disability fall under the 2010 Equality Act.

There is a definite pattern that has emerged over the last 2 years with regard to action being taken against inaccessible websites. The end result of the case against Beyoncé's website is almost of little consequence individually – it has already drastically increased awareness over the importance of sites being accessible and the potential ramifications if they aren't.

Now although the prospect of being sued and having to pay fines or take action to remediate an inaccessible website is a reasonably big motivator, it shouldn't be the only reason you consider accessibility.

Competitive advantages

Of course, accessible design has other practical benefits too. You don't always have to be sued in order to make the news for accessibility – there is also the potential to achieve very negative, or positive, press coverage. In May 2018, upgrades to HSBC's online banking experience inadvertently prevented users with blindness and low vision from accessing their bank accounts online. Users complained that what used to be a "simple process has now become unreliable" and forced them to switch to telephone banking which took much longer.[18]

While this was happening, Barclays capitalised and drew attention to their strength in this area. They contacted the BBC and, in the very same article that reported HSBC's failings, were able to demonstrate that Barclays "involves disabled people right from the start, as part of its development and testing process."[19] In this case, Barclays achieved both positive media publicity for being inclusive and also a wave of new customers, all for doing the right thing.

The possibility of financial gain is also clear. At the end of 2016, the BBC reported that retailers could be "missing out on £249bn because many are inaccessible to disabled customers,"[20] and a slice of that sum is certainly not the worst outcome for taking access needs into consideration.

With everyone on the Internet competing for users, as well as making sites easier and more enjoyable to use, some have noticed other benefits. For example, accessible design has been known to make websites rank higher in search engine results.[21] It can also save costs on retrospective redesign: while it is possible to adapt a site to make it accessible (we'll get to this later), it is always cheaper to build accessibility in than having to go back and change it later, especially when there is legal action involved. Then there is the added bonus that accessible sites, being easier to use, typically require less support for users. People with neglected access needs often make up a large part of your audience who will get in touch for help. Minimising barriers means fewer phone calls, shorter queues, and lower costs.

Unfortunately, despite obvious (and mounting) practical benefits, in recent years accessibility has remained an afterthought, or more accurately, it's been considered but not acted upon, often due to time constraints. There is a common belief that the amount of work doesn't properly match the percentage of users it will cater for. This may seem harsh, but in the fast-moving world of campaigns, product releases, and tight deadlines, developers and designers find themselves with a serious time deficit.

Here's an interesting thought though. A campaign that suffers from these constraints will still spend time making a site work in older, outdated browsers and devices to cater to a small portion of the audience that still use them.

As of right now, for every person using Internet Explorer 10 or older in the United Kingdom, there are six people with significant sight loss.[22]

Browser support is easier to handle than ever; we have higher usage in popular modern browsers, and dwindling numbers using the older, unsupported versions of browsers that so frequently cause hours of debugging and support. Microsoft themselves, as of January 2016, only support Internet Explorer version 11 (the last version) and their new browser Edge. So, while we're in the process of limiting support for older technology, why not put that time to better use by turning our attention toward making our sites inclusive?

Why approach accessibility in a disability-driven way?

This book presents a practical approach to accessibility, clearly outlining needs and solutions. It is designed to be both a guide now and a source of future reference for you as you move forward. You can read it from start to finish (which would be lovely), or you can skip to particular chapters if you're currently focusing on a particular access need in your work.

I raise this because cases have often been brought against sites by charities for particular disabilities, or center around particular access needs. As a result, understanding users' specific needs is key to ensuring that you're actually addressing the barriers they face.

It is worth mentioning that just as W3C have said that WCAG "doesn't address the needs of people with all types, degrees, and combinations of disability,"[23] this book cannot cover every single access need either. It does, however, extend what WCAG has covered and allows you to practice noticing accessibility needs by allowing you to become familiar with a range of them. Obviously, if a particular disability, either permanent or temporary, isn't covered here, that doesn't mean that it's not of consequence.[24]

Thankfully though, once you start addressing accessibility from so many different perspectives, you will also begin to notice similarities and consistencies appear when catering for different disabilities – access needs often overlap. For example, providing more time for users on pages where they submit content benefits those with motor disabilities, severe anxiety, or learning difficulties like dyslexia, but for different reasons. By removing one barrier (in this case, a short timer), you empower and include a wide range of users.

The overlap between access needs and disabilities we focus on in this book means that even if a user has a disability we do not cover, many of the proposed solutions will still be relevant. It is also always worth remembering that **access needs are user needs**; accessible design won't just help people with disabilities, it will improve the Web for everyone.

This is where the power of this book truly lies. By the time you finish reading, you will be familiar enough with a range of access needs (and how to cater for them) to always work with them in mind. It's this combination of knowing how to identify barriers and then remove them that will ultimately allow you to provide truly inclusive web experiences.

Notes

1. Vint Cerf, *The Internet is for Everyone,* Speech to
    the Computers, Freedom and Privacy Conference,
    (07/04/1999) <www.itu.int/ITUD/ict/papers/
    witwatersrand/Vint%20Cerf.pdf> [accessed
    01/03/2019] – Original quote edited slightly. "The
    Internet is for everyone – but it won't be until it's in
    every home, in every business, in every school, in
    every town and every country on the Globe, Internet
    can be accessed without limitation, at any time and
    in every language."

2. Vint Cerf, in *Internet Becomes a Lifeline for the Deaf,*
    by Tami Luhbi, New York Times, (12/02/1998),
    <https://archive.nytimes.com/www.nytimes.
    com/library/cyber/week/021398deaf.html>
    [accessed 01/03/2019].

3. ibid.

4. Vint Cerf, in *Internet inventor: Make tech accessibility
    better already,* by Joan Solman, (10/04/2017),
    <www.cnet.com/news/internet-inventor-vint-
    cerf-accessibility-disability-deaf-hearing/>
    [accessed 01/03/2019].

5. Tim Berners-Lee in World Wide Web Consortium
    Launches International Program Office for Web
    Accessibility Initiative, (22/10/1997), <www.w3.org/
    Press/IPO-announce> [accessed 01/03/2019].

6. Understanding WCAG 2.1, W3C, (26/02/2019),
    <www.w3.org/WAI/WCAG21/Understanding/>
    [accessed 01/03/2019].

7. Web Content Accessibility Guidelines (WCAG), W3C, (05/06/2018), <www.w3.org/TR/WCAG21/> [accessed 01/03/2019].

8. James Buller, in interview by Ashley Firth, (26/02/2019).

9. *What's New in WCAG 2.1,* W3C, (2019) <www.w3.org/WAI/standards-guidelines/wcag/new-in-21/> [accessed 01/03/2019].

10. *Web Content Accessibility Guidelines (WCAG),* W3C, (05/06/2018), <www.w3.org/TR/WCAG21/> [accessed 01/03/2019].

11. Vint Cerf, in *Internet inventor: Make tech accessibility better already,* by Joan E. Solsman, (10/04/2017), <www.cnet.com/news/internet-inventor-vint-cerf-accessibility-disability-deaf-hearing/> [accessed 01/03/2019].

12. James Buller, in interview by Ashley Firth, (26/02/2019).

13. Disabilities, World Health Organisation, <www.who.int/topics/disabilities/en/> [accessed 01/03/2019].

14. *Beyoncé's Web site The Focus of an Accessibility Lawsuit,* Bureau of Internet Accessibility, (09/01/2019), <www.boia.org/blog/beyonces-website-the-focus-of-an-accessibility-lawsuit> [Accessed 01/03/2019].

15. Caren Decter, *ADA Web site Accessibility Lawsuits: What Advertisers need to know,* (06/12/2018), <https://advertisinglaw.fkks.com/

post/102f6xu/ada-website-accessibility-
lawsuits-what-advertisers-need-to-know>
[Accessed 01/03/2019].

16. *Disabled access to web sites under UK law,*
     Out-Law, (2011), <www.out-law.com/en/topics/
     tmt--sourcing/e-commerce/disabled-access-to-
     websites-under-uk-law/> [accessed 06/03/2019].

17. ibid.

18. Sally Abrahams & Lee Kumutat, *Blind customers
     locked out by bank web upgrades,* BBC
     News, (06/05/2018), <www.bbc.co.uk/news/
     business-43968736> [Accessed 01/03/2019].

19. ibid.

20. Chris Rourke, *UK Retailers Still Failing to Meet Web
     Accessibility Standards,* Econsultancy, (14/02/2017),
     <https://econsultancy.com/uk-retailers-
     still-failing-to-meet-web-accessibility-
     standards/> [Accessed 01/03/2019] & Gemma-
     Louise Stevenson, *Shops are 'dumb' for ignoring
     disabled customers,* BBC Newsbeat, (21/12/2016),
     <www.bbc.co.uk/newsbeat/article/38370149/
     shops-are-dumb-for-ignoring-disabled-
     customers> [accessed 01/03/2019].

21. Rebecca Sentence, *Why accessibility is key for search
     and visibility,* Search Engine Watch, (25/02/2016),
     <www.searchenginewatch.com/2016/02/25/
     why-accessibility-is-key-for-search-and-
     visibility/> [accessed 01/03/2019].

22. 6 x 1 research data. Over 2 million people in the
     UK have blindness or site loss:

     NHS, *Vision Loss,* <www.nhs.uk/conditions/vision-
     loss/> [accessed 01/03/2019]. UK population as of
     2018 = 66.57 million. 2 million from 66.57 million =
     2.996%. 2.996% of UK population with blindness or
     site loss (2 million used)= 1,994,437.

     Combined percentage of IE 5.5-10 users via
     https://caniuse.com/usage-table = 0.5%. 0.5% of
     UK population using IE 5.5-10 = 332,850. Outcome:
     Nearly 6 times as many people in the UK suffer from
     loss of vision than use IE versions 5.5-10.

23. *Web Content Accessibility Guidelines (WCAG)*, W3C,
     (05/06/2018), <www.w3.org/TR/WCAG21/> [accessed
     01/03/2019].

24. Haydon Pickering, *Apps For All: Coding Accessible
     Web Applications*, Smashing Magazine, <https://
     shop.smashingmagazine.com/products/apps-for-
     all> [accessed 01/03/2019].

CHAPTER 2

Blindness

Around 360,000 people in the United Kingdom are partially sighted or severely sight impaired (legally blind).[1] This, of course, creates a specific set of access needs – blind users must be able to access the Internet without visual information.

When faced with a site that has neglected those access needs, these users encounter barriers. Not only is this exclusion unfair and discriminatory, but it also contributes to loss of independence. It was this particular type of exclusion that formed the basis of the lawsuit against Beyoncé's website and (most likely) of the United Kingdom cases brought by the Royal National Institute of Blind People last year too.[2]

Contrary to common belief, visual impairments need not be a barrier to using the Internet. If websites are well designed, it is easy to include users with sight loss, who can have just as rich an online experience as anyone else. In fact, the Internet is arguably richer for blind users when one considers its empowering potential as a previously untapped source of information, services, social contact, and entertainment.

In this chapter, you will learn about the barriers that people with blindness face when using the Internet and the solutions you can put forward to help remove those barriers. This chapter is also unique when compared to most others in this book, as blindness is the only disability that has one fairly unambiguous technology linked with it – screen readers. If you're able to make your site work effectively with a screen reader, you will empower almost all the blind users that visit your site.

© Ashley Firth 2019
A. Firth, *Practical Web Inclusion and Accessibility*,
https://doi.org/10.1007/978-1-4842-5452-3_2

Screen reader software

In a survey conducted on screen reader users around the world in 2017, nearly 96% experienced blindness or a visual impairment.[3] This shows the captive audience screen readers hold and that they're the best (and only real) means of removing barriers for blind users: designing for blindness currently means designing for screen readers.

First though, a bit of context. Screen readers are pieces of software that "read out" information on a page, either out loud or through a braille display. They have become much more prominent in the last decade, and while once upon a time only costly third-party software was available, there is now free software available for every major operating system. This proliferation of screen-reading technology has been great for users, but also for developers, allowing them to hear a site they may have only ever seen before.

Refreshable braille displays, unfortunately, have remained very expensive, costing thousands of pounds. Recently, however, this has begun to change, and in late 2018, the RNIB began selling a display (the Orbit Reader 2.0) for around £500.[4] This is partly why online braille adoption is so low when compared to audio screen reader use. It's worth noting that braille is, however, incredibly important for blind users' independence: studies suggest that 80% of blind people who are employed can read braille, and braille is still the only way that deafblind users can browse the Internet.[5] The good news though is that if you make your site accessible for screen readers, it requires no extra changes for braille – a refreshable braille display simply presents the content using raised mechanical pins instead of speaking it out loud.

Although different screen readers have different features, they all rely on good web design to work smoothly. In fact, in 2017, when 1,800 screen reader users were asked what would have "the biggest impact on improvements to web accessibility," a whopping 85.3% said "more accessible websites," as opposed to "better adaptive technology."[6]

This clearly shows that users believe that the responsibility lies with designers and developers to take their needs into account when building a website, as opposed to relying on the software to navigate around those mistakes.

So, what can you do?

Perceive, navigate, and interact

There is a wide range of things required to make screen readers more accessible, and we will be categorising them into three key areas:

- **Perceive**. Whether content is accurately displayed to a user

- **Navigate**. Whether a user can effectively move through that content

- **Interact**. Whether a user can freely engage with that content

I've set them out in this order because the process acts as somewhat of a waterfall – to navigate through content, a user must first be able to recognise it, and in order to interact with content, they must first be able to navigate it properly.

Just a quick point to raise before we dive in: our focus on making sites screen reader–friendly means that this chapter will contain quite a few code examples, and is the most technical chapter in the book. Therefore, please don't be alarmed if you can't engage with every suggestion here, or understand all the code – you will still be able to follow the intention behind it, and you won't have to worry about this after this chapter.

As I mentioned in the introduction, this book is designed for a range of disciplines and levels of experience and won't explain anything unnecessary. These code examples will be useful for developers, but I've worked hard to ensure that they complement the points being made, as opposed to complicating them. For those interested, you will be able to find the code for both examples mentioned in this chapter in the "Chapter 2" folder of the Github repository (`https://github.com/Apress/practical-web-inclusion-and-accessibility`). As I've mentioned before though, there will be web links in this chapter too, so you can see the examples in action – you can also find links to all of the practical examples in this book at `https://inclusive.guide/examples`. Either way, these examples help explain each solution, and you can use them in your sites or use them as conversation starters with developers you work with.

Using ARIA

ARIA (Accessible Rich Internet Applications) was a spec, created by W3C, to improve the accessibility of applications by providing extra information to screen readers through code. Screen readers are already quite good at understanding a web page, but adding ARIA roles provides screen reader users with more information, more context, and greater interactivity.

ARIA roles are a good place to start because they allow blind users to identify what part of the website they are on. If they didn't exist, as screen reader users moved through a page, they would hear lots of content with little context. ARIA roles are therefore especially relevant to making sure readers can **perceive** content – the first of our three requisites for screen reader accessibility. To understand how screen reader users perceive the Web, and why ARIA roles are useful, we have to understand a little about how websites work.

Websites are built using a language called HTML that forms the content displayed on a page. These pages are made up of a series of tags – the most common being a `<div>` tag. These represent a division (hence the name) or a section in an HTML document. They act as containers, so that you can group content such as text, lists, and images inside them.

This is an easy format to follow for website building, but the main issue for accessibility is that you don't really know what's in a `<div>` tag until you actually interact with the content; it could be a menu, a footer, a sidebar, or anything else really.

This isn't a big deal if you can see the page, as a language called CSS can be used to transform that same <div> tag visually into all those different features we mentioned previously. CSS stands for Cascading Style Sheets, and it's the code used to style HTML – to customise the visual look and feel of a web page. The problem arises when you hear the site instead. If you were to navigate around a site comprised solely of `<div>` tags, you'd simply hear a screen reader read out the content, without helpfully signposting what part of the page you're on.

ARIA provides some of that helpful signposting.

Now, ARIA is a large topic, and I won't be able to cover all of its uses here. If you're interested to know more after reading this chapter, W3C has a fairly extensive document that goes into more detail.[7] What I will do though is run through some practical instances where the simple addition of ARIA can improve blind users' experiences. You'll therefore be able to see just how easy ARIA attributes are to add and, because the implementation is so consistent, you'll also know how to add others you come across that are relevant to your work.

ARIA is split into two main sections – the first being roles and the second being states and properties. Roles are added to help users understand the purpose and importance of content within a page. They can help identify large, important parts of a page like a navigation menu, provide context for common site features that HTML doesn't understand (like a set of tabs), or alert uses when other content is added to a page (like a modal dialog). States and properties are known collectively as "ARIA attributes" and are used to give information about how pieces of content are related to each other, highlight changes in status, and generally provide more granular information (we will get to this later).

The important benefit of using all of these is their ability to alter how a screen reader recognises a page's content – and give far greater context to the user. Let's start with a simple example – you can add an ARIA role by simply assigning a role attribute to a tag like so:

```
<div role="banner">
```

And just like that, a screen reader will announce this section as a "banner" (the place where you'd store your logo/menu/search bar, etc.) – something HTML previously wouldn't have recognised.

These are known as "Landmark Roles" and once you've added them to page, a lot of screen reader users will use them to navigate, as they can help show where important actions and information will likely be.

Here are a few common roles that you can add to areas of a page in the same way:

- banner – Typically the "header" of your page

- region – A significant part of the site containing content

- main – The primary area of content on your site

- navigation – Used to identify groups or a list of links which are intended to be used for navigation

- contentinfo – Typically the "footer" – containing information such as copyrights and policy documents (such as accessibility statements!)

Adding these five areas to your page could be done in a couple of minutes and instantly provides info that helps a blind user know where they are and what they are interacting with. This is a powerful tool but has to be used carefully – announcing an element as something it isn't could create more confusion than if you'd done nothing at all. For instance, if you stated that an element was a menu and it didn't contain a list of menu items, a screen reader user would be lost.

Applying ARIA attributes

As we mentioned earlier, styling with CSS can be used to create the impression that elements are something they aren't, such as a custom toggle or checkbox for example. This is popular amongst websites because unique, custom site design catches user's attention and makes sites memorable. However, if you do this without applying ARIA attributes, screen readers will only be able to read out the tags that you've used – they won't read the feature out as a checkbox, for example, as they can't comprehend it. What ARIA does is provide a screen reader, and its user, with a way to **perceive** and **interact** with that feature.

Google's new reCAPTCHA verification button is a good example of this. You have probably encountered CAPTCHA before, but just to make sure, they are tests that let websites know that you are, in fact, a real user.[8] Previous versions of CAPTCHA required users to decipher garbled text and were notoriously inaccessible – in a 2017 survey, screen reader users voted CAPTCHA the single most annoying thing on the Web.[9] Google therefore used ARIA to present users with a custom "checkbox," making reCAPTCHA screen reader and keyboard accessible and replacing the need to type up semi-indecipherable text embedded into an image that blind users couldn't see. After this change, they could also offer alternative ways to verify for blind users.

They accomplished this with a <div> tag with a role of checkbox,[10] meaning it can behave like a checkbox from a screen reader's perspective while not actually being one:

```
<div tabindex="0" class="checkbox" role="checkbox" checked
aria-checked="true">
  I'm not a robot
</div>
```

You can't "check" a <div> normally because it isn't a checkbox, but you can "check" a <div> with a role of checkbox on it.

Therefore, if you're creating a design that contains a unique or custom way for a user to input information or a decision such as this, ensure that you have the correct ARIA role to allow *all* users to do that.

Components

Now, a screen reader can understand a custom checkbox, because it inherently knows what a checkbox is, but what about recognising things a screen reader has never heard of? In addition to modifying roles (like turning a "div" into a "menu" for a screen reader user), ARIA can also help identify things that don't exist in HTML at all, like some tabs, or a slider. These are common user interface components (or "widgets") used in sites, and ARIA can help a screen reader user identify them too.

As an example, here is the code for a "slider" – a popular component that allows users to specify a number within a certain range by clicking and dragging a slider. By default, this component has no way of letting a screen reader know what the range is, or what the current value is. We can make it accessible by adding three ARIA attributes like this:

```
<label for="slider">Volume</label>
<input type="range"
  id="slider"
  min="1"
  max="100"
  value="50"
  step="1"
  aria-valuemin="1"
  aria-valuemax="100"
  aria-valuenow="50">
<output for="slider" id="volume">50</output>
```

This may seem a little intense, and understanding the actual code isn't essential, but the attributes make it easy to follow. The `<input>` itself accepts a minimum and maximum value, along with the current value. We simply add the three ARIA roles: `valuemin`, `valuemax`, and `valuenow`. As the user moves the range input, both the native and ARIA values will update automatically. This will give a screen reader user instant feedback on the value they've selected. I've built a practical example that will allow you to hear this in action with your screen reader of choice turned on. You can find it in the "Chapter 2" folder of the Github repository, and you can also check it out live at `https:// inclusive.guide/examples/aria`.

Not only can ARIA roles allow you to expose blind users to the same content that a sighted user sees, they also allow you to optimise that content for those users. We will now look at some other ways you can do that, by providing more context, clearly outlining actions, and even removing content that could otherwise detract from the core information on a page.

aria-live

Firstly, you can use ARIA to provide up-to-date information with the aria-live attribute. It can be added to tags that you know will contain content that will change, perhaps based on certain actions, that a user should be notified about. This role will inform assistive technology as soon as its contents change.

You often see messages like this appear as alerts at the top of a page, to let users know that an action has succeeded or failed.

```
<div aria-live="assertive">
  <span>Status: Uploading</span>
</div>
```

However, a blind user may have moved past that part of the page, and they'll be unaware of the status change, as will the screen reader. With this tag in place though, a screen reader will interrupt the content a user is listening to in order to inform them of the change.

It's important not to overuse this tag, as it could lead to a very disjointed experience riddled with interruptions. It's also key to avoid applying aria-live to large areas of content and reserving it for small, specific, and important page changes. When added correctly though, it can provide a user with invaluable contextual information.

aria-label

ARIA labels provide features with context and are especially useful for explaining what a button, for example, will do. Knowing what will happen after an action is taken is hugely beneficial to users. Here, we accomplish this by adding a simple description to an otherwise vague button action using aria-label:

```
<button aria-label="Submit information and move to next
page">Submit form</button>
```

aria-hidden

Sometimes it can be just as important to hide content as it is to label or annotate it. Aria-hidden is really handy for hiding components that are on a page for purely visual purposes, such as decorative images and presentational icons. It also helps with text related to that content, so people using screen readers don't have to spend time listening to it needlessly:

```
<p aria-hidden="true">This content is hidden from screen
readers.</p>
```

It's important to ensure that this content provides absolutely no important information for users using assistive technology before hiding it, as a screen reader will then make no attempt whatsoever to read it out.

Support

Every role in ARIA is generally well supported across modern browsers, and when they aren't, they don't pose any harm to a website's layout – they're simply ignored. This means that, when added correctly, they take only a few moments to implement and have no downside.

HTML5 implicit mapping

As we covered, a `<div>` tag could mean anything to a screen reader unless additional context is provided. ARIA roles are good for bridging some of these accessibility issues, but they don't solve the underlying confusion caused by HTML. However, the latest version of HTML helped with this issue a little. HTML5 introduced "named" tags with predefined meanings. These allow developers to use tags like `<header>` and `<nav>` to represent areas of their site when before they had to use `<div>` and an ARIA role. These new tags help screen reader users understand the layout of a website and mean your site can handle part of your accessibility challenge for you.

Take the following example of a `<div>` with ARIA added to tell screen readers that it's a menu:

```
<div role="navigation" title="Main menu">
```

HTML5 allows you to replace this with

```
<nav>
```

and assistive technology is able to determine the type of content you are displaying in the same way.

Earlier in the chapter, we saw a list of ARIA roles and their meanings. Using HTML5, you could replace the need for those particular examples by using the following tags instead of a `<div>`:

banner – `<header>`

region – `<section>`

main – `<main>`

navigation – `<nav>`

contentinfo – `<footer>`

I highly suggest looking through the ARIA spec online to explore all the possible additions you can make.[11]

Heading structure

Users with visual impairments use headings both to understand what is on a page (**perceive**) but also where they are on a page and to move around it (**navigate**). Recent studies show that 67.5% of screen reader users prefer to navigate by headings when they are looking for information on a lengthy page.[12]

To make this as easy as possible, all headings on a web page should have a hierarchy, beginning with the most important header and moving down, and a site's code should reflect that. In HTML, the most important title is an `<h1>` (heading level 1) tag. This is usually the title of the page as it's the single most useful piece of information. These numbered heading tags can go all the way down to `<h6>`, and you should drop down to a lower heading tag each time you display subheadings inside a section that already has a heading.

Figure 2-1 provides an example of a typical heading structure.

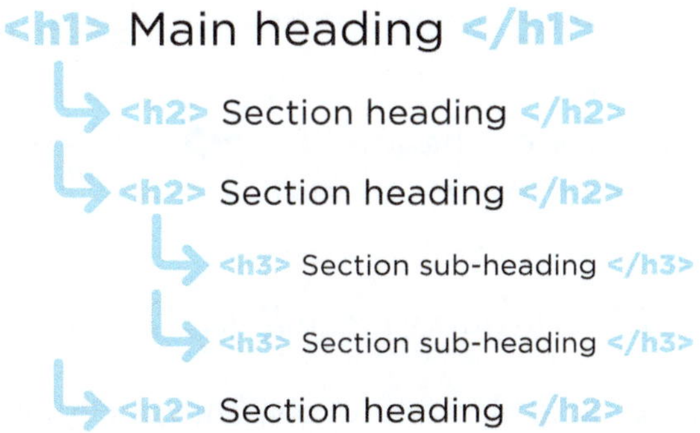

Figure 2-1. *A diagram of how the heading hierarchy on a web page should work*

As you can see, not every heading requires subheadings, but it's important that every heading with an equal or higher rank start a new section, and that headings with a lower rank start new subsections that are part of that higher-ranked section.

You can use as many or as few of these as you like, but they *must* start with an <h1> and should always be used in order.[13] This is because heading tags denote importance to screen readers, and disordered headers may well confuse a user about what content relates to what section. Proper heading structure also benefits the SEO of your page (how well your site performs with search engines).

Styling headers

With this in mind, it's important that you use these heading tags to display page headings, rather than using other tags and relying on where you position them to infer meaning. For instance, if you're adding a title above some text, it needs to be in a heading tag followed by text as seen in Figure 2-2.

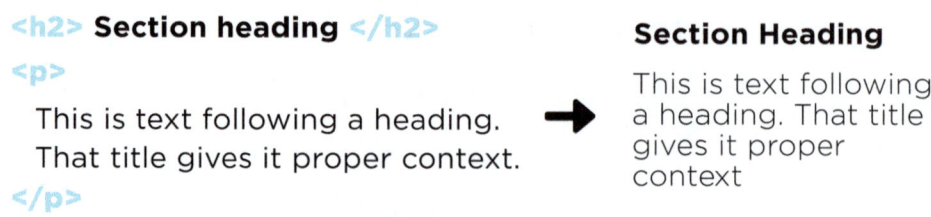

Figure 2-2. *An HTML heading tag, followed by a paragraph tag*

This both displays the hierarchy of content visually and provides the distinction between the title and the paragraph correctly to a screen reader. However, if an incorrect tag is used, but it's placed in the same spot a title would go and styled to look like one, like in Figure 2-3, this can cause problems.

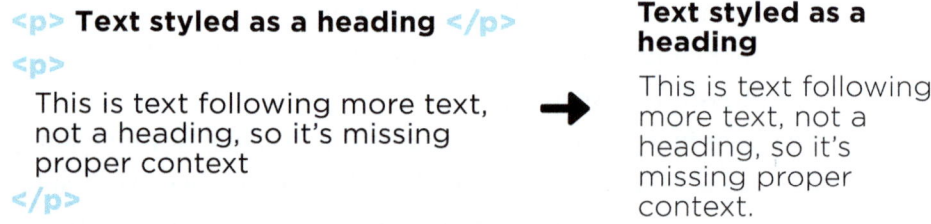

Figure 2-3. *A paragraph tag acting as a heading, followed by another paragraph tag*

It displays the same visually on a web page but, for screen readers, there is no difference between this "styled" heading and any other piece of text – it would just read the fake "heading" out as text without explaining that it's the heading of the whole section. The result is a potential lack of context for those listening to the page. Using the wrong tag also inhibits proper navigation for those that like to move around a page by its headings – the screen reader won't recognise it as a header and so the content could be completely skipped over.

aria-labelledby

A header can also help provide a good signpost for a piece of content larger than itself. Earlier we discussed how landmark roles can help screen readers understand the role and purpose of a web page's main areas.

Using `aria-labelledby`, we can improve this further by tying the tag with its title, like so:

```
<section aria-labelledby="goldfish-header">
  <h2 id="goldfish-header">Everything you need to know about
  goldfish</h2>
  <p>More content here</p>
</section>
```

The result is that when it reaches the section, a screen reader software will now read out something along the lines of

"Section. Everything you need to know about goldfish"

which provides a lot more context for users who wish to navigate quickly in this way.

Semantic markup

validity is a good first step towards accessibility

—W3C[14]

The same people that created WCAG also encourage (and allow you to check) if you've written your HTML correctly. Errors such as unclosed tags and incorrectly ordered heading tags can result in the page being displayed in strange and unexpected ways. These errors won't be consistent either, as different browsers behave in different ways, so valid code helps create a consistent experience for all of your users.

31

There are many online checkers that allow you to submit a pages URL, or upload a file directly, and it will return any validation errors and warnings that it finds – W3C also provide one themselves![15]

Testing heading structure

You can check this easily using a heading map generator. When run on a page, this generates a tree based on the headings on your page (similar to the visual example I displayed earlier), and highlights any that are out of place or have been skipped entirely. Here is an example (Figure 2-4), based on the "ARIA roles and headings" practical example available to you on Github (which you can view at `https://inclusive.guide/examples/aria`):

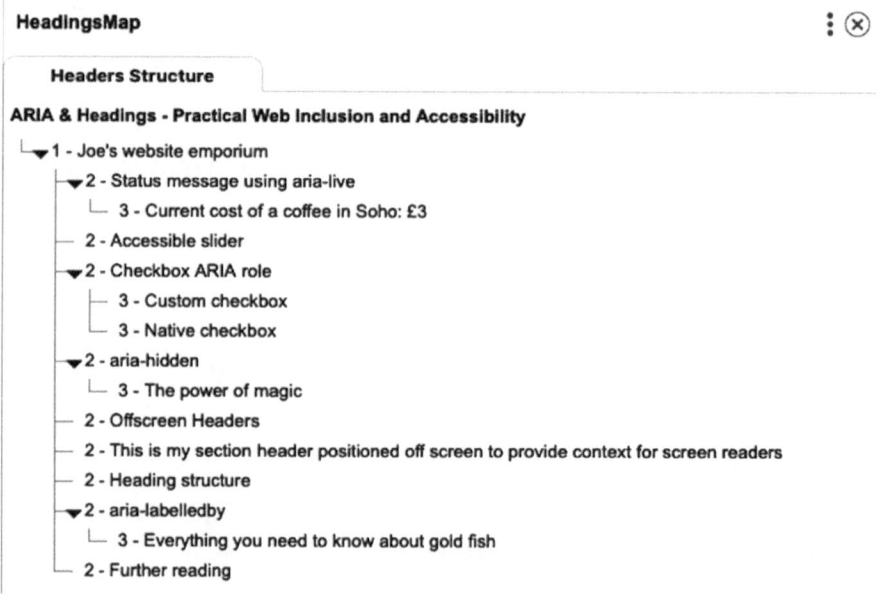

Figure 2-4. *An example of a web page's heading structure, visualised as a heading map with a tree-like layout*

Off-screen headers

After you've tested the heading structure of your website, you may have found that certain sections lack context as they don't have (and in many cases, don't need) a header. From a design perspective, it's OK to have areas where contextual information is inferred visually through the content around it rather than explicitly stated, but you *will* need to add explicit context for screen readers.

To achieve this, you can create a header that is visually hidden with a "class" but will still show up on a screen reader. This preserves the useful signposting that allows screen readers to **navigate** a page as we've covered, without impacting a page's design.

To do this, you first create the title with a regular heading and a class you can reference in your styles:

```
<h2 class="screenreader-only">This is my title</h2>
```

Then you add the following styles to position the header off of the page. This means that the title will never be seen visually, but will be read out by a screen reader in the position you've placed it on your page:

```
.screenreader-only {
    clip-path: inset(100%);
    clip: rect(1px 1px 1px 1px); /* IE 6/7 */
    clip: rect(1px, 1px, 1px, 1px);
    height: 1px;
    overflow: hidden;
    position: absolute;
    white-space: nowrap; /* added line */
    width: 1px;
}
```

This isn't always necessary, but some sections accidentally end up without headings because sighted users can recognise the wider meaning of a piece of content without the need for consistent headers. A designer may also omit a header because they make that same visual connection between content and context that other sighted users do, without realising the consequences for blind users. For screen reader users though, these headers are always necessary.

Note   If you use a popular framework in your website such as Bootstrap, they often have utility classes such as this built in, allowing content for only screen readers and allowing only assistive devices to focus on it. It's always worth checking the documentation of your framework of choice before adding your own, as these projects are actively maintained and so adapt as the Web changes.

Linear layouts

Understanding how screen reader users **navigate** often requires sighted users to use their imaginations. Blind users typically don't navigate with a mouse, so they generally move through a page in one direction – as it is read out – from the beginning to the end.

How users navigate

Navigation is dictated by the various ways in which users typically engage with the content of a page. You can have a screen reader simply read the content of a page to you how as it finds it, which is handy for long-form text and articles. Users can adjust something called "verbosity" which is speech feedback that gives information about where they are in a page and describes features like tables that might help build up a mental picture. Screen reader users can also choose whether content is read out a line, word, or letter at a time – which is useful as people might need to hear the same thing several times over.[16]

Users, however, hardly ever move through an entire page in order. Think about how you typically navigate a page. You don't normally engage with every single piece of content from the top to the bottom. Instead, we're always trying to extract key information, like links or actions, that give you an indication of what point the page is making or what is being asked of you.

Screen reader users are no different. They typically use the "Tab" key to move between the content of a page. As we saw earlier, they can also navigate by content type, such as headings, links, and actions. It's worth noting that one of screen reader users' biggest complaints are "keyboard traps" – tabbing into part of a page that you then can't get out of. This is covered in Chapter 4 (Motor Disabilities), so if you want to learn more, head over there.

Interestingly, users with refreshable braille displays navigate pages in much the same way that other screen readers do, and so the same design solutions apply. They can use little "rocker switches" above each refreshable braille character to send the cursor to a specific space on the page.

Ultimately, navigation preference varies from user to user, but all methods require that the layout – the order of the page – makes sense.

What is a linear layout?

You can get a very literal understanding of what order a page is read out by a screen reader in by removing the styles from a page and seeing what you're left with. For instance, in Figure 2-5 is the same site with and without CSS styles applied to it.

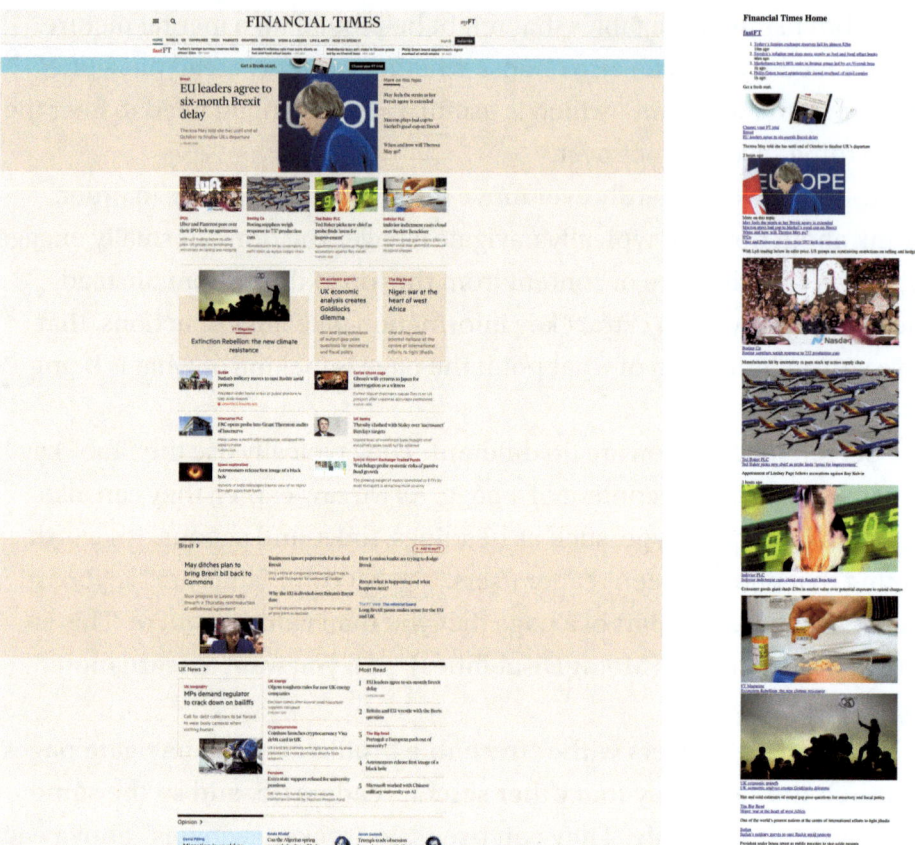

Figure 2-5. *A comparison of a web page's layout, first with CSS applied and then without*

The picture on the right shows the content a screen reader user would experience. When you navigate this way, you begin to realise the order in which content is read out can often differ from how it appears visually. CSS makes it possible to create intricate layouts and designs in order to make a web page more attractive to its audience, but taking this idea too far can end up excluding certain users.

Before any styling takes place, marked-up content should follow a simple, linear layout. However, it's possible to unintentionally lose this logical flow through styling, and you wouldn't know unless you were a screen reader or keyboard-only user. Try removing the styles from a page on your site. Does it still make sense? Can you discern the sections from one another? Can you identify the core actions you're asking your users to perform? It's key that this still makes sense.

You need to avoid the assumption that it's obvious that two pieces of content are related or that one follows another, simply because they are close to one another visually. Content must be read out in an order that makes sense.

Mobile devices

Interestingly, a more linear layout can be especially useful for mobile screen reader users.[17] A survey by WebAIM shows that 88% of screen reader users also used screen readers with their touch-screen mobiles.[18] There are a series of gestures that mobile screen reader users employ to navigate a page instead of tabbing: for example, flicking two fingers down the screen to hear content on the page read out from the beginning, a single tap to bring a button or link into focus, and a double tap to activate a button or link. Notably, rather than listening to the page in order, one command involves tracing one finger around the screen, either top to bottom or side to side, to explore the interface, hearing the screen reader speak what's under your finger.[19]

This last point shows that the physical placement of content on the screen can be just as important as it is for sighted users – related content should be placed close together on the page. Similarly, having a linear order that you can scan down with one finger works well.[20]

With mobile use now typically on par with, or exceeding, desktop use, it's just as important to consider accessibility for mobile sites too.[21] Indeed, designers are starting to think about it before anything else.

"Mobile first," as the name suggests, means that designers start designing a website for mobile devices which have more restrictions in terms of screen size and then expand its features to cater for a tablet or desktop version – this is visualised in Figure 2-6, where the site's content is stacked on a smaller mobile device and the layout then adjusts to make use of the increased screen space on a desktop. It has become a prominent layout strategy for designers, as it forces you to decide what the most important pieces of information on your page are and to lay them out in a way that works well on a small screen. This lack of screen real estate actually allows all users to focus on one piece of content at a time, rather than having to digest a complicated layout.

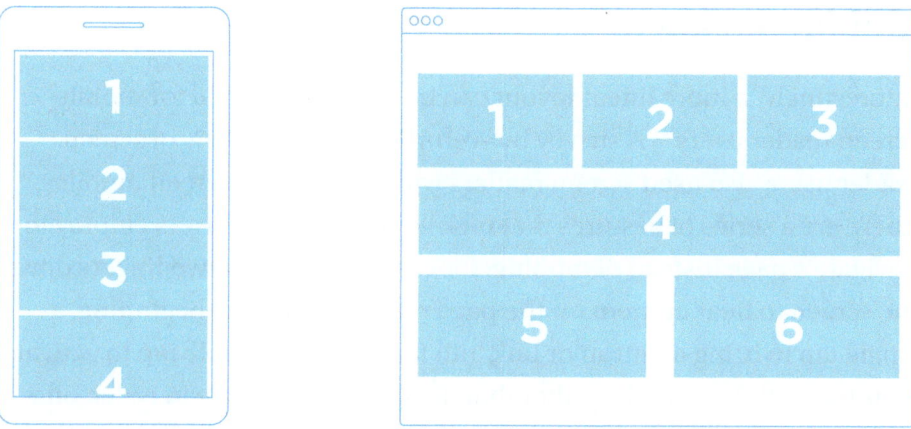

Figure 2-6. *A representation of a linear, mobile-first design: a layout that stacks on a mobile device in the correct order and a more complicated layout on a bigger desktop screen*

This is another good example of how designing for accessibility can help all users: creating an unambiguous layout that is capable of adapting to all screen sizes will ensure everybody avoids confusion.

"Skip to main content" link

As the name suggests, the "Skip to main content" link allows screen reader users to skip past common, repetitive content (usually a header and/or menu) so they can get straight to a page's unique content. This is a great little tool – helping users **navigate** a page and **interact** with the content more easily. Over half of screen reader users regularly use the "skip to main content" feature,[22] and they have the added benefit of helping people with motor disabilities navigate using a keyboard too.

Most web users are unaware of these links because they are usually only obvious when you need them – they are hidden visually but suddenly appear when you tab to them. If you're interested, try heading to some sites you use frequently and hitting "tab" once you arrive. In many examples, you'll see a previously hidden link appear from nowhere and offer to send you down to the unique content by pressing "Enter". For those listening to a web page using a screen reader, it will be the very first item they hear.

Sites usually have a common menu or header at the start of every page, so not having a skip to content link can leave screen reader users listening to the same content again and again or having to skip through elements and guess where a page's unique content starts. In cases where a navigation element contains many sub-menus and items, a user could be waiting for minutes at a time while the screen reader runs through them all.

Instead, you can make a simple link to bypass all that common content in three easy steps (you can skip these steps and head to the practical example I've built for you if you'd prefer – available in the "Chapter 2" folder of the Github repository, or live at `https://inclusive.guide/examples/skip-to-content`):

1) Add your new link as the first piece of content inside your page's body and have that link point to a section containing your page's main content:

```
<a class="skip-to-content" href="#content">Skip to main
content</a>
...
<main id="content">
    ...
</main>
```

Notice that in the figure above, the link is navigating to "#content". Links that begin with a hash symbol allow you to navigate to part of the same page with a matching ID – in this case, a `<main>` tag with the ID of "content".

2) Now the link exists, we want to hide it visually. We achieve this by positioning the link off the screen – the same technique we used for off-screen headers:

```
.skip-to-content {
    position: absolute;
    top: -400px;
}
```

At this point, only screen readers will be presented with the option to use the link as it's completely hidden visually.

3) Optimising for keyboard-only users

To finish off the link, we need to make a small addition for those only using a keyboard to navigate. We style the link so that when you 'focus' on it (the state that occurs when you "tab" onto content), it will reappear on the page ready to be used:

```
.skip-to-content:focus {
    position: relative;
    top: 0;
}
```

That's all there is to it.

As with all practical examples in this book, I've created a working example for those who would like to insert it directly into their site, or use it as a proposal or conversation starter. As I mentioned earlier, it's available in the "Chapter 2" folder of the Github repository, or you can view it at `https://inclusive.guide/examples/skip-to-content`. For this example, I've created two pages with the same menu: one has a "skip to main content" link and one doesn't. I'd recommend opening the page without the link first, and using a screen reader to listen to the page. You'll quickly discover just how long it takes to get to the main content. Then, try out the page with the feature above, and see how one link and the push of a button can save you trouble and time!

Link placement

The 'Skip to main content' link is usually placed in the top left-hand corner of a web page as that is the first thing a keyboard or screen reader would engage with. It's important to make the link or its focus style obvious, because it could well be missed by sighted motor-impaired users; they're forced to tab through common content anyway (we'll discuss focus styles in more depth in Chapter 4).

Alt tags

Alt tags are a property that you'll hear about several times throughout this book, because they are useful to so many users. They are added to images in order to help users understand what they are unable to **perceive** or

interact with, particularly if they they have low or no vision and they're using a screen reader. This is a simple but fundamental point. If you display imagery, or in any way rely on imagery to convey meaning, you need to provide what's called "alt" text, which is text that a screen reader can read out for those who can't see the image itself. Take this banner as an example:

```
<img src="images/stock-graph.jpg" alt="A graph about stonks"/>
```

Now this example provides a small piece of information about the image, but if you went on to speak in detail about information held in the image without providing better alt text, screen reader users would still end up quite confused.

This is a common trap that people working on a site can fall into – you may not actually *notice* the mistake because providing *any* alt text will satisfy the WCAG rules, but what you've added doesn't always help explain the image. As we've talked about, you sometimes need to go beyond a WCAG rule and think about what's actually going to help a user.

With this in mind, here is a further improvement:

```
<img src="images/stock-graph.jpg" alt="A graph showing the steady increase in stock price for Apple over the last 5 years"/>
```

Now we've ensured that the text actually describes what is in the image, rather than a simple declaration of what it is.

A lack of alt text was a consistent problem on Beyoncé's website in the lawsuit brought against her company, and is particularly important on e-commerce sites – if the user can't see an image of the product on sale, they need it properly described.

Context

Alt text is always worth auditing and checking, and it requires a slight shift in thinking. This is because content creators will often place relevant images next to text. They will then sometimes accidentally make no direct reference to that image's contents in the text while simultaneously relying on that image to help explain the meaning of those words.

Take this example:

"The shaft is one of the longest in recorded history, and can move back and forth at impressive speeds."

What do you think this is talking about? There are a few obvious answers, but none that I'd commit to print. This text refers to an image, but without an alt tag specified, a blind user would have none of that important context (they may even think that they've stumbled onto a different site unintentionally).

This particular example is actually talking about the elevators in the Empire State building.

Even if you're dealing with existing content, alternative descriptions are incredibly easy to add - just one attribute and some text. This is also possible if you're maintaining an existing site with a content management system, such as WordPress, because there's usually a field to add a description when you upload or edit an image.

A quick note about alt text in relation to the ARIA roles that we covered earlier: if you've added `aria-hidden="true"` to an image, it would be contradictory to then add alt text. This is because decorative images must be coded in a way that can be ignored by assistive technology, and the accepted method is to actually leave the alt text blank in order to not cause confusion.

The good news is that sites are now encouraging content creators to think about alt tags more frequently. You may have noticed that when you upload an image to Instagram, it now offers you the ability to provide proper alt text by tapping the corner of the image, thereby making its core media more accessible. Facebook have followed suit and have even developed an algorithm to try and describe what's in an image if a user doesn't provide alt text.[23] With large social networks placing an emphasis on this, it's more likely than ever to become commonplace on all websites. Don't get caught out!

The lang attribute

In order to **interact** with content, blind users have to be able to understand what language is being read out. This may sound obvious, but the relevant attribute is often forgotten. The lang (language) attribute is used to specify the language that the text on the page is written in. For example, in order to explain that the following text is written in English, we would set the lang tag to "en" – this is because the tag accepts the ISO language code for the language you're representing (you could actually extend it to "en-gb" to represent British English):

```
<html lang="en">
    <body>
        ...
        <p>This content is written in English and, thanks to
        the language tag, a screen reader knows this!</p>
    </body>
</html>
```

This feature is consistently overlooked because it makes no immediate visual difference to a web page when it is added – it doesn't change the language of your text. However, for a browser, setting the lang of a page will ensure it offers to translate the content if it doesn't match the user's specified language. This prevents both blind and sighted users from having to try and read content written in a language they don't understand.

If a piece of text is purposefully written in a different language to the rest of your page, you can simply specify a different language for that section using the same attribute. Here is a piece of French writing inside of our English page, marked up so a screen reader user will understand when they reach it:

```
<html lang="en">
    <body>
        ...
        <p>This content is written in English and, thanks to
        the language tag, a screen reader knows this!</p>
        ...
        <p lang="fr">J'ai des petites jambes comme un
        pingouin!</p>
    </body>
</html>
```

In this example, setting the extra lang attribute allows a screen reader to provide correct pronunciation and accent for the English text and then switch language profile to French – rather than attempting to read French with English pronunciation (like me in my French lessons at school). It's an incredibly simple thing to add, but a big win for users.

Forms

Whatever the purpose of your website or app, you're likely to be using at least one form, whether for gathering information, sign-ups, or carrying out a transaction. A badly designed form can have a huge impact on the experience of every user and cause particular problems for people with accessibility needs.

In a highly competitive online market, an inability to receive customer information through a screen reader, and/or by using solely a keyboard, could result in a loss of traffic, and business to competitors.

As Chris Moore describes in the blog series "accessibility and me":

> *Some of the other barriers I face are unlabelled form elements or items that can't be reached without a mouse. It is very frustrating when you start a transaction like online shopping and you are not sure what needs to be entered into a form field or you are unable to activate the button to checkout. Situations like that force me to close the window and then find a more accessible competitor.*[24]

Forms are a key place where users abandon user journeys, and an easy, accessible form will increase conversion rates. This should be more than enough to convince someone that testing this user journey for accessibility issues is a worthwhile endeavor – showing colleagues that certain users can't actually *make it* through a form on your site is usually a big wake-up call.

One of the issues here is something called `tabindex`, which is a simple attribute that can tell a page that it should be possible for a user to focus on, and interact with, a feature via the "Tab" key. We will focus on this more thoroughly in Chapter 4 (Motor Disabilities), so if you're experiencing real problems with this, I would recommend consulting there.

Proper labelling/identification

As you may have noticed from Chris Moore's comments, he also mentions "unlabelled form elements." Users should be able to understand what a form field is asking for through a screen reader; otherwise, they'd be left simply guessing what they should input.

A "lack of adequate prompting and labeling" prevented users on Beyoncé's website from accessing the "goods and services" on the site – purchasing merchandise in this instance.

If you don't properly label form elements, a screen reader will try and guess what is required to prevent confusion. It will go and look for text to the left and above form fields, to see if nearby text might help indicate what the form field is for. However, the screen reader is only guessing and might associate the wrong form field with the wrong information. Most commonly, a label for a form element *has* been provided, but there has been no coded connection to make this obvious to blind users – it's purely visual.

The solution here lies in something called the for attribute, which pairs a form field with a label to describe it. It does this by adding a value on a label that matches up to the id attribute of a form element to create a connection, like so:

```
<form>
  <label for="first_name">Enter your first name</label>
  <input type="text" id="first_name">
</form>
```

This is one of the many examples where improving accessibility improves all user's online experience - knowing exactly what each form field needs you to enter prevents a lot of annoyed users!

Large click areas

An added bonus is that when the for attribute is properly set, a user can then click on the label to interact with the form field as well as the field itself. This larger hit area is easier to interact with. Take Figure 2-7 for example: If the label is linked to the checkbox correctly, a user would be able to check or uncheck it by clicking, tapping, or tabbing on the text as well as the checkbox itself:

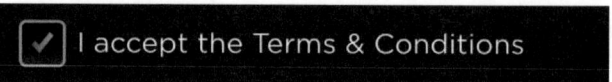

Figure 2-7. *A ticked checkbox, next to a label saying, "I accept the Terms & Conditions"*

This helps those with low vision, or even people with hand tremors, use form elements by preventing the need to be precise in their actions.

Displaying error messages at the top of a page

You may have experienced a scenario like this before: you fill out a form, hit submit, only to find that you stay on the page and nothing seems to have changed. You then investigate the page to find that there is an error message displayed somewhere else on the page that you didn't expect and weren't navigated to. Now imagine this scenario but without being able to see the screen. Here, screen reader users are left to try and find out what happened by searching around. This, again, will often drive users elsewhere.

Luckily the solution can be found in something we've already covered – ARIA. By creating a section with either the aria-live attribute set to "assertive," or the role attribute set to "alert," you can populate that section with a status message for the form that is read out to the user as soon as something changes (e.g., which inputs have errors and why). The section's position on the page doesn't matter, only the attribute, which means that you can position it wherever you would like visually without negative accessibility effects. You can also provide both positive and/ or negative feedback in the same place ("Form submitted successfully" vs. "there was a problem submitting your form") and the user will hear it immediately.

Conclusion

Hopefully the areas we have covered here will have helped you to understand how blind users interact with a web page. At the end of each chapter, I will encourage you to do one thing: try the solutions out for yourself. As I mentioned in the introduction to this chapter, blindness is unique among the disabilities we will cover in this book because there is one main tool that most blind users use to engage with a website, and a version of that tool is available on every major operating system for free. This makes engaging with technology and interacting with the Web the way a blind user does, very easy to achieve. Indeed, 77.8% of screen reader users see free or low-cost screen readers as viable alternatives to commercial screen readers, which shows the high level of usage these free versions have. We'll cover a range of different screen readers in the chapter on Tools and QA (Chapter 11).

Testing a screen reader can be a shock at first. It's a completely new way of navigating the Web and requires complete concentration (when you only receive audio information, distractions like phone calls can cause you to completely lose your place). Despite this, I encourage you to put yourself in the same position as your users – perhaps seek some screen reader training or spend bit of time with a screen reader user. At the very least, you should go to some of the sites that you use most regularly and see how screen reader-friendly they are.

The secret here is little and often. The more you practice specific screen reader shortcuts and gestures, the less daunting they become to test. Through practice, you should also understand some of the main barriers that screen reader users encounter, and how to make sure that they can **perceive**, **navigate**, and **interact** with everything on your site. We certainly haven't covered every corner and caveat of the topic, but you've now had your first taste of approaching web content from a different perspective and engaged with the challenges that it can bring. Even though you might not know every solution, you should be able to start spotting problems, and think independently about what you can do to help empower, and include blind users.

Notes

1. *Blindness and Vision Loss,* National Health Service, (2019) <www.nhs.uk/conditions/vision-loss/> [accessed 10/04/2019].

2. *Disabled access to web sites under UK law*, Out-Law, (2011), <www.out-law.com/en/topics/tmt--sourcing/e-commerce/disabled-access-to-websites-under-uk-law/> [accessed 06/03/2019].

3. WebAim, *Screen Reader User Survey #7,* (21/12/2017), <https://webaim.org/projects/screenreadersurvey7/> [accessed 07/04/2019].

4. Royal National Institute of Blind People, *Introducing the Orbit Reader 2.0,* (27/09/2018), <www.rnib.org.uk/orbit-reader-20> [accessed 10/04/2019].

5. Al Thompkins, *Decline in Braille Use 'Threatens Literacy'*, Poynter, (10/01/2010), <www.poynter.org/reporting-editing/2010/decline-in-braille-use-threatens-literacy/> [accessed 10/04/2019].

6. WebAim, *Screen Reader User Survey #7,* (21/12/2017), <https://webaim.org/projects/screenreadersurvey7/> [accessed 07/04/2019].

7. W3C, *Using ARIA,* (27/09/2018), <www.w3.org/TR/using-aria/> [accessed 07/04/2019].

8. Derek Featherstone, *The accessibility of Google's No CAPTCHA*, Simply Accessible, (04/12/2014) <http://simplyaccessible.com/article/googles-no-captcha/> [accessed 07/04/2019].

9. WebAim, *Screen Reader User Survey #7*, (21/12/2017), <https://webaim.org/projects/screenreadersurvey7/> [accessed 07/04/2019].

10. Derek Featherstone, *The accessibility of Google's No CAPTCHA*, Simply Accessible, (04/12/2014) <http://simplyaccessible.com/article/googles-no-captcha/> [accessed 07/04/2019].

11. W3C, *Accessible Rich Internet Applications (WAI-ARIA) 1.1,* (14/12/2017), <www.w3c.org/TR/wai-aria-1.1/> [accessed 07/04/2019].

12. WebAim, *Screen Reader User Survey #7*, (21/12/2017), <https://webaim.org/projects/screenreadersurvey7/> [accessed 07/04/2019].

13. There are actually a few specific situations where leading with a heading tag below an <h1> is acceptable. For example, for three column layouts, it is possible to have a <h2> heading before the main content's <h1> tag if the main content is in the center column.

14. W3C, *Validity and Accessibility,* (01/07/2005) <www.w3.org/WAI/GL/2005/06/validity-accessibility.html> [accessed 12/04/2019].

15. W3C, Markup Validation Service, (2013), <https://validator.w3.org/> [accessed 12/04/2019].

16.   DeafAction, *Guide to Accessible Information,*(08/2014) <www.deafaction.org.uk/wp-content/uploads/2014/08/Guide-to-Accessible-Information.pdf> [accessed 12/04/2019].

17.   Ed Horsford, *Research with blind users on mobile devices,* (09/06/2016), <https://accessibility.blog.gov.uk/2016/06/09/research-with-blind-users-on-mobile-devices/> [accessed 12/04/2019].

18.   WebAim, *Screen Reader User Survey #7,* (21/12/2017), <https://webaim.org/projects/screenreadersurvey7/> [accessed 07/04/2019].

19.   Ed Horsford, *Research with blind users on mobile devices,* (09/06/2016), <https://accessibility.blog.gov.uk/2016/06/09/research-with-blind-users-on-mobile-devices/> [accessed 12/04/2019].

20.   ibid.

21.   Statcounter, *Desktop vs Mobile vs Tablet Market Share Worldwide,* (July 2019), <https://gs.statcounter.com/platform-market-share/desktop-mobile-tablet> [accessed 12/04/2019].

22.   Whenever they're available 15.8% ∗ Often 16.4% ∗ Sometimes 27.8% ∗ Seldom ∗ 21.6% ∗ Never 18.4% ∗ WebAim, *Screen Reader User Survey #7,* (21/12/2017), <https://webaim.org/projects/screenreadersurvey7/> [accessed 07/04/2019].

23.   Shaomei Wu, Jeffrey Wieland, Omid Farivar, Julie
       Schiller, *Automatic Alt-text*, (02/2017)
       `<https://research.fb.com/wpcontent/`
       `uploads/2017/02/aat_cscw2017_camera_`
       `ready_20161031-2.pdf>` [accessed 12/04/2019].

24.   Chris Moore, *Accessibility and me: Chris Moore*,
       (01/07/2016) `<https://accessibility.blog.gov.`
       `uk/2016/07/01/accessibility-and-me-chris-`
       `moore/>` [accessed 12/04/2019].

CHAPTER 3

Low Vision and Colour Blindness

Recently, there has been a lot of work on accessibility for blind users, but the vast majority of users with sight-based access needs actually have other forms of visual impairment. The World Health Organisation (WHO) estimates that there are 39 million people living with blindness in the world, but 246 million people with low vision (86% of all visual impairments).[1] In the United Kingdom, the NHS estimates that 300,000 people have severe sight loss, while 2 million experience low vision.[2] These figures account for visual impairments that interfere with a person's ability to perform everyday activities.[3]

The figures are so large because there are many different variants of low vision with many different causes. In this chapter, we will continue with our functional, disability-driven approach – focusing on visually impaired users' various access needs, the barriers they face, and what you can do to help them.

It's important to consider that not everyone sees in the same way. A famous example of this was "the dress," shown in Figure 3-1, an argument that gripped the Internet a couple of years ago.

© Ashley Firth 2019
A. Firth, *Practical Web Inclusion and Accessibility*,
https://doi.org/10.1007/978-1-4842-5452-3_3

Figure 3-1. *A photograph of "the dress" – an image that became a viral Internet sensation when viewers disagreed over whether it was coloured blue and black or white and gold*

This image prompted endless debates online and caused members of the scientific community to investigate the photo for fresh insights into colour vision. Now, the confusion wasn't caused by a form of visual impairment, but it did turn mainstream attention toward the idea that people can view the same image in different ways. It gave many people (myself included) who saw the dress as yellow and gold a direct insight into what it's like to view content differently to the way it appears to others (it was eventually decided that the dress was black and blue).[4]

This chapter will draw attention to five main areas of visual impairment that you should keep in mind.

- **Clarity**. Many users experience problems with "visual acuity" which means they have foggy, blurred, or unclear vision.

- **Field of vision**. Many users experience impairments that restrict certain parts of their field of view (e.g., glaucoma leads to peripheral vision loss and macular degeneration leads to central vision loss).

- **Light sensitivity**. Users with conditions such as albinism can experience "photophobia" and find it extremely difficult to work with bright screens and bright content.

- **Impaired contrast sensitivity**. Those with diabetic retinopathy, or again glaucoma for example, have problems perceiving low contrast.

- **Perceiving Colour**. People with various types of colour blindness, for example, often have no problem with visual acuity or their field of vision but can miss out when designs rely on colour to convey meaning.

In order to cater for these impairments effectively, there are two main approaches, or major themes that underpin this chapter. First, we'll look at how to provide a strong accessible foundation for all users with low vision. Starting with magnification, we'll see that there are a plethora of design choices that will, for example, make text clearer, contrast better, and features less colour-dependent for these users. This, in turn, will also help ensure a base level of accessibility for everyone else.

The second thing you can do to dramatically improve accessibility – our second theme – is to allow a degree of customisation. Because there are so many types and combinations of visual impairment, sometimes there is simply not a one-size-fits-all solution for users. Low vision is one of the rare areas of accessibility where fixing one barrier can actually create another for a different user. The solution, as we shall see, is to facilitate a degree of customisation.

Magnification

Magnification is used to increase the size of content, either by zooming in on an entire page or into a particular area. This feature is available in all major browsers, but specialist software can extend this functionality to other areas of computer use.

This has become a common part of many visually impaired users' setup because they have different needs to most other people, and having some control over how a website appears to you can be incredibly useful. Being able to "zoom" – choosing how large the features of a website appear – is a great example. Zooming in can be helpful for those with visual acuity problems (blurry vision) from conditions like cataracts and diabetic retinopathy, and zooming out can help users with glaucoma – which causes a loss of peripheral vision, sometimes described as being like "looking through a straw." Without zooming, content will appear at sizes many can't engage with. These barriers can similarly impact those who suffer from migraines, and can also affect you more as you get older. Again, addressing these barriers will therefore empower a lot of other users. There are, however, also some issues that can occur when using magnification that do need to be solved.

Horizontal scrolling

When users increase the size of content and it doesn't adjust to fit the size of the screen, that content spills over the side of the screen's viewport, forcing a user to scroll horizontally to read text, in addition to the usual vertical movement.

> *it is frustrating when content on web pages does not reflow when I increase the font size or reduce the window width...I'll often give up reading rather than excessively scrolling my zoomed view back and forth.*[5]

This is by far the biggest barrier associated with "nonresponsive websites" (websites that don't adapt to the size of the screen, even when magnified).

Tracking

Horizontal scrolling interferes with "tracking" – our ability to follow lines of text, including getting from the end of one line to the beginning of the next. This dictates how quickly and freely we can read content, and having a page that fails to adapt to larger content affects tracking ability immensely, as accessibility consultant Molly Watt (who has a visual impairment) explains:

> *If a website layout is spread out horizontally and I cannot zoom, it becomes extremely exhausting to scroll across and back and forth every line to read one paragraph. I often give up with this.*[6]

The discomfort described here happens when magnification interferes with tracking, and it can impact all of us.

Text overflow

Horizontal scrolling is arduous, but not being able to do it at all is even worse. When users choose to zoom, some pages can even cut off text altogether. This happens when sites use CSS to intentionally prevent horizontal scrolling. If the property `overflow-x: hidden;` has been applied, this tells the page to hide any content that may be outside of the screen's viewport on the X-axis, making it physically impossible to scroll horizontally. This is typically used when a page's layout contains a piece of content that is accidentally bigger than the screen width, creating a permanent horizontal scrollbar that is visible to the user. Applying this overflow rule hides that scrollbar but renders the content inaccessible to those using magnification. If you use, or find, this rule in your site, I would recommend removing it and fixing the underlying layout issue instead.

Testing zoom

To check whether this happens on your site, try using your browser to increase the zoom to 200% (Cmd + on Mac, Ctrl + on Windows). This is what WCAG deems as the acceptable *minimum* you should allow your users to zoom to in order to be AA compliant. What you will (hopefully) see is your content made twice as large, with headings and text resizing accordingly. The page layout may have shifted around a little, but the content should all still be on the page. If it is, then hooray! This site is using at least one aspect of responsive web design.

Responsive web design

Responsive web design is an approach that aims to move past previous design limitations, forcing pages to adapt to users' browsing choices – as opposed to users adapting to them instead. This type of flexibility eliminates the horizontal scrolling issue by delivering "fluid" web page layouts, rather than a static layout with one defined size. By making your website responsive, it also allows a page's content to adapt to the screen size of any device. You can achieve this through settings sizes as percentages of a page rather than explicitly setting sizes for content that could end up being too big when zoom is increased. You could also use "breakpoints" to size content and alter layouts but only at certain screen sizes, or you could simply not apply sizing at all. Content would then adapt to fill the space by default. This provides optimal viewing across a wide range of devices – it adapts as neatly to a mobile or tablet as it would on a desktop. You may have seen the layout of a page change, with content "stacking" or "reflowing" to adjust to the limited space, when you resize a screen or view a site on a mobile device. If your site isn't responsive, however, the layout won't adapt to different screen sizes or users who zoom to make content bigger.

Both of the issues raised above are solved by responsive web design. Having a "fluid" width prevents users having to resort to **horizontal scrolling** and, when correctly coded, the same fluidity applies to text. This allows users to adjust their zoom and create both a comfortable line length and number of characters per line while leaving **tracking** unaffected.

This approach helps cater for nearly every access need that we'll cover in this book in one way or another, and nowadays you'd be hard pressed to find a good enough reason for a newly built site not to be "responsive." However, responsive web design is still less common than you may think. In 2015, Akamai found that only 12% of the top 10,000 sites on the Web (based on traffic) were responsive, with that figure dropping to 10.5% for the top 100.[7]

Now the rate of mobile adoption has undoubtedly impacted this figure in recent years, but it tells us that responsive web design is still not implemented as a standard. Given the benefits it holds for all users (especially those with low vision), and the focus this area has received since WCAG 2.0 (ensuring minimum zoom levels and that content can be read on a small mobile device), making sure your website is responsive is well worth the time. From a usability point of view, it also creates a far better experience compared to an unresponsive, static website.

Preventing zoom

There was a dangerous notion going round a few years ago that said: if you had a responsive design, it was perfectly OK to prevent users from being able to zoom on that page.[8] I mean why not? You've gone to the trouble of adapting your site for all screen sizes after all, and its inclusion would avoid horizontal scrolling. This unfortunately meant that many sites went on to implement responsive web design but also to block all zooming with the following tag:

```
<meta name="viewport" content="width=device-width,
initial-scale=1.0, minimum-scale=1.0, maximum-scale=1.0,
user-scalable=no">
```

This is the embodiment of the two themes we discussed at the start of the chapter, and why allowing custom magnification is still important even after you've implemented accessible features: making your site responsive provides a good level of accessibility that will help users with a range of barriers, but it in no way guarantees that you've solved all access problems for every person. You must still allow users a degree of control over their experience on your site – in this case, the option to zoom.

For this reason, if you spot this tag in any site that you work on, I'd recommend removing it; you simply can't guess what users want to do, and they may be viewing your site on a device that you've never tested. If you use the following version of the <meta> tag, you'll ensure that zooming on your site is possible:

```
<meta name="viewport" content="width=device-width,
initial-scale=1">
```

It's time we stop disabling a very useful feature by default. Nobody can be *that* confident their layout works for everyone.

Point of regard

There are a handful of other things you can do to help users once they have zoomed in. The "point of regard" or "focus area" is the area of a screen that a user is focusing on. If a user has low vision and needs to zoom in order to view content, that point of regard becomes focused on a much smaller area. If an action then alters that point of regard again, but only temporarily, it can cause the user to lose their place and become confused and frustrated.

A good example of this is content that only appears when you hover over a certain area. Imagine you were zoomed in and hovered over an acronym to view it's meaning. If the popup that appeared was bigger than the view you currently have (due to zooming), you would then have to scroll to read the new content. However, because the content only appears on hover, as you scroll, the mouse will cease to hover over the acronym and so the content disappears. Another example would be trying to fill in a form where the question is on the very left, the input field is beneath, and the submit button is far right – when "zoomed in," the user will struggle to locate the button.

To combat this, you could show content to the user with a click, tap, or toggle rather than by hovering. These states require an action to dismiss them as well as initiate them, so the user will be able to scroll to view content without it disappearing as their focus shifts.

Navigation

Given the wide range of visual impairments, the ways in which people with low vision navigate a site are incredibly varied.[9] Nevertheless, there are a few things you can do to make navigation easier for a large portion of users, especially people with impaired visual acuity, who have opted to use large text and so have room for little else in their field of view. Once again, these solutions help remove barriers in another area of accessibility – they are very similar to those we suggested in the last chapter to help blind users navigate mobile sites (see Chapter 2). Responsive web design allows content to adapt to a smaller screen size, but this reordering could accidentally isolate some content. You should place related information close together and features in consistent positions to ensure that finding and understanding them is easy. In most cases, it is best if you also make sure that the following is true:

- Feedback is in close proximity to the user's visual focus (i.e., form validation next to the form itself rather than, for instance, at the top of a page).

- Dialog boxes and pop-up messages appear within the users point of regard (close to where the user opens them from).

- Users are informed of new information that may be outside of their view — such as a new browser tab opening in the background or an alert message in response to an action.

Accessible text

We've seen how adaptive content can help low-vision users to read text more easily, but there is a lot more you can do to help. Firstly, a sensible base font size can help remove the need for constant magnification and relieve a source of ongoing pain for users. To do so, we first need to learn about the "pixel."

A pixel is a unit of measurement, created specifically to be used on the Web. Although there are many different measurement options available in CSS, pixels became popular because they offer a degree of consistency. Rather than trying to deal with inches, centimeters, points, and picas that people had used before the Web on the same page, people began using pixels as standard. The W3C described it as the "magic" unit when it was released, because users could treat one pixel in code as one pixel on a screen.[10]

Everyone knew what size things would be, and that size would be the same in every browser your website was viewed in. Figure 3-2 shows a title, sized using pixels, that will display as 16px in size regardless of where you viewed it.

This is a 16px title
Size: 16px

Figure 3-2. *A 16px title, created using pixels*

And so everyone began to use pixels, for everything.

Relative units

However, even when W3C introduced the pixel, they didn't recommend using it for text. Instead, they recommended using "rem" or "em." These are "ephemeral units," whose sizes are relative to the default font size of the device or browser that content is viewed on. For example, 1 "em" is equal to 100% of that default font size, so if you have a browser with a base font size set to 16 pixels, then 1 em = 16 pixels. Then 2 em would be 32 pixels, as its 200% of the sizing, and so forth. By doing this, you could ensure that your text size was, at the very least, a reflection of what the software or hardware a user was using had decided was appropriate.

This point is really important. Most modern desktop browsers now have the same default base font size of 16 pixels (about the same size as text printed in a book – accounting for reading distance),[11] which would be the "root" size that "em's" would take into account. That 16px is not true of every device though. A good example is the Amazon Kindle, which has a much higher base font size than a browser because it makes content easier to interact with on the smaller screen.

Now, the base font size of devices and browsers being set in pixels is OK – it's websites that need to ensure that they're setting sizes relative to that root size, rather than their own explicit pixel values.

Let's use our title example to show the difference. Here are two titles, one using pixels and the other using "em's," where the user's default font size is set to 16 pixels:

```
.pixel {
    font-size: 16px;
}

.em {
    font-size: 1em;
}
```

In Figure 3-3, they happen to be the same size. However, if the user decided to increase their base font size to 20px to make content easier for them to read, based on the same code as previously mentioned, then it would be different as shown in Figure 3-4.

User's default font size: 16px

This is a 16px title
Size: 16px

This is a 1em title
Size: 16px

Figure 3-3. *Two titles both sized at 16 pixels, one created in pixels and the other using relative units (em's)*

User's default font size: 20px

This is a 16px title
Size: 16px

This is a 1em title
Size: 20px

Figure 3-4. *A title sized at 16 pixels that hasn't scaled with an increase in a user's font settings, and a title now sized at 20 pixels using em's that has*

The "em" sizing has factored in the user's preference and altered its size, but the pixel layout was completely unaffected by the user's choice.

Stop using pixels

Because pixels have absolute size, they don't scale in response to user preferences. Setting text in pixels means that it will ignore any type of user preference set on the device or browser. If the user's browser has a default font size of 16px and you set your text to 14px, it will display as 14px. If the user's mobile device has a default font size of 18px, it will still display as 14px. If the user has chosen to increase the default size text on that device to 20px, it will *still* display as 14px. Using pixels ignores all of it.

Again, this has to do with customisation:

> *Some people need larger text in order to perceive letters. Although increasing size is most common, some people with tunnel vision and good visual acuity may prefer smaller letters so they can see more words at a time.*[12]

Either way, using pixels for text sizing would clobber every change they attempt to make through their device settings, leaving them to resort to the more manual task of zooming or just leaving your site altogether. WCAG states that users should be able to "change the text size (font size) of all text, without zooming the entire interface."[13] If you're setting all of your font sizes in pixels, you're not catering for this user need.

Screen sizes

> *"Now that hardware is changing and pixel densities are growing, pixels are struggling to find relevance as the stable unit they once were."*[14]

There is also the problem of pixels being referred to as the "magic" unit. People were told to think of one pixel in code as one on the screen, and although this may have been true decades ago, screens have advanced significantly, and pixels have not. The truth is:

Pixels in CSS are *not* equivalent to real screen-sized pixels anymore.

There is now a much wider variety of devices, resolutions, and display ratios available. The idea put forward to simplify things has done the opposite. As such, you'll see devices with high pixel density display something two or three times smaller than it's shown on a browser because explicitly defined sizes simply will not adapt to larger screen resolutions.

The result of these two points is this: pixels don't make too much sense as a stable unit of measurement on the Web anymore. Despite this, pixels continue to be very commonly used for text (and all sizing) on a page. Using relative units gives users the freedom to adapt your content to best suit the way they enjoy browsing the Web and give devices the opportunity to actually do that.

Raise your base font size

With all of that in mind, it's also worth asking whether everyone would need to increase their font size themselves if an acceptable size was chosen for a website in the first place.

It's fair to say that not everyone knows how to change their browsers font size, let alone do it on their mobile device, tablet, or any other device they happen to own. Yet these people would often benefit most from a standard change in font size.[15]

If the process of transforming your whole site from using pixels to relative units such as "em's" in one go is too much, a good first step is simply increasing the font size you're currently displaying if it's below the 16px benchmark most browsers deem to be the reasonable reading size. If you set a higher base font size, you can make it as easy as possible for most people to read it.

Indeed, research conducted by Google and IBM showed a marked increase in reading speed and ease of reading as font sizes on pages increased, so increasing this value on any existing site is a great quick win.[16]

Line height

Line height is the vertical space between two lines of text. Specifically, it's the exact distance between two adjacent baselines, and it can be just as important as font sizing. Imagine trying to read reading multiple lines of text where each line blurs and overlaps with the text below and above it? It would require an unnecessary amount of extra concentration.

To give just one example, a study about typography and accessibility noted that: "Increased line height did significantly reduce the error rate for simulated macular degeneration."[17]

Most users will immediately notice that there's something wrong with your text, even if they can't put their finger on what it is.

Line height is usually best defined as a percentage of the font size in order to ensure readability,[18] with somewhere between 140 and 180% being optimal for accessibility – WCAG sits neatly between this bracket, suggesting 150% at least.[19]

Remember, you need to set line height using em's for the same reasons we discussed with font sizes – if the font size on your site was increased through a user's change in settings, but the line height was set as a fixed pixel size, lines of text would start overlapping with each other and it would render the text completely unreadable. For example, Figure 3-5 shows some text where the font has been increased to twice its original size through user settings, but where a line height was set explicitly with pixels that therefore doesn't scale.

"Space is big. You just won't believe how vastly, hugely, mind-boggingly big it is. I mean, you may think it's a long way down the road to the chemist's, but that's just peanuts to space."

Figure 3-5.   *Text on multiple lines overlapping with one another, due to having a font size much bigger than its line height*

Instead, we should use the em unit again but set it to be a percentage greater than the font size:

```
body {
    font-size: 1em;
    line-height: 1.5em;
}
```

Using the preceding code, if a user's default font was set to 16px, their font size would be 16px (as we mentioned previously, an em unit is equal to the base font size of a browser or device by default, so in this scenario 1em = 16px) and their line height would be 24px (150% of the default 16 pixel font size equals 1.5em). However, if a user increased their default font to 20px, their font size would be 20px, and their line height would be 30px.

Letter spacing

The spacing between your letters and words are usually less of an issue than size or line height, as they're handled by the font that you choose and aren't edited as often (although it can be edited using the letter-spacing property).[20] You should, however, avoid aligning content in a "justified" style – stretching each line so that it reaches both edges of its column, as shown by the block of text on the right in Figure 3-6.

"A towel is about the most massively useful thing an interstellar hitchhiker can have. Partly it has great practical value. You can wrap it around you for warmth as you bound across the cold moons of Jaglan Beta; you can lie on it on the brilliant marble-sanded beaches of Santraginus V, inhaling the heady sea vapors; you can sleep under it beneath the stars which shine so redly on the desert world of Kakrafoon; use it to sail a miniraft down the slow heavy River Moth; wet it for use in hand-to-hand-combat; wrap it round your head to ward off noxious fumes or avoid the gaze of the Ravenous Bugblatter Beast of Traal (such a mind-boggingly stupid animal, it assumes that if you can't see it, it can't see you); you can wave your towel in emergencies as a distress signal, and of course dry yourself off with it if it still seems to be clean enough."

"A towel is about the most massively useful thing an interstellar hitchhiker can have. Partly it has great practical value. You can wrap it around you for warmth as you bound across the cold moons of Jaglan Beta; you can lie on it on the brilliant marble-sanded beaches of Santraginus V, inhaling the heady sea vapors; you can sleep under it beneath the stars which shine so redly on the desert world of Kakrafoon; use it to sail a miniraft down the slow heavy River Moth; wet it for use in hand-to-hand-combat; wrap it round your head to ward off noxious fumes or avoid the gaze of the Ravenous Bugblatter Beast of Traal (such a mind-boggingly stupid animal, it assumes that if you can't see it, it can't see you); you can wave your towel in emergencies as a distress signal, and of course dry yourself off with it if it still seems to be clean enough."

Figure 3-6. *Left aligned and justified text side by side, showing the inconsistent spacing between words that the latter causes*

Justified text looks neat, but creates different sized spaces between every word on every line of text. Having no consistent gap between each letter makes it more challenging for users to read. Text aligned to the left (displayed by the block of text on the left in the above Figure) is proven to be easier to read.

Font choice

The final takeaway, and perhaps the easiest, is that you are less likely to run into issues if you've chosen a "commonly" used font – a font available in all modern operating systems. Users can become accustomed to reading text in certain styles after being exposed to them on many different sites. Now, having a custom font for your headers can add a unique dimension to a brand or page design, but adding that same font to the main body of text can throw up barriers that simply don't need to be there. Here is a list of some widely available and therefore commonly used fonts:

- Arial

- Georgia

- Courier New

- Tahoma

- Times New Roman

- Trebuchet

- Verdana[21]

When it comes to text, keep it simple!

Contrast ratio

Contrast is the difference in luminance (the intensity of light emitted from a surface) between two adjacent or overlaid colours. Strong contrast is incredibly useful for people with impaired contrast sensitivity, which includes some users with cognitive impairments,[22] and many types of low vision: from those with visual acuity impairments like cataracts to field-of-vision issues like macular degeneration and glaucoma to those with colour blindness.

By comparing the difference in luminance (brightness) between the two colours, you can work out a contrast ratio. The more dramatic this contrast is, the easier it will be for most users to perceive that content.

Contrast issues can be tricky to spot sometimes, especially if you've been designing for or working with a certain brand or colour scheme for any length of time. Luckily contrast levels are easy to test, and there is a widely accepted benchmark. WCAG states that the contrast level between foreground and background colours should be at least 7:1 for regular body text (typically 16 pixels to match most web browsers) to be AAA compliant (the highest level), and 4.5:1 for AA compliance (the base level). Here, accessibility is also tied to the size of text (as we just covered), so it's important to consider both. For example, the required contrast ratio for AA reduces if the text size is larger:

WCAG 2.0 level AA requires a contrast ratio of 4.5:1 for normal text and 3:1 for large text – Large text is defined as at least 14 point (typically 18.66px) and bold, or 18 point (typically 24px).[23]

A low contrast ratio means that users have trouble reading your content, particularly if it's a large body of text.

Studies suggest that good contrast helps with many types of low vision[24] but is especially important to those with glaucoma or cataracts, as well as certain colour-blind users, who may have trouble focusing on text coloured similarly to the background.

It's important to walk the line between maintaining the aesthetics of a design or brand that you've created while not compromising the content or experience for those with visual difficulties. In this scenario, there are two points that are worth thinking about and discussed in the next sections: clear contrast and offering a change.

Good contrast helps users without visual impairments

As we've said before, if you design for users with a specific access need, you end up benefiting all users. Users that suffer from migraines, who are trying to read the content with screen glare, or who are very tired will all benefit from a stronger contrast ratio. As we get older and our vision starts to naturally deteriorate, this consideration is also valuable.

Accordingly, having a low contrast ratio will negatively impact all your users. Consider the three levels of contrast for the standard text size of 16 pixels shown in Figure 3-7: failing (3:1), AA compliant (4.5:1), and AAA compliant (7:1):

3:1
"Time is an illusion. Lunchtime doubly so."

4.5:1
"Time is an illusion. Lunchtime doubly so."

7:1
"Time is an illusion. Lunchtime doubly so."

Figure 3-7.   Three examples of text and background colour contrast levels – the first is a failing level, the next is AA compliant, and the last is AAA compliant

As the contrast between text and foreground increases, so too does the ease at which you can read it. It's worth noting that these values are merely the *minimum* contrast that you should aim for – having a contrast level over 7 is not only completely possible but good news!

You could always offer a change

One approach that requires work but can have brilliant results is, again, allowing for customisation within your design. This way you don't end up alienating your users for the sake of design but can still maintain your brand.

This can be especially useful, because:

> there may not be one solution that fits [with] regards to visually impaired users. Accommodations for the needs of one user may work against the needs of another user.[25]

For example, we've spoken about the benefits of having a high contrast ratio, but because contrast relies on levels of light, people who suffer from photophobia (light sensitivity) can feel discomfort or pain from clashing bright colours.[26] It should be noted that these contradictions are a rare occurrence when designing with accessibility in mind.

The W3C (who wrote WCAG) has attempted to address these contradictions. Their findings, and their suggestions, are somewhat vague though. They state the importance of providing high contrast for legibility and recognise there can be situations where, for example, a user can both require high contrast to engage with content and simultaneously experience photophobia. They eventually do encourage customisation as a solution, but when explaining what shape that customisation should take, they suggest:

any strategy for remediation must employ a multi-treatment approach to address sets of functional limitations that have contradictory treatments when addressed singularly.[27]

Got that?

Me neither.

Thankfully, steps can be taken to reconcile these different access needs. In this case, accessibility is preserved by offering users a choice, but we can be even more specific.

I once tackled this issue on a project I was working on. When speaking to customers who had low vision (and some that had dyslexia too), some mentioned that they didn't enjoy reading the regular communications that we emailed them. The typical design style for this project was white text on a dark blue background. Now although this site fully passed AAA WCAG standards for contrast ratio, customers had reported trouble reading or focusing on the content.

This was another example of a website being WCAG compliant but still not fully addressing the access needs of users – customers were still having trouble engaging with content. We had to make a decision.

The line of thinking we took was this: These emails were being sent to customers regularly, asking them to either engage with their contents or perform an action. It was also content going to *their* inbox for only them to view.

Our solution was to allow each customer to invert the colours of the communications they were receiving, meaning they could choose an alternative option of dark text on a light background; the contrast levels between the two are essentially identical, but the former created a barrier that wasn't there in the latter. More importantly, it helped them engage with the communications more freely. Figure 3-8 shows an example of an email we send our customers, both with and without the inverted colour scheme option applied.

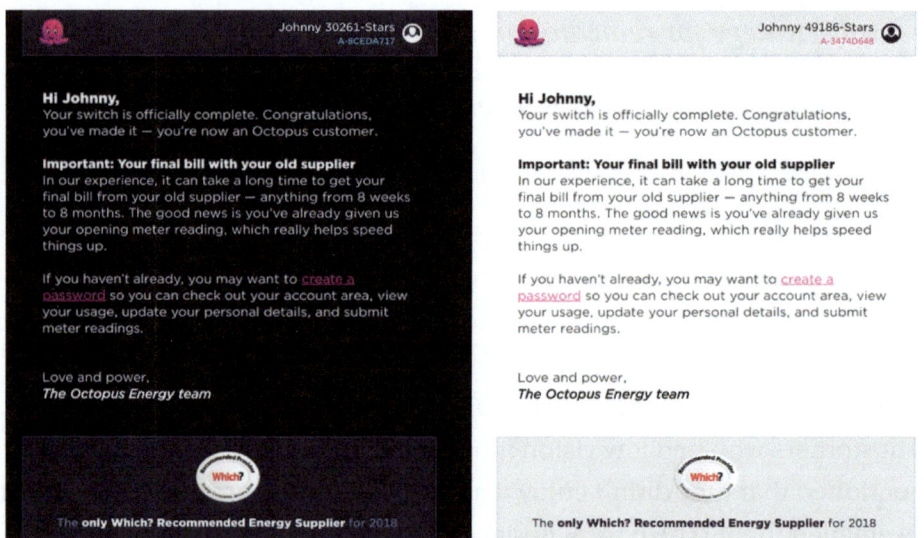

Figure 3-8. *Two examples of the same customer communication: one with the standard colour scheme of light text on a dark background and the other with an inverted colour scheme of dark text on a light background*

The feedback was hugely positive and we've since had many users without low vision enable the mode, simply because they preferred receiving their content in that style.

Of course, your regular brand should have WCAG-compliant contrast ratios anyway – you shouldn't use accessible alternatives as an excuse to neglect your original design.

Computer contrast

This logic can also be applied by users to their entire computer as well! Since 'macOS Mojave', Apple's operating system, allows easy switching to a dark theme if users prefer it. Windows offers many different equivalents, and Windows high contrast mode has long been used to transform sites to a high contrast style to allow for easier interaction. All these developments show that the idea of customising to meet user needs is becoming a consideration in every facet of our online lives.

The changes mentioned previously, and settings that provide light text on a dark background, create a strong contrast but with a lower level of luminance, because the dominant background colour becomes darker, placing the stronger white light on smaller, individual pieces of content. Users with albinism or macular degeneration often benefit from these settings as it provides a far less light-sensitive environment while still being easy to read. Moreover, the ability to change settings at any point allows users to adapt their experience depending on what impairments they are experiencing most strongly at the time (albinism can often have more of an impact at the beginning of the day, whereas macular degeneration is typically more prominent at the end of the day).

As with the changing their base font size though, users would have to know that these settings, or software, exist and how to use them. Why not avoid the risk and preemptively provide this consideration for your users? Users are generally grateful when you take their potential needs into account. It's one of my personal favorite accessibility considerations, and

I've created a simple example of this for you in the practical example for this chapter (available on Github in the "Chapter 3" folder and to view at `https://inclusive.guide/examples/theme-change`) (Figure 3-9).

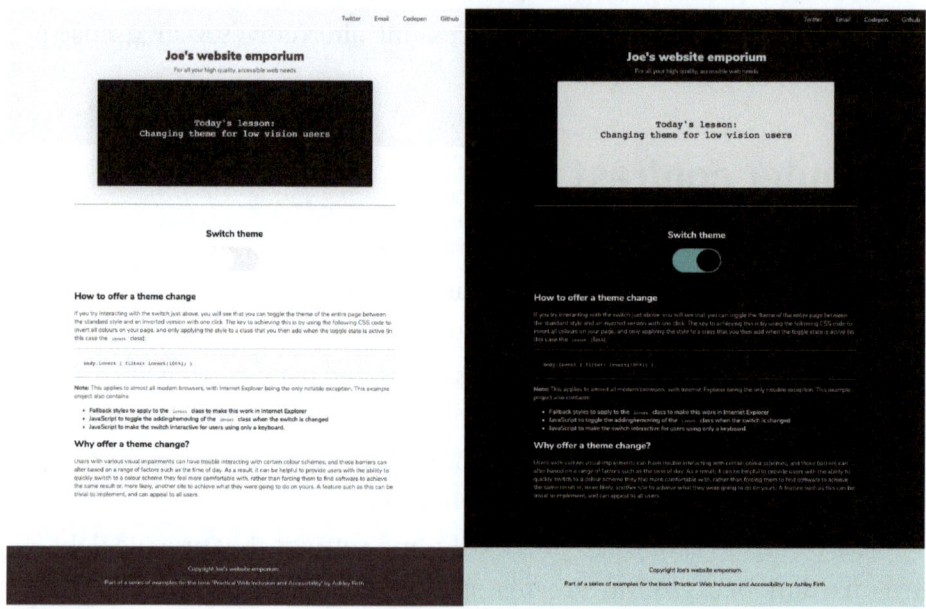

Figure 3-9. *Two screenshots taken from the "theme change" example for this book – first of the standard theme of the page and the second with the inverted theme*

It's worth noting how useful this is for long form articles or blogs that involve a lot of text.

For those maintaining an existing site, this may seem like a time-consuming rewrite; however, depending on the browsers you support, it could be a lot easier than you think. This is because CSS has a `filter` property available that can create a whole range of different visual effects. One possible method is `invert` which, as the name suggests, inverts the colours of any section you apply it to. Therefore, we can simply add the following CSS:

```
body.invert {
    filter: invert(100%);
}
```

Then when the user opts to change theme and clicks the button the `invert` class is added, every colour on the page will be immediately inverted, offering an oppositional theme with one line of styling.

The `filter` property has over 93% browser support, with Internet Explorer being the only notable browser that doesn't support it.[28] If IE still accounts for a large percentage of your audience, then this solution is still possible but requires a little more work – you would need to apply overriding rules inside the `invert` class for the contents of your page. Again, I have demonstrated this in the practical example.

Testing

I have found that contrast ratio accessibility is especially easy to test for. This is covered at length in the chapter on Tools and QA (Chapter 11) if you're ready to test your sites.

Colour blindness

Colour-based barriers are especially important because they frequently exclude a specific group of visually impaired users. Colour blindness (also known as colour vision deficiency) is common, affecting approximately 1 in 12 men (8%) and 1 in 200 women in the world. In Britain, this means that there are approximately 3 million colour-blind people (about 4.5% of the entire population).[29] Colour also affects contrast ratio, and many users with low vision also experience dull colours, so this section is important for them too.

Different types of colour blindness

Your eyes' retinas contain two types of light-sensitive cells called rods and cones. Rods work in low-light conditions to help your vision at night, but cones work in daylight and are responsible for colour discrimination. Scientists believe that issues with one or more of these three cones (red, blue, and green) causes colour blindness.[30]

It's important to ensure that your colour scheme works for the multiple types of colour blindness users have. There is a wide range of types, but we'll focus on two of the most common – red–green and yellow–blue confusion.

Red–green confusion

This is the most common, and well-known, type of colour blindness.[31] However, within this spectrum, there are four main types of red–green confusion:

- Deuteranopia and deuteranomaly (also known as green-blind) – reduced sensitivity to red light and missing or reduced ability to see green hues. Deuteranopes are more likely to confuse

  - Mid-reds with mid-greens

  - Blue–greens with grey and mid-pinks

  - Bright greens with yellows

  - Pale pinks with light grey

  - Mid-reds with mid-brown

  - Light blues with lilac

– Protanopia and protanomaly – "L-cones" are missing
   or defective. The user cannot see reds. Protanopes are
   more likely to confuse

- Black with many shades of red

- Dark brown with dark green, dark orange, and dark
  red

- Some blues with some reds, purples, and dark
  pinks

- Mid-greens with some oranges[32]

This does not mean that these people cannot perceive reds or greens
entirely. They simply have a harder time differentiating between them.
It would be easy for someone with a red–green deficiency to tell the
difference between a light green and a dark red, for example. It depends –
at least in part – on how dark the colours are.

Don't use colour to infer status

The challenge arises because red and green are commonly used to infer
positive or negative messages. Take the following status messages in
Figure 3-10 from a form submission for example.

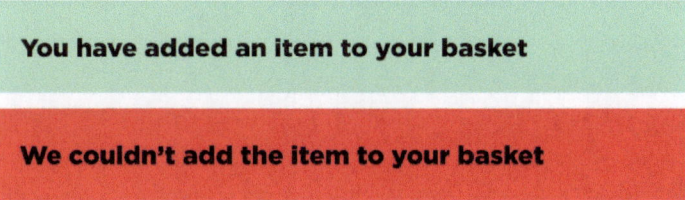

Figure 3-10. *Two alerts, one positive and one negative, both where
colour is the primary way in which status is displayed*

If you're able to view reds and greens correctly, you can easily make the distinction between the positive and negative messages. However, this is roughly how a user with deuteranopia would see the messages in Figure 3-11.

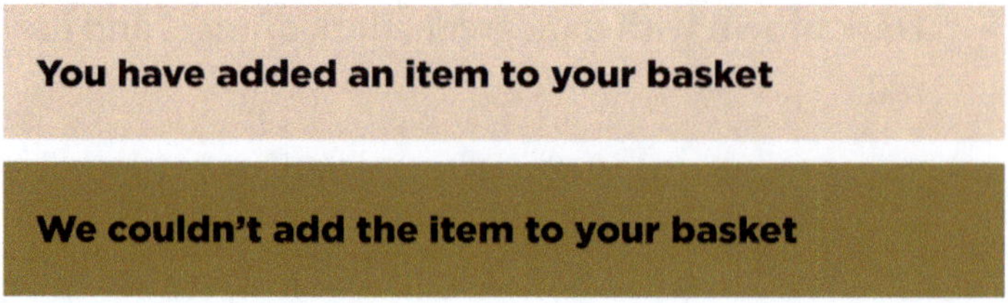

> **You have added an item to your basket**

> **We couldn't add the item to your basket**

Figure 3-11. *The same two alerts but how they would be seen by someone who has deuteranopia. The lack of a clear green or red makes the alert's meaning harder to discern*

Suddenly the contents of the alert could be misconstrued (particularly if it's negative and unexpected).

The key is to use colour as a compliment and not a crutch. A reliance on colour can create a hugely confusing experience for users who have difficulties perceiving colour and sometimes result in a complete loss of contextual meaning. This makes it more important to ground status with a message and/or icon. Both provide immediate feedback to a user without relying on colour (Figure 3-12).

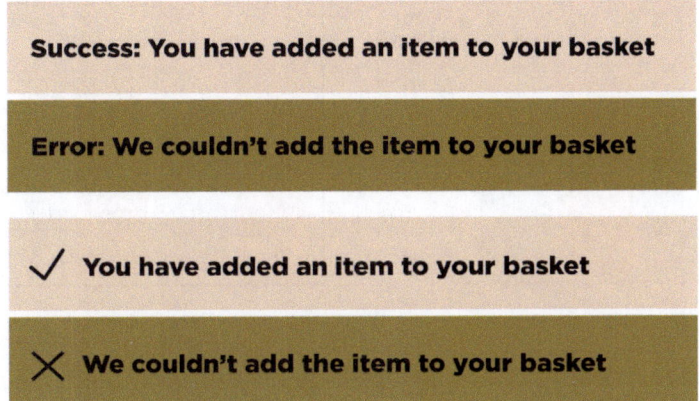

Figure 3-12. The status messages now use either "Success" and "Error", or a tick and a cross icon, so the meaning of the message doesn't rely on colour

Yellow–blue confusion

- **Tritanopia or tritanomaly** – Users have typical red and green vision but have trouble distinguishing yellow and red from pink, and blues appear greener.

Colour is often used to signify different segments of a graph – include adequate labelling where colours are necessary. Diagrams and infographics are common offenders.[33]

The ramifications of yellow–blue confusion are worth keeping in mind, particularly for content that uses many colours to differentiate between content. A good example of this would be a typical bar chart, where colour is used to match bars up to a legend of names.

If you tested many graphs against various strains of colour blindness, you'd likely have trouble determining which segment represents which part of the data, even with a legend there to provide more context. For instance, Figure 3-13 shows what a bar chart using a range of colours would look to someone with tritanopia.

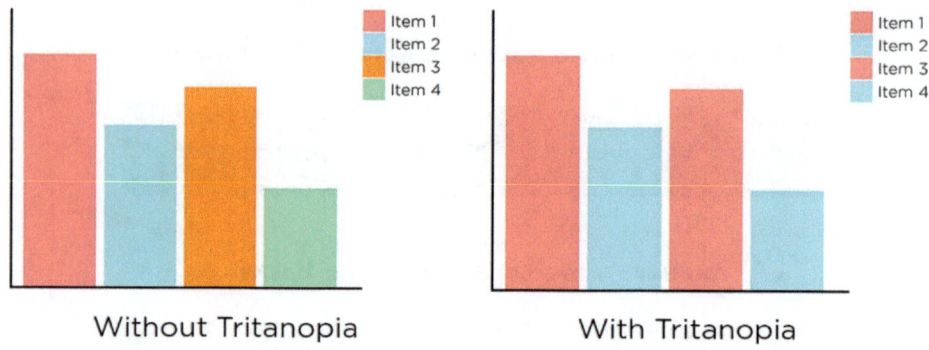

Figure 3-13. *A comparison of how a bar chart using multiple colours looks with and without tritanopia*

Some colours don't change, but it's much more difficult to distinguish between others. If you provide an additional way of differentiating between data sets rather than just relying on colour, the graph becomes immediately accessible for those with colour blindness. Figure 3-14 shows the same graph, but with different patterns added to each bar so that the bars and legends appear unique even without colour.

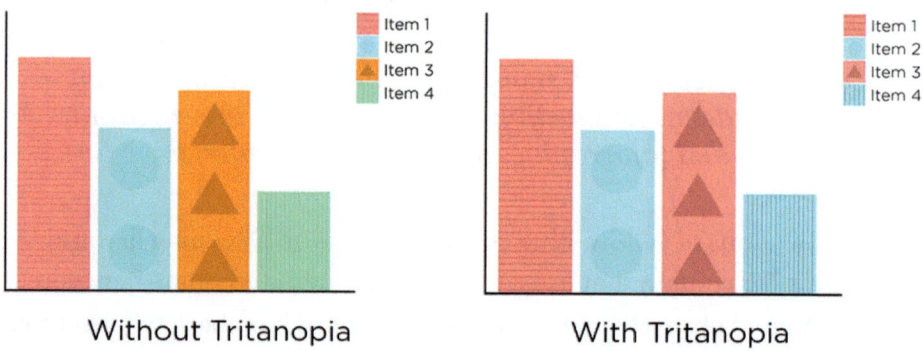

Figure 3-14. *The bar chart now uses patterns to help all users discern between the different bars without the need for colour*

Monochromacy

This is the rarest and most severe form of colour blindness and prevents
the user from seeing anything but black, white, and shades of grey.[34] These
users are worst affected when we choose to convey meaning solely through
colour, and there are occasions when the meaning of a feature relies
heavily on colour:

> *If the purpose of posting the image is to communicate some-
> thing about the colours in that image, then it is important to
> provide some other way of understanding the information.*[35]

The best example I've seen is WebAIM's monochrome London
underground route map shown in Figure 3-15.[36]

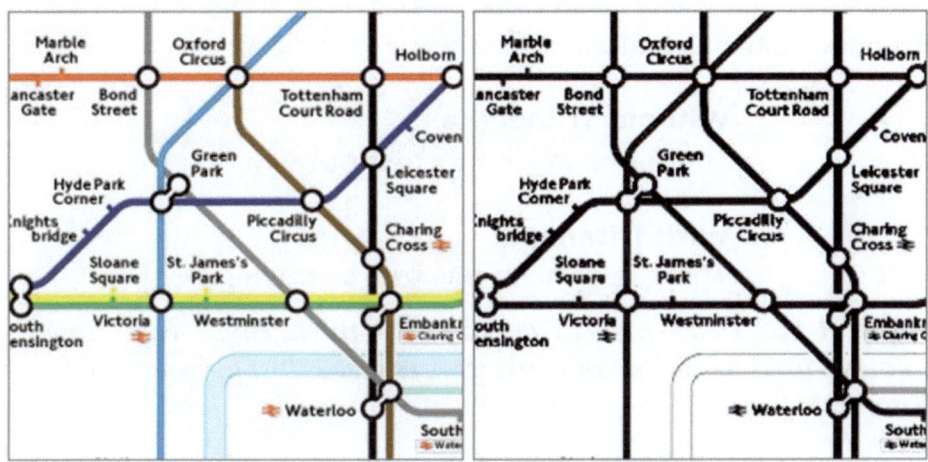

Figure 3-15. *A small piece of the London underground map as
someone without a visual impairment would see it and then how
someone with monochromacy would see that same image*

Here, a user with monochromacy must rely on techniques we've covered such as descriptive alt text, differentiating the different lines through patterns, annotation, or text next to the image to help them distinguish between the routes.

I raise these different variations of colour blindness simply because this impairment can encompass such a wide range of things visually, meaning that it's very likely that users are seeing your site from thousands of slightly differing perspectives. The reality is that you won't be able to create a colour scheme that can be fully interpreted by everyone, which makes it vitally important that you don't rely on colour to convey meaning.

Links

It's worth mentioning a particularly common colour-related issue that impacts multiple colour-blind users: Links, as seen in Figure 3-16, often rely on colour for identification.

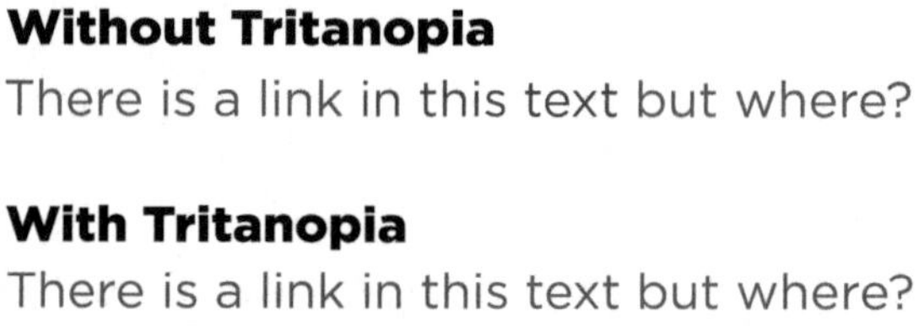

Without Tritanopia
There is a link in this text but where?

With Tritanopia
There is a link in this text but where?

Figure 3-16.   Two sentences with a link in them. However, as only colour is used to display the link, its presence is lost for users with tritanopia

By default, link text is underlined, making it accessible, but underlining is often removed using CSS for aesthetic reasons and the distinction is lost. Ensure that you keep your underlining. There is also a WCAG contrast requirement specifically for link text to avoid examples like the previous ones.[37]

Testing

My personal favorite accessibility testing tool is a piece of software called Sim Daltonism.[38] When installed, it allows you to quickly see what people with multiple types of colour blindness see, allowing you to test your sites as you're building them and act on the results quickly. Head to the Tools and QA chapter (Chapter 11) to read more about it.

Conclusion

Some solutions proposed in this chapter have certain caveats to them, due to the fact that each visual impairment can affect users on such different levels and in wide-ranging ways. However, by instilling a solid basis of accessibility for as many visual impairments as you can, and providing users with the tools to customise their web experience to suit their needs, you will have ensured your site caters to its users, and not vice versa.

Notes

1. W3C, *Accessibility Requirements for People with Low Vision*, (17/03/2016), <www.w3.org/TR/low-vision-needs/> [accessed 25/04/2019].

2. NHS, *Blindness and vision loss,* (08/06/2018), <www.nhs.uk/conditions/vision-loss/> [accessed 25/04/2019].

3. W3C, *Accessibility Requirements for People with Low Vision*, (17/03/2016), <www.w3.org/TR/low-vision-needs/> [accessed 25/04/2019].

4. Wikipedia, *The Dress*, <https://en.wikipedia.
    org/wiki/The_dress> [accessed 25/04/2019].

5. James Buller, *Accessibility and me: James Buller*,
    Accessibility in government blog, (22/08/2016),
    <https://accessibility.blog.gov.
    uk/2016/08/22/accessibility-and-me-james-
    buller/> [accessed 25/04/2019].

6. Molly Watt, *Accessibility and me: Molly Watt*,
    Accessibility in government blog, (09/01/2017),
    <https://accessibility.blog.gov.
    uk/2017/01/09/accessibility-and-me-molly-
    watt/> [accessed 25/04/2019].

7. Guy Podjarny, *RWD Ratio in Top 100,000 websites –
    refined*, (09/01/2014), <www.guypo.com//rwd-
    ratio-in-top-100000-websites-refined>
    [accessed 25/04/2019].

8. Adrian Roselli, *Don't Disable Zoom*, (05/10/2015),
    <http://adrianroselli.com/2015/10/dont-
    disable-zoom.html> [accessed 25/04/2019].

9. Moreno, et al. *Exploring the Web navigation
    strategies of people with low vision*, (14/09/2018),
    <https://dl.acm.org/citation.cfm?id=3233845>
    [accessed 25/04/2019].

10. Bert Bos, *EM, PX, PT, CM, IN...*, W3C, (26/09/2018),
    <www.w3.org/Style/Examples/007/units.
    en.html> [accessed 25/04/2019].

11. Oliver Reichenstein, *The 100% Easy-2-Read
    Standard*, iA, (17/11/2006), <https://ia.net/
    topics/100e2r> [accessed 25/04/2019].

12. W3C, *Accessibility Requirements for People with Low Vision*, (17/03/2016), <www.w3.org/TR/low-vision-needs/> [accessed 25/04/2019].

13. W3C, *Accessibility Requirements for People with Low Vision*, (17/03/2016), <www.w3.org/TR/low-vision-needs/> [accessed 25/04/2019].

14. Scott Kellum, *A Pixel Identity Crisis*, A List Apart, (17/01/2012), <https://alistapart.com/article/a-pixel-identity-crisis/> [accessed 25/04/2019].

15. Jakob Nielsen, Guesses vs. Data as Basis for Design Recommendations, (07/06/2009) <www.nngroup.com/articles/guesses-vs-data/> [accessed 25/04/2019].

16. David Beymer, Daniel Russell, Peter Orton, *An Eye Tracking Study of How Font Size and Type Influence Online Reading*, (2008), <www.bcs.org/upload/pdf/ewic_hc08_v2_paper4.pdf> [accessed 25/04/2019].

17. Erica McCoy, *Accessible Web Typography for the Visually Impaired*, (05/2018), <https://mdsoar.org/handle/11603/10871> [accessed 25/04/2019].

18. Tom Clarke, *Best UX practices for line spacing*, JUSTINMIND, (27/11/2018) <www.justinmind.com/blog/best-ux-practices-for-line-spacing/> [accessed 25/04/2019].

19. W3C, *Understanding Success Criterion 1.4.12*: Text Spacing, <www.w3.org/WAI/WCAG21/Understanding/text-spacing.html> [accessed 25/04/2019].

20. W3Schools, *CSS letter-spacing Property*, (2019)
     <www.w3schools.com/cssref/pr_text_letter-
     spacing.asp> [accessed 25/04/2019].

21. WebAIM, *Fonts*, (2019), <https://webaim.org/
     techniques/fonts/> [accessed 25/04/2019].

22. A, Ridder et. al., *Impaired contrast sensitivity is
     associated with more severe cognitive impairment
     in Parkinson disease*, (07/10/2016), <https://www.
     ncbi.nlm.nih.gov/pmc/articles/PMC5222688/>
     [accessed 25/04/2019].

23. WebAIM, *Contrast Checker*, (2019), <https://
     webaim.org/resources/contrastchecker/?fcolor
     =fff&bcolor=000> [accessed 25/04/2019].

24. Michael Christen and Mathias Abegg, *The effect of
     magnification and contrast on reading performance
     in different types of simulated low vision*, (2007),
     <https://bop.unibe.ch/index.php/JEMR/
     article/view/3523> [accessed 25/05/2019].

25. Erica McCoy, *Accessible Web Typography for the
     Visually Impaired*, (05/2018), <https://mdsoar.
     org/handle/11603/10871> [accessed 25/04/2019].

26. Greg Bullock, *The Ultimate Guide to Photophobia
     and Light Sensitivity*, (08/11/2018),   [accessed 25/04/2019].

27. W3C, *Overview of Low Vision*, (09/02/2016), <www.
     w3.org/WAI/GL/low-vision-a11y-tf/wiki/
     Overview_of_Low_Vision> [accessed 25/04/2019].

28.   Caniuse, *CSS Filter Effects,* (07/2019) <https://caniuse.com/#search=filter> [accessed 25/04/2019].

29.   Colour Blind Awareness, *Welcome to the Colour Blind Awareness site,* (2019), <www.colourblindawareness.org/> [accessed 25/04/2019].

30.   Colour Blind Awareness, *Causes of Colour Blindness,* (2019), <www.colourblindawareness.org/colour-blindness/causes-of-colour-blindness/> [accessed 25/04/2019].

31.   National Eye Institute, *Facts About Color Blindness,* <https://nei.nih.gov/health/color_blindness/facts_about> [accessed 25/04/2019].

32.   Colour Blind Awareness, *Types of Colour Blindness,* (2019), <www.colourblindawareness.org/colour-blindness/types-of-colour-blindness/> [accessed 25/04/2019].

33.   Hampus Sethfors, *Colorblind Accessibility on the Web – Fail and Success Cases,* axess lab, (06/09/2017), <https://axesslab.com/colorblind-accessibility-web-fail-success-cases/> [accessed 25/04/2019].

34.   Colblindor, *Monochromacy – Complete Color Blindness,* (20/07/2007), <www.color-blindness.com/2007/07/20/monochromacy-complete-color-blindness/> [accessed 25/04/2019].

35.   WebAIM, *Visual Disabilities*: Color-blindness, (2019), <https://webaim.org/articles/visual/colorblind> [accessed 25/04/2019].

36.   WebAIM, *Visual Disabilities*: Color-blindness, (2019), <https://webaim.org/articles/visual/colorblind> [accessed 25/04/2019].

37.   W3C, *G183: Using a contrast ratio of 3:1 with surrounding text and providing additional visual cues on focus for links or controls where color alone is used to identify them,* (2016), <www.w3.org/TR/WCAG20-TECHS/G183.html> [accessed 25/04/2019].

38.   Michel Fortin, *Sim Daltonism,* (2019) <https://michelf.ca/projects/sim-daltonism/> [accessed 25/04/2019].

CHAPTER 4

Motor Disabilities

People with motor impairments generally experience a partial or total loss of function of a body part and are affected by chronic pain, poor stamina, muscle weakness, lack of muscle control, or paralysis.[1] These impairments impact millions of people but there has been very little research into the exact number. Microsoft commissioned the last major study, based in the United States, and found that roughly 7% of working age adults have a severe dexterity difficulty that would likely force them to seek alternative methods for navigating the Web.[2]

Motor impairments can have many medical causes, from physical trauma, like spine injuries or amputations, to neurological and nervous disorders like strokes, multiple sclerosis, cerebral palsy, Parkinson's, and motor neuron disease.

In this chapter, however, we'll continue with our functional approach: focusing on how best to support users with these challenges, not their causes. We ask: how do different motor impaired users, with a range of access needs, approach navigating and interacting with the Web? It should be noted that while Chapters 2 and 3 (Blindness and Low vision and Colour blindness) focused on helping users **perceive, navigate, and interact** with a site, this chapter mainly concerns on the two latter themes.

This chapter encompasses a wide range of design considerations because of the multitude of different ways that motor-impaired users interact with sites. We currently recognise the keyboard and mouse combination as the "common" form of interaction with a computer, but the creation of the first mouse came long after that of the first computer.

© Ashley Firth 2019
A. Firth, *Practical Web Inclusion and Accessibility*,
https://doi.org/10.1007/978-1-4842-5452-3_4

In their inception, computers had no mouse. Instead, data was entered by typing commands on a keyboard – the exact way that many users with motor impairments still interact with a computer today. It wasn't until Apple released the Macintosh in 1984 (alongside the rise in popularity of the graphical user interface – or GUI) that using a mouse became standard.

Given that a keyboard-only interface was the first "common" method of interacting with computers, it's disappointing that today many websites don't support keyboard-only interaction as well as they should. We'll start by looking at how you can identify this problem and then discuss how to fix it.

Traditions, however, are changing, and these days, touch screens are nearing complete adoption. Touch screens condense all external input sources such as the keyboard or mouse into one interface that accepts multiple forms of interaction (such as gestures). This (further) raises the importance of considering access needs and tackling barriers faced by users whose setups are based on "pointer-based" interaction. This includes touchscreens, a mouse, joystick, head wand, and more.

We will also cover other alternatives, such as voice to text software (also known as dictation software), which offer users the ability to make their voice the primary source of input for their device. Toward the end of the chapter, we will also look at helping users who, like the late Steven Hawking, travel the Web using a single switch.

Finally, there are a number of solutions that can improve the online experience for a range of motor-impaired users in different ways. We will finish by examining some solutions that remove barriers for all motor-impaired users.

Keyboard-only navigation

Have you ever tried using a website without a mouse? It's harder than you might think, particularly when trying to perform actions across multiple pages such as signing up for or purchasing something. Some users that have motor disabilities often only use a keyboard to interact with a computer: this includes amputees; many users with Parkinson's disease, which affects roughly 127,000 people in the United Kingdom;[3] and some of the United Kingdom's 1 million users who experience tremors.[4]

The most common method of keyboard-only navigation relies on the Tab key, which moves the user sequentially between elements on a page that can be focused on and interacted with. When you're focused on an element using the keyboard, by default an outline appears to reflect that. Figure 4-1 shows a button with and without keyboard focus.

Figure 4-1. *A picture of a button and then that same button with keyboard focus style applied*

You may have seen this before. The latter indicates that a user can perform an action on the element and can be initiated with a keyboard as well as a mouse.

Now, keyboard-only users will usually tab from one feature to the next as part of their navigation; however, most will not tab through an entire page in order to navigate through it. Much like screen reader users that we covered in the chapter on blindness (Chapter 2), keyboard-only users utilise search and 'skip to main content', and make use of personalised shortcuts to move around pages.

It's still important to ensure that tabbing through a page is possible though, and this relies on correct code and ensuring that your content is ordered sensibly. Most browsers are very good at allowing keyboard interaction with elements such as buttons, links, and form inputs. However, sometimes design and user experience use custom components and features that need to be built using different tags, but still require user interaction, and these need to be just as accessible. An example of this is when a calendar widget is used for date input – these usually prevent manual date entry and so need to be altered to be accessed via keyboard.

For this reason, we will now spend a little time explaining how to make a site keyboard-only accessible.

Tabindex

If a user is unable to navigate and interact with your content with a keyboard alone, it falls under WCAG's "denial of keyboard access"[5], and was another major issue raised in the lawsuit against Beyoncé's website. Using `tabindex` will save you this trouble!

You can use `tabindex` to ensure that important content can be focused on and help the user quickly move past content that doesn't require interaction. We mentioned it briefly in the chapter about blindness (Chapter 2), but don't worry if you've never come across this before. Tabindex is an attribute that simply allows you to set two things, and the clues are in the name:

Tab – determines whether an element is "focusable" or not for a user using the Tab key to navigate.

Index – The order in which focusable content is presented on a page.

With this, you can ensure that motor and visually impaired keyboard-only users have access to all the relevant information on a page, in an order that is both clear and logical.

The good news is that if you use correct markup, certain interactive elements are focusable by default. For example, if you use a `<button>` tag to represent a button (as opposed to a `<div>` styled to look like a button with custom markup), the computer will recognise it as a focusable element. This means that a user will be able to move through a page, from top to bottom (and back up using Shift + Tab), without you having to make any changes to your code. Here is a list of essential elements which receive focus by default because they require action from the user:

- `<a>` – A link in HTML. As long as it has somewhere to go (defined with an `href` attribute), it can be focused through tabbing.

- `<button>` – A button.

- `<input>` – A field inside a form is defined as an `input`, and they all have focus set by default (apart from hidden inputs).

- `<select>` – A dropdown (when focused using the keyboard, you can navigate through the options using the arrow keys).

- `<textarea>` – A text box, often used for long-form comments and bigger than a usual `input`.

So why would you need tabindex if interactive elements can be tabbed to already?

Fantastic question. It's comforting to know that keyboard-only users already have the power to engage with all of the typical features of a web page, but there are certain scenarios where adding, altering, or even removing tabindex from certain elements can improve the experience. These are achievable through the three values that the `tabindex` attribute takes:

0

The 0 value lets the page know that the element you have set this attribute on should be focusable but in "sequential" order – wherever it is on the page in relation to other elements, it'll be available via "Tab" as it reaches it. This means your custom components (e.g., a button) made from tags that aren't interactive by default (like a `<div> tag`) can now be focused just like a real button. What the 0 value also does is specify that it can be tabbed to. Figure 4-2 below shows this – here there are two `<div>` tags that can't be "tabbed" to by default, but one has become part of the tabbing order as it has the `tabindex` attribute:

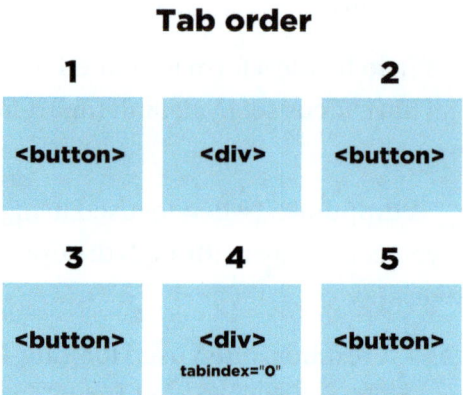

Figure 4-2. *A diagram showing the tabbing order of buttons. One `<div>` tag is ignored, while the other is added to the order as it has the `tabindex` attribute added to it*

As `tabindex` wouldn't be set by default on a non-native element such as the first `<div>` previously, a user navigating via the Tab key would not be able to interact with it passing over it instead. With `tabindex` however, you can provide that focus.

1 or greater

This dictates that elements should be both focusable and focused on in a specific order that you've chosen, regardless of where the element is positioned on the page. Tabbing priority is set in ascending order (so 1 means it's the first thing to be navigated to, and a number bigger than 1 would be navigated to after). Figure 4-3 shows an example of how this can be used to create custom tabbing orders.

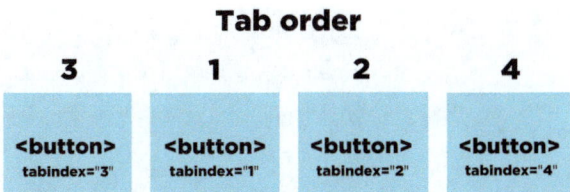

Figure 4-3. *A diagram of a custom tabbing order being dictated by the tabindex attribute*

Given the example, simply reordering the buttons would remove the need to set a custom tabindex order and would likely make it easier for users to understand as they'd no longer be moving through content in a nonlinear way.

In my experience, there is hardly ever a good reason to dictate a custom tabbing order, and if you find yourself doing this, then you need a strong justification. It's best to use a value of "0" and not specify a custom tabindex order – as it matches how a user typically navigates content.

-1

A negative tabindex value removes the element from the sequential flow we just mentioned, so a user can't tab to it. However with this attribute applied, when it is needed, it can still have focus applied to it through code. This is very useful for elements that should not be tabbed to all the time, but that may need keyboard focus in certain situations depending on a user's behavior on the page.

The classic example of this is a modal or dialog window, as shown in Figure 4-4.

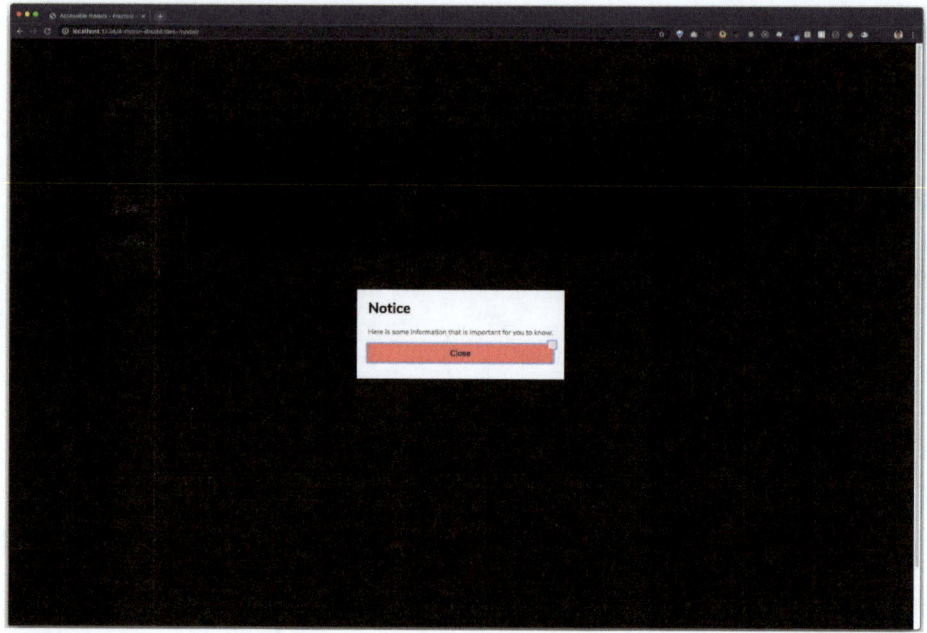

Figure 4-4. *A picture of an active modal*

As a modal only appears when a user opens it, the content is typically hidden when they first arrive on the page. We therefore don't want the content to receive keyboard focus by default, as the user may end up tabbing content they can't see.

However, when a user opens the modal, causing the hidden content to appear, the contents should now receive keyboard focus, allowing the user to Tab around it and not the rest of the elements on the page. We will tackle this challenge in more detail when we go through creating accessible modals a little later.

Testing

Try heading to one of the sites you're involved with and navigate a page using just the keyboard. You'll likely discover two things:

1) It's a lot harder to get things done with just a keyboard than you'd expect.

2) Sometimes you're not sure where you are on the page.

Checking whether your core journeys can be accomplished without the use of a mouse is a great access need test-case that you can try without the need of any special applications or test suites. For the second point, a great first step is ensuring that you have clear, consistent focus styles.

Focus styles

Take a look at Figure 4-5 – remember this image from earlier in the chapter?

Figure 4-5. *A picture of a button currently receiving keyboard focus with the default focus style*

This is what a focused element looks like by default. An element receives focus when you have tabbed to it or interacted with it. It provides a universal sign that the user is focused on this part of the page.

It's fairly common, however, to not see this blue outline, because many designers and developers consider it unsightly. Simply applying the following styling (CSS) code removes the focus indicator completely.

```
*:focus { outline: 0; }
```

Here, again, we need to tread the line here between creating an aesthetically pleasing site and providing an acceptable degree of usability for users who interact with content in a different way.

Now, removing a focus style may not pose a problem to someone navigating freely with a mouse, but without a focus style, those navigating via the tab key are left guessing where their focus is. It is therefore important to replace the standard focus style with one of your own if you decide to remove it. Nice alternatives to the typical outline rule can be created using a strong box shadow on the element, or applying a change to the background or border colour. Anything at least equally as obvious as what was there.

This is especially important because, as we've covered, only certain parts of a page are "tabbable," so a keyboard user's movement depends on how many interactable elements are present on the page and how far apart each of them are.

No two sites are designed in exactly the same way, and content is often placed in wildly varied locations. Given this inconsistency, having a clear focus style is invaluable. If users are unsure of where they've just moved to, having a focus style that stands out provides landmarks on the page, which can help users focus their attention on the right content.

However, focus styles are not just useful in the context of a whole page – they can be equally helpful when identifying position in a small area. For example, Figure 4-6 shows two identical menus currently focused on the same item. The only difference is that the second menu displays a focus style on the active element:

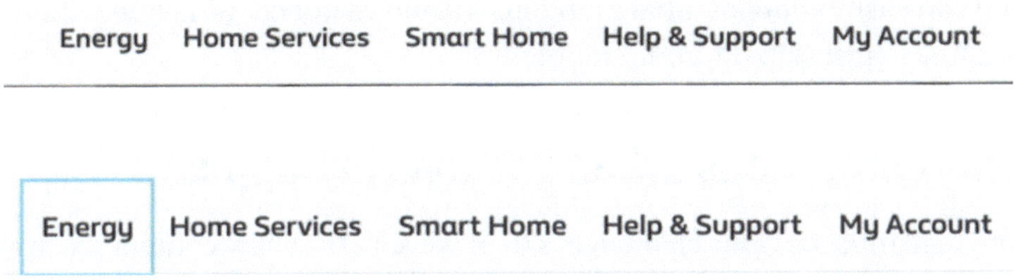

Energy   Home Services   Smart Home   Help & Support   My Account

Energy   Home Services   Smart Home   Help & Support   My Account

Figure 4-6. *A picture comparing two menus focused on the same item – one with a focus style and one without*

Imagine you're a keyboard-only user and you're aiming to interact with one of these menu items. In the first example, you're left to guess which link you're on and could potentially end up heading to pages you weren't trying to navigate to. Now, a menu is a feature that is (usually) always present on a page, but there can be even more serious issues with content that is overlaid or injected into a page. Let's talk about how to make features like that more accessible.

Accessible overlays

As we mentioned earlier, overlays like modals are common features (and pitfalls) online. Keyboard-only users can hit barriers when a page's content is altered by a user's action, like using a button, but the content that appears is impossible to interact with.

Let's take a look at some of the challenges these actions pose, and how we can make them more accessible. We'll go through the process of creating a modal that can be triggered, interacted with, and closed, using a keyboard-only setup, thereby ensuring that the process of displaying new content can be achieved accessibly.

Before we get started, I have already created this modal example for you to play with in the practical example for this chapter (found in Github under the "Chapter 4" folder, and live at `https://inclusive.guide/examples/modal`). I'd still recommend reading through this section so that you can easily spot potential problems – if you're not code-inclined, then feel free to just skip the code snippets.

Changing focus when the overlay appears

The first, most obvious challenge is to make sure that new content receives focus when it appears on the page, so that the user can both navigate that content and close it if they're not interested. Figure 4-7 is an example of this I encountered recently.

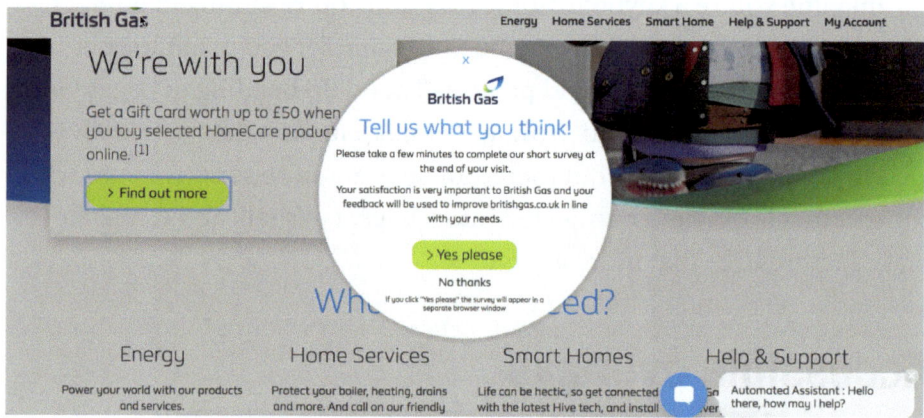

Figure 4-7. *A picture of a feedback modal overlaid on a page, but with keyboard focus still on the content beneath it*

While browsing the site, an overlay was added to the page without prior warning, but once it had appeared, I couldn't interact with it using the keyboard. As you can see in the image, my keyboard focus remained on the button below – pressing "tab" was still cycling me through the content of the page beneath it. Even more unfortunately, the message was asking for feedback on the site and its ease of use. Oh, the irony.

In WebAIM's 2017 screen reader survey, "Screens or parts of screens that change unexpectedly" moved from 7th most problematic web feature in 2009 to the 2nd most problematic in 2017. This is a prime example.[6] You need to be wary of changing focus when you overlay content on a page. If you don't, keyboard-only users won't be able to navigate to it. This amounts to taking over the user's page without their permission and then, without tab index, refusing to give it back. This is what is known as a keyboard trap.

Keyboard traps

A keyboard trap happens when a keyboard-only user is caught within a specific piece or group of content and then can't get out of the situation that the page has placed them in.

This most commonly occurs through a misuse of tabindex, or when content is added to a page and keyboard focus is either not moved to the new content, or is taken away from the web page's original content, but doesn't allow you to leave or close it.

It sounds like a rare occurrence, but has become increasingly common due to the 2018 GDPR regulations on data protection. These rules require sites using cookies to prompt users to accept that behavior when they first visit the site, and this is often accomplished by presenting an overlay modal that the user must accept in order to dismiss it. From a design perspective, it ensures that the rest of the user's time on the site can be free of popups, but the unfortunate truth is that, when created incorrectly, these can stop those users from engaging with the content at all.

Because of how common this is, WCAG actually has a success criterion in its spec for how to avoid creating a keyboard trap, and it's a requirement for their lowest level of compliance (A). Their spec states that you have to be able to move to and from a component using only the keyboard and, if you can't achieve this through the Tab key, you need to explain how to do so.[7] It's important to raise this here as it's the first of many solutions that improves the accessibility of a site for either multiple access needs, or users as a whole, by starting with just one access barrier.

105

You can solve this problem by using code to apply focus to the modal when it's opened, thereby preventing the issue with the feedback modal shown above. What specifically you decide to focus on within the modal is up to you, but it should be steered by the purpose of the modal and the content within it. For example if it holds information that doesn't require interaction, perhaps assigning focus to the button that closes the modal is the way to go, or if it's an overlay containing a form such as "log in" (as our example does), it's more beneficial going straight to the first form input – Figure 4-8 displays an example of the latter:

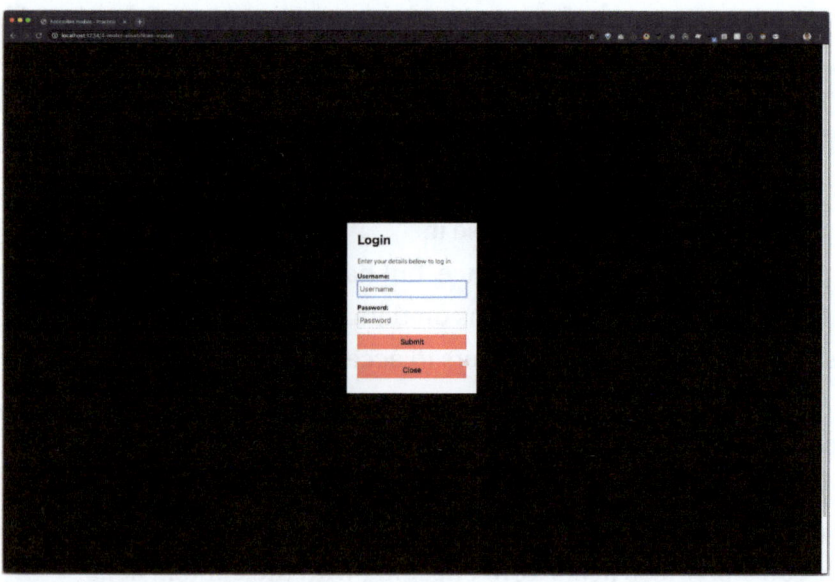

Figure 4-8. *A picture of a login modal window, with keyboard focus on the first form input*

Assigning focus to the first focusable element typically works better, as you will see in the practical example. This is because it can be used for both the first element of a form, or the modal's close button if it's only the element with focus in the content - both focusable elements.

Keeping tab focus inside the new content

Being able to move through the content in the now visible overlay makes it accessible and prevents a keyboard trap, but the other content on the page can still be navigated to. As a result, a user may end up tabbing through the content in the modal and continue onto the content below the overlay. As they now can't see that content due to the overlay, the user still ends up losing their place and isn't sure why. Strangely, you actually do want to form a kind of keyboard trap here: you want to allow focus to **only** exist on the visible modal content while that modal is open.

You can do this in one of two ways. First, you could temporarily hide all content that isn't in the modal while it's active, thereby ensuring that there is nothing else available to tab to. This is because hidden content isn't focusable on a web page. Again, for those reading that are not developers, feel free to skip past the code examples in the next few pages.

```
// JavaScript
// Hide all immediate children of the body tag that isn't the
modal
$('body > *:not('.modal')').addClass('modal-hidden');

/* CSS - make non-modal content invisible */
.modal-hidden {
    visibility: hidden;
}
```

This approach makes sense if your design prevents users from seeing the content underneath your modal – if they can see it though, then that content disappearing when the modal opens could seem strange.

An alternative solution is to add a small script that finds all content in the modal that can be focused on (links, buttons, elements with `tabindex` set, etc.) and create behavior that "loops" users through only those elements. This means that if a user is focused on the last focusable element in the modal and hits tab, instead of shifting them onto the content underneath, it would place focus back on the first focusable element of the modal. Likewise, if someone backward tabs (shift + Tab) while focused on the first focusable element, it would focus them on the last focusable element.

```
// If it's a tab or back-tab handle the movement
const tab = 9;
$(window).on('keydown', (e) => {
    switch(e.keyCode) {
        case tab:
            if (e.shiftKey) {
                Modal.handleBackTab(e);
            } else {
                Modal.handleTab(e);
            }
            break;
        default:
            break;
    }
});

...


handleTab: function(e) {
// If someone is on the last focusable element in the modal and
presses tab,
// Shift the focus to the first focusable element in the modal
  if (document.activeElement.isEqualNode(lastModalFocus)) {
    e.preventDefault();
    $(firstModalFocus).focus();
  }
},
```

```
handleBackTab: function(e) {
// If someone is on the first focusable element in the modal
and is hitting shift and tab to tab backwards,
// Shift the focus to the last focusable element in the modal
  if(document.activeElement.isEqualNode(firstModalFocus)) {
    e.preventDefault();
    $(lastModalFocus).focus();
  }
}
```

I have implemented this approach into our practical example as it's the more involved of the two, code-wise, but it's a simple switch to the other approach using the previous code should you prefer that.

Allow the user to close the new overlaid content

We've touched on this already, but once the user is in the modal, they must be able to close it without using a mouse. You can offer this behavior in a range of ways to cater to everyone:

- **A "Close" button.** This is the obvious first option. In our example, we immediately apply focus to it for the second of our two modals. This means that, with one key press, users can return to the page content. The button is often seen as an "X" icon positioned in a corner, but a "Close" button is more explicit.

- **Clicking outside of the modal content**. Now although this approach doesn't work for keyboard-only users, it certainly helps provide a way of closing the modal without the need to accurately press a specific button; clicking anywhere outside of the modal content will close it. This is incredibly useful for "pointer-based" users who suffer from motor impairments but still navigate with a cursor in some way. We will cover this in more detail in a moment, but for now, we achieve this by calling a `closeModal` function whenever a click occurs on the overlay, except for when the click is focused on the modal content:

```
initModalCloseWithNavMask: function() {
// Allow for the modal to be closed by clicking outside
of the content,
// but don't close if a click occurs inside of the
content
  $('.modal').on('click', function() {
    Modal.closeModal();
  });

  $('.modal > div').on('click', (e) => {
    e.stopPropagation();
  });
}
```

- **Hitting the escape key**. This has become a very common user behavior to close content and so adding it to our modal, even if many people don't use it, is still of value. In this case, we can add to our code from the previous challenge of maintaining focus in the modal, to initiate an action if the escape key is hit:

```
const esc = 27,
      tab = 9;

// Check for keyboard input
// If its the escape key, close the modal
// If it's a tab or back-tab handle the movement
$(window).on('keydown', function(e) {
```

```
    switch(e.keyCode) {
        case tab:
            if (e.shiftKey) {
                Modal.handleBackTab(e);
            } else {
                Modal.handleTab(e);
            }
            break;
        case esc:
            if ($('.modal.modal-open').length > 0) {
                Modal.closeModal(e);
            }
            break;
        default:
            break;
    }
});
```

Allow the user to return to where they were before the content appeared

Finally, once a user has interacted with your overlaid content, the focus should be returned to the place they initiated the modal from. This is easy, as when the user first opens the modal, you can store the element that initiated it. Then when the user closes the modal in any way, you simply return focus to that same button:

```
const trigger;
openModal: function(target, button) {
    ...
    trigger = button;
}
```

```
closeModal: function(e) {
...
    // Return focus to the original button that was clicked
    button.focus();
}
```

Now, if you've overlaid content without user interaction, returning them to where they were is tricky. As the user didn't cause the content to appear and, in order to be accessible, you will have moved the keyboard focus to the overlay, you may be unable to tell where their attention was. One thing you can do is get the code you're running to check if the user is focusing on any content at the time. You can then store that in the way that we have above and return them to it. However, they may not have been focusing on anything at the time, in which case you may need to resort to applying focus to the first focusable element on the page. This is better than nothing but has the added possibility of annoying users by taking over the page and then returning them to a completely different part of it. This raises the broader question of whether it's a good idea to inject content unannounced into the page in the first place (I believe the answer is a resounding "no").

Third-party software

This is a good point to finish this section on, as it's worth noting that barriers like this could be present on your site without you realising. Popups appearing without warning may seem like a specific example, but many sites choose to add some third-party software, perhaps to handle their GDPR-compliant cookie popup, or to gather feedback as we saw in the example above. If you do this, you could be inflicting a keyboard trap on your users that you didn't create, but that can lead to negative feedback about the accessibility of your site from excluded users. For this reason it's good to check if any third parties you use are injecting content into your site (A/B testing, chat apps, social sharing, etc.) and, if so, if they're doing it accessibly – it may not even be your own development that cause barriers. Now that we've covered a few ways to make content more accessible for keyboard-only users, let's look at some other ways in which users with motor impairments interact with the Web.

Pointer-based gestures

Some motor-impaired users prefer to **navigate** and **interact** with content on the Web using pointer-based gestures. This might involve pointing and clicking with a mouse, but these users often tire quickly, are less precise, or are prone to making mistakes. Other users (e.g., with milder arthritis or tremors) may use specialist mice or joysticks to mitigate these problems. Catering for point-based gestures requires us to consider a number of different access needs to those experienced by keyboard-only users.

It's worth noting that, although using the mouse has become the most traditional way of navigating the Web in a pointer-based manner, it's far from the only way. The introduction of touch screens opened up a plethora of other options, whether operated by hands, feet, or like some of the United Kingdom's 30,000 people with cerebral palsy – using head wands and mouth sticks.[8]

For those involved in making websites, all of these "pointer-based" forms of touch interactions are indecipherable from one another – all we can see from analytics is that the user is on a mobile device. This is equally true for those using computers, where point-based navigation can be achieved with a mouse alternative, like a joystick, or even eye tracking.

It is always worth remembering that these users may not be able to make certain gestures, like dragging and dropping, or pinching to zoom on a touch screen. We need to avoid this assumption that interactions are always carried out by the common mouse and keyboard combination. The key is to reduce the need for precision in the actions you ask users to make.

113

Large hit areas

The first thing you can do is to check that the areas where users perform actions, such as clicking buttons or checking checkboxes, are big enough and do not require large degrees of precision to operate.

This is another design pattern that would help the Web as a whole. All users would have a much larger margin for error, avoiding a great deal of frustration.

This is especially important on mobile devices where fingers, or other methods of input, often offer even less precision than a mouse cursor and use much smaller screens than standard monitors. Furthermore, interactions on a mobile device (e.g., a head stick tapping the screen) can obscure part of the screen from the users view.

WCAG have specified a minimum target size of 44 pixels x 44 pixels[9], but this doesn't mean that everything on your site should be square – if you use 44 pixels as a minimum for one axis, making the other larger will also make the target easier to hit. An example would be buttons on a mobile screen that designers often adapt to fill a high percentage of a screen's width while ensuring the minimum 44-pixel height – as Figure 4-9 shows.

Figure 4-9. *An illustration of two target areas on two mobile devices – the first as a 44px x 44px square and the other whose width adapts to fill the screen*

Both satisfy WCAG, but one seems a lot easier to interact with. It's worth noting that this WCAG rule is to satisfy their highest compliance level (AAA). However, given how easy it is to implement and the obvious benefits of doing so, I think it's something to seriously consider adding.

Now this isn't such an issue for keyboard users, as the tab key will focus on the button whatever the size. However, making the hit area bigger will always help to make the action easier for everyone to complete, as it makes the target area more visible, which is particularly useful for users with low vision.

Pointer cancellation

The last point leads nicely to pointer cancellation – another great rule added in WCAG 2.1.[10] Pointer cancellation matches this book's inclusive approach because as well as providing support for pointer-based users with impairments, it also safeguards a much wider group of people, allowing for a degree of human error.

What's even better is that nearly everyone who's used the Web has likely experienced this without even realising. Imagine the following scenario:

You're on a website purchasing a new book (after you've finished reading this one naturally). You reach the final page of the checkout journey, and just as you click the "submit order" button, you realise that the delivery address is set to your ex's house. Awkward. However, you haven't lifted your finger from your mouse/phone screen just yet, and so you slowly slide your finger/cursor away from the button and then lift your finger. The interaction on the button didn't register, and you've saved yourself an unpleasant phone call.

How is this possible? The answer is that this "click" is made up of both an "up event" and a "down event." A "down event" is registered the moment a tap is initiated, and if this type of event activated the "submit order" button above, the order would have been submitted instantly.

This is why the second "up event" exists. Unlike the down event, this event only happens when the "up" motion of finishing a tap/click is complete (it waits for the user to finish the whole action). This will allow users to cancel unintended actions midway through.

Undoing the action

Even after initiating actions on an up event, users may wish to cancel the action. For example, if that sudden moment of clarity had happened on the checkout page after they'd clicked the "submit order" button, they might still want to undo it.

As W3C explains, users should be able to

> "abort the function before completion or to undo the function after completion"[11]

Buttons can be pressed accidentally by someone with tremors while trying to scroll or by someone with a head wand who has missed their target, which reminds us to think about human error even after interactions have passed.

Google Mail introduced a great example of this, displayed in Figure 4-10, whereby immediately after clicking send on an email, the following notification appears.

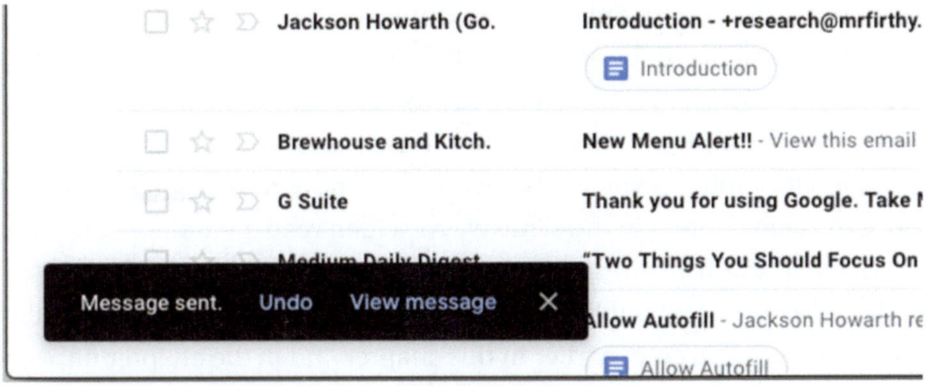

Figure 4-10. *An example of Google Mail's "undo sent message" feature*

This small (keyboard accessible) box provides users with the ability to swiftly undo this action. It's also becoming more common for eCommerce sites to let people know exactly how to reverse the purchase they've just made on the order success page. Cancelling actions is especially useful for point-based users – but is also a step towards considering all users' circumstances.

Now, both keyboard and pointer-based inputs are types of physical interaction, but not all motor-impaired users operate in this way. In fact, there are those that use only their voice.

Voice to text

Voice to text is another increasingly common form of navigation, especially among users with chronic pain, or arthritis (which affects over 10 million people in the United Kingdom alone).[12] Rani Nayyar, who experiences osteoporosis and fibromyalgia (which causes chronic pain) explains:

> *I use Dragon Naturally Speaking software due to the problem with my hands. It was recommended to reduce the use of the keyboard and mouse.*[13]

117

Other users (e.g., people with quadriplegia),[14] rely on voice to text to a much greater extent though. Almost all voice-to-text users use Dragon naturally speaking (a recent survey shows that nearly 90% use a version of Dragon).[15] Simply put, this software responds to voice commands that allow you to scroll, activate links, dictate text, move the cursor, and also move through content in the same way a screen reader would.

Given that voice-to-text users often navigate in a similar way to keyboard-only users ("tabbing" between content), a lot of the accessibility solutions we've covered, earlier in this chapter and in the chapter on blindness (Chapter 2), apply here. Here is a quick checklist if you're currently focused on optimising for speech software – all of these also provide tangible benefits to users without motor impairments:

- **Focus to show place** – If a user explicitly states which link to navigate to, displaying a focus style that shows that the command was successful is important.

- **Visual order and tab order** – With voice-to-text software navigating similarly to keyboards and screen readers, there's another good reason to provide a logical and linear order for content.

- **Alternative text (alt text) should match images** – For example, if an image of a printer is used to display a link to print a document, the user will probably use the command "Link print" to activate it. However, if the alternative text does not match that, the command won't be recognised and the link will not be activated.

- **Use form labels** – Many voice command users complain about difficult forms, and correctly labelled form elements make this interaction much easier. Without this, the user is forced to rely on "tab" voice command or guess what the designer or developer has called that form field.

- **Use Semantic Markup** – As we mentioned in Chapter 2, you should make sure that you are using the right HTML to reflect the feature that you are building. For example, if a user gives the command "click button" on a button that was made using a `<div>` tag instead of the native `<button>`, nothing will happen.

- **Avoid content that appears on hover** – We discussed this in the last chapter, as it causes issues with zooming software and creates a small "point of regard" area for users. In this case, voice commands are usually used to initiate a full interaction such as a click. A hover action, however, is based on focus and therefore usually undone the moment a user focuses elsewhere. For example, if a menu opens on hover, it may close before the user can engage with one of the links inside of it.

- **Making target areas larger** – You may think that, much like keyboard-only navigation, the target area for an element such as a button wouldn't matter if you're using speech software. However, some voice-to-text users also use a feature called "mouse grid." After using this command, a numbered 3 x 3 square grid will appear on the page, as you can see in Figure 4-11.[16]

Figure 4-11. *A picture of an active MouseGrid on a web page*

The user will then say the number closest to the content they want to interact with. Once they've done that, a new 3 x 3 grid appears in their chosen square, and they can select again. Figure 4-12 displays an example of this enhanced view.

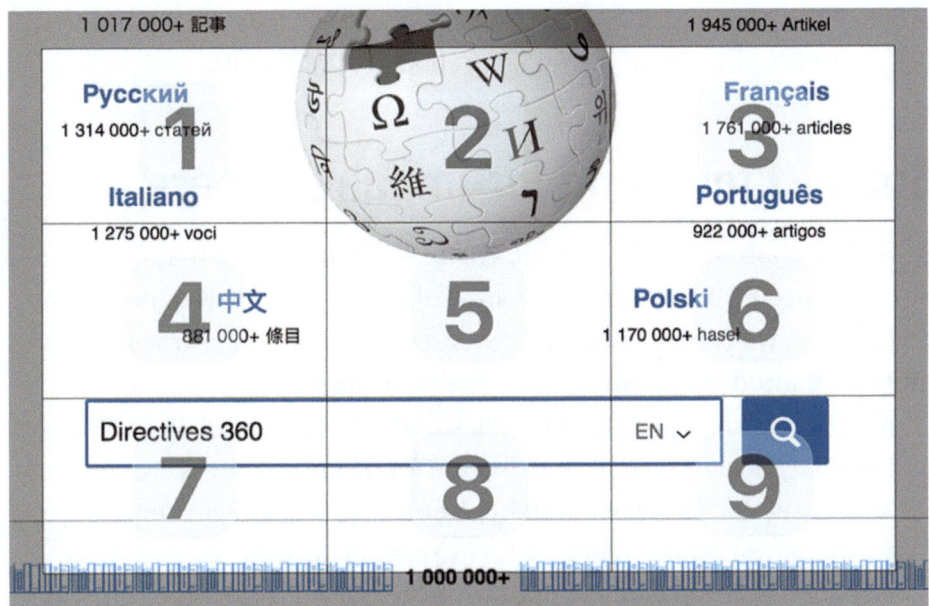

Figure 4-12. *A picture of an enhanced MouseGrid on a web page after user interaction on the first grid*

This verbal magnification continues until the grid is small enough that the user can click on their target.

MouseGrid can be used to overcome one or more of the barriers we've mentioned above but, more simply, some motor-impaired users may just prefer to navigate in this way. Again, we want to avoid making assumptions about how users choose to interact with content. As a result, making target areas for interactive elements such as buttons, links, and forms bigger proves very useful. Bigger targets are also a big win for voice-to-text users who use specific commands to steer the cursor, like "move cursor 50 pixels left" because it increases their accuracy too.[17]

One final big improvement, which will also help blind users, is to ensure websites don't ever play audio or video unexpectedly. As you can imagine, this can severely interfere with voice recognition software – even the act of trying to pause the noise on the page can be tricky in this situation. Instead, you should always provide a link/button to activate audio.[18] WCAG's original 2.0 spec has a rule about how to handle content like this[19], and we'll be covering it properly in the Imagery chapter (Chapter 8).

Support for all motor-impaired users

As we keep pointing out, there are changes you can make that will impact not only specific users but a wide array of users with different needs. In this section, we cover several improvements you can make that assist all motor-impaired users, and many other users too.

Of course, some people naturally stand to benefit more than others, and so it is quickly worth noting that the following solutions are some of the most useful fixes you can put in place for an often neglected group of motor-impaired users – people who use switch devices.

Steven hawking, who had **amyotrophic lateral sclerosis** (ALS) – a form of motor neuron disease, famously used a digital, on/off, "sensory switch" in his cheek to interact with the Web. He wrote at a rate of about one word a minute until autosuggest came along and doubled his writing speed. Besides sensory switches, switches can be buttons, like those on the side of your phone, sip-and-puff machines, or even camera switches in IOS products, operated by tilting your head.

If you want to imagine how switch users navigate and interact, a focus style jumps across the screen, or on-screen keyboard, and you need to wait until it's at the feature or letter you want to click on and then activate the switch.

If Stephen Hawking were to have scrolled on an iPhone using the switch device that he wrote 17 books on, there's a good chance that he would have had to do the following:

> 2 quick clicks to bring up an interaction menu
>
> 1 click to select the row with scroll button
>
> 1 click to select the scroll button
>
> 1 click to select the row with scroll down button

1 click to select the scroll down button

1 click to go back to the main menu

1 click to close the interaction menu.[20]

Switch users can use the Internet like anybody else as long as they have been catered for but obviously find it incredibly time consuming. Given the patience required, the solutions below become especially important, and every one of the following fixes holds value for all users too.

Short timeouts

Timeouts can generally occur after a certain period of inactivity to prevent fraud or unauthorised access (in the case of a user's account) or to allow for items in a basket to be made available to others (in the case of an online shop). They often result in progress in a journey or inputted information being lost. However, an inability to alter or extend the time allowed to complete actions can often be worse – leading to hastily completed actions, inviting human error, causing frustration, and excluding motor-impaired users (as well as a range of others) who work more slowly. It's therefore worth considering the following accommodations.

Extend a timeout

The main issue with timeouts related to motor-impaired users is that they usually fail to accommodate those who cannot complete the action before the predefined time limit is reached – all users may be indecisive about purchasing what's in their basket, for example, but some users need more time to finish the journey once they've decided. This affects motor-impaired users with head wands and switches, to cognitive impaired users who require longer to comprehend and complete tasks, or even those using screen magnifiers, mentioned in the last chapter, who take longer to scroll. Now, there are varying levels of success here. WCAG states that you should provide the ability to extend the deadline by at least ten times the initial time you provided,[21] with a prompt at least 30 seconds before the end of the timer. Inside this prompt, there should be a way to easily choose to extend the timer; otherwise, the same problem could occur – this is required for level A compliance. A more involved solution (to achieve AAA compliance) could be allowing the user to reauthenticate after a long time away and continue their journey without having lost the data they've already submitted.[22] This is ideal but of course is a bigger job. It's worth evaluating the nature of your journey and the effort required to complete it, to determine which solution would be most applicable.

Provide shortcuts

Due to the effort required to navigate a page with a motor impairment, it's always worth looking at a page and working out if there are steps that could be taken in order to make the process easier to undertake.

It's worth mentioning that there actually is a framework that exists in website development to provide shortcuts within a web page for users. It's called accesskey and has been part of HTML for years. The initial concept was to allow developers to specify a shortcut that, when pressed, would navigate the user to that part of the page. For example, you could set accesskey="s" on a search input, and so pressing "s" would provide keyboard focus to it.

However, because any key could be assigned to any type of action on the page, this created a whole host of inconsistency problems between sites, and made it too risky for anyone to add.

Components

Because accesskey failed as a general concept, the idea of providing shortcuts in a sensible way that provides value for users is somewhat limited to what you can do with individual components, and so should be thought about on a case-by-case basis depending on the components on your site.

We mentioned the "skip to main content" link in Chapter 2, and our practical example explained that this link would appear as the first focusable element if a user was navigating the page using a keyboard.

Another good example involves converting a series of manual address inputs into a postcode lookup list that the user can select their address from. Components like these often require additional effort for developers (in this case more so than the simple implementation of a regular form field), but in comparison to the pain of misspelled and unformatted addresses, along with the time taken to fill it all out, it's almost certainly a net gain.

This point is also relevant for those suffering from dyslexia or other learning difficulties, accounting for human error in the information they input (we will go into this more in Chapter 6).

Motion actuation

Motion actuation describes the performance of certain actions by physically moving a device, and is the subject of a success criteria for accessible websites introduced in WCAG 2.1. It is also especially valuable for those that use mounted devices for ease of use.

For example, the iPhone has a feature where shaking the device will undo something you've just written. This presents an accessibility issue because the feature may be unintentionally activated by turbulence, for example, a mounted wheelchair on a bumpy bus. This also poses problems for users with Parkinson's, for example, who experience hand tremors and other unintentional movements.

To remove this access barrier, there must be a way to switch the feature off, either on the web page or the device (to prevent "accidental triggering of functions"), and of achieving the same behavior using another method.[23] There must be an action that can undo what the motion-based feature does. For the iPhone example, this is the cancel button that appears when the "shake to undo" feature occurs, and prevents a situation where users are punished when this happens unintentionally.

This criterion is aimed at devices but there are many ways that sites can leverage a device's mechanisms such as the accelerometer or cameras, and it's been used on sites to provide features based on gestures such as tilting, shaking, or gesturing to a camera. These are exciting innovations, but they often exclude users with motor-based impairments – so it's important to design customer journeys that don't rely on them to complete an interaction.

Orientation

Orientation is relevant here, as it may not be possible to alter the orientation of a mounted device. Web content must therefore be visible to users regardless of whether they're viewing in portrait or landscape, as sites that only offer one orientation are noncompliant and inaccessible.

It may sound like a weirdly specific scenario, but when mobiles were introduced, users often had to change orientation to view content, as many sites didn't respond to a change in screen width. Figure 4-13 displays an example of this – because you can use CSS to detect a device's orientation, many companies decided to force their users to change their device orientation to view content rather than make their website responsive. This meant that, often, sites viewed in portrait mode would display the following message.

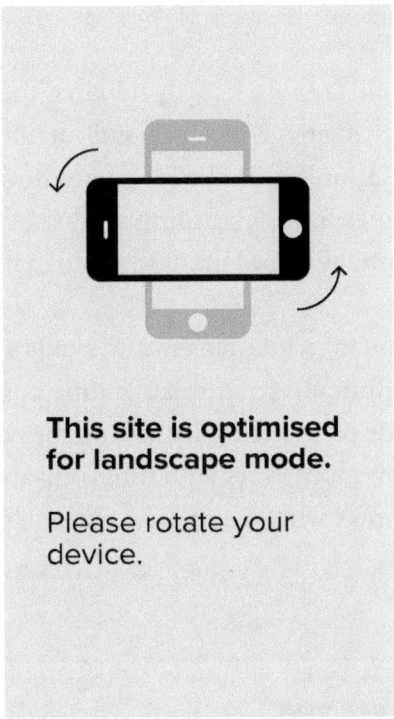

This site is optimised for landscape mode.

Please rotate your device.

Figure 4-13. *An example of a web page, displayed in portrait mode, asking the user to rotate their device to view the content*

In this case, "optimised" actually means "our old site will only fit this orientation – we haven't designed for portrait." Today, portrait mode is, of course, the standard for most mobile phones, so this caused problems. The solution, as mentioned in Chapter 3, is responsive web design. If your site can adapt to any screen size, it can therefore adapt to multiple orientations. Again, this also avoids the dangerous assumption that users can easily switch between portrait and landscape.

Autofill

The usefulness of autofill is more heavily debated than you may think. On the face of it, autofill seems entirely useful – it allows users to store information that they input frequently (most commonly addresses and passwords) in their browser, which prompts them every time they arrive at an address or login form, allowing them to paste that content rather than rewriting it every time.

This cuts down time for a lot of users and holds an added benefit for those that find typing difficult, strenuous, or time consuming – such as those using head wands or switches. By default, browsers allow this, and from the perspective of many users with motor disabilities, it can be a big win. Figure 4-14 shows what a common autofill looks like on Google Chrome.

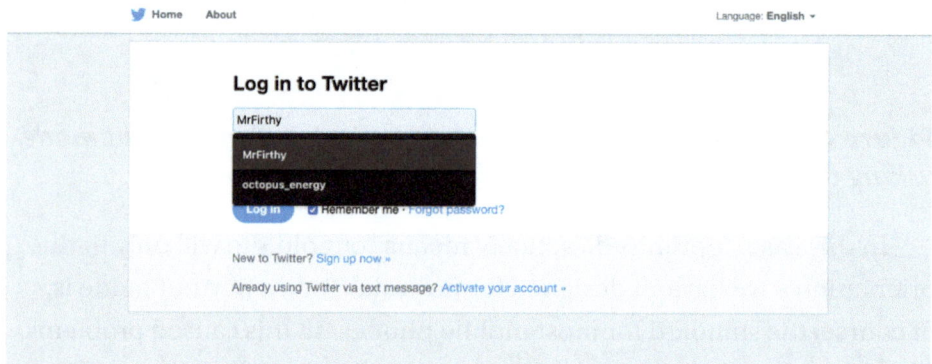

Figure 4-14. *An example of Google Chrome's autofill feature, as a user logging into Twitter*

So why is there a debate?

Well, although autofill can save some typing time, many people have raised the argument that browsers frequently store data in incorrect fields which, when inputted, can either force users to have to delete what was auto-filled and replace it, or end up submitting data in the wrong fields without noticing (thereby causing potential delivery or billing issues). Furthermore, having browsers hold sensitive information becomes a problem if a user's device is stolen and their personal information is offered up by a browser.

From an aesthetic perspective, any input on a form that has been automatically filled switches its background colour to a light blue (it used to be light yellow but changed in a recent update). This lets the user know which inputs have received information. This colour deliberately clashes with most colour schemes in order to stand out, and so has the potential to negatively impact a design. You might think that people would be hesitant to remove this useful feature for the sake of a colour scheme, but remember people also frequently remove the small blue outline caused by the focus style.

What makes this debate even trickier is that those who build sites have the power to completely remove autocomplete using one attribute:

```
<input type="text" name="address-line-1" autocomplete="off" />
```

Just like that, the user's browser will not allow autocomplete.

My personal opinion is that autocomplete should be allowed, and this is because there is a reasonable solution for all of the concerns previously raised:

- Each user can choose not to store their information in autofill, but turning it off through code makes that choice for every user.

- It's reasonable not to want the wrong information in the wrong form fields. However, a combination of good form validation (ensuring a postcode can't appear in a telephone number field for example) and allowing a user to check both after the initial autofill and on a review page means that this isn't a good-enough reason to turn it off for people who may rely on it.

- I wholeheartedly agree that sensitive data shouldn't be stored in a browser, and I include passwords in that category alongside credit card information. This is why password managers are so important and on the rise in terms of popularity. Keeping data in an application specially designed to keep it safe is the safest choice, and turning off autocomplete impedes a password manager's ability to insert content into forms when called upon.

- In response to the light blue background that autofilling creates, you can use CSS to alter its appearance to a more palatable colour, just as we mentioned that you could for the focus style. The following would change the background for auto-filled inputs in Google Chrome and Safari (Firefox doesn't support this at the moment unfortunately):

```
input:-webkit-autofill {
    background-color: black;
}
```

Note   It's important to choose a colour with a high-enough contrast that the user can read the pre-filled information displayed by autofill without issue.

Conclusion

Motor disabilities create a range of access needs that require careful consideration. Having covered a variety of different ways in which users with various motor impairments interact with the Web, hopefully you now feel as though you both understand some of the barriers faced by them and know how to spot them in your sites and journeys.

We've also learned how to remove some common barriers. We looked at how to avoid excluding motor-impaired users from content that they might not be able to interact with using the `tabindex` attribute, how to avoid trapping them *in* content (and out of it) when new features such as modals and overlays take over a page, how to handle autofill, timeouts, and to avoid motion-based actions like tilting and shaking that many users may not be able to perform. Overall, you should now know how to accommodate a range of input methods and navigational techniques in order to make your sites as accessible as possible.

Notes

1. International Neuromodulation Society, *Motor Impairment*, (2019) <`www.neuromodulation.com/ motor-impairment`> [accessed 08/05/19].

2. Microsoft and Forester Research, *The Wide Range of Abilities and Its Impact on Computer Technology*, (2004), <`http://download.microsoft.com/download/ 0/1/f/01f506eb-2d1e-42a6-bc7b-1f33d25fd40f/ researchreport.doc`> [accessed 08/05/19].

3. NHS Inform, *Parkinson's disease*, (2019) <`www. nhsinform.scot/illnesses-and-conditions/ brain-nerves-and-spinal-cord/parkinsons- disease`> [accessed 08/05/19].

4. National Tremor Foundation, *Essential Tremor Information*, <`https://tremor.org.uk/public/ downloads/O6qdN/Booklet.pdf`> [accessed 08/05/19].

5.   W3C, *Keyboard Accessible: Understanding Guideline 2.1,* (2016), <www.w3.org/TR/UNDERSTANDING-WCAG20/keyboard-operation.html> [accessed 08/05/19].

6.   WebAim, *Screen Reader User Survey #7,* (10/2017), <https://webaim.org/projects/screenreadersurvey7/> [accessed 07/04/2019].

7.   W3C, *No Keyboard Trap: Understanding SC 2.1.2,* (2016), <www.w3.org/TR/UNDERSTANDING-WCAG20/keyboard-operation-trapping.html> [accessed 08/05/2019].

8.   Assistive Technology Guide, *Mouth/Head Stick/Pointers,* <https://at-aust.org/items/2899> [accessed 08/05/19] + Cerebral Palsy Sport, *Cerebral Palsy Key Facts and Statistics,* <www.cpsport.org/resources/cerebral-palsy-key-facts-and-statistics/> [accessed 08/05/19].

9.   W3C, *Understanding Success Criterion 2.5.5: Target Size,* (2016), <www.w3.org/WAI/WCAG21/Understanding/target-size.html> [accessed 08/05/2019].

10. W3C, *Understanding Success Criterion 2.5.2: Pointer Cancellation,* (2016), <www.w3.org/WAI/WCAG21/Understanding/pointer-cancellation.html> [accessed 08/05/2019].

11. W3C, *Understanding Success Criterion 2.5.2: Pointer Cancellation,* (2016), <https://www.w3.org/WAI/WCAG21/Understanding/pointer-cancellation.html> [accessed 08/05/2019].

12. NHS, *Arthritis,* (14/12/2018), <www.nhs.uk/
conditions/arthritis/> [accessed 08/05/19].

13. Rani Nayyar, *Accessibility and Me*, Accessibility
in Government Blog, (19/09/2017), <https://
accessibility.blog.gov.uk/2017/09/19/
accessibility-and-me-rani-nayyar/> [accessed
08/05/19].

14. Joe Meyer, *Spinal Cord Injury Update,* (2010),
<http://sci.washington.edu/info/newsletters/
articles/10_sum_speech_rec.asp> [accessed
08/05/19].

15. Chris Moore, *Results of the 2016 GOV.UK assistive
technology survey*, accessibility in government,
(01/11/2016), <https://accessibility.blog.
gov.uk/2016/11/01/results-of-the-2016-gov-
uk-assistive-technology-survey/> [accessed
08/05/19].

16. Nuance, *Mousegrid*, <www.nuance.com/products/
help/dragon/dragon-for-mac6/enx/Content/
Navigation/MouseGrid.html> [accessed 08/05/19].

17. Nuance, *Mouse Commands*, <www.nuance.com/
products/help/dragon/dragon-for-mac6/enx/
Content/Navigation/MouseCommands.html>
[accessed 08/05/19].

18. Trenton Moss, *Improving Accessibility for Motor
Impaired Users,* (2007) <www.webcredible.com/
blog/improving-accessibility-motor-impaired-
users/> [accessed 08/05/19].

19. W3C, *Audio Control: Understanding SC 1.4.2*, (2016)
     `<www.w3.org/TR/UNDERSTANDING-WCAG20/visual-`
     `audio-contrast-dis-audio.html>` [accessed
     08/05/19].

20. Hampus Sethfors, *I Used a Switch Control for a
     Day, 24 Accessibility*, (18/12/2018), `<www.24a11y.`
     `com/2018/i-used-a-switch-control-for-a-day/>`
     [accessed 08/05/19].

21. W3C, *Timing Adjustable: Understanding SC 2.2.1*,
     (2016), `<www.w3.org/TR/UNDERSTANDING-WCAG20/`
     `time-limits-required-behaviors.html>`
     [accessed 08/05/19].

22. W3C, *Re-authenticating: Understanding SC 2.2.5*,
     (2016), `<www.w3.org/TR/UNDERSTANDING-WCAG20/`
     `time-limits-server-timeout.html>` [accessed
     08/05/19].

23. W3C, *Understanding Success Criterion 2.5.4:
     Motion Actuation*, (2016), `<www.w3.org/WAI/`
     `WCAG21/Understanding/motion-actuation.html>`
     [accessed 08/05/19].

CHAPTER 5

Deafness and hard of hearing

Hearing loss is extremely common. According to the World Health Organisation, more than 5% of the world's population – 466 million people – are deaf or hearing impaired, with 11 million of those people residing in the United Kingdom.[1] It's thought that by 2050, over 900 million people around the world (1 in 10) will have a hearing impairment.[2] With deafness set to become more prominent, we need to ensure that more attention is given to the barriers that these people could face.

Deafness affects people of all ages and does so in different ways. Some people are born without the ability to hear, while others lose their hearing later in life. As a result, some users learn to read and write English while being able to hear. Others, however, who were born deaf or hearing impaired, often find this much more difficult, but might be more proficient at British Sign Language, or reading lips. There are also several forms of hearing impairment that don't constitute a complete absence of hearing, including conductive hearing loss (where sound is muffled), perceptive deafness (where sound is distorted), various types of tinnitus, and auditory agnosia (where it is difficult to distinguish between sounds).[3] At a glance, these users experience similar access needs – auditory information must be communicated in alternative ways. In reality, there is far more to it, and it's important to remember that different deaf users have different preferences about how they receive this information.

© Ashley Firth 2019
A. Firth, *Practical Web Inclusion and Accessibility*,
https://doi.org/10.1007/978-1-4842-5452-3_5

Of the 11 million people in Britain who are deaf, over 150,000 use British Sign Language (BSL) as their preferred language, not English.[4] Since 1970, sign language has come to play an increasingly central role in the cultural unification of the British deaf community.[5] I spoke to Áine Jackson of the British Deaf Association, and she explained that:

> *These users often do not feel disabled and argue that they run into barriers due to a lack of understanding and services delivered in their first language. Deaf users can be considered a linguistic and cultural minority, a part of a community with a rich heritage and identity.*[6]

Remember that in the introduction, we discussed the World Health Organisation's change in the definition of "disability" from a "personal attribute" to a conflict between a person and the society they live in. Many BSL users don't want their deafness to be treated as a disability, they want people to understand that they have a different (and neglected) set of access needs when compared to hearing people, and this speaks to the essence of this book.

In this chapter, we will look at how to design with their access needs in mind, helping to remove those unnecessary barriers. The solutions in this chapter will empower BSL users, other hearing-impaired users, and a whole host of others, from people who speak another language to those who simply find reading difficult.

Nevertheless, providing a solution that works for all these users is a challenge and requires a delicate balance of considerations. This is because some of the typical methods have restrictions – the ability to provide sign language translators on videos is often restricted by the size of the video and the cost it incurs, and providing captions on video and audio raises the question of catering for those who have trouble understanding written English.

The good news is that many of these solutions can be added to content that already exists. We'll begin with, and largely focus on, creating and adding accessible subtitles and captions – tools that hold the greatest potential for providing access to previously inaccessible content. Because the way to achieve this (through code) has seen near global adoption across different browsers, we can provide this content in a way that better caters to the needs of deaf and hard-of-hearing users than was possible before.

We'll then look at the importance of the content itself and how to include options that cater for the various preferences of different deaf and hard-of-hearing users, which leads us on to advancements in this area from video streaming sites like YouTube. From communicating with customers to dealing with autoplay, barriers for deaf users often crop up unexpectedly, and this chapter will prove that it's important to be proactive when addressing common pitfalls that make understanding information harder than it should be.

Subtitles vs. closed captioning

Video and audio have grown online massively in recent years, and ensuring that yours are accessible has never been more important. If your videos have any sort of audio that holds meaning, then deaf and hard-of-hearing users are missing out on that information. Do you remember how we fixed existing inaccessible images in Chapter 2, by adding alt tags as another way to interact with them? It's time to do the same for videos!

You'd be forgiven for thinking that updating existing videos would be harder than adding `alt` tags to images, but really it only involves adding one tag, and a file with a format that's easy to understand. The main difference is that the amount of content you must describe depends entirely on the length of your videos. Before we get into the implementation though, it's worth briefly getting to know the different methods for describing audio content in written form. These are captions and subtitles, and understanding the difference can be tricky.

In the United Kingdom and, in fact, in many countries, the two words are often used interchangeably, with captions sometimes referred to as subtitles for the hard of hearing. However, elsewhere, people draw more concrete distinctions.

Captions, for Americans (and interestingly, also the W3C), are a word-for-word transcription of what is being said, in the same language as the audio. They also contain auditory information that isn't spoken but that helps the user to understand the context of the video. This could include indications of actions, music, and sound effects. For W3C, captions are described as being intended for deaf and hard-of-hearing users. Subtitles, on the other hand, only include words that are spoken and can be translated into other languages. W3C argue that subtitles are designed for hearing users who want the dialogue provided in text form as well.

The problem is, while it is useful to make a distinction between the two, these definitions make some unnecessary and confusing assumptions.

One big problem is that this definition assumes that subtitles are "for" hearing users and captions are "for" deaf users. Lisa Herrod, a user experience consultant who has written extensively about designing for deaf users, disagrees. She argues that both options are useful for deaf and hard-of-hearing users in different ways.

> *As a transcription, captioning is simply the written form of spoken words and sound effects, including slang, colloquialisms, modifiers, and wordplay—which... can be very difficult for deaf, HOH, and Deaf people who struggle with English as a second language.*[7]

In other words, captions are not "for" *all* deaf users, because, as we shall see in a moment, the word-for-word language can be confusing.

Similarly, Herrod goes against the W3C to point out that subtitles should not always be a word-for-word transcription of what is spoken – they should be considered translations, which allows us to change the text:

Subtitling, which is a translation, provides an opportunity to use words that are closer to the signs a Deaf person would use. However, it is important to note that typically, native sign languages have no natural written form.[8]

Here, subtitles can help some deaf users who prefer altered English, especially those who understand English poorly, or as a second language (we will explain how to write like this in more detail later in the chapter). Just as captions shouldn't be considered "for deaf users," subtitles shouldn't be seen as existing "for" hearing users.

It's clear that instead of emphasising a distinction based on who they are "for," we instead need to emphasise a difference in purpose. There's "translation" (changing text – sometimes into a different language – so it can be better understood) and "transcription" (writing down text word-for-word).

Moving forward, we will simply refer to captioning as providing extra contextual information and subtitling as containing the spoken content, but with the option to translate that content (into another language, or into more accessible text in the same language) using the most appropriate words for the task. These options should be seen more as preferences: some deaf users, for example, prefer "deaf-friendly" subtitles, while others are more comfortable with word-for-word transcribed English captions. For example, Todd Wright, a bilingual deaf user, explains:

I would prefer all subtitles and/or captions be more like literal translations with transcribed sound effects – I view media with full English captions as I do understand English very well.[9]

The key is to offer both captions, and subtitles translated into "deaf-friendly" English. For maximum accessibility, it is also especially useful to provide a combination of the two (subtitles with speech translated into "deaf-friendly language," combined with added contextual information).

Caption actions

You often see an indication like this in captions, wrapped in square brackets, like so:

```
[spits milk]
```

This infers information that isn't speech but helps the user greater understand the context of the video.

Furthermore, you'll often see captions positioned in different places over the course of a video to indicate who is speaking at a certain time. Subtitles, on the other hand, are positioned in the center and at the bottom of the screen at all times.

All of this is intended to provide a catered experience to users who cannot hear and break through barriers that aren't solely tied to the words in the video. Imagine each of the following scenarios while watching a movie with no sound:

- Characters in a movie have their backs to the camera and so it's not clear who's speaking.

- A glass smashes off-screen that draws attention, but the viewer cannot hear the sound.

- The soundtrack in a movie scene turns ominous but there is no dialogue.

Here, subtitles alone would leave a user with only part of the experience. You can easily see the difference captions make when by enabling them and turning the sound off. Netflix offers subtitles and captions in multiple languages as content is available in so many countries and to help those with hearing-related access needs enjoy content.

Both captions and subtitles are available in two forms: open and closed. Open means they are overlaid permanently on the screen and cannot be turned off, whereas closed means typically they are off by default but can be turned on at will by the user.

Helping all users

Captions and subtitles are another set of solutions that have proven useful to users with a wide range of access needs. Research has found that enabling subtitles helps improve comprehension of a language you're learning, and many people have taken to using them as a means of testing themselves.[10]

The W3C have argued that subtitles can also help some cognitive-impaired people. This is because it provides content in more than one format. When used simultaneously, multiple formats increase the likelihood of understanding and positive engagement, as users don't have to rely on a single source of information.[11]

Both formats also help hearing users engage with content without sound – either through being in a noisy environment or by being in a quiet environment where they are unable to play the sound.

Finally, creating transcripts can make your site easier to find on Google and makes it easier for other people to translate your content into other languages, as there is a written copy of content that would otherwise be inaccessible.[12]

Which should I apply?

It's worth thinking about the content of the video and ensuring that any important context wouldn't be lost if you were to purely transcribe speech and nothing else. Including both a captioned track that "transcribes" the contents of media, one that "translates" the text into "deaf-friendly" language, and a hybrid that includes both, creates choice for the user and caters to the widest possible set of access needs.

The good news is that, despite their different purposes and benefits, accessible subtitles, captions, and a mix of the two are implemented in the same way technically, and the change in how you format the content between the two types is minimal. So, whichever challenge relates to your site, we'll be tackling it.

<track> element

We added alt tags to images in Chapter 2 to provide a description of content for people who can't perceive images. Now, we're faced with a similar challenge but for audio and video. Luckily, HTML5 allows us to solve the problem for these users by adding subtitles for a video using the <track> tag:

```
<video controls>
    <source src="videos/video.mp4" type="video/mp4">
    <source src="videos/video.webm" type="video/webm">
    <track label="English" kind="subtitles" srclang="en"
    src="captions/vtt/video-en.vtt" default>
    <track label="Deutsch" kind="subtitles" srclang="de"
    src="captions/vtt/video-de.vtt">
</video>
```

For those that haven't seen this type of code before, this is how a video is added to a page in HTML. Let's quickly look at the three tags that are being used here:

`<video>` – The "parent" element that wraps the other tags. It tells the page that it will be displaying a video.

`<source>` – This tag holds the path to the actual video file that the page will display. A video can have multiple sources to account for different video formats, because some browsers will only display videos with a certain format.

`<track>` – The tag we're most interested in. This is what allows us to add our own subtitles and captions.

Now let's take a closer look at the attributes of the `<track>` tag we're focusing on, and the ways you can customise it:

- `label`: This provides the title for the track you've provided. Users will see this when they select a caption option.

- `src`: The path to your caption file.

- `kind`: Quite simply specifies the type of file. As we mentioned earlier, there is a difference between subtitles and captions, and so you can specify which type your file is through this. Other notable types are "chapters" which are provided to help users navigate to particular parts of audio or video and "descriptions," which provide a description of the visuals of a video if it's obscured or the user can't see it due to blindness or low vision. This is more useful when there is little to no dialogue in the video.

- `srclang`: The language that the captions or subtitles are provided in. This follows the same ISO country code format we mentioned in our work with the `lang` attribute in Chapter 2. Our above example has `en` for English and `de` for German. This is an important point to make, as you can provide multiple `<track>` files in order to provide captioning for a range of languages. This means that, by adding captions for a range of languages, you can also remove an access barrier present for users whose first language is not the one that your content is written in. If the `kind` attribute is set to "subtitles," you must set a `srclang`.

- `default`: following on from the last point, you can specify the default language that captions should be provided in (if you have supplied multiple options). This comes into effect if the user's preferences don't indicate that another track would better suit them – such as language preferences on their device/browser.

Much like going back through your site and adding `alt` tags to images, `<track>` is a big win for sites that already have video or audio on their site. Rather than undergoing the costly and time-consuming process of remaking videos in order to overlay captions onto it, you can simply create your own and add them retrospectively. We've seen how the file is added, so let's look at how to make the `.vtt` file itself.

WebVTT files

So, what is a `.vtt` file? WebVTT stands for Web Video Text Tracks Format, and these files allow you to write your very own captions for any videos you have on your site.

.vtt layout

The files that contain the actual caption data are simple text files. They follow a specified format and can be made without any knowledge of coding in an application like TextEdit or Notepad. You provide them in the following format:

```
WEBVTT

00:00:00.500 --> 00:00:03.500
Run run run as fast as you can

00:00:03.600 --> 00:00:05.000
You can't catch me
I'm the gingerbread man
```

You simply specify the start and end time for the part of the video you want to annotate and then add the words spoken within that time frame. You can also place this text over multiple lines if you want. That's it. You could save the code above as a .vtt file, add it to your audio or video using the <track> tag, and the first 9 seconds of it would display that text at those times. Figure 5-1 shows what this should look like.

Figure 5-1. *An example of WebVTT captions*

Different formats

It's worth noting that .vtt isn't the only format that can provide captioning for video and audio. There are a range of different formats that were created and adopted by different video platforms, but they all mostly follow the same format with a couple of minor style tweaks. For instance, this is an example of an .srt caption – another widely known format:

```
1
00:01,000 -> 00:04,000
-This is the common sloth in its natural habit

2
00:05,000 -> 00:09,000
-It moves very slowly along a branch
-in
```

As you'll see, it's nearly identical to the WebVTT example above – the main differences are the formatting of the times (srt uses commas between seconds and milliseconds, instead of full stops), and numbering captions is mandatory.

Popular sites like Youtube, Vimeo, and Netflix all support both .srt and .vtt, so you can't really go wrong with either.[13] However, as of 2019 WebVTT has a global browser support of nearly 93%[14] and is recommended by the W3C.[15] It also has a much broader set of features, allowing you to customise captions to fit your content, and user's needs, better. Let's get into some of the formatting options that WebVTT alone supports.

Styling subtitles

Providing text tracks for audio and video is a good first step, but, much like a web page itself, styling with CSS can really elevate both their aesthetics and usability. You may want the text to match your site's style, or for the captions to work a little harder to help those using them to better understand the content.

Browser support for WebVTT styling still varies, but due to the rapid adoption of the file format, adding some of these features to your .vtt files will provide you with a bit of futureproofing. As soon as a browser starts supporting them, you'll have an advantage, and if a browser doesn't support them, it'll simply ignore the custom tags and display the text normally anyway – let's go through some of these rules.

cue

The first rule that can be styled is the cue rule – this is what each line of text in a .vtt file is known as. Using cue, you can add styling rules that will apply to every caption or subtitle shown. Figure 5-2 shows the result of the code below – turning the caption text red and the background white:

```
video::cue,
audio::cue {
      color: red;
      background-color: white;
}
```

Figure 5-2. *The same caption as the previous example but styled with red text and a white background*

Formatting

There are a few simple tags that WebVTT recognises which work on every major browser:

- `<b>` (Bold) – Allows you to place emphasis on certain words

- `<i>` (Italics) – Allows you to italicise parts of text

- `<u>` (Underline) – Allows you to underline areas of a sentence

However, in Google Chrome and Safari, you can take this a little further and apply styling changes directly to these tags, thereby allowing you to change their appearance beyond these default styles. In the code below, you can see a line from a WebVTT file with bold (`<b>`) and italic (`<i>`) tags. The CSS below targets those tags to change their styles. Figure 5-3 shows these changes taking effect.

```
WEBVTT

00:00:08.100 --> 00:00:10.500
<b>I'm</b> not the monster here. <i>You are</i>.
```

```
/* CSS */

video::cue(b),
audio::cue(b) {
     color: blue;
}
video::cue(i),
audio::cue(i) {
     color: green;
}
```

Figure 5-3. *Parts of captions styled using the bold and italic tags*

Positioning

Beyond the aesthetic changes to captions, you also have control over where text is displayed on your video. You can achieve this with a range of attributes, all of which work in modern browsers.

position and **line**

As seen in Figure 5-4, these two rules decide where captions are positioned. `position` is responsible for the X-axis, and `line` is responsible for the Y-axis.

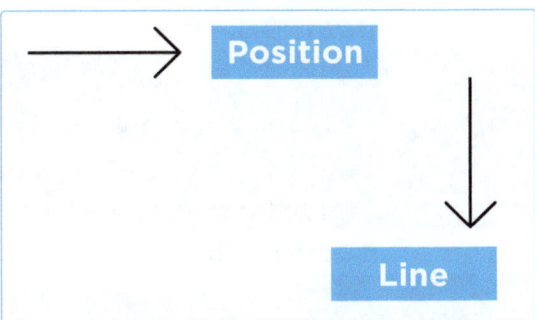

Figure 5-4. *A diagram showing how the* position *and* line *attributes affect the positioning of captions*

position is represented using a percentage (0%– 100%), which can also be used for line, but *line* can also be a number which represents how many lines from the top (if the number is above zero) or bottom (if the number is below zero) the caption should be. These rules can be applied to every caption through CSS, or on a per-caption basis by adding the rule to a specific cue just after the end time. In Figure 5-5, you can see how different percentage values change the position of several captions:

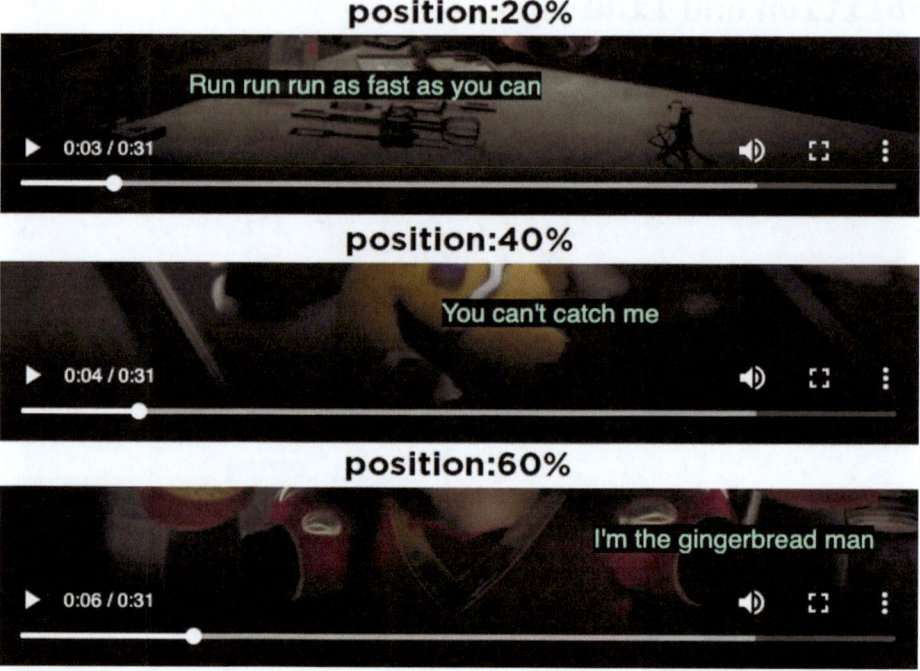

Figure 5-5. *A visual representation of captions positioned in different places using the* `position` *attribute*

This isn't useful if you're adding "translations" without captions, as they're always positioned in the center and at the bottom of the screen, but it is useful when positioning captions. These rules allow caption content to be closer to the person who is speaking if there's more than one person visible in the video, or if the mouth of the person speaking isn't visible, for example.

Align

This specifies the alignment of the caption text. It can be `start` (left), `center` (middle), or `end` (right) (shown in Figure 5-6) and can be applied to each cue individually.

```
00:00:04.100 --> 00:00:06.000 align:center
You can't catch me
```

Figure 5-6. *Captions aligned left, center, and right based on the* align *attribute set*

Size

The size attribute dictates how much of the screen your captions take up. This is always specified as a percentage (0%–100%). For example, the code below reduces the size of the caption box, with the result shown in Figure 5-7.

```
00:00:06.300 --> 00:00:012.600 size:10%
You can't catch me
```

Figure 5-7. *A caption displayed as one word per line, due to the* size *of the caption being set to 10% of the screen*

It's worth considering whether you should reduce the size of your captions or subtitles though, as it can be difficult to read more than two lines at a time.[16]

Future features

The following features are part of the WebVTT spec but are currently not widely supported. They are, however, worth thinking about because of their potential to provide greater understanding for users in the future. I have provided an example of each of these in the practical example for this chapter, but you will see varying results for now until their support becomes more commonplace:

Voice spans

VTT files also allow for "voice spans" to distinguish certain subtitles. For example, the following markup:

```
00:00:00.000 -> 00:00:08.000
<v Walter>I am the danger</v>
```

This will allow you to consistently style text spoken by a particular person, such as a character or narrator. This is especially useful for dialogue, as you won't have to apply the same styling rules to every part of the file in which a certain character speaks. The style for the above would look like:

```
video::cue(v[voice='Walter']) {
    color: white;
    background: red;
}
```

Classes

Applying a `classname` will allow you to style a piece of text in the same way that you can use CSS to style any other element with a class. The syntax is a little different to the other examples, but the results are the same:

```
<style>
    /* CSS */
    .my-class {
        color: purple;
        text-transform: uppercase;
    }
</style>
```

```
WEBVTT
01:23:00.000 -> 01:23:04.000
<c.my-class>Get busy livin', or get busy dyin'</c>
```

:past and :future pseudo elements

These two selectors allow you to style captions that happen either before or after the video's current playtime. A good example of this is karaoke, where it's handy to have a sense of timing related to a line of text. Take the following example:

```
WEBVTT

00:00:14.500 --> 00:00:21.000
I've<00:00:14.500> tried to<00:00:16.000> be fair<00:00:18.000>
to<00:00:18.750>you<00:00:20.250>creatures
...
/* CSS */
video::cue:past {
    color:grey;
}
video::cue:future {
    color:pink;
}
```

Here, you can see a timestamp assigned to certain parts of the sentence. As the video or audio reaches a particular point, the text that came before will be grey, and the text yet to come would be in pink, which Figure 5-8 shows.

Figure 5-8. *Captions displaying text in grey that is in the past (based on the point in the video) and pink for words in the future*

Karaoke is quite a niche example though. A handier use for this functionality is that you can use the timed captions to more accurately match words *as someone is saying them,* so that users deaf can engage with physical gestures as well as the text. This is useful because it helps users build up a greater sense of context. For example, deaf and BSL users "rely heavily on facial expression to convey essential meaning and emphasis."[17] The key is having shorter and more frequent captions rather than bigger ones that last longer. This allows users to understand gestures, follow with greater ease, and not focus on just the text because they're unsure how long it'll be present on screen – preventing them from getting overwhelmed. This is a better example, as karaoke would mean providing captions for an audio track and not video – but now let's go through how to handle that too.

<audio> tag and captions

Providing captions for audio files is especially important, as this form of media only conveys information via sound and would otherwise be completely inaccessible to hearing-impaired users – video at least compliments audio with visuals. However, there is one big problem – at the time of writing, captions don't really work at all with audio. They ignore the <track> tag in all major browsers (despite recognising that it's there).[18]

The good news is that we can work around this problem, using the <video> tag. What we can do is provide an audio file such as an MP3, specify that as the type, and the <video> tag will simply play audio:

```
<video class="audio" controls>
    <source src="media/audio.mp3" type="audio/mpeg">
    <track label="English" kind="subtitles" srclang="en"
src="vtt/audio.vtt" default />
</video>
```

This makes sense, as the <audio> and <video> tags both use the same <source> tag, and both extend from the native media element. This is great news for accessibility but does come with a slight drawback. As captions display at the bottom of a video by default, and because an audio track has no video to display, the captions can often end up displaying underneath the browser's native video controls.

There are a couple of ways to combat this issue. First, you could provide a thumbnail or "poster" image for the audio, which is shown as a fallback when no video is present:

```
<video class="audio" controls poster="images/poster.jpg">
```

This gives the <video> tag the height it needs to avoid displaying captions below the controls.[19] An alternative to avoid visuals is to explicitly set a height for the video element serving the audio, and then using the line attribute, we mentioned earlier to position the captions at the top of the <video> instead of the bottom:

```
/* CSS */
.audio {
    height: 120px;
}
```

```
WEBVTT

00:00:08.100 --> 00:00:10.500 line:1
I'm not the monster here. You are.
```

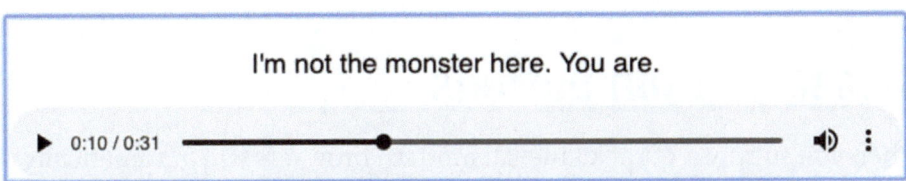

Figure 5-9. *A custom audio player using the* <video> *tag, a fixed height, and positioned captions*

Remember line:1 means that the caption should be displayed one line from the top of the video. I have created both implementations in the practical example, so that you can see both in action and decide which works best.

Practical example

What is hopefully clear from looking at all of these attributes is that there are ways to cater to pretty much every preferred style of displaying captions and subtitles. You can now have full control over positioning, styling, colours, and the direction the text is read – even allowing users to sing along to it. There should, therefore, never be an issue where you are unable to accurately describe what is happening in audio or video within a .vtt tag.

I have added examples of each of these features into this Chapter's practical example, including a demonstration of how this works for audio as well as video. For those who are interested in the code you can check it out on Github in the "Chapter 5" folder, or if you just want to see it in action, you can view it at `https://inclusive.guide/examples/webvtt`. Again, what's great about this implementation is that you don't necessarily have to change anything about the content you already have – it's really easy to add captions or subtitles as an extra file and your site will immediately become more accessible. Now that you know how to add captions and subtitles for both video and audio yourself, let's briefly cover how users can control them, and how they're handled in a large video–based website like YouTube.

Closed caption buttons

When you supply a `<track>` file, all modern browsers will automatically display a button to toggle the subtitles/captions on and off (or choose between the multiple languages that you have provided). You see the same on sites such as YouTube or Vimeo. This means that you don't have to build this functionality yourself – you're rewarded with it for providing a `.vtt` file! Figure 5-10 shows the expanded version of the caption button on a native video player.

Figure 5-10. *An example of a browser's default closed caption button*

This is a brilliant accessibility gain, but you may not always want to display captions – overlaying captions or subtitles on your media for every user would be unnecessary. Fortunately, this is easy to handle and can be controlled by one attribute on the `<track>` tag – `default`. If you don't provide a `default` track, the video won't display the captions by default and instead requires the user to turn them on via the "closed caption" button. Not providing a default also makes sense from the perspective of not making assumptions about your user's language of choice.

YouTube

As we mentioned before, major streaming platforms such as YouTube and Vimeo, and media players such as VLC and iTunes support the ability to upload the WebVTT captions we just created. This means you can make your content more accessible even when it's not hosted on your own site using the `<video>` tag. YouTube, however, actually creates captions for videos that are uploaded to their system themselves:

> *YouTube can use speech-recognition technology to automatically create captions for your videos. These automatic captions are generated by machine-learning algorithms.*[20]

You can view these by clicking the "CC" button next to the full screen icon, and Figure 5-11 shows how they are displayed.

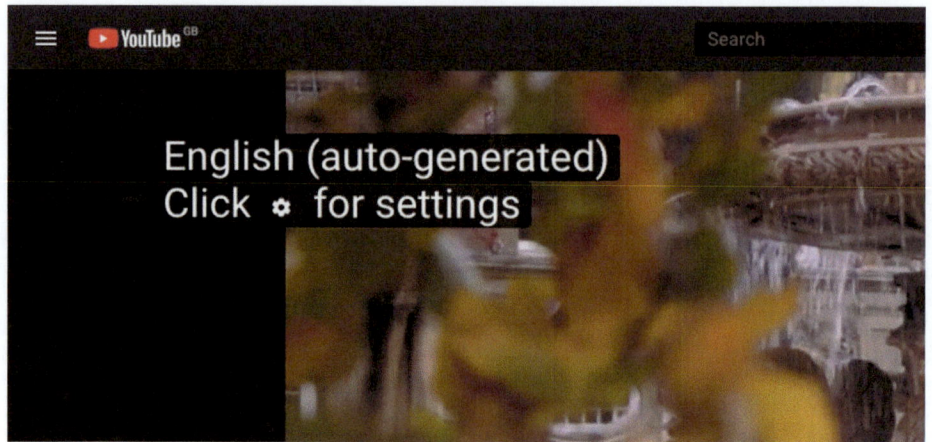

Figure 5-11. *The message displayed on a Youtube video when you enable closed captions and they've been generated using YouTube's algorithm*

This is seriously impressive and provides an excellent baseline of accessibility on one of the most visited websites in the world. However, Youtube does state that "the quality of the captions may vary" as the algorithm gets smarter. It's therefore worth going over the captions that have been created for your content and making any necessary changes if some have been incorrectly created.

It's possible to do this through YouTube's "Video Manager" (shown in Figure 5-12) where you can edit both text and timings that have been generated automatically.

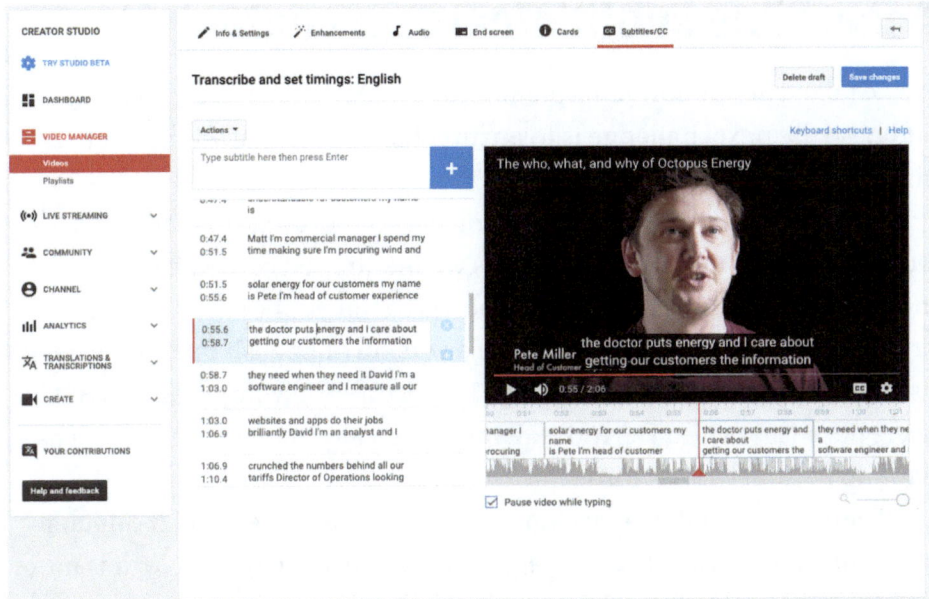

Figure 5-12. *The YouTube manager page that allows you to alter the generated captions for your video*

You can also choose to download and edit the captions YouTube have generated, which are provided as an `.sbv` file but bears a heavy resemblance to the `.vtt` files we covered earlier:

```
0:00:03.529,0:00:08.970
We started octopus energy to be
fairer to customers
```

```
0:00:08.970,0:00:13.380
to make it digital the way it should be
and because it's so important we move to renewables
```

Accessible subtitle/caption content

We've talked about how to implement subtitles and captions for video and audio, so the next challenge is to ensure that the content within them is also accessible.

Some deaf users who can read English comfortably are happy with word-for-word captions. However, as we mentioned earlier, it can be incredibly useful to translate (as opposed to transcribe) your subtitles, providing the option to have them in a version of English that many deaf users will find easier to understand. This is especially important to BSL users because, as Lisa Herrod explains: "typically, native sign languages have no natural written form."[21]

There are several reasons that native BSL users often find it difficult to understand word-for-word transcribed English. For example, it is more difficult to learn English without sounding out the words, and BSL is very different from written English – words that sound the same in English will often have very different BSL signs, and BSL has its own grammar structure. A phrase like: "How old is your friend?" might be expressed as "Friend yours how old?"

How a deaf user prefers to receive accessible information often depends on what they consider to be their first language. As we mentioned at the start of the chapter, many native BSL users consider BSL their first language, and so would benefit most from on-screen BSL signing. There are many organisations that you can commission to create BSL titles for your content, as this approach isn't as easy to implement as closed captions and subtitles. The result, as Áine Jackson of the British Deaf Association explained to me is that:

> most web content accessibility guidelines do not make adequate provision for sign language users to access content in sign language as a first language. While there is limited good practice happening with some organisations and charities, this is very much the exception and not the rule.[22]

If signed translation is not an option, perhaps due to cost, then Lisa Herrod recommends:

a combination of captioning (to transcribe sound effects) and subtitling (written translation, with a focus on users with sign as a primary language) is most effective.[23]

Some companies are willing to translate audio into BSL-friendly subtitles which are easier for these users to understand. Where this still isn't possible, there are still some important steps you should take yourself to ensure that your subtitles are more accessible for Native BSL signers. These all revolve around writing in a way that is more accessible to these users. It's also important to remember that deaf users for whom English is their first language often still struggle with written English and as a result typically have a lower reading age (a common way to estimate someone's reading ability, measured against the average ability of people of different ages). Research about this is disappointingly rare, but a famous report in 1979 found that deaf school leavers had an average reading age of around 9 years old. A more recent report from 1996 found that with modern teaching techniques, this had only risen to around 13 years old.[24] Therefore, the solutions we are about to propose are also extremely useful for removing barriers for these users, who might not sign BSL but will still benefit from more accessible English:

- **Avoid puns** – Words that mean the same thing in English tend to have very different signs in BSL – and puns relies on understanding the sounds of the words to make sense. Unless a deaf user has a very strong grasp of written and spoken English, hearing puns can become quite confusing. For example, the phrase "time flies like an arrow, fruit flies like a banana" could be difficult to understand, due to the different meanings of the word "flies" – especially for BSL users who have different signs for flying and insects.[25]

- **Synonyms** – English has more synonyms than almost any other language, while BSL uses very few gestures to describe the same thing. It can sometimes be useful to use a more common synonym if you were thinking of using an obscure one.

- **Text speak** – (i.e., C U L8er). Again, to understand what the letters mean here, you have to understand how they sound, which isn't an option for many deaf users.

- **Avoid colloquialisms/idioms** – A lot of idioms, like "once in a blue moon" do not carry over to BSL well – it is difficult to know whether they should be taken literally, and therefore they might not be understood.[26]

- **Clear simple speech** – This is especially important due to a lower average reading age in deaf users. We will talk in more detail about plain English in Chapter 6, as this is also relevant when catering for various cognitive impaired users.

If possible, deaf and BSL-friendly English should be used across your entire site. This is part of a much wider accessibility requirement – writing clearly. BSL-friendly language includes several aspects of "plain English." Writing accessible English is especially worth it when you consider that it will make your writing much easier to understand for those with dyslexia, autism, and cognitive impairments.

Writing accessible English shouldn't be mistaken for "dumbing down" content though, it's more about making content clearer:

There seems to be a perception by some people that subtitles for the Deaf use dumbed-down language. However, I've always perceived the language to be based on the English equivalent of the signs that would have been used had an interpreter been present. Of course, this means that the grammar continues to follow an English pattern, but it seems to me that the subtitles are likely to be more accessible to a wider audience.[27]

Summarising audio and video content

Providing a short summary of what is in your media can be just as useful as adding captions and will allow *all* users to decide whether they want to engage with it or not. Here's an example from a hearing-impaired user called Ruth, talking about watching an Aretha Franklin performance on Facebook:

I see her playing the piano and I think, 'What song is she playing? There's absolutely no description. It's not that I need to hear every word, but sometimes I have no idea what's happening.[28]

This is another method that is similar to `alt` text for images but holds particular benefit to those with a hearing impairment.

Providing a transcript

Another way of distilling media in a way that includes deaf users is to provide a full transcript of content that includes audio. This is less commonly seen on sites, as it has the potential to be quite a lengthy body of text, and (in the case of videos) because captions allow users to read each part of the transcript in isolation while also watching the media. Despite this, the approach can have its benefits (users can read in their own time), providing content in another way that doesn't exclude users offers them the freedom to choose. You can accomplish this without doing any extra work by generating a transcript based on the contents of your WebVTT file, meaning that you get two accessible features for the price of one! There are a range of converters available online that accept .vtt as a format (which I'll cover in more detail in Chapter 11 "Tools and QA").

Unexpected or Automatic Audio

Deaf and hard-of-hearing people may have a hard time gauging how loud videos are, particularly when they play automatically or unexpectedly. "You see a video on your Facebook feed and there's no sound," explains Ruth in the same interview. "If you click on it to make it big, the sound plays, but you don't realise. Sometimes I have my hearing aid off and I feel like the video is blaring out sound."[29]

Interestingly, autoplaying video on mobile devices was prohibited for a long time, largely due to the user being inadvertently forced to download the contents of a video using their roaming data the moment they arrive on a page. However, this suppression didn't extend to desktop computers where it's still very much possible through the autoplay attribute on videos.

When this happens, it can cause embarrassment for deaf users, and so if you intend to autoplay video on your site, you should couple it with another attribute: muted. Doing this ensures that even if a video has started playing without the user's knowledge, it won't blare out sound too:

```
<video autoplay muted>
    ...
</video>
```

Linear Layouts

Deaf users are used to relying entirely on their sense of sight, and are therefore more susceptible to being confused by badly or illogically designed websites. We covered linear layouts and clear heading structures extensively in Chapter 2 to help those who cannot interact with the visual aspect of a site, but the same solutions apply to users that rely *solely* on visual information.

Ensuring that your headings are descriptive and have a clear structure reduces the risk of a deaf user encountering problems with the only means that they have of interpreting content on web pages:

> *I rely so much on visual information... If they weren't [clearly structured], I'd feel very lost because I completely rely on reading for understanding.*[30]

I won't cover the same ground again; if you want to know how to cater for this issue, head to Chapter 2, but I wanted to raise this as a consideration in this chapter as it's not a barrier that many would associate with users who can "see" a site.

When content in its various forms (headings, paragraphs, lists, etc.) becomes harder to interact with (through either incorrectly coded sites or because their default style has been altered through design), those using screen readers, for example, have ARIA roles to help appropriately signpost and highlight types of content. For those interacting through sight alone though, this property doesn't help.

Correctly coded sites, and layouts that display content in a linear, unambiguous way, are good practice and help everyone, including people who are reliant on a single source of information online (visual input). Now, these users can encounter a major barrier when their need for visual information isn't respected. A prime example of this happens when a company only allows them to get in contact via the telephone – a medium that simply doesn't accommodate for them. We'll now discuss what you can do to combat this access need.

Servicing customers without a telephone

Barriers can crop up in unexpected places, and sometimes you have to be proactive to spot them. For example, customer contact pages are one overlooked area where deaf users are often excluded. Here, placing your company's phone number, or requesting a user's, can be useful for some people, but if it is the only channel of communication, it can exclude others. We covered the following example in the introduction, but to recap, here's James Buller again (Head of access needs at the United Kingdom Home Office), talking about testing the United Kingdom's online passport registration process:

> *We did some testing with D/deaf people. Initially the query was why would you do that, there's no audio involved in the service? But we decided to check anyway... [The subject] was going through the form, and there had been no big problems until she got to the most boring page on the site – the contact page. It asked her to 'provide a phone number' and she did, but also wanted to write 'I'm D/deaf please don't call me.' In this case, it wouldn't let her submit an answer with both numbers and text in it. When we tested this page against WCAG it passed, but on human terms, it was not accessible because we did not provide her with that option.*[31]

You should ensure that you offer multiple means of communication so as not to exclude a certain demographic. This also involves avoiding reliance on voice recognition (particularly with banking) which will often disrupt an otherwise accessible user journey.[32] This will be good for accessibility and for your business!

Providing alternatives

In research conducted by data company Harris Interactive, they found that 75% of customers believe it takes too long to reach a customer service agent.[33] Nobody likes a long wait on hold, and customers are getting used to having multiple options when it comes to getting in touch – ranging from email and live web chat, to communication through popular social networking sites like Facebook.

In 2020, an organisation can be considered outdated if it offers only a phone number as a method of communication. Your customers should be able to contact you in a mode of communication that is accessible to them and meets their needs. Email seems like the natural alternative to the phone, as it doesn't require an audible interaction. However, some people still want the instant responses that phones offer. In this case live chat, or even a Facebook messenger integration can provide the best of both worlds, and younger customers often feel more comfortable and familiar with live chat than they do with phone support.[34]

Doing this allows you to effectively communicate with your customers, but also allows them to do the same to you. This freedom often results in them taking the time to provide more feedback on how you're doing in general which is invaluable.

Text relays

One other (often overlooked) option that many deaf users find useful is the Next-Generation Text Relay. This service connects a hearing person on a standard phone line with a deaf person using a textphone (a special type of phone with a keyboard and display). "An operator acts as an intermediary and will type what is spoken and speak what is typed."[35] However, Áine Jackson explains that:

It is common when using next generation text relay to contact a service provider that frontline staff are not aware of this service and that it can be used and will refuse to accept or interact with a call.[36]

If your website relies heavily on customer contact, you should ensure that your staff know that this is an option.

For the benefit of all your customers, you need to provide multiple ways for them to communicate with you. We will explore this topic in depth in the "Communication" chapter (Chapter 9).

Conclusion

In this chapter, we've looked at catering for users with hearing-based access needs. We've learned about subtitles and captions, the differences between them, the preferences that different hearing-impaired users have, and how to implement both yourself using WebVTT. We've discussed how to make the most of these technologies by sizing, styling, and positioning captions for added effect and how to add these improvements for audio as well as video. We then turned our attention to the content of these subtitles and captions and focused on how to make the words you use accessible through plain language and deaf-friendly text. Finally, we moved away from captioning and explored an array of other accessibility issues – from preventing unexpected audio by muting videos that autoplay, to making sure that you can communicate with deaf customers effectively. Hopefully this chapter has encouraged you to review your audio-based media but has also helped you understand that truly catering for deafness and hard of hearing involves more than that.

Notes

1. Government Digital Service, Saleem: profoundly deaf user, (25,10,2017), <www.gov.uk/government/publications/understanding-disabilities-and-impairments-user-profiles/saleem-profoundly-deaf-user> [Accessed 24/05/2019].

2. Andrea Popescu, Web accessibility for hearing impairment, Medium, (17/08/2018), <https://uxdesign.cc/web-accessibility-for-hearing-impairment-3f49fc7b5a34> [Accessed 24/05/2019].

3. Thomas O. Willcox, Gregory J. Artz, Auditory System Disorders (2007), <www.sciencedirect.com/topics/pharmacology-toxicology-and-pharmaceutical-science/central-hearing-loss> [Accessed 24/05/2019].

4. Government Digital Service, Saleem: profoundly deaf user (25,10,2017), <www.gov.uk/government/publications/understanding-disabilities-and-impairments-user-profiles/saleem-profoundly-deaf-user> [Accessed 24/05/2019].

5. Auditory Disabilities, WebAIM, (2019), <https://webaim.org/articles/auditory/culture> [Accessed 24/05/2019].

6. Áine Jackson, (British Deaf Association research and policy coordinator) Interview with author, (16/05/2019).

7. Lisa Herrod, Deafness and the User Experience, A List Apart, (12/08/2008), <http://alistapart.com/article/deafnessandtheuserexperience/> [Accessed 24/05/2019].

8. Lisa Herrod, Deafness and the User Experience, A List Apart, (12/08/2008), <http://alistapart.com/article/deafnessandtheuserexperience/> [Accessed 24/05/2019].

9. Todd Wright, in Deafness and the User Experience, A List Apart, (12/08/2008), <http://alistapart.com/article/deafnessandtheuserexperience/#comment-14519> [Accessed 24/05/2019].

10. REV, Subtitles vs. Captions: What's the Difference?, (09/01,2019), <www.rev.com/blog/subtitles-vs-captions> [Accessed 24/05/2019].

11. WSC, Video Captions, (23/01/2019), <www.w3.org/WAI/perspective-videos/captions/> [Accessed 24/05/2019].

12. TED Translators, OTP Learning Series 05: Subtitle Length and reading speed, (08/04/2014), <www.youtube.com/watch?v=ckm4nOBWggA&amp=&list=PLuvLOOYxuPwxQbdq4W7TCQ7TBnW39cDRC> [Accessed 24/05/2019].

13. REV, Closed Caption File Format Guide for YouTube, Vimeo, Netflix and More, (21/03/2019), <www.rev.com/blog/close-caption-file-format-guide-for-youtube-vimeo-netflix-and-more> [Accessed 24/05/2019].

14. Caniuse, WebVTT, (08/2019), <https://caniuse.
     com/#search=webvtt> [Accessed 24/05/2019].

15. W3C, WebVTT: The Web Video Text Tracks
     Format, (04/04/2019), <www.w3.org/TR/webvtt1/>
     [Accessed 24/05/2019].

16. DeafAction, Guide to Accessible Information,
     (08/2014), <www.deafaction.org.uk/wp-content/
     uploads/2014/08/Guide-to-Accessible-
     Information.pdf> [Accessed 24/05/2019].

17. Lisa Herrod, Deafness and the User Experience,
     A List Apart, (12/08/2008), <http://alistapart.
     com/article/deafnessandtheuserexperience/>
     [Accessed 24/05/2019].

18. Ian Devlin, WebVTT and Audio, (13/12/2015),[Accessed 24/05/2019].

19. Marty McGuire, Native HTML5 captions and titles
     for audio content with WebVTT, (17/10/2017),
     <https://martymcgui.re/2017/10/17/native-
     html5-captions-and-titles-for-audio-content-
     with-webvtt/> [Accessed 24/05/2019].

20. Google Support, Use automatic captioning,
     (2019), <https://support.google.com/youtube/
     answer/6373554?hl=en-GB> [Accessed 24/05/2019].

21. Lisa Herrod, Deafness and the User Experience,
     A List Apart, (12/08/2008), <http://alistapart.
     com/article/deafnessandtheuserexperience/>
     [Accessed 24/05/2019].

22.   Áine Jackson, (British Deaf Association research and policy coordinator), Interview with author, (16/05/2019).

23.   Lisa Herrod, Deafness and the User Experience, A List Apart, (12/08/2008), <http://alistapart. com/article/deafnessandtheuserexperience/> [Accessed 24/05/2019].

24.   DELTA, Reading and the deaf child, <http:// deafeducation.org.uk/home/family-support/ reading-and-the-deaf-child/> [Accessed 24/05/2019].

25.   Erika Cancio-Bello, The Sources of Deaf Humour, (Swarthmore, Pennsylvania, 2015) <https:// scholarship.tricolib.brynmawr.edu/bitstream/ handle/10066/16212/Cancio-Bello_thesis_2015. pdf?sequence=1> [Accessed 24/05/2019].

26.   Lisa Herrod, Deafness and the User Experience, A List Apart, (12/08/2008), <http://alistapart. com/article/deafnessandtheuserexperience/> [Accessed 24/05/2019].

27.   Lisa Herrod, Deafness and the User Experience, A List Apart, (12/08/2008), <http://alistapart. com/article/deafnessandtheuserexperience/> [Accessed 24/05/2019].

28. Ruth MacMullen, in Sounding out the web: accessibility for deaf and hard of hearing people [Part 1] by David Swallow, (13/02/2017), <https:// developer.paciellogroup.com/blog/2017/02/ sounding-out-the-web-accessibility-for-deaf-and-hard-of-hearing-people-part-1/> [Accessed 24/05/2019].

29. Ruth MacMullen in Sounding out the web: accessibility for deaf and hard of hearing people [Part 2], by David Swallow, (20/03/17), <https:// developer.paciellogroup.com/blog/2017/03/ sounding-out-the-web-accessibility-for-deaf-and-hard-of-hearing-people-part-2/> [Accessed 24/05/2019].

30. Ruth MacMullen in Sounding out the web: accessibility for deaf and hard of hearing people [Part 2], by David Swallow, (20/03/17), <https:// developer.paciellogroup.com/blog/2017/03/ sounding-out-the-web-accessibility-for-deaf-and-hard-of-hearing-people-part-2/> [Accessed 24/05/2019].

31. James Buller, Interview with the author, (24/02/2019).

32. Áine Jackson, (British Deaf Association research and policy coordinator), Interview with author, (16/05/2019).

33. Harris Interactive, in Help Scout, 75 Customer Service Facts, Quotes & Statistics, <www.helpscout. com/75-customer-service-facts-quotes-statistics/> [Accessed 24/05/19].

34.   Comm100, Millennials Prefer Live Chat for Speed
       and Convenience, (2019) <www.comm100.com/
       resources/infographic/millennials-prefer-
       live-chat-speed-convenience/> [Accessed
       24/05/2019].

35.   DeafAction, Advisory Services Good Practices
       Guide, (06/2016), <www.deafaction.org.uk/
       wp-content/uploads/2016/08/Deaf_Action_
       Money_Matters_June16_pages.pdf> [Accessed
       24/05/2019].

36.   Áine Jackson, (British Deaf Association research
       and policy coordinator), Interview with author,
       [16/05/2019].

CHAPTER 6

Cognitive Impairments

In this chapter, we'll explore a wide range of access needs that belong to users with impaired cognitive functions. We will largely focus on comprehension of language, as it effects a wide variety of cognitively impaired users – looking at how to make the written content you create as accessible as possible. We'll talk about how to structure that content, choose the words that make it, and how best to display them.

We'll then move onto different needs. We'll think about the benefits of clear iconography, avoiding ambiguity, and how to ensure that your pages and your users' experiences with them aren't overly "complex". We'll touch on web features that affect a user's visual and visual-spatial comprehension, as well as their executive function, focus, and memory. We'll do so through tackling a range of barriers and covering a range of solutions – from breadcrumbs and sitemaps that can aid a user's comprehension of your site's structure and give them the control to properly navigate it, to self-contained actions that prevent confusion, and autocomplete that does not punish human error.

First though, let's define what we mean by cognitive impairments, so that we can best understand how to cater for them.

© Ashley Firth 2019
A. Firth, *Practical Web Inclusion and Accessibility*,
https://doi.org/10.1007/978-1-4842-5452-3_6

Defining Cognitive Impairments

Cognitive disabilities can take many forms. Clinical diagnoses include autism, Down's syndrome, dementia, dyslexia, ADHD, and a whole host of other impairments and learning difficulties. They also impact a huge amount of people. For example, 700,000 people in the United Kingdom are currently considered to be on the autism spectrum,[1] and as many as 10% of the population are expected to have dyslexia.[2]

Robert McDowell, author of the recent, cutting edge "Neurodiversity and Digital Inclusion" report, explained that although these conditions are common, it is often difficult to understand and identify cognitive impairments. As a result, they are "sometimes referred to as hidden disabilities."[3] However, he also explains that "not only are cognitive differences hidden, they have in many ways been ignored," and despite being given more attention in recent years, this rings true for accessibility too. Cognitive impaired users have been "woefully neglected when compared with the work done for other users online."[4]

Recently, many have sought to fix this lack of attention, including the "neurodiversity" movement, which McDowell references in the title of his report. This movement argues that there is no "neuro-normal" mind, and instead there are "a broad spectrum of human minds that interpret and experience the world in different ways."[5] From within their framework, conditions like ADHD, dyslexia, dyscalculia, and autism are simply examples of neurodiverse minds – part of a spectrum of minds, on which everybody has different strengths, weaknesses, and access needs. I spoke with Robert McDowell about his work, and he told me that "paying attention to accessibility for neurodiverse users will, by definition, cause you to make things clearer and better, and easier to use."[6]

This movement raises two points that are relevant to this project. Firstly, it strongly argues that "disabilities" only arise when users' access needs are ignored, creating barriers. This focus on catering for access needs, and the fact that they can arise for anyone, echoes our approach in this book. Secondly, cognitive impairments are a contentious topic. A lot of ink has been spilled in debates over how to categorise, diagnose, and talk about them, and these boundaries are constantly changing.

For example, some have pointed out that it is difficult to include "more severe" cognitive disabilities in the neurodiverse model. Writers like Twilah Hiari have argued that by putting too much of an emphasis on what society can do to accommodate users, proponents of neurodiversity have taken the focus away from individuals whose impairments might be eased by treatment.[7]

Others have tried to reconcile these views. Speaking predominantly about people with autism, writer Patrick Dwyer argues that:

> *Neurodiversity was not about denying the idea that there are real, medical and neurological differences in autistic people, nor denying the idea that these differences themselves cause suffering and that they might need to be addressed on those grounds. Neurodiversity merely called attention to the value that can be found within neurodivergent minds and cautioned against the dangers of an automatic attempt to eliminate such diversity.*[8]

I raise this because I understand the benefit of shedding light on ideas like neurodiversity, and the research that it has inspired, but also because this book does not take sides. I understand that each person's approach to their disability is unique and they may not want to be categorised in this way. Whether a user considers their access needs predominantly a product of diversity or impairment, and whether they seek treatment or not, our focus in this book remains solely on making navigating and interacting with the web easier for them and everyone else.

As opposed to focusing on medical categories, we will continue as we have done throughout this book by focusing on the access needs created by **functional disabilities**, which "ignore the medical or behavioral causes of the disability and instead focus on the resulting abilities and challenges."[9]

Now, in this chapter, some of the access needs are a little more difficult to understand than in prior chapters. For example, it is much easier to understand that somebody might have trouble perceiving a shape because they have low vision, or experience colour blindness, than it is to understand that somebody might have trouble actually recognising and understanding what a shape is, or means, because of a visual cognitive impairment. This is part of what Robert McDowell meant by these being "hidden disabilities."

What's more, it's sometimes more difficult to clearly *categorise* these access needs, separating them from one another. Again, when we talked about visual impairments, for example, it was easy to tell the difference between needs based around blindness and colour blindness. However, as we shall see, this is harder with cognitive impairments, with overlap between barriers experienced by users who struggle with language and memory-based impairments, or visual comprehension and visual–spatial-based impairments. This is another big reason why there is so much debate in this area on how to classify cognitive impairments.

Because of the way I've chosen to approach accessibility in this book, and because there is less consensus on how to categorise these access needs, I have composed my own way of grouping them. Having looked at the latest reading and reports, supported by suggestions from charities, and inspired by existing work from organisations like the W3C who now have a Cognitive and Learning Disabilities Accessibility Task Force (COGA), [10] these groups are:

- Language comprehension
- Visual comprehension
- Visual–spatial comprehension

- Executive function and focus

- Memory

Now of these areas, we'll direct most of our attention to the first one. This is because language comprehension holds the potential for you to help a huge range of cognitively impaired users – it's estimated that 15–20% of the population has some form of difficulty with text or language comprehension.[11] However, as the chapter progresses, we will also come across examples and useful tips for catering for each of these other areas too. I believe that by organising these needs in this way, you will easily be able to identify different types of barriers and solutions when catering for cognitive-impaired users.

Language comprehension

Let's begin with a point that may seem obvious but many sites often struggle with – providing content that is simple to follow and feasible to read for as many people as possible.

Plain English

The most valuable of all talents is that of never using two words when one will do.

—Thomas Jefferson

Ironically, this quote is a little wordier than it needs to be, but the sentiment still stands.

Plain English means writing clear, concise, well-organised content – essentially writing in an accessible way.[12] It is especially useful to people with impairments that impact language comprehension. This includes the 10% of the British population with dyslexia and those with conditions like aphasia (a language-based impairment that often results from a stroke).[13] It also, however, benefits users with impairments that impact language less directly, like those with visual impairments or difficulties with other forms of comprehension and reasoning (like some users with Alzheimer's or Down's syndrome).[14]

The importance of accessible writing may seem like one of the most obvious points raised in this book. After all, who wouldn't write in plain English? Unfortunately, this happens surprisingly often. At some point, you will have come across text that feels harder to read or engage with than usual. The fact that you can tell that there's something wrong without knowing exactly what it is draws attention to the importance of being clear and concise.

It also shows that exclusionary prose can have an impact regardless of expertise or how comfortable someone is with reading. Moreover, when you consider that, shockingly, the average reading age across the United Kingdom is only 9 years old, it becomes clear that a considerable group of users can benefit from uncomplicated writing.[15]

Interestingly though, these benefits are not confined to those that find reading difficult. A 2012 study by Christopher Trudeau found that 80% of participants preferred sentences written in plain English.[16] This makes a lot of sense because when we encounter a subject we are not familiar with, there can be a lot of specialist terms and phrases. Here, people can get bogged down in understanding the words themselves rather than the point they're meant to be making. Surprisingly though, the study also found that experts, despite understanding these specialist terms, vastly preferred the writing to be plain and jargon-free for ease of reading too.

There are two main areas to look at when we talk about plain English. The first concerns the structure of the text and how it's organised, and the second is to do with word choice.

Structure

Research has found that people on average only read 20–28% of text on a web page, and the pressure on the brain to understand content increases for every 100 words you put on a page – even on pages with as little as 100 words of content, on average a user will only read half of that.[17] Therefore, paying attention to how you structure your content, especially on longer pages with more of it, can really help keep users focused.

The Center for Plain Language is a nonprofit that helps government agencies and businesses write clear and understandable communications. They explain that:

> *When you create material in plain language, you also organize it logically for the audience. You consider how well the layout of your pages or screens works for the audience. You anticipate their questions and needs.*[18]

This is largely because a clear structure prevents your reader from becoming overwhelmed and allows them to understand contextual information clearly – they can easily see where one of your points ends and another begins, and identify the most important information on the page. This is also tied to the creation of a linear page layout, as it organises content logically, from top to bottom. This idea can be broken down granularly – from a section's heading, to the paragraphs within it, down to the individual sentences within those paragraphs.

Headings

If you write headings that help readers predict what comes next, it creates a structure that allows readers to quickly and confidently find the information they are looking for. We've mentioned this before when talking about how screen reader users often navigate using headings. Good examples include:

- Questions that the user may ask themselves – "What is the purpose of plain language?"

- Simple statements that aren't ambiguous – "The purpose of plain language"

Whereas the following styles of heading make it harder for users to navigate:

- Introducing new terms for the very first time in the heading (unless it's part of a question)

- Headings that are dozens of words long instead of a succinct statement – "Everything you need to know about how to create good headings as part of using better plain English"

- Vague headings that don't help the user understand what a section is about

Paragraphs

Underneath these headings, the content should be broken up into short sections as opposed to large paragraphs. This offers "stopping points" for the reader, allowing them to digest what they've read or to take a break. Forcing a user to read through a 20-line paragraph takes a toll. As a guide on how large to aim for though, research conducted by the United Kingdom government suggests a paragraph shouldn't be more than five sentences long.[19] Equally, you should take into account where the "natural" stopping points are – you shouldn't cut a paragraph midway through an idea or point.

Sentences

Inside your paragraphs, your sentences should be "short but logical." Doing so avoids the need for the user to hold too much information in their head at once and makes them less likely to get confused by content, or how it's laid out. The United Kingdom government's accessible writing guidelines explain that even if plain language is not used, the sentence can still be accessible if it's reasonably short, as "people with moderate learning disabilities can still understand sentences of 5 to 8 words without difficulty."[20]

Guiding sentences

You can also achieve better sentence comprehension by trying to write what is known as "guiding sentences" (or "front loading content"). This involves placing the most important content at the beginning of a sentence, so you know what is being talked about right away, making it easier to grasp. An example is that the following sentence:

> *"'Designing Accessible User Experiences' is a new course that will be offered this August"*[21]

is typically easier to read than

> *"There is a new course offering coming this August called 'Designing Accessible User Experiences.'"*

Because the course itself has been introduced first, you know what is being talked about from the outset, as opposed to finding out that "something" is starting in fall and then having to work out what it is.

Supporting content in multiple formats

If you can provide content in a range of formats (other than just text), you can significantly increase the likelihood that a user with linguistic comprehension difficulties like dyslexia or aphasia will be able to engage with it.

Good examples include using images (as long as they have `alt` text added) and diagrams to compliment written content, rather than inadvertently creating a wall of text in only one format. Not only does including other formats make pages look more appealing to engage with, but it makes reading them more manageable for those with dyslexia. It breaks up a page in a similar way to headings, providing a clear journey through the page and regular places to stop.

In the last chapter, we talked about how captions can help users understand audio and video by introducing another channel for them to receive information. The same principle applies for all types of content. For example, you could apply a colour and/or pattern to different sections to separate or theme different information (as long as you don't rely on colour alone to convey that meaning). If you provide information in a range of formats, it increases the likelihood of one of them being comprehended.

Having looked at how to structure written content, let's look at the changes we can make to the text itself. To do this, it's useful to know how users typically interact with words and why word choice matters.

Word choice

Children quickly learn to read common words and become familiar with a primary set of 5,000 words, and a secondary set of around 10,000 words. These words are used every day, and children are comfortable with most of them by the time they are 9 years old.[22] Once they've become familiar with these, they actually stop reading the words and start recognising their shapes instead, which allows them to read much faster.

Now, although your vocabulary will grow, you will always be comfortable reading from those base 5,000 words. When writing content, you can make the most of this ability by using more common words, and using them in a plain, concise way, to ensure that users will not encounter barriers with your text.

Research suggests, however, that cognitive-impaired users read in a very different way. For example, people with both moderate learning disabilities and **visual comprehension impairments** find it more difficult to recognise the shape of words – those with dyslexia are a prominent example (this issue is common enough that a font called Dyslexie has been specifically designed to aid reading and comprehension online for those with dyslexia).[23] Users who experience this issue are "more likely to read letter for letter – they do not bounce around like other users."[24] Using plain language can therefore have huge benefits. We mentioned earlier that many cognitive-impaired users can understand a standard sentence of 5–8 words; however, by using common words you increase this dramatically – helping these users understand sentences of around 25 words. This could significantly offset the barriers usually faced by language-impaired users.

Use familiar language

We talked about using familiar language a little in the last chapter when it came to writing "deaf-friendly" English, and many of the same ideas apply. You should try and avoid complicated words, jargon, idioms, and figures of speech (such as "once in a blue moon"). The last point is especially useful because users with autism, for example, are more likely to attempt to interpret these phrases literally.[25]

Also think about shorter words and less obscure synonyms for other words where you can, and don't be afraid to leave out details that don't help or may distract readers, even if they are interesting. This is good practice for all writing and will make your written content clearer.

Avoid using so many large words

Research into content design found that when you use a longer word of 8 or 9 letters, users are more likely to skip the shorter words (3, 4, or 5 letters) that follow it.[26] As a result, if you make a habit of consistently using longer, complicated words, they are likely to require unnecessary attention and increase the chances of users skipping large parts of your content. This affects comprehension and encourages disengagement, and it's needless. Take this sentence for example:

"The recently sanctioned alterations to Transport for London's seasonal timetables should not be displayed before 1st January 2020."[27]

There's a lot going on here, but the most important word in the sentence is "not" – you should *not* display the new transport timetable before this time. However, because of the lengthy words that precede it, that vital word is more likely to be overlooked. The "not" is far more obvious in a sentence like this:

"Do not display the new Transport for London timetable before 1st January 2020."

Use an active voice

Sentences that use an active voice are especially clear. This happens in sentences where the subject performs a stated action – thereby placing a clear focus on that action to readers. A sentence such as "You must create an accessible website by Friday" is more comprehensible than "An accessible website must be created by Friday" as it clearly involves the reader as a character.[28]

Provide definitions

Acronyms and long, difficult words are sometimes unavoidable, particularly when talking about specialist subjects (or when you want to avoid writing the same five or six words multiple times in one block of text). Still, you should remember to explain what they mean. Not doing so can be confusing for readers, causing them to disengage out of frustration.

Firstly, you can do this with code. This involves wrapping an acronym or specialist term in an "abbreviation tag" – allowing you to provide an explanation of it:

```
<abbr title="Accessibility">a11y</abbr>
```

Once you've done that, the word will, by default, display with a small dotted underline (as shown in Figure 6-1). Then when the user hovers over, taps on, or tabs to the word, the meaning will be displayed in a tooltip next to the cursor (as shown in Figure 6-2).

A11y

Figure 6-1. *An example of how an abbreviation tag displays on text*

Figure 6-2. *When a user hovers over an abbreviation tag, the meaning appears in a tooltip next to the cursor*

Fun fact: a11y is the shortened term for accessibility. It was created to make it easier to type out, and '11' represents the eleven letters between 'a' and 'y' in accessibility.

Alternatively, you can simply write the definition next to the acronym in brackets or in prose such as "otherwise known as...." This is better suited for those of you who control the content of a site but who don't have access to the code – perhaps through a CMS (otherwise known as a content management system). See what I did there?

Pay attention to text style

There are a range of text styles that can be used to draw attention, such as **emboldening** or CAPITALISATION to draw emphasis, *italicising* to denote meaning, and <u>underlining</u> to advertise an action of some sort (a link or a description of the word).

Styling like this can be used to make sure important words are not overlooked. Take the transport timetable example from earlier:

> *"The recently sanctioned alterations to Transport for London's seasonal timetables should **NOT** be displayed before 1ˢᵗ January 2020."*

Now the "not" is far more obvious. This shouldn't in anyway supersede our point about avoiding consistently large words, but it can be used to ensure content is **not** misunderstood.

It should, however, be noted that excessive use of these text styles can be confusing to users with impairments like dyslexia, as we mentioned above, as they can make words look less familiar – they're useful, but in moderation.

We've now discussed how to structure the content on your sites, how to choose the words that make up that content, and how best to display those words – but what about when there is simply too much content for certain cognitive-impaired users to contend with? Let's delve briefly into a way that you can help them interact with content, or at the very least set their expectations.

TL;DR's

TL;DR is an acronym that stands for "too long, didn't read." It began its life as a deadpan response to a very long post on an online forum. The point was simple – your content is too long for me to interact with. This is a point we've made throughout this chapter: large amounts of info can be overwhelming and difficult for many users to get through, including people with impaired language comprehension. You can help reduce this by putting the recommendations we mentioned above into action and keeping content as concise as possible, but sometimes longer content is unavoidable. In those situations, one particularly useful solution involves providing a heavily summarised version of existing content – enabling those with reading difficulties to still extract useful information from your content.

After its first use, TL;DR's became popular and were commonly seen accompanying long posts in the early 2000s. They were made famous by sites such as Reddit and 4Chan, where content often centers around longform posts and discussions. Now, you'd be hard-pressed to find a long post without one. They're created by extracting the core information from the content into a single sentence and placing it at the bottom of any long post, allowing readers to take away the key point(s).

This is a useful feature, but it may not always be possible to condense the main takeaways of a long-form article or blog post into a single sentence. This doesn't mean that the act of providing a brief overview of the content isn't useful though; it simply needs altering slightly. There are a couple of ways you could adopt a TL;DR.

1) Switch the position

We can switch position, so the TL;DR is above the content instead of below it. Because people who are unfamiliar with TL;DR's won't know to look at the bottom of the article to find it, a reader may either only find it once they've read all of the content (thereby rendering it pointless for them) or, unfortunately, they could leave the page without interacting with the content. This is particularly true for people with cognitive impairments like dyslexia who are more likely to be put off by a long, unbroken page of text.

2) Switch up the content

It doesn't always have to be a sentence – a list of points is still much smaller and easier to digest than a full article.

But Ashley, won't it ruin the surprise of what's in the content?

On the contrary, summarising content doesn't mean you have to fill it with spoilers or oversimplifications. You could use your TL;DR to explain the main points on a page or raise some new questions that are secondary to the main title that might convince the user to stay and read the content. Think of it as an extended advert for your content that is more likely to convince a reader to stay and read it once they've arrived on the page. Here's an example for an article about Snooker:

- We'll be taking a look at how Snooker is trying to reinvent itself
- We speak to Barry Hearn, Chairman of World Snooker about its progress
- The key to its revival came from an unusual place...

This TL;DR includes the main point of the article (i.e., it contains an interview with the head of Snooker) and even an anecdotal line to grab the reader's attention. Beyond these access needs, a TL;DR simply shows an appreciation for people's time – understanding that they may want to know what they're getting into before they start.

Reading time

This same thought has gone into the "reading time" feature, which lets people know quickly how long it would normally take someone to get through what's on the page (as shown in Figure 6-3).

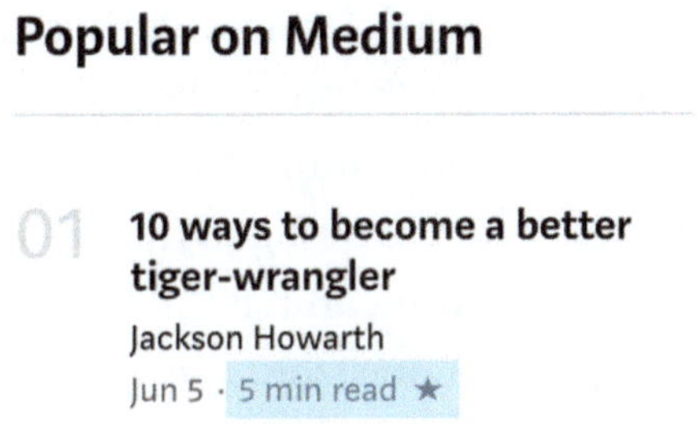

Popular on Medium

01   **10 ways to become a better tiger-wrangler**
Jackson Howarth
Jun 5 · 5 min read ★

Figure 6-3. *An example of Medium's "read time" – shown following each article*

Of course, everyone reads at different speeds, but if users read faster or slower than average, they can still extrapolate to determine how long it will take. Again, it's useful for setting user expectations and allows them to interact with your content in a hurry.

Of course, words are not the only content on a page that a user can engage with to understand information or perform actions. Let's talk about the power of using clear iconography on your sites and the potential drawbacks for users if you get it wrong.

Clear iconography

Using icons can be a neat way to display a status or action without the need for excessive amounts of text. They can be especially useful for users with language processing impairments, as they provide another medium for these users to receive information through. Obvious examples include symbols like a cog to represent "settings," a magnifying glass to represent "search" functionality, or the "hamburger" icon to represent a menu.

However, an overreliance on icons, beyond the obvious few, can lead to exclusion. It is difficult to connect many icons that are currently used online to their associated action. This barrier is felt keenly by users with impaired **visual comprehension** (e.g., visual processing disorder, or VPD, and dyscalculia – which can affect a user's ability to imagine, understand, and remember shapes). Users with these access needs have trouble identifying images, comprehending the meaning behind them, and associating them with a given action. This is also true of those with low tech literacy and who aren't often exposed to the Web or web-based icons often enough to understand their meanings.

This is made worse by the inconsistent use of icons online. A user's understanding of an icon is based on previous experience and, confusingly, the same icon is often used to represent different actions on different sites. Therefore, users are left unsure as to whether the meaning they believe an icon represents is accurate. Here are a few common examples, starting with Figure 6-4.

Figure 6-4. *A "speech bubble" icon*

The speech bubble icon is used quite widely. Although its style is tweaked slightly between sites, it's meaning changes far more drastically. It means "View post and comments" in an Instagram feed but then means "Add a comment" when a user is on an individual Instagram post. It also means "View messages" on Facebook, "Reply" on Reddit, and "Start a thread" on Slack. Next is the "pencil" icon, shown in Figure 6-5.

Figure 6-5. *A "pencil" icon*

This icon is used inside a square to mean "Create a note" in Apple notes but means "View drafts" in Outlook. It is also commonly used to represent an "edit" action on many sites (and in Google's "material design" library). Third and finally, Figure 6-6 shows the "arrow" icon.

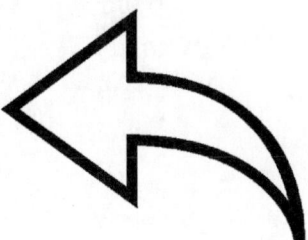

Figure 6-6. *An icon of an arrow, pointing upward and left*

This is my least favorite icon, used to represent "Share a post" on LinkedIn, "Undo an action" in Word processing programs like Google Docs and Microsoft Word, "Back" on social media sites like Twitter, and "Reply" in email platforms like Outlook Google Mail. Although some of these actions are somewhat related, and you might be able to guess what the icon means from context, it's still a guess - and an (incorrect) assumption that everyone else would be able to make that intuitive leap too.

Custom icons

Then there's the case of using custom icons you've created yourself. Untested, these are often open to interpretation and invites misunderstanding, meaning that your attempt to make a page less cluttered can cause confusion. I would caution that if you look at one of your own icons for long enough, its meaning can seem obvious – but it won't be to others. This idea isn't confined to the Web either – it's visible everywhere, and a problem for everybody. Household appliances, for example, are a goldmine of ambiguous icons – Figure 6-7 shows a dial on a washing machine.

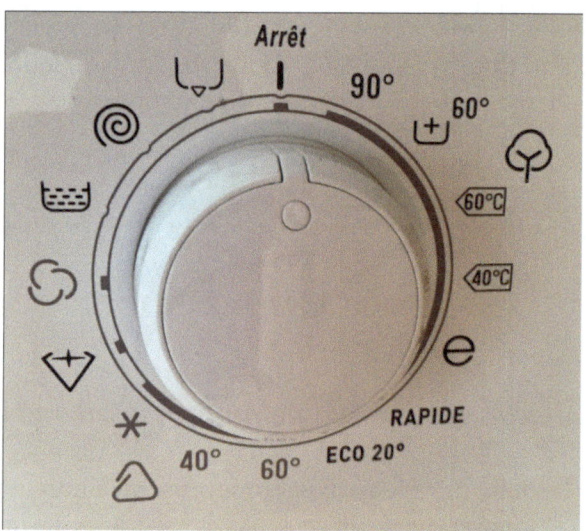

Figure 6-7. *An image of a dial on a washing machine, surrounded by ambiguous icons*

I genuinely have no idea what some of these mean and icons are supposed to *remove* the need for extra text.

How do we combat this?

This ambiguity means that icons currently cannot be relied upon to convey meaning by themselves. Designers should therefore ensure that there is another way to understand what an icon means. This is commonly handled with a label underneath or next to the icon. A study by user testing found that when users were presented with icons that were also labelled, they were able to correctly predict what would happen when they tapped the icon 88% of the time. As soon as the label was removed, the comprehension of those icons dropped to 60%.[29] Again, this problem gets exponentially worse when you create icons yourself. The same tests found that for unlabelled icons that were unique to the app, users only had a 34% success rate when guessing what they were for.

Despite all of this, icons are still heavily used within websites. There are also many different ways in which they can be added to a site. So, it's important that we know how to make them accessible. We'll be covering all of this in the chapter on "Imagery" (Chapter 8).

It's now time to think about how the mixture of content and visuals can come together to create a site that is overwhelming and even damaging to users with cognitive impairments. We'll look at what makes a "complex" page, what you should avoid having on your pages for this reason (with some unpleasant examples), and ways in which you can instead provide a sense of control and ease to your users.

Avoiding complex pages

As we mentioned in Chapter 2, most users (without blindness or low vision) primarily engage with the Web using visual information – by looking at the screen. So far this chapter, when designing for users with **visual comprehensive** impairments (like dyscalculia or dementia), we have focused on iconography, due to trouble understanding actions represented visually. If we take a step back though, it becomes clear that page layouts and experiences are primarily interpreted in a visual way, and so, when badly designed, they can also cause difficulties for these users. There are two sides to this – the complexity of the layout itself and a complexity of experience.

Complex layouts

If your layout forces users to work hard to follow or identify content – because of irregular positioning, direction, or size – you create unnecessary barriers between your user and what they want to engage with. This relates to the point we made earlier about how users only read a fraction of a page's content, because complex layouts prevent them from "skimming" comfortably. Figure 6-8 shows a screenshot of the website for "Suzanne Collins books."

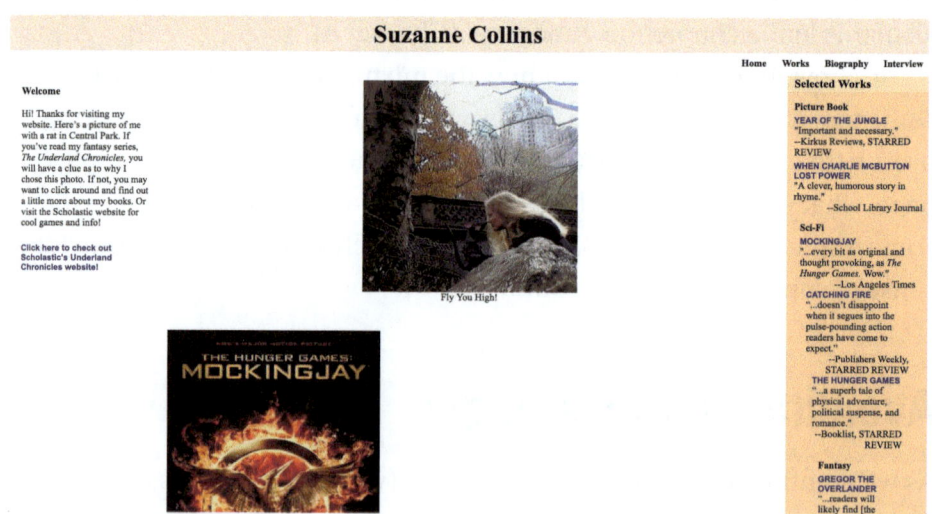

Figure 6-8. *The home page layout of "Suzanne Collins books." Content is scattered everywhere without a particular order or linear flow*

Suzanne Collins is the best-selling author of *The Hunger Games* trilogy. Understandably, her website receives a high amount of traffic as people look for more of her work. What they find when they reach the home page is shown in the image above. Content does not flow in a linear manner. Instead, information is scattered everywhere, in a range of formats, which draws a user's attention from place to place in a confusing manner. Users are confronted by a page that, in many ways, looks broken.[30]

Again, mobile-first approach is a good solution for this and also reflects the change in user behavior over recent years – with over half of all site traffic coming from mobile devices since 2016.[31] These layouts are typically easy to follow, with most having a single column, and without an overwhelming number of elements on display at any one time. Learning to make the simplest layout (thanks to the smaller screen size of mobile devices) and then scaling your design up is a good approach to web design in general. It forces the site to take on a simpler feel and provides users with only one or two things to focus on at a time. Once that's done, designers can then ask serious questions about whether components really ever needed to be sprawled all over bigger screens simply because there was room to do so.

Beyond the unique layout of any one site, there are a few key components that you can find on almost all web pages. Users with impaired visual comprehension benefit when you consistently position these features where they would commonly expect to find them. For example, users are used to finding the main menu, or at least the icon to open the main menu, of a site at the top of the page – both on mobile and desktop devices. Adhering to this consistent design pattern really helps, even when the rest of the page's content may be a little nonlinear. When writing about dementia, a condition that can significantly impact **visual comprehension** and **memory**, Ability.net also identified "the Home button, the search box, and a sitemap" as essential navigation items. When these are positioned in a consistent way, everybody wins.[32]

Complex experiences

Overcomplicated or unpredictable experiences can also impact cognitively impaired users who are easily overwhelmed. In a world of popups, adverts, and multimedia content, the core content of a page can be obscured or inaccessible, even if the layout is simple. For some users with autism, for example, providing too much information at once or asking them to complete multiple actions simultaneously, can potentially cause stress, anxiety, and even physical pain:

> *If I get sensory overload then I just shut down; you get what's known as fragmentation...it's weird, like being tuned into 40 TV channels.*[33]

Busy pages with a range of different pieces of content vying for attention can prove especially overwhelming. Take a look at Figure 6-9, from gaming site "Games Radar."[34]

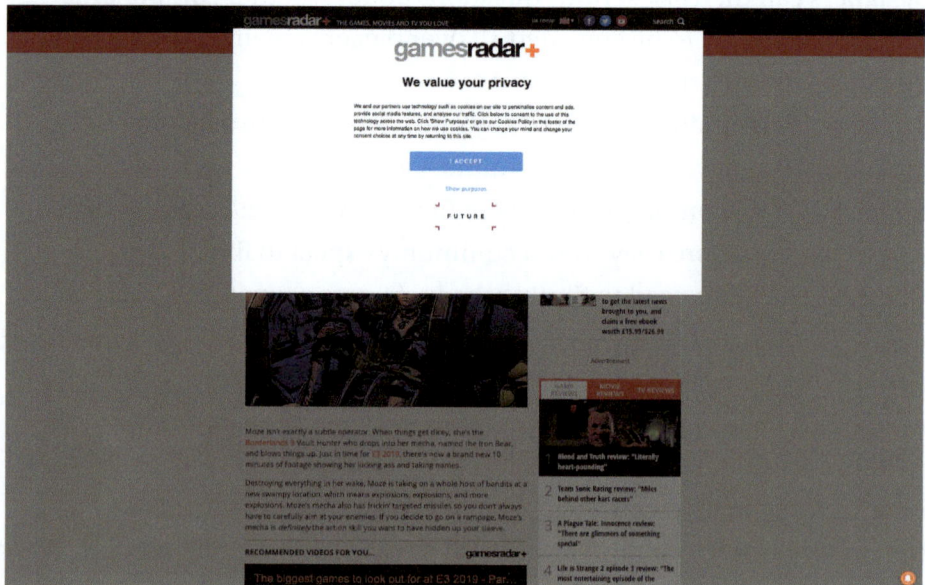

Figure 6-9. *An overlay on a site that appears as soon as the page is loaded, asking the user to accept the use of cookies*

The user is immediately greeted by this as they arrive, followed quickly by that shown in Figure 6-10.

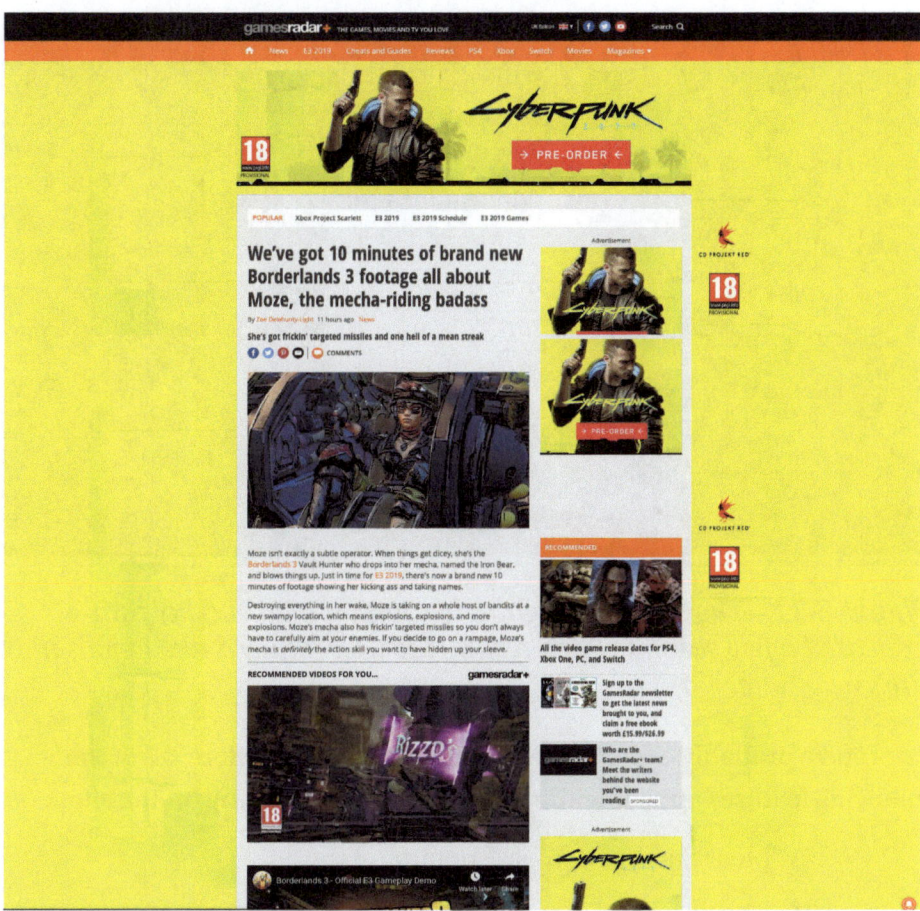

Figure 6-10. *The same site as above but with adverts now loaded at the top and sides of the content in a bright colour, alongside multiple images, and an autoplaying video*

A few seconds later, another modal appears automatically (shown in Figure 6-11).

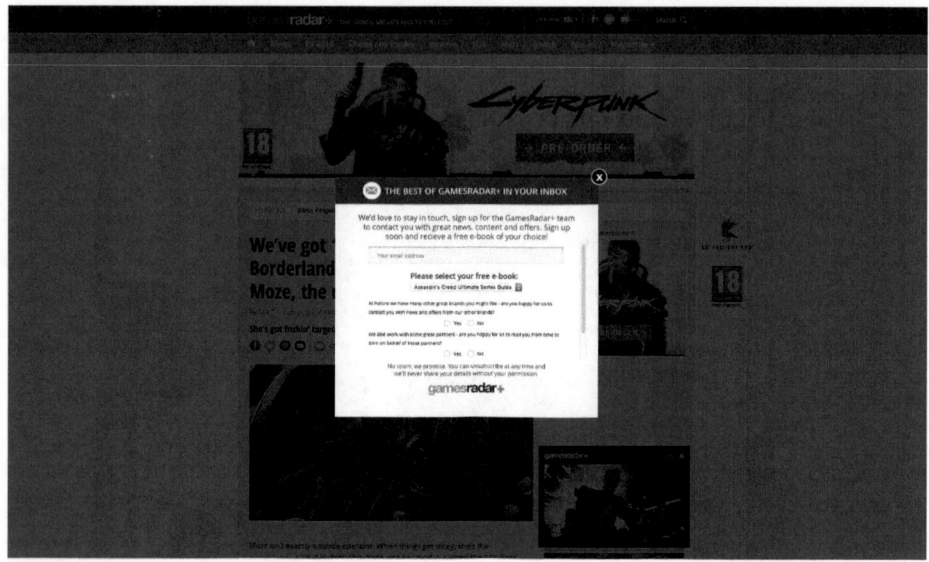

Figure 6-11. *The same site again, but with a new overlay that appeared a few seconds later, asking the user if they'd like to join the site's newsletter*

You've probably experienced sites like this before. Here, all of the following features appear within a few seconds of arriving on the site:

- A "please accept cookies" popup

- An advert at the top of the page

- Adverts down both sides of the page showing different content

- A video that plays automatically

- A sudden change in background colour, to a vibrant yellow, because of an advert

- A range of images with text

- A popup encouraging them to subscribe to their newsletter

- A popup, asking permission for the site to send the user notifications, even when they're not on the site

That's a lot to take in. Of this list, ads are often the most off-putting, as they're usually completely unrelated to the content of the page and take longer to load than the rest of the content. As a result, many users, including those with heightened sensory awareness, often block ads to prevent themselves from being overwhelmed. Unfortunately, sites that display ads often combat people doing this by resorting to *another* form of interruption – shown in Figure 6-12.

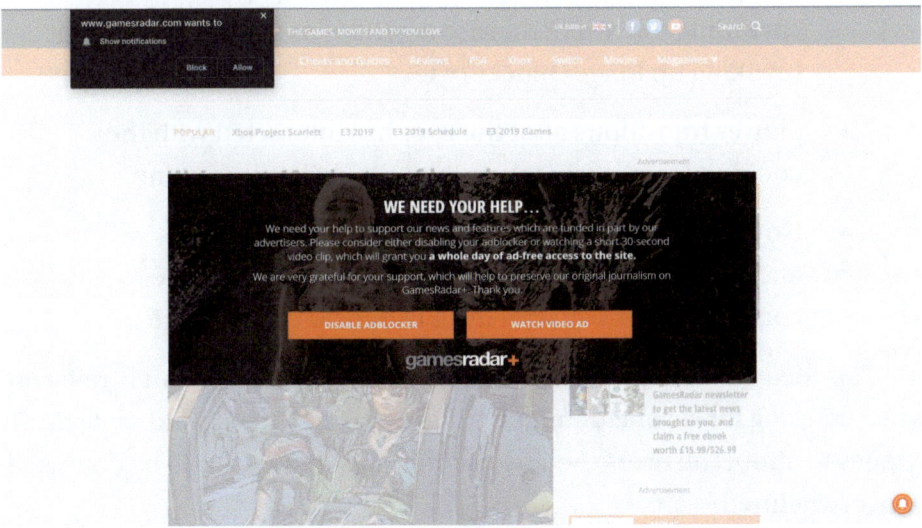

Figure 6-12. *An overlay that appears on the site to ask the user to disable the advert blocking extension that they have active, as well as a popup asking the user to accept the site's request to show them notifications*

It's a struggle to wade through all these distractions before you even reach the content, and afterward the layout itself is affected by the need to work around these components. There is often nothing wrong with any of these components individually, and I understand they can impact revenue and conversion, but they also often create an unpleasant experience, putting off customers too. A balance therefore needs to be found. Some possible solutions include

- Synchronising the content of the adverts so that they show a consistent message

- Advertising with videos but removing autoplay (as we've covered already)

- Questioning whether banner images are necessary alongside other imagery at the top of the page and spreading the rest of those images out as a way of breaking up longer blocks of text

- Slower transitions after the user has interacted with the cookie popup, easing them into the different content

- Not having a newsletter advert take over the page and instead making sure it appears at the end of the content, or more discreetly in the corner of the page

This idea of creating logical, simplistic layouts and content is relevant when catering for several different groups of access needs and realistically applies to almost all users; people visiting sites don't want to be confused or overwhelmed.

As an added bonus, choosing not to load adverts from external sites improves loading speeds (as you're not waiting to load extra code for popups or for multiple server calls for images), making your site quicker. According to statistics from Google, over half of mobile users abandon a site if it takes more than 3 seconds to load,[35] so avoiding those components on your page increases the chance that people will hang around to see it.

Breadcrumbs

We have just seen how some users with visual impairments can find it especially difficult to navigate a confusing, overcrowded page layout. However, another group of users with cognitive access needs also often have trouble with navigation. These users experience **visual–spatial impairments**, which affect orientation, as well as a user's ability to understand or imagine maps and models. This can affect some users with dyscalculia, VPD, and Alzheimer's, for example. These users can easily become disoriented when moving around a page, and we have already discussed a number of suggestions that will improve their online experiences when we covered linear layouts and mobile-first design. What we haven't yet discussed is how to help **visual–spatial**-impaired users who become disorientated when navigating between series of pages that make up a larger website.

Breadcrumbs let a user know where they are within a series of pages, allowing them to navigate within a wider website. There was recently a discussion on the popular designer's hub "Designer News" simply titled "Are breadcrumbs still a thing in 2019?"[36] They concluded that breadcrumbs are being added to sites less frequently but that they are still incredibly useful.

Firstly, they're still recommended by WCAG in multiple rules. One of the main rules is "location" – breadcrumbs allow you to provide "multiple ways of navigating" a site, which helps when the user is unsure of their location within it.[37] Secondly the Baymard Institute, who conduct independent web usability research, ran a study with various e-commerce websites and found that breadcrumbs remain a vital tool for helping users navigate. They then studied 50 of the top e-commerce websites and found that, despite their usefulness, 94% had what they called "sub-par breadcrumb implementation," with nearly a quarter having no breadcrumbs at all.[38]

There are two main types of breadcrumbs: hierarchical and historical.

Hierarchical

This is the most common type of breadcrumb. They help show users the position of their current page within the hierarchy of the site and are most often used to navigate between items within a certain category, as Figure 6-13 shows.

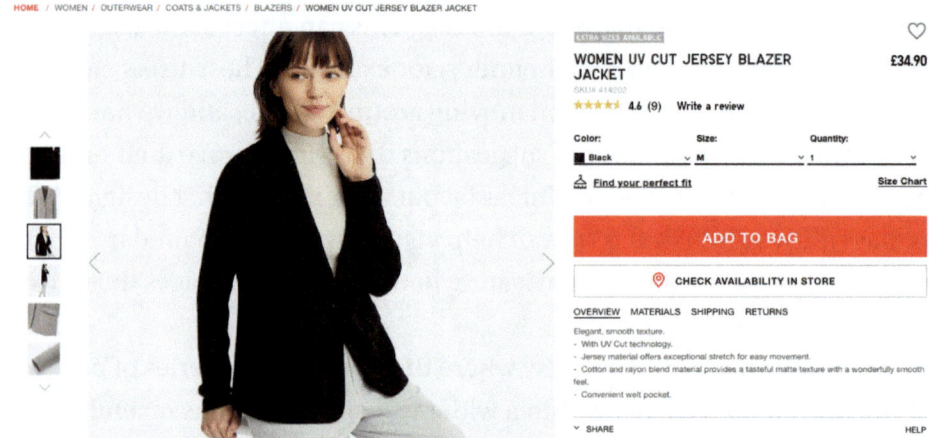

Figure 6-13. *A screenshot of a product page on the Uniqlo website, with a set of hierarchical breadcrumbs at the top*

Not only do they provide a clear indication of a user's position within a site, but they help the user understand what else is available around them. It also creates a contextual menu that helps users navigate content that's more closely related to what they're currently viewing, rather than forcing users to use a main menu. In the previous example, a user could decide to go and look at other blazers, jackets, women's clothing more generally or go back to the home page, without having to search for any of those pages.

This means users with **visual–spatial** cognitive impairments don't have to try and picture a sequence of pages, or their path through them in their head – it is always on the page with them. This is linked to a success criterion in WCAG 2.0 called "Multiple ways" that ensures that users can find content on a website in more than one way. A user may have trouble interacting with one method of finding content (e.g., a menu) in which case links in a footer, or a set of breadcrumbs, would prevent them from getting stuck. As we mentioned earlier, they may also have trouble understanding their location within a site, in which case this solution helps too.

Without providing breadcrumbs, the user is forced to make what is called "drastic scope jumps" such as going all the way back to the main menu if they want to explore related content. This doesn't make for a great user experience, and for those that become lost easily due to issues with orientation or comprehending visual information, a lack of granular navigation could be exclusionary. This applies to much more than e-commerce sites – it can help users navigate to related pages of any content that may be organised in subcategories. For example, hierarchy-based breadcrumbs could help users discover related content in blogs through tags assigned to posts, or in frequently asked questions (FAQs) organised by topic.

Another good reason to add breadcrumbs revolves around helping users who come across your content from outside the site. It's entirely possible that, rather than reaching certain pages on your site by drilling down from one section to another, users will have found it via a search engine, or perhaps through an advert, or another site that's mentioned yours. You can't assume that the user has reached the product page above, for example, after visiting the "women's clothing" page, then the jackets section, and finally the product itself. It's just as possible that they've seen it on a blog or advert, or have simply used a search engine to find it.

Therefore, breadcrumbs provide contextual information that a user who has just arrived on the site won't otherwise have. Without breadcrumbs, they wouldn't immediately know what other pages are on the site, or their position within those pages. In this respect, breadcrumb navigation *invites* users to explore related content (i.e., look at other jackets on the page), rather than simply leaving your site. It "blends site taxonomy and user behaviour into a single functional element."[39]

Historical

Now that we've started to think about the different journeys a user could take to get to your website, let's think about the different types of journey they can take within it. Going back to the example of an e-commerce website, a user going through a checkout process will likely not benefit from a breadcrumb menu that is based on page hierarchy, such as

Home ➤ Shopping ➤ Checkout

Instead, it'd be more useful to have:

Basket ➤ Shipping Address ➤ Payment Details ➤ Review

This is an example of a historical breadcrumb, which provides quick links to get back to places the user has been while on your site. This is, of course, possible with the "Back" button on a browser, but that's restricted to moving one page at a time, whereas breadcrumbs allow you to go back multiple steps or stages. It also means you can potentially keep filters and state inputted by the user which the browser's back button can't always accomplish. Adding breadcrumbs again accomplishes the "multiple ways" WCAG rule, as people can use those links instead of hitting "back" multiple times or restarting the journey completely. This is particularly useful for users with **impaired working memory** (like those with dementia), who find it difficult to carry information from one page to the next. Breadcrumbs remind them "of the route they've taken to get to a page, and [allow them] to see which section they're currently in."[40]

With both hierarchical and historical breadcrumbs providing different but equally useful features, the Baymard Institute recommend that you implement both types. It's important that you review the sections and journeys within your site to see whether a breadcrumb menu could be useful. Before breadcrumbs existed on sites though, there was a consistent way for users to see every page that was on a website in one place (although they aren't used in this way as much anymore) – let's talk about sitemaps.

Sitemaps

A sitemap is a file and/or page, written in code, that lists all of a website's pages – providing a complete overview of a site's structure. They were common in the early days of the Web, as a site would only contain a handful of pages and there wasn't always links between them. In recent years, though, the number of pages in a typical site has risen drastically, and the rise of online blogs and shops has meant that a sitemap could hold hundreds (or thousands) of pages. This has meant that sitemaps are nowhere near as easy to use as they once were.

This is partly why sitemaps are now geared more toward helping search engines find and index pages. The Google sitemap XML protocol was a landmark change for this, where they advised sites to build the file for this purpose and had their search engine look for it by default.[41] Its existence doesn't affect your page's ranking in searches, but it does ensure that search engines are aware of all of the pages you have (and want them to see), allowing them to appear in search results. Moreover, it makes it easier to track how frequently your website is updated and records the last time any changes were made (useful as search engines prefer to display recent, relevant content in their searches).

All of this aside, the fact that sitemaps provide every link in the same serialised format without the need to go searching for all of them in different menus and journeys means they're still useful for accessibility purposes. Again, this goes back to WCAG's "multiple ways" which recommends you provide more than one way to navigate and find content – if users know that they can locate content within a site from the same consistent place (Google requires it to be at the root directory of every website – i.e., mywebsite.com/sitemap.xml), they can easily find what they're looking for. W3C even say so themselves:

> *A person with cognitive disabilities may prefer a table of contents or site map that provides an overview of the site rather than reading and traversing through several Web pages.*[42]

A user with cognitive impairments would therefore be able to engage with one file to find a page, should they have trouble understanding a user flow or traversing numerous menus and sub-menus they aren't used to. They may well prefer not to do this, but at least they would have the choice. As they hold benefits for search engine optimisation, and make a site a little more accessible, sitemaps are well worth the effort.

Now, part of what made sitemaps so appealing was that they allowed you to see every page on a site and know exactly where you were going if you clicked on a particular page – every action made sense by itself. On many sites, this is no longer the case – actions may be part of a wider journey, or be embedded within the flow of a sentence, and it may not be immediately clear what a particular action is or what it is asking a user to do. With that in mind, I'd like us to touch briefly on how (and why) to ensure that your site's actions are "self-contained."

Self-contained actions

"Self-contained actions" are actions (like links or buttons) that users can understand in isolation from other content on the page, rather than relying on the content around them to provide context. The term was raised in a study about web accessibility for users with autism, where it mentioned that having information that was self-contained was particularly useful for users with sensory processing disorders (SPD),[43] and reduced the time needed to concentrate on a task – an issue that could apply to any user. Links with text like "click here" may make sense as part of a sentence, but seen by themselves, it's difficult to know exactly what would happen if you interacted with them. Describing actions so that they make sense on their own can remove barriers for a wide range of cognitive-impaired users. For example, they help users with language comprehension impairments or visual impairments who struggle to understand or recognise vague language. They also help **visual–spatial** impaired users who have trouble navigating, because they allow them to more easily identify where they want to go within a website.

If users come across an action that is vague and nondescriptive, this can lead to a stressful and negative experience. Take the following two buttons shown in Figure 6-14 – both responsible for submitting details in a form.

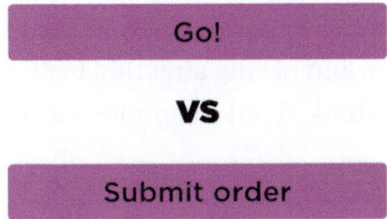

Figure 6-14. *A comparison of two buttons by themselves, one with text where the result of the action is unclear ("Go!") and one where it's clearer ("submit order")*

Only one of these two buttons makes any sense by itself. You need to check if, when read completely in isolation, the action makes sense and informs a user of what will happen if they interact with it. Phrases like "click here" and "get started" may seem obvious given the content and text around them but are ambiguous and say very little independently. On the other hand, links such as "Attach files" or "Subscribe to newsletter" are clear, concise, and unambiguous.

This a slam dunk when it comes to catering for a group of users with cognitive-based access needs that we have not yet discussed in this chapter. Self-contained actions help those with **reasoning impairments** understand what task they are meant to be doing and how to do it, and users that have difficulties with **executive function** (planning and execution) identify the next step they should take to accomplish their goal. They also help those with ADHD to **focus** on the task at hand and can remind **memory-impaired** users about what they were doing.

They're actually also useful for people using screen readers. This is because there is usually a break between a screen reader reading out the content of a sentence and the text in a link (they are two different elements after all), so the context of the sentence can be forgotten. Therefore, having to wait a few seconds and then hearing a link entitled "click here" will almost certainly cause confusion and force the user to reread the previous sentence.

Again, there are many overlaps between access needs despite different reasoning behind them, and paying attention to clarity benefits everyone. With this in mind, let's think about a common issue on the Web for all of us – human error.

Autocomplete

Issues with human error are common across the Web. For example, Microsoft conducted research in 2011 and found that users made spelling mistakes in 10–20% of searches.[44] However, the effects of an unforgiving site are felt more keenly by those with cognitive impairments. Again, this is an issue for users who have language-based access needs, but it also has a huge impact on those with **memory impairments** like dementia.

To combat this, you need your site to be as error tolerant as possible, and a large portion of these pain points are revealed when content is inputted. I often find myself typing too quickly and placing letters in the wrong order, so if a site can compensate for these small and very human errors, it will prevent unnecessary frustrations.

Features such as autocorrect (automatically correcting common spelling errors) come as standard in a lot of devices and operating systems and can be very useful, but another great innovation that you can add yourself is autocomplete.

Autocomplete is often seen on form inputs and attempts to "guess" what a user has started to type. It provides options that they can select from, based on the information the user has already provided, and offers to complete the entry for them. It's important to note that autocomplete is only as smart as the data behind it – usually pulled from a database or a list of potential results in a site's code. Still, it can often help users find results more quickly, especially if they have trouble remembering what they are looking for or how to spell it. This can also help people with ADHD or autism, who often become overwhelmed by too many options.

The latter can be caused by form elements that contain long drop-downs, for example, selecting a country from a list of every country on Earth. Examples like this are a perfect candidate for autocomplete, as it filters those options the moment a user starts interacting.

This approach encapsulates one of the new success criteria that the Cognitive and Learning Disabilities Accessibility Task Force (COGA) added into the recent WCAG 2.1 update. It's called "Identify Input Purpose" and refers to the ability to programmatically determine the purpose of an input field in order to make collecting data from a user easier. Here, they explain how autocomplete can also help users with dyslexia and dyscalculia:

Supermarket assistant with dyslexia and dyscalculia:

Problem: My address is so complicated. There's lots of numbers and long words. It's hard to type it all without making mistakes.

Works well: I love websites that can automatically fill it all in for me. Then I don't have to work so hard to get the numbers and spelling right.[45]

This can be a powerful feature, but there is a catch – autocomplete often still requires a degree of precision to use. This is because, by default, many of the libraries used to add autocomplete aren't great at accommodating human errors. As a result, their usefulness depends on the way a user searches, and errors inputting content can actually offset the time saved by implementing autocomplete, as a user would need to delete the incorrectly entered content before retyping it in order to find the correct option. This is what I call "strict search" and, when implemented in this fashion, can make the process longer than inputting content regularly.

"Strict" search

A good example of this is the most frequently used autocomplete library on the Web – jQueryUI Autocomplete (which is part of jQuery's larger UI library).[46] This is easy to implement, but as we mentioned earlier, it only returns results for queries that are spelt correctly, as opposed to returning results that are close to an intended answer. If we were hypothetically trying to search for the country "Croatia" from a list of every country, using this library, here are the search examples that would return it as an option (with the result shown in Figure 6-15):

- Cro (typing the start of the word, with the letters in the correct order)

- Croatia (the country name itself, spelt correctly)

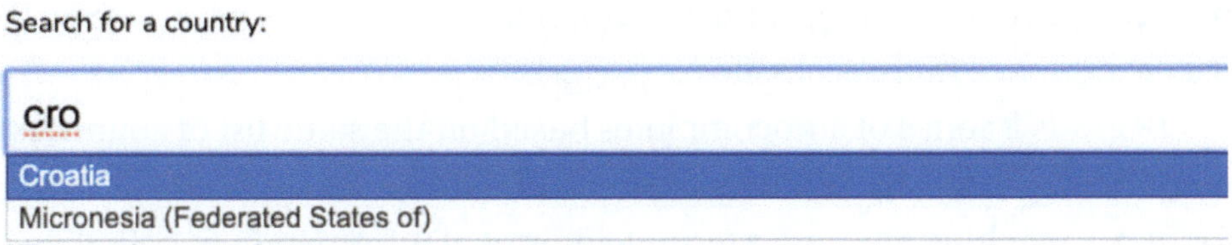

Search for a country:

> **cro**
>
> **Croatia**
> Micronesia (Federated States of)

Figure 6-15. *Strict search accurately returning "Croatia" when the user has entered "cro"*

It does what it should when the correct information is submitted, but it's not lenient to human error (shown in Figure 6-16).

Search for a country:

> croasha

Figure 6-16. *Strict search returning no results when the user has entered an incorrect spelling of Croatia – "croasha"*

"Fuzzy" matching

You've probably seen autocomplete on sites like Google and Amazon, and you've probably also seen they're good at "guessing" what you're searching for. This is known as "fuzzy" matching (or approximate string matching to be technical).

Fuzzy matching can search for results in a list like the example above, but also in a far more lenient way, without relying on an exact match with content that has already been inputted. It includes misspelt words, the correct letters that are in the wrong order, or alternative spellings of a word (i.e., something that "sounds" phonetically like the word).[47]

Not only that, but fuzzy matching can take in associated or related information for each search result, rather than just the word itself. For example, if a user is searching for a book, they may want to search by author, or ISBN number – not just by title. These are all common user

217

behaviors when searching, and allowing them on your site will make your user experience more accessible.

Below is a series of autocompletes based on the same list of countries mentioned previously, but with a couple of differences – this one allows for fuzzy matching and can interpret additional information to help the user find the result they may be looking for. In this case, it allows users to search by ISO country code as well as the country itself. Here are just a few examples of entries that a user could write in the form field to return Croatia as the top result:

- Cro (typing the start of the word, with the letters in the correct order)

- Croatia (the country name itself, spelt correctly)

- Croasha (misspelling of the "tia" at the end)

- Coratai (all of the letters in "Croatia", but in a completely wrong order)

- Roatia (missing the first letter, likely from a quick-typing error)

- HN (the ISO country code)

- Crosha (a misspelling)

- Crowaysha (written as the word sounds)

- Croaysha (same as above)

And many more I likely haven't thought of.

Figures 6-17, 6-18, and 6-19 below show a few of these scenarios working successfully with a fuzzy matching search:

Search for a country or ISO code:

cro
Croatia
Costa Rica
Colombia
Romania

Figure 6-17. *Fuzzy search accurately returning "Croatia" when the user has entered the start of the word – "cro" – the same as strict search*

Search for a country or ISO code:

croyasha
Croatia
Costa Rica
Canada
Colombia

Figure 6-18. *Fuzzy search accurately returning "Croatia" when the user has entered an incorrect spelling based on how the word is said – "croyasha"*

Search for a country or ISO code:

coratai
Croatia
Costa Rica
Colombia
Canada

Figure 6-19. *Fuzzy search accurately returning "Croatia" when the user has entered all of the correct letters for the word but in the wrong order – "Coratai"*

Types of "fuzzy" searching

I didn't create the logic for "fuzzy" searching; I'm merely showing how implementing better searching methods can benefit a wide array of users. I will, however, provide examples of them in this chapter's practical example, so that you can easily recreate the behavior and implement it into your own sites. As always, you can find the code for the practical example on this book's Github repository (in the "Chapter 6" folder), but if you'd simply like to see it in action, you can visit `https://inclusive.guide/examples/autocomplete`

There are two popular approaches to fuzzy searching.

Jaro–Winkler distance algorithm

This algorithm measures how many characters there are in common between the text that the user has entered and a list of possible autocomplete options.[48] This combats human error in the form of spelling mistakes but also takes into account instances where a user incorrectly spells a word after sounding it out but has got a fair amount of the letters correct. For example, Croatia is pronounced "cro-ay-sha" which, despite being the incorrect spelling, has 5 of the 7 letters in common with the correct spelling.

This is the approach used in the previous images, and in this chapter's practical example, using a library called Missplete. The code was created by a developer called Xavi Caballé. In the practical example, you'll find links to his work.

Levenshtein distance – Fuse

The Levenshtein distance (also known as edit distance) is the minimum number of single-character edits (insertions, deletions, or substitutions) required to change one word into another.[49] In this case, it compares what the user has entered against the list of possible options and determines how it could get to a result with the fewest edits. The most commonly used version of this with autocomplete was created by Kiro Risk, a Software Engineer at LinkedIn, who created Fuse JS. Although I didn't use this approach in the practical example, I *have* added links to it there if you're interested.

Which should I use?

Both provide a significant improvement on standard "strict" searching by allowing for human error and by allowing the search to associate multiple pieces of information with each result. In research conducted on both, Jaro–Winkler was considered the faster of the two approaches,[50] but the Fuse library is more heavily supported as a project. In my opinion, there is little difference between the two, so you can simply choose which library fits most neatly with your needs.

Whichever you choose, it's clear to see that fuzzy searching holds the potential to help more users.

Conclusion

Hopefully the five areas we have covered here have made it easier to explore and understand an area of accessibility that is still very much fluid and up for debate. As I mentioned at the start of this chapter, the access needs experienced by cognitive impaired users are hard to place into distinct areas. Many needs span multiple areas and overlap with the needs, barriers, and solutions mentioned in other chapters too.

Despite this, this lack of clear distinctions has its benefits. In the introduction to this book, I mentioned that by regular practice at identifying access needs and barriers, you can become adept at identifying these issues in your work and therefore seeing how you can cater for a wide range of users. Now that we are a few chapters in, I hope you have started to catch some of the overlaps that have been cropping up.

As a useful recap, here are some solutions that we've covered in this chapter that overlap with access needs we've covered in other chapters:

- TL;DR's can be useful for screen readers, particularly if they're positioned at the top, as these users can read the summary before deciding whether to engage with the rest of the content. They can also help users in a rush who don't have time to fully engage with all of the content.

- In "Motor disabilities," we mentioned the importance of shortcuts for keyboard-only navigation (such as "skip to main content"), and breadcrumbs provide another excellent option. These quick, context-based links allow a user to quickly tab to a related page without searching through a large menu.

- Some users with dyslexia have trouble reading on certain foreground/background colour combinations (such as white text on a black background) even though it has a high contrast ratio. We mentioned this briefly in the chapter on "Low Vision and Colour Blindness," but the same access needs, and emphasis on using colour in a positive way, are mentioned in the "Plain English" section. Here, we discussed how slightly different coloured backgrounds on different sections of a page can help split up content and provide "natural stopping points."

- Similarly, we looked at how bright contrasting colours can overwhelm some users with Autism – a barrier that can also exclude users with photosensitivity.

- "Unexpected autoplay" was a discussion topic in the last chapter about "Deafness and Hard of hearing" but was also relevant in this chapter because of the effect it has on those with heightened sensory awareness. It's capable of contributing to the "complex experiences" that overwhelm some users with autism.

- Sitemaps provide a consistent format for displaying lists of pages on a site and, aside from providing an alternate way to navigate for cognitively impaired users, they can also help Blind and Low Vision users through their consistent layout for screen readers to digest.

It's worth taking a little time to think about each of these and other crossovers you might have spotted. No chapter is completely isolated from the others in this book, in exactly the same way that no disability or access need is isolated from other user needs. Just as cognitive impairments can be known as "hidden disabilities," many of these overlapping benefits can help you cater for "hidden needs" – things you hadn't considered because it wasn't immediately obvious that they applied to a specific area or disability, but that can still improve a user's experience on the Web. The more that you begin to think like this, the more needs you will tackle, and the better you will get at seeing more than one benefit. Accessibility is iterative, and practice is key.

Notes

1. National Autistic Society, *Autism facts and history,* <www.autism.org.uk/about/what-is/myths-facts-stats.aspx> [accessed 14/06/2019]

2. British Dyslexia Association, *About us,* <www.bdadyslexia.org.uk/dyslexia> [accessed 14/06/2019].

3. Robert McDowell, *Neurodiversity and Digital Inclusion,* (12/2018), <https://econsultancy. com/reports/neurodiversity-and-digital- inclusion/>[accessed 14/06/2019].

4. Robert McDowell, Interview with author, (04/04/2019).

5. Robert McDowell, *Neurodiversity and Digital Inclusion,* (12/2018), <https://econsultancy. com/reports/neurodiversity-and-digital- inclusion/> [accessed 14/06/2019].

6. Robert McDowell, Interview with author, (04/04/2019).

7. Twilah Hiari, *Neurodiversity is dead. Now what?* (08/04/2018), [accessed 14/06/2019] <www. madinamerica.com/2018/04/neurodiversity- dead-now-what/> [accessed 14/06/2019] .

8. Patrick Dwyer, *The Misrepresentation of Neurodiversity*, Autistic Scholar, (27/11/2018), <www. autisticscholar.com/the-misrepresentation- of-neurodiversity/> [accessed 14/06/2019].

9. WebAIM, *Cognitive*, (2019), <https://webaim.org/ articles/cognitive/> [accessed 14/06/2019].

10. W3C, *Cognitive Accessibility User Research*, (2015), <www.w3.org/TR/coga-user-research/> [accessed 14/06/2019].

11. WebAIM, *Cognitive*, (2019), <https://webaim.org/ articles/cognitive/> [accessed 14/06/2019].

12. Plainlanguage.gov, *What is plain language?*   [accessed 14/06/2019].

13. NHS, *Aphasia*, (08/02/2018), <www.nhs.uk/
    conditions/aphasia/> [accessed 14/06/2019].

14. W3C, *Cognitive Accessibility User Research*,
    (15/01/2015), <www.w3.org/TR/coga-user-
    research/> [accessed 14/06/2019].

15. Claudia Cahalane, *How to avoid losing one million
    customers with inclusive digital design for dementia*,
    ability.net, (05/04/2017), <www.abilitynet.org.
    uk/news-blogs/how-avoid-losing-one-million-
    website-customers-inclusive-digital-design-
    dementia> [accessed 14/06/2019].

16. Donna Maksimovic, *Plain English... Write less,
    say more*, Companies House Blog, Gov.uk,
    (01/10/2018), <https://companieshouse.blog.
    gov.uk/2018/01/10/plain-english-write-less-
    say-more/> [accessed 14/06/2019].

17. Neilsen Norman Group, *How Little Do Users Read?*,
    (05/05/2008), <www.nngroup.com/articles/how-
    little-do-users-read/> [accessed 14/06/2019].

18. Center for Plain Language, *about*, (2019), <https://
    centerforplainlanguage.org/about/> [accessed
    14/06/2019].

19. Government Digital Service, *Content design:
    planning, writing and managing content*,
    (05/09/2019), <www.gov.uk/guidance/content-
    design/writing-for-gov-uk>[accessed
    14/06/2019].

20. Government Digital Service, *Content design: planning, writing and managing content,* (05/09/2019), <www.gov.uk/guidance/content-design/writing-for-gov-uk>[accessed 14/06/2019].

21. Harvard University, *Use plain language,* (2019), <https://accessibility.huit.harvard.edu/use-plain-language> [accessed 14/06/2019].

22. Government Digital Service, *Content design: planning, writing and managing content,* (05/09/2019), <www.gov.uk/guidance/content-design/writing-for-gov-uk>[accessed 14/06/2019].

23. Dyslexie font, (2019), <www.dyslexiefont.com/> [accessed 14/06/2019].

24. Government Digital Service, *Content design: planning, writing and managing content,* (05/09/2019), <www.gov.uk/guidance/content-design/writing-for-gov-uk>[accessed 14/06/2019].

25. Ian Stuart Hamilton, *People with Autism Spectrum Disorder Take Things Literally,* (04/07/2013), <www.psychologytoday.com/gb/blog/the-gift-aging/201304/people-autism-spectrum-disorder-take-things-literally> [accessed 14/06/2019].

26. NHS Inform, *NHS inform style guide,* (2019), <www.nhsinform.scot/campaigns/nhs-inform-style-guide> [accessed 14/06/2019].

27. Government Digital Service, *Content design: planning, writing and managing content,* (05/09/2019), <www.gov.uk/guidance/content-design/writing-for-gov-uk> [accessed 14/06/2019].

28. Center for Plain Language, *Five Steps to Plain Language,* (2019), <https://centerforplainlanguage.org/learning-training/five-steps-plain-language/> [accessed 14/06/2019].

29. Hannah Alvarez, *Making Your Icons User-Friendly: A Guide to Usability in UI Design,* User Testing Blog, (04/08/2015), <www.usertesting.com/blog/user-friendly-ui-icons/> [accessed 14/06/2019].

30. Suzanne Collins, *Welcome,* <www.suzannecollinsbooks.com/> [accessed 14/06/2019].

31. Eric Enge, *Mobile vs Desktop Traffic in 2019,* Stone Temple, (04/11/2019), <www.stonetemple.com/mobile-vs-desktop-usage-study/> [accessed 14/06/2019].

32. Claudia Cahalane, *How to avoid losing one million customers with inclusive digital design for dementia,* ability.net, (05/04/2017), <www.abilitynet.org.uk/news-blogs/how-avoid-losing-one-million-website-customers-inclusive-digital-design-dementia> [accessed 14/06/2019].

33. National Autistic Society, *Sensory differences*, <www.
     autism.org.uk/about/behaviour/sensory-world.
     aspx> [accessed 14/06/2019].

34. Gamesradar, *Home,* (2019), <www.gamesradar.com/
     uk> [accessed 14/06/2019].

35. David Kirkpatrick, Google: *53% of mobile users
     abandon sites that take over 3 seconds to load,
     MarketingDive*, (12/08/2016), <www.marketingdive.
     com/news/google-53-of-mobile-users-
     abandon-sites-that-take-over-3-seconds-to-
     load/426070/> [accessed 14/06/2019].

36. Martin Petersen, A*re Breadcrumbs still a Thing
     in 2019?,* (2019), <www.designernews.co/
     stories/98937-are-breadcrumbs-still-a-thing-
     in-2019> [accessed 14/06/2019].

37. W3C, *Location,* (2016) <www.w3.org/TR/
     UNDERSTANDING-WCAG20/navigation-mechanisms-
     location.html> [accessed 14/06/2019]

38. Jamie Appleseed, *Baymard Institute, E-Commerce
     Sites Need 2 Types of Breadcrumbs (68% Get it
     Wrong)*, (07/2014), <https://baymard.com/blog/
     ecommerce-breadcrumbs> [accessed 14/06/2019].

39. Jamie Appleseed, *Baymard Institute, E-Commerce
     Sites Need 2 Types of Breadcrumbs (68% Get it
     Wrong)*, (07/2014), <https://baymard.com/blog/
     ecommerce-breadcrumbs> [accessed 14/06/2019].

40.   Claudia Cahalane, *How to avoid losing one million customers with inclusive digital design for dementia,* ability.net, (05/04/2017), <www.abilitynet.org.uk/news-blogs/how-avoid-losing-one-million-website-customers-inclusive-digital-design-dementia> [accessed 14/06/2019].

41.   Sitemaps, *Search Engine Giants Adopting the XML Protocol,* (2019) <www.xml-sitemaps.com/about-sitemaps.html> [accessed 14/06/2019].

42.   W3C, Understanding Success Criterion 2.4.5: *Multiple Ways,* <www.w3.org/WAI/WCAG21/Understanding/multiple-ways.html> [accessed 14/06/2019].

43.   Antonina Dattolo, Flaminia L. Luccio & Elisa Pirone, *Webpage accessibility and usability for Autistic Users, a Case Study on a Tourism Website,* (2016), <https://core.ac.uk/download/pdf/80136806.pdf> [accessed 14/06/2019].

44.   Huizhong Duan Bo-June (Paul) Hsu, *Online Spelling Correction for Query Completion, Microsoft,* (03/2011), <www.microsoft.com/en-us/research/publication/online-spelling-correction-for-query-completion/?from=http%3A%2F%2Fresearch.microsoft.com%2Fpubs%2F148103%2Fwww11-onlinespellingcorrection.pdf> [accessed 14/06/2019].

45.   W3C, What's new in WCAG 2.1, <www.w3.org/WAI/standards-guidelines/wcag/new-in-21/#135-identify-input-purpose-aa> [accessed 14/06/2019]

46.   jQuery user interface, *Home,* (2019) <https://
      jqueryui.com/> [accessed 14/06/2019].

47.   Technopedia, Fuzzy Search, (2019), <www.
      techopedia.com/definition/7356/fuzzy-search>
      [accessed 14/06/2019].

48.   Wikipedia, *Jaro-WInkler distance,* <https://
      en.wikipedia.org/wiki/Jaro%E2%80%93Winkler_
      distance> [accessed 14/06/2019].

49.   Nikhil Babar, *The Levenshtein Distance Algorithm,*
      (02/10/2018), <https://dzone.com/articles/the-
      levenshtein-algorithm-1> [accessed 14/06/2019].

50.   Peter Christen, *A Comparison of Personal Name
      Matching: Techniques and Practical Issues,* The
      Australian National University, <http://citeseerx.
      ist.psu.edu/viewdoc/download?doi=10.1.1.65.7
      311&rep=rep1&type=pdf> [accessed 14/06/2019].

CHAPTER 7

Mental Health

Design is what mediates our interaction with the internet. It's the language we read it in. It's not too much to ask that that language is comprehensible and honest.[1]

Of all the disabilities we have discussed so far, mental health impairments have arguably seen the biggest increase in exposure over the last few years. Consequently, at the time of writing, the way we think about mental health is in a state of flux. While some mental health disorders, like depression and anxiety, are fairly well understood, the way we categorise and define other conditions is constantly changing – just like many of the cognitive impairments mentioned in the last chapter. The definitions of conditions like schizophrenia or psychosis, for example, have changed a lot over the last few decades and can refer to a wide variety of experiences.

The charity Money and Mental Health estimates that "In any given year, one in four people will experience a mental health problem which can affect their cognitive and psychological functioning".[2]

Again, this a fluctuating number. For example, in their "Fundamental facts about mental health" paper published just months before, the Money and Mental Health foundation said that: "Nearly half of adults believe that, in their lifetime, they have had a diagnosable mental health problem, yet only a third have received a diagnosis."[3] This variance is rooted in a large number of factors. Experiences can vary substantially from person to person, across different conditions, at different times in a person's life, and even differing understanding whether their symptoms constitute a mental health condition. As Money and Mental Health's Merlyn Holkar told me:

> *Everybody's mental health will get better and worse over time – it could be that somebody has had a breakup or a financial problem that has recently just made things worse. People might not tell you that they are experiencing these symptoms.*[4]

This creates a situation that differs from catering for most other access needs, where we cannot always confidently identify people affected by mental health issues. At the same time, research has found that "consumers experiencing mental health problems are systematically disadvantaged...and are more likely to pay over the odds, experience poorer services, and are more likely to end up in financial difficulty."[5] With these points in mind, we can start to address these needs by first understanding which features are exacerbating these symptoms online.

Dark patterns

In 2018 the Norwegian Consumer Council published a paper called "Deceived by Design." In it, they highlighted some of the tactics used by sites like Facebook, Google, and Microsoft to "manipulate" users into disclosing information and relinquishing their privacy online. This included using certain language to alter decisions, prompting "take it or leave it" questions, and hiding actions deep inside account menus. The report concluded that these actions were implemented in their online experiences "to a degree that we consider unethical."[6]

Just over 6 months later, following the advent of GDPR (General Data Protection Regulation), Google was hit with a £44 million fine.[7]

Now although this fine is, on the face of it, directed at regulating privacy, the same practices manipulate users, and the lack of transparency causes distress. Online deceit exploits human behavior, and those with mental health problems can be more sensitive to this exploitation.

In this case, Google was found to have "pre-ticked" certain form fields – forcing people to opt out rather than opt in and to have disseminated important information across multiple pages, making it difficult to find. These are just two examples of "dark patterns." This phrase, coined by UX specialist Harry Brignull, describes features crafted to "trick" users into doing things they may not want to do but that benefit the business.[8]

There are a lot of techniques used online that are designed to "nudge" users into behaving a certain way. These practices are known to increase conversion, retention, and most other metrics that sites measure success by, which explains why they're so popular. It's also difficult to legislate when it comes to leveraging human psychology, and so holding businesses accountable here is hard to do.

Encouraging a user to do something isn't necessarily the problem (all sites do this in some way); it depends on *how* sites do it. As the Norwegian consumer council explain:

> *the use of exploitative design choices, or "dark patterns", is arguably an unethical attempt to push consumers toward choices that benefit the service provider.*[9]

Dark patterns create negative experiences which can be amplified for those with mental health-oriented access needs: for example, those who struggle with a lack of motivation, those susceptible to periods of impulsivity that cause them to make quick (and sometimes poorly judged) decisions, and those who suffer from anxiety. Other access needs might even arise from the treatment of these symptoms: WAI explain that "medication may have side effects including blurred vision, hand tremors, and other impairments" which can also increase how sensitive these users are to dark patterns.[10]

Another problem is that this sort of behavior isn't monitored or regulated. Indeed, despite the recent rise in awareness, there isn't an agreed set of rules for helping those with mental health issues online. WCAG 2.1 doesn't explicitly mention mental health disorders, and COGA (Cognitive Accessibility Roadmap and Gap Analysis), mentioned in the last chapter, is still working on gap analysis to understand the state of web accessibility and what to recommend.[11]

You don't have to do the same thing as other companies though and, in fairness, sometimes dark patterns have manipulative consequences that go beyond what their creators intended. Beyond dark patterns, barriers for those with mental health issues are also often thrown up unintentionally and so it's important to know how to spot them and how to reach and support these users more generally. Fully understanding the effect that certain web features have on users with mental health problems can lead you to make better decisions when catering for these users.

What we're going to talk about

Harry Brignull says that "the best defence against dark patterns, is to be aware of them,"[12] so that's what we'll do. I want to approach this chapter through the dual lens of both catering for those with mental health disorders more generally and avoiding dark patterns. Pulling together work from government bodies, research groups, mental health charities, and users themselves, we will address several areas, organised by the following themes:

- **Dark pattern** – Whether a particular barrier is rooted in a manipulative technique used to either encourage or discourage a user action.

- **The symptom(s)** – The symptoms that a barrier can generate or aggravate and how these are compounded for people with mental health issues. It's worth briefly noting that mental health disorders can have cognitive impacts that are identical to those mentioned in the last chapter, affecting planning, reasoning, memory, and attention.[13] Therefore, to fully cater for these users, I would recommend reading over the last chapter as well as this one if you haven't already.

- **Solution(s)** – Solutions we can implement to avoid these issues, or simply actions to avoid. This will also include some examples of those that have approached this in a way that empathises with users.

These access needs should be thought of in relation to all users. In fact, many of these patterns will be situations that you can relate to directly and have been impacted by. This helps to put yourself in the situation of these users and ensure that your sites are doing everything they can to make their experience online a positive one – let's get started.

Dark pattern: Complicated journeys and dead ends

Harry Brignull (who coined the term "dark patterns") also coined the term for a particular pattern – a "Roach Motel." This is a user experience that is very easy to get *into*, but very difficult to get out of.[14] A classic example of this would be the act of deleting an account or cancelling a subscription. Businesses often believe it is in their best interests to make these journeys as hard as possible to discourage users.

Let me take you through a scenario. At the time of writing, if you wanted to close your account with Amazon, you'd likely start looking for the action under the "Your account" section (Figure 7-1).

Your Account

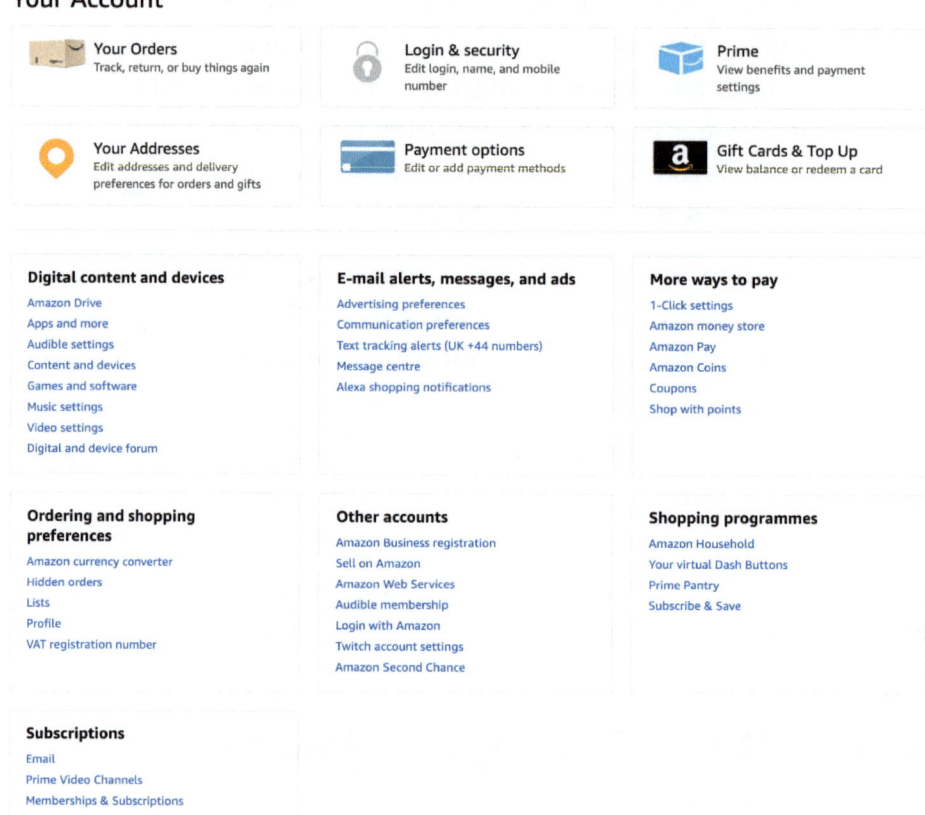

Figure 7-1. *A picture of the links in Amazon's "Your account" section*

But it's not there, not in any of those links. Here is the journey you'd need to take:

1. You scroll to the bottom of the page and select "Help" out of the two-dozen links there.

2. Of the 16 categories on the "Help" page, you need to select "Contact us".

3. Of the four tabs that appear there, you have to select "prime or something else".

4. From the drop-down under "something else", you have to select "login & security".

5. From the next drop-down that appears, you have to select "close an account".

6. Once here, you have to contact them directly to actually perform the action (this is a whole other problem and we'll get to it later).

This is both a dead end (an action that is not where you'd expect it to be) and a complicated journey (six separate actions, many of which would require extensive searching before you find the option that would take you to the next step).

Behavior like this was part of what prompted Google's GDPR fine, as the regulator found that "relevant information is accessible after several steps only, implying sometimes up to five or six actions."[15] This indicated they were hiding information, "nesting" it deep in sub-pages in a way that was needlessly complicated.

Content or actions are not always hidden solely by their position in a layout though – they can be hidden in other ways. Take the example shown in Figure 7-2, found by a user on the booking site lastminute.com.

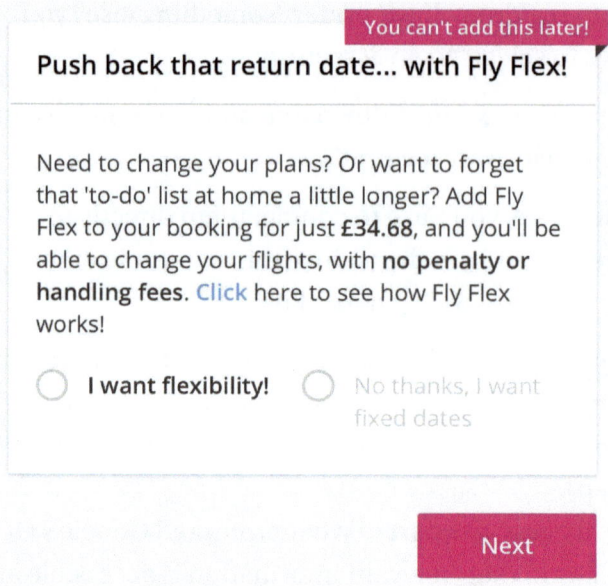

Figure 7-2. *A pair of radio buttons, where one option looks inactive*

At first glance, it doesn't look as though you have a choice – one option appears inactive (thanks to its "greyed out" styling). If you were completing the journey quickly, perhaps becoming tired in the process, you may instinctively select the other option and move on. However, the option that is supposedly "inactive" – not purchasing the upgrade – can still be selected, as Figure 7-3 shows.

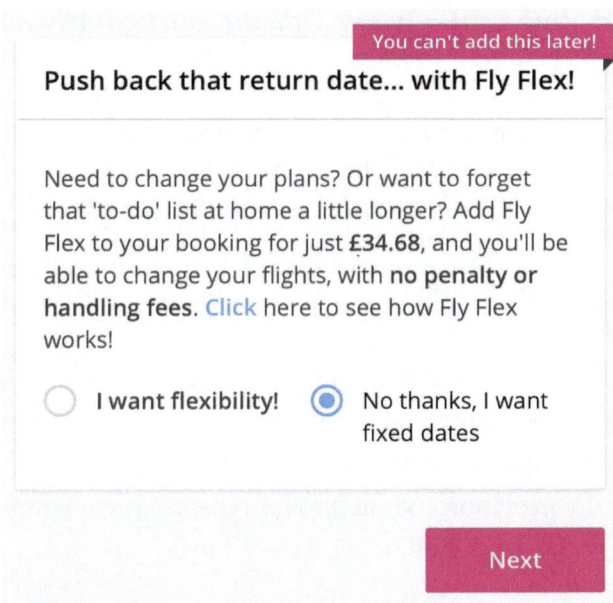

Figure 7-3. *The same pair of radio buttons, but with the seemingly inactive option selected*[16]

This is a small feature, but it can create confusion.

Symptom

Online journeys can be daunting, and companies hope that users will give up and go along with what the site wants. That's what complicated sitemaps and various "dead ends" are designed to do.

Anyone would have trouble navigating deeply nested pages or struggle to remember account security details. However, for those with conditions such as depression who are prone to experiencing a debilitating lack of motivation, or users with panic disorders who are experiencing high levels of panic and confusion, these actions can be nearly impossible to complete. For example, Money and Mental Health reported that:

For many, this is simply too difficult, particularly when they are unwell. When depressed, people often lack the motivation to pursue hobbies and other pleasurable activities. At these times, engagement in essential service markets can require superhuman levels of effort. Eight in ten (82%) of our survey respondents said they found the thought... exhausting.[17]

Users with mental health issues are also especially prone to disengagement.

Complicated journeys also impact users with conditions like schizophrenia, who might have trouble mentally mapping out how pages relate (known as impaired visual–spatial comprehension – which we mentioned in the previous chapter). When discussing his report with me, Merlyn Holkar also described how this technique can cause "information overload":

Some mental health problems can affect your 'attention switch' and other cognitive faculties that you use when you are scanning between different things to try and find the information that's appropriate to you... if there's a website and it has a header with ten different columns dropping down, and you're trying to find a specific thing but you just don't really know what it is, and there's too many things for you to know what to look up.[18]

Not only does this affect users with these conditions – the act of having to find information or complete actions inside a complicated journey can actually make these symptoms worse.[19]

Solutions

You must ensure that common or popular actions are easy to find and initiate. According to W3C, people with mental health issues benefit from "clearly structured content that facilitates overview and orientation,"[20] so a good start involves making sure your main source of navigation (commonly found on every page, such as a main menu) is easy to engage with. It should prioritise core tasks, features, and information and hero those – rather than featuring lots of complicated sub-menus. Take a look at the two menus shown in Figure 7-4.

Figure 7-4. *A visual comparison between two menus – one with both high-level menu items and several sub-menu items and one with just the high-level items*

The latter provides a clearer overview, whereas the former – showing the other items from the offset – makes it harder to know where to begin. This is the difference between "flat" and "deep" navigation patterns.[21] You can always make sub-items available when you interact with a main item (e.g., through a click or tab). This is just as effective, because users would be able to understand the sub-items within the context of the main item they fall under. Another good point is to hero a single navigation item if it is the most common action that your users take, shown in the second menu of Figure 7-5. This could be starting a journey they're likely looking for (i.e., "get a quote"), or a useful reference point if they want to engage with you ("get in touch").

Figure 7-5. *A visual comparison between two menus – one where all menu items are the same and the other where one item is singled out visually*

There is a lot of discussion online about good vs. bad navigation, so I won't go into this deeply; but if you have a lot of menu items, then a great feature to accompany the downsizing of your menu can be making use of a clear "Help" or "frequently asked questions" section. As Merlyn correctly pointed out: 'a lot of users know that the right information is on there somewhere' – it's about making it as easy as possible to find it.[22] A robust "Help" section should mirror common user queries, with pages like "I can't understand my bill" or "where can I change my card details?" Giving users access to a search function that can provide these answers, rather than forcing them to navigate a help section, is even better. By anticipating needs like this, you create a flatter site structure and also make your pages easier to find if someone were to search for that same question through a search engine instead.

Common journeys

While journeys like closing an account may only need to happen once, other journeys can take a greater toll because they are used more frequently. For some users, even the act of logging in can be a barrier, raising questions like:

- "What email did I sign up with?"
- "Do I remember my password?"
- "If I reset it, how long would that take?"
- "Will the email end up in spam?"

Sometimes these steps are unavoidable, and that's because the risk of exposing sensitive data is simply too great. However, it's good to actively think about whether common journeys could be accomplished in fewer steps than they currently require, even if that requires a little more work on your end.

Digital bank Monzo did this with their login process, which now requires only an email address be remembered by the user to log into the app. Once they submit that, a "magic link" is sent to that inbox that logs them in. Users still need to know their pin to use the money in their account (which is good for security purposes), but that's easier to remember than a long password.

I've encountered a similar issue at Octopus Energy while reviewing the journey users take when submitting meter readings. It's something that is required monthly, and after receiving an email reminding customers, they would need to remember their login details to access their dashboard, head to the "meter reading" area, and then submit them. We spoke to customers and found that the number of steps involved meant that customers were not submitting readings and therefore receiving potentially inaccurate bills.

We reviewed the journey and realised that no sensitive data was required when submitting a reading. Moreover, the submission page itself also checked that the reading submitted was within a reasonable threshold of the previous one to prevent fake submissions. This meant that a login wasn't necessary to allow the user to complete the journey.

As a result, we created an anonymous link that we'd email to users every month with their reminder. By clicking this link, they could submit the reading without login details, reducing the time needed to complete the action dramatically. It particularly helped our users that have issues with memory by removing the need to remember a password (e.g., those with dementia). It also aided people with anxiety, who often like to minimise the time spent on sites they aren't familiar with and, more generally, any user looking to complete required actions as quickly as possible.

Since introducing the feature, the percentage of people submitting their first meter readings increased by 24% to 80% of all customers while also reducing the amount of issues created through inaccurate bills. Double whammy!

Setting expectations

Anxiety is experienced by many people (in 2013, there were 8.2 million cases of anxiety in the United Kingdom) but especially users with generalised anxiety disorder, panic disorder, phobias, and post-traumatic stress disorder (PTSD).[23]

Uncertainty is closely linked to anxiety, and uncertainty online can be a big problem – largely due to the sheer volume and variety of content out there. The Web is home to such a wide range of sites – built using different technologies, at different times, during different phases of design and development. As there are no consistencies between these factors, there is no guarantee about how a site is going to appear – one website may design a user journey one way, while another may take a different approach. Of course, some common journeys require similar information (e.g., delivery and payment info will likely be required for an online shop), but even then, this can be asked for in a plethora of ways, over varying amounts of pages and steps.

This makes every experience on a new site a journey into the unknown. For many users, this leads to anxiety, which can prevent them from making their way through a journey effectively, or from even starting one. This can manifest in several ways, from a fear that something bad might happen if the user makes a bad decision or does something wrong, to confusion about how far along they are in a journey, how much further they have to go, and what information they might need.[24]

The solution to this lies in setting a user's expectations correctly. There are two main ways to accomplish this: priming messages and signposting.

Priming messages

Priming messages are used to set a user's expectations ahead of the next step in a journey. After the user completes the action(s) on a page, it's important to explain what will happen next (rather than leaving users confused).

Let's take a look at two buttons (Figure 7-6), each taken from different sites but both at the point in their respective journeys that the next step will be the "payment" page.

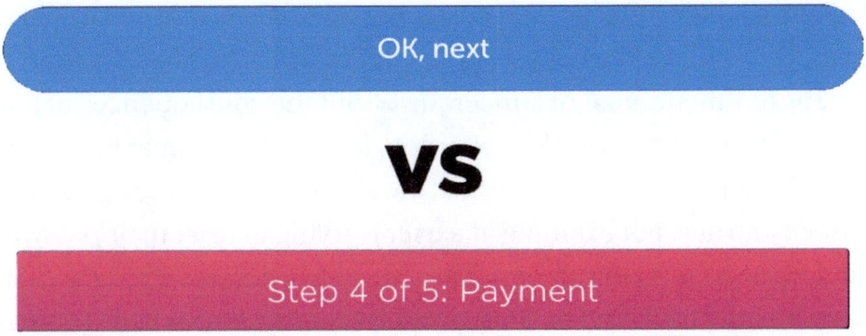

OK, next

VS

Step 4 of 5: Payment

Figure 7-6. *A comparison of two buttons – one that simply says "OK, next" and the other that lets the user know the number and name of the next step in the journey*

The first says nothing. The user doesn't know what "next" means in this context, in the same way that people don't know what a link entitled "click here" will do. At least in the case of the link, the text that comes before it can provide some context.

Conversely, the second option tells users what to expect in the next stage of the journey and also lets them know how far along in the journey they are. This all helps set their expectations for what's to come. It can also mean that users don't have to work as hard to motivate themselves, which can be an issue for those with depression. This is because breaking down tasks into easily understandable chunks removes some uncertainty about how long a task is going to take, and therefore, the worry that the task could go on for what seems like forever.[25]

Priming messages away from your site

The United Kingdom Home Office created a series of simple "do's and don'ts" posters in 2017 to offer guidance on how designers and developers can make sites more accessible for users with certain access needs. We'll cover these properly in Chapter 11 ("Tools and QA"), but recently they added one to their collection on designing for anxiety, and according to them, your online journeys shouldn't leave users "confused about next steps or timeframes" or "uncertain about the consequences of their actions."[26] We've just covered "next steps", but the reason that timeframes are mentioned is because sometimes the steps on your site are only *part* of a user's journey. For example, if a user is trying to reset their password, it could involve receiving an email they need to interact with, or an SMS alert, or even a phone call to confirm their identity. In this case, you can help to set expectations by letting them know:

- What the next step is

- When they should receive these communications

- When they should next expect to hear from you

- What will be expected of them when they hear from you

- What to do if they don't receive a message

The key here is to be upfront and truthful about time frames – if it'll take an hour, then tell users that. Promising shorter wait times will only result in frustration for users when it doesn't happen. People are happy to wait longer if they expect that to begin with. Event strategist Íse Murphy explains this well in her experiences with physical queues:

> *If it had been more realistic, then no one would have grumbled and we would have happily stood there waiting because they had set our expectation levels. Giving us accurate and timely information would have allowed us to make our own decisions. This makes us happy because we feel respected.*[27]

Signposting

Beyond priming for the next action, signposting the main stages of an entire journey can also provide a handy reference point (and source of calm) for users making their way through. Providing context in this way, as seen in Figure 7-7, shows progress and also reduces journey drop-off as people can set their expectations accordingly.

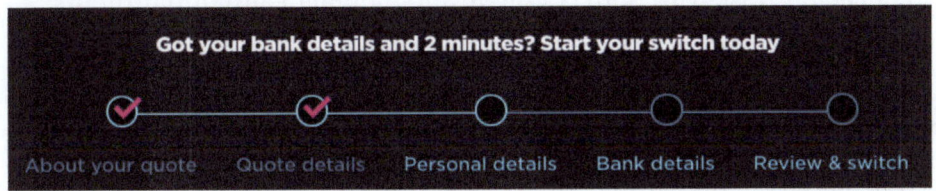

Figure 7-7. *A timeline from a checkout process that shows the user how far they've progressed and which steps are left to complete*

In the journey timeline above, you can see what the steps are, but also how far you've come already and how far there is left to go. This can help users make a decision about when to complete the journey, given what's left to do, and whether they have the right information in order to complete those steps – these are some of the main concerns we raised earlier. Sarah Drummond, founder of the agency Snook, which develops design patterns for mental health services, has talked about how you must "prepare people by providing what information is needed for... the journey they are embarking on."[28] This allows for a sense of "confidence and readiness." Priming messages facilitate preparation for each step, and this simple feature provides it for the whole journey.

This has also been known to help users who suffer with attention impairments – a symptom associated with mental health problems such as ADHD and panic disorders and results in a difficulty concentrating. Activities such as comparing products, scrutinising charges, or filling out lengthy forms require a lot of attention to complete correctly. Knowing exactly what these activities are, and how many of them are present in an online journey beforehand, can allow users to plan when they want to complete it – which reduces the chances of them abandoning it out of frustration and not trying again.

This ties into the historical breadcrumbs that we covered in the last chapter. The combination of providing good signposting of progress in your journeys and enabling users to interact with the various steps and navigate between them, creates a feature that is both reassuring and practical for those with both cognitive and mental health impairments.

Dark pattern: Forced urgency

We've just seen how setting honest expectations can help users understand and complete the journey they are about to go on. Now we are going to look at how some sites manipulate users into rushing these journeys by creating a false sense of urgency.

Travel site booking.com has been frequently cited as an example of a journey that unduly forces a sense of urgency on users. After searching for a hotel in London for a weekend, at the time of writing, I found all of the following messages on the *same page*:

- "In high demand – only 1 room left on our site!"

- "Booked 10 times for your dates in the last 24 hours on our site."

- "1 other person looked for your dates in the last 10 minutes."

- "In high demand" in big red letters – two lines below a badge that says the exact same thing.

- "33 other people looking now."

- "Last chance! Only 1 room left on our site!"

- "89% of our listings are reserved on these dates."

- "Prices have been increasing on your dates over the past 3 days."

Alone, these messages could be considered informative. Eight of them, however, add up to form an intense experience. To compound this worry and urgency, they also show rooms that you "just missed" (shown in Figure 7-8).

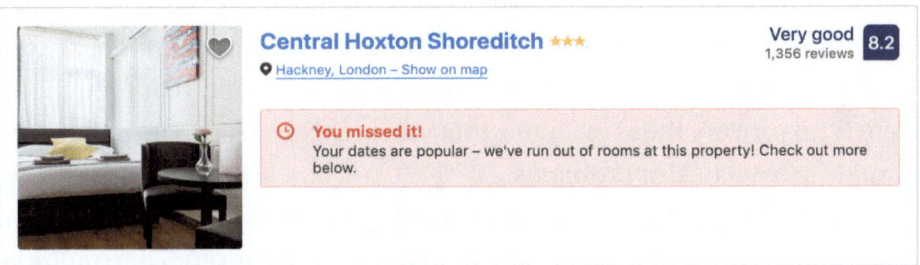

Figure 7-8. *A screenshot from booking.com, where a message is informing the user that they've missed the opportunity to book a certain room*

Even if you had no intention whatsoever of booking the room, you now have a sense of urgency forced upon you, playing on a fear of missing out – look how quickly everything is selling! Imagine if you don't get a great deal![29]

There are examples of this all over the Web. Ticketing websites, for example, often work with even more time-sensitive sales. A recent addition are "virtual queues" – loading screens that update every couple of seconds to let you know how many people are queueing behind you. This increases the urge to complete the purchase as you suddenly become aware of a group of people who are ready to take your tickets if you don't act quickly.

Symptom

While these intrusions can be a source of irritation and stress for many people, they can be complete showstoppers for people with mental health disorders that cause them to feel anxiety, which include generalised anxiety disorders, panic disorders, and psychosis – often need to take their time when completing actions. Rushing these can make them "feel pressured to make decisions more quickly than is comfortable for them,"[30] aggravating their symptoms.[31]

Similarly, features like this also prey on paranoia, encouraging people to act instinctively rather than taking the time to consider the wider context.

Paranoia is "thinking and feeling as if you are under threat even though there is no (or very little) evidence that you are,"[32] and it can be a symptom of many mental health problems.

Finally, these patterns can also encourage impulsive behavior that may be harmful in the long run. Impulsive behavior is a symptom of conditions like borderline personality disorder (BPD). It can compel users to make decisions that negatively affect their life without properly examining them (e.g., making impulsive purchases).[33] This is precisely what actions with time constraints encourage – a sense of urgency and a fear of missing out.

Software developer Roman Cheplyaka actually did a deep dive into booking.com's online practices in 2017, and found that, when you look into the information behind the messaging, there's nothing at all to worry about – it's the nature of the messages themselves (their wording, appearance, etc.) that gives the impression that you need to act immediately. There's a particular button on the site that says "someone just booked this" next to a particular listing. However, when interacted with, "just booked" was actually 4 hours ago. The notification itself appears a few seconds after the page is loaded though, giving the (incorrect) impression that it's appearing in real time.[34] This is capable of alarming users with paranoia, for example, and convincing them to react immediately, perhaps even rashly, in response to the information.

Solutions

Here, our solution echoes a recommendation from the "Motor disabilities" chapter about timers on a site, where giving the users more control over timed tasks made inputting information easier. You need to give users enough time to complete an action, and this applies to decision-making as well as setting impractical time limits.

If you bombard users with multiple sources of information, even information that you think is useful, they could end up making a decision they're not happy with. This could result in complaints, requests for refunds, and losing repeat customers – you potentially increase conversion, but almost certainly reduce customer happiness as a result.

As I mentioned earlier, these pieces of information are not always added to deliberately manipulate the user. Sometimes it can simply be the unfortunate cumulative outcome of testing lots of small features on a page to see if they increase engagement or conversion, and then applying them all together. As a user on the popular development forum Hacker News explains:

> *This is what A/B testing does to a popular site. You test for immediate customer engagement but cannot (easily) test long-term customer loyalty. This is why booking.com has become the largest online hotel booking site in several continents. Nevertheless, I think it will eventually be their downfall.*[35]

It's important to review your journeys and ensure that adding features for the sake of conversion hasn't created a situation where you're pressuring users through your funnel as quickly as possible. You don't want them to regret the decision they've made with you.

You should look at your journeys and if they overencourage the user to rush an action, then simply choose the most compelling argument and emphasise that. This is similar to the logic behind setting expectations. You should stress the importance of the action and then cede control to the user – knowing that the page's simplicity will give them freedom to choose.

Reviewing information

Let's return briefly to this image from setting expectations (Figure 7-9):

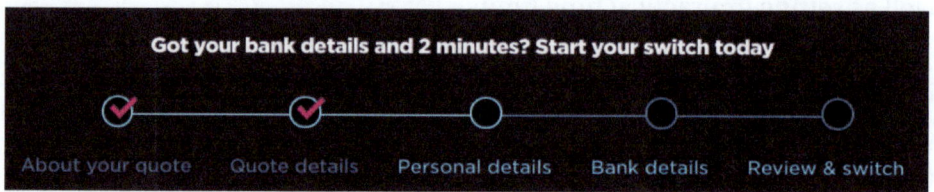

Figure 7-9. *A timeline from a checkout process that shows the user how far they've progressed and which steps are left to complete*

Another point worth mentioning here involves the final step on the diagram above. If you are asking a user to provide information over multiple stages or site pages, it's important that you give them the opportunity to review the information they have provided before they submit it to you, or at the very least allow them to return to previous pages in the journey to review and alter information. This means users can avoid worrying about the answers that they gave. In Figure 7-9, the final page is reserved for giving users a chance to review the steps they've completed. This is important, so let's delve into it a little more.

Not having the chance to review submitted information can cause users to worry. This is partially because unreliable memory is a very common symptom of many mental health problems, like schizophrenia, for example, and can also be a side effect of some treatments.[36]

Reviewing information can also help those with obsessive compulsive disorders (or anxiety disorders) who might wish to check whether they have made a mistake several times.

WCAG 2.1 covers this feature in a new section about "Error prevention."

Being able to review, and then alter and/or revoke, actions such as submitted information and product choices prevents errors and empowers the user. WCAG states that this benefits users with "all disabilities who may be more likely to make mistakes," but realistically it should actually say "all users."[37] We are all susceptible to human error and, while features like autocomplete can safeguard against some incorrect submissions, mistakes can still be made in other areas.

Some dark patterns, however, can even be employed during a review page.

Dark pattern: "Sneak into basket"

When you add something to your basket, some companies add another item automatically, putting the responsibility on you to remove it. This is known as inertia selling or "sneak into basket" selling. The dark patterns website uses domain hosting company GoDaddy as an example, where adding a domain to your basket automatically puts privacy protection into the basket with it.[38]

These "hidden cost" tactics are designed to capitalise on the sunk cost effect – the idea that if a user has put enough effort into the process already, they'll more likely accept a surprise charge than leave the journey. Equally, users that are lacking motivation or are tired out from having gone through several pages to get to the review page may not even notice the changes and simply finish the process.

Symptom

This tactic is often combined with the forced urgency that we mentioned earlier. For example, knowing that others are queueing behind to get tickets and that there are only a few left plays on the users' potential anxiety to increase profit. All of this makes ambiguous costs such as "management" and "handling" fees – which only appear on the review page – difficult to refuse.

Solution

The solution to this dark pattern is very simple. Make sure that any charges the user has to pay are obvious upfront, and don't put anything in their baskets that they didn't add themselves.

Giving users the opportunity to revert full actions

A lot of physical shops offer easy returns without negative repercussions if the user changes their mind, and where possible, the same should be true of online commitments.

This is an example of where applying friction is actually beneficial to the user. Although it involves adding another step, the opportunity to review and revert decisions could, and perhaps should, be applied to every possible consequential action – from the short term (checking submitted information) to the long term (returning purchases).

The bank Monzo had some research conducted on their behalf that found that users that experience Bipolar disorders

> *tended to overspend on needless items — often late at night — while in a manic phase, only when morning came to be faced with this reality. With no way to remedy their mistake, people can then find themselves slipping into a depressive state. That is a dangerous, daunting place to be.*[39]

To combat this, Monzo added a feature called "review late-night spending" which notifies the user the next day about purchases made late at night and asks them whether they'd like to review it. This provides users with a degree of control and, in the instances where a return or refund is possible, makes the process easy enough that it doesn't require a lot of motivation to complete. Even asking if a user is happy with their purchase is a good way of reaching out to check that they're comfortable with their actions. It could also lead to a positive review if they are.

Dark pattern: Confirm shaming

Confirm shaming is the act of framing a decision that the user has to make in such a way that saying no to it could "shame" them, or make them feel bad about their choice. It's an approach that has become applied to actions of every kind online, from discount offers to appeals for newsletter signups. The switch from offering a traditional "Yes or No" choice is due to the fact that framing questions in this way can result in more people choosing the option that the business wants – increasing anything from signups to retention rates. However, it can have a negative impact on users and make you look bad while doing it. Here's an example: Figure 7-10 shows how Amazon frame the option of not buying Amazon prime.

Join Amazon Prime

Get Unlimited One-Day Delivery on Millions of
Eligible Items

ately for   No thanks, I don't want Unlimited One-Day Delivery

Figure 7-10. A screenshot of the "decline" message on an Amazon prime advert, stating "No thanks, I don't want Unlimited One-Day Delivery"

Not only is the option of declining the prime offer relegated to a much smaller link than the signup button, but it turns something that shouldn't be difficult to dismiss into something users have to focus on, and take action. With the user now engaged and in the right mindset to make a decision, the wording associates negativity with that action, encouraging them to accept the other choice for fear of missing out or making a bad decision. You're not just saying no, you're saying no to unlimited one-day delivery!

There is an entire site called "Confirm Shaming" that is dedicated to calling out this type of dark pattern and sharing them publicly as a way of dissuading others from doing it.[40] Their examples range from subtle put-downs to outright name calling. Here are a few examples I found:

Choosing not to sign up for a beginner's guide to gardening:

"No thanks, I know everything about gardening"

Choosing not to enter your email address to get 15% off an order:

"No thanks, I'm not into savings"

Choosing not to disable advert blocking on a website

"I am a bad person"[41]

Symptom

Statements like this can deeply affect users with social anxiety (also known as social phobia).[42] As the NHS explains, people with social anxiety often fear criticism and have low self-esteem, and every one of these examples play on that. With anxiety being such a widespread symptom, this can also affect those with generalised anxiety disorder, panic disorder, PTSD, and social anxiety.[43] As Money and Mental Health explain, these users "often find it more difficult to shop around or leave a service that isn't right for them for fear that something bad might come of the decision."[44]

These tactics are also often used to supplement complicated journeys. For example, here are the options in a popup confirming if a user wants to cancel their gaming subscription (shown in Figure 7-11).[45]

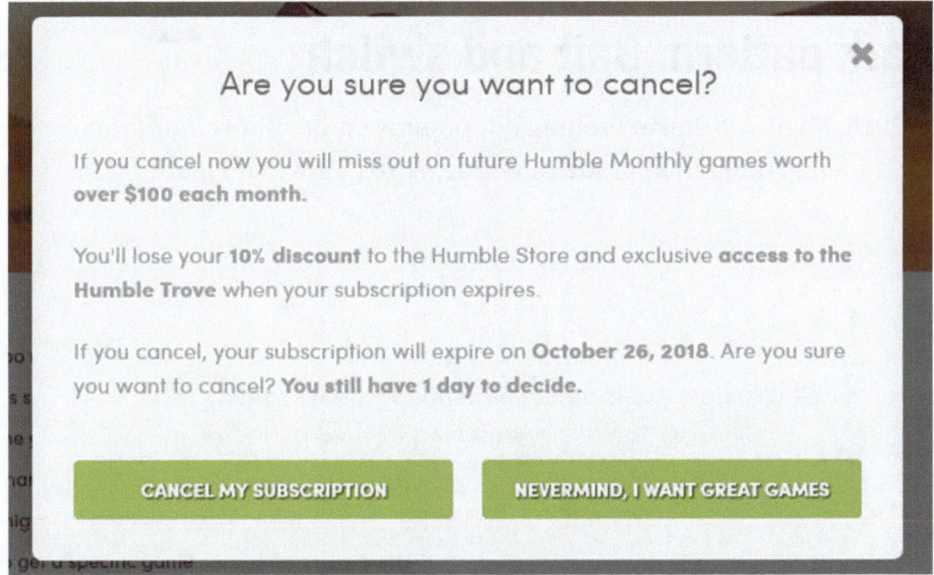

Figure 7-11. *A screenshot of a popup asking the user to confirm that they want to cancel their gaming subscription. The "no" option is worded "Nevermind, I want great games"*

Solution

In both cases, you can clearly see how the option that the site doesn't want to happen is intentionally worded to either shame or scare the user, whether they mean to or not. Here, those who are susceptible to feeling embarrassed, humiliated, or judged negatively have their access needs used against them, simply because they don't want to sign up to a newsletter or give out their details. Even if they choose not to perform the action, they've still had to face the decision. We spoke in the last chapter about choosing language that is plain, particularly for actions, but you must also ensure that those words don't shame or manipulate users. The Confirm Shaming website describes doing this as "hot garbage," and I'm OK with printing that in a book and standing by it.

Dark pattern: Bait and switch

In 2016, Microsoft started rolling out popups on people's computers, encouraging them to upgrade to Windows 10 (shown in Figure 7-12).

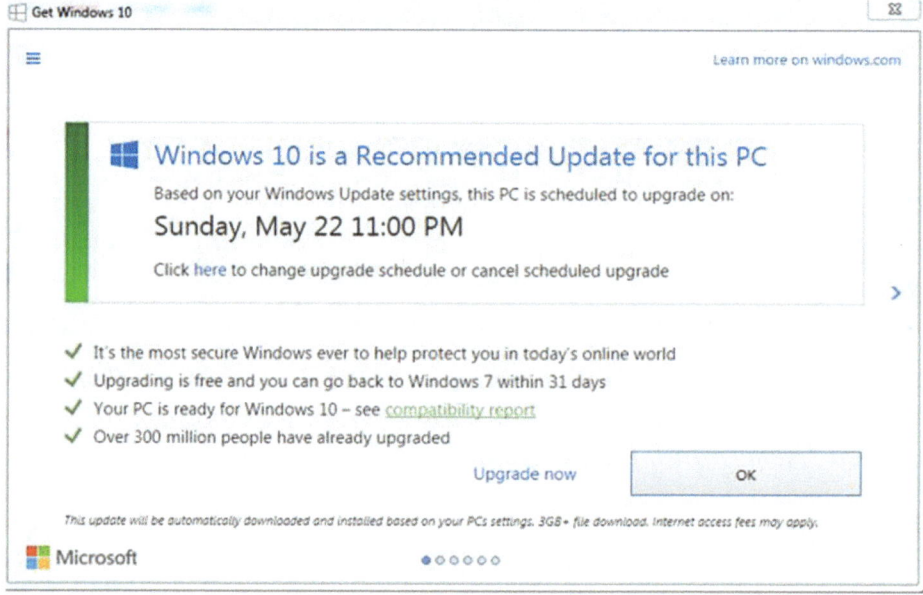

Figure 7-12. *A screenshot of a popup that appeared on Windows computers – recommending that they upgrade to Windows 10*

This is a fairly routine call to action, but over time the frequency of the popups increased. It started appearing as a "recommended upgrade" for users, and unlike the Confirm Shaming we just spoke about, this popup didn't have two "Yes or No" style buttons. Instead, it had one button that recommended you start the install, and only a small default "X" icon in the corner of the popup to close it.

Poor form perhaps, but still nothing heinous. Despite the increased frequency and change in wording, many users still weren't upgrading and instead dismissing the popup when it appeared.

You see where this is going, right?

Then, in a particular popup, they changed the behavior of the universally known "X" icon which, on every one of the previous popups, closed the window. Instead, clicking the icon actually scheduled the upgrade process. By doing this, they deliberately cashed in on the action that these users had been performing so consistently for nearly a year: hitting the "X" icon to close it. This same tactic is actually used by viruses, where closing actions can trigger unexpected behavior that does the opposite of what you would expect.[46]

The backlash was massive, and because of this, an immediate patch was created to revert the change.[47] Chris Capossela, Microsoft's Chief Marketing Officer, said

> *within a couple of hours of that hitting the world, we knew that we had gone too far.*[48]

It's highly unsurprising that there was uproar about this behavior, particularly from a company as big as Microsoft.

Symptom

The "X" icon represents one of the few universally identifiable online actions, and because of this, people trust that it will behave consistently between sites, browsers, and even operating systems. If this doesn't happen, it can trigger a range of symptoms. The most immediately obvious is stress. Stress can commonly occur when we experience something new or unexpected, or when we feel as though we have little control over the situation.[49] Although not considered a condition in itself, stress can exacerbate mental health problems like anxiety or depression, and equally *having* a mental health problem can induce stress itself.

Similar tricks have been pulled without changing the functionality of a site, where the action itself stays the same, but the wording is changed. A classic example involves inverting the option to opt out – using wording like "tick if you do *not* want to receive promotional material." People are used to leaving this box unchecked because it typically results in an endless stream of marketing emails, but here, failing to do so leads to the same outcome.

Following on from the idea of complex online experiences in the last chapter, parts of a site that compete for your attention and then behave in strange and unpredictable ways when users interact with them can leave users feeling stressed, tricked, and powerless. Users may have already had to expend a lot of effort to get through a journey and already be unsure or frustrated. Behavior like this can especially create a sense of panic in anxious or paranoid users who find online processes stressful, leaving them worried that they may not have understood something properly, or feeling like the company is trying to trick them (in the case of Microsoft, they'd have been right).

Solution

The solution here is another slam dunk – actions need to be consistent for everyone, especially when they use components that users will be used to interacting with already. The result of tricking more people into upgrading their operating system wasn't worth the backlash that Microsoft received, and the same applies to any site that attempts to leverage the learned behavior of a user to make them perform an action they don't want to out of pure instinct.

WCAG have a rule simply named "consistent identification" for this reason. It states that

People who learn functionality on one page on a site can find the desired functions on other pages if they are present.[50]

This refers to actions within your site specifically; ensuring that if you lay out a way of doing something on your site, that behavior is consistent across all pages.

I'd challenge you to look at this principle through a wider lens though. As a site on the Web, I think you have a responsibility to ensure that if you choose to use a common icon, it represents the action that a user would expect. Failure to do so garners you a bad reputation and an experience that doesn't feel intuitive to users.

Having covered a range of dark patterns, the symptoms they evoke, and some solutions on how to identify and handle them, let's now turn our attention to another issue that commonly effects users with impaired mental health. It might not strictly be a dark pattern itself, but it can still form part of a dark pattern and evoke similar symptoms.

Communication anxiety

Let's briefly return to the journey a user might take when deleting an account on a site. After going through pages and pages of menus, dropdowns, and options to close an Amazon account, the final step used to require a phone call with someone at Amazon to finalise its closure. You couldn't complete the action yourself, you actually had to speak to someone.[51]

This is a massive barrier for many users with impaired mental health. As Merlyn Holkar and Katie Evans explain:

Many people with mental health problems, particularly anxiety disorders, are phobic about using the telephone. This can be a significant barrier to market engagement, particularly where customers must make a telephone call to cancel an existing contract.[52]

Access needs such as social anxiety and panic disorders mean that many users experience difficulties communicating with their providers, managing their accounts, and getting support when problems develop. It can also affect those with cognitive impairments, such as autism, as it "involves impairments of social communication and interaction abilities."[53]

For some, being forced to use an unsuitable communication channel can trigger panic attacks or suicidality:

I have massive anxiety about talking to strangers on the phone. I frequently end up feeling exhausted or at worst suicidal afterwards.[54]

Why do this?

Many users feel (quite rightly) that the phone process may not be easy – the person on the other end may not immediately comply with what you're asking them to do, and instead try to persuade you not to leave, to try a different type of account, to reduce the frequency or amount of the payments you're making; anything to stop you from actually leaving. They often have the same intention as those who create complicated journeys and dead ends online – it's another barrier designed to wear the user out and make them less keen to leave or cancel.

Reach users where they feel comfortable

Different people prefer different communication channels. Just as some people cannot answer the phone, some people will not open post, and others do not trust web chat. The reasons can be quite personal, and so providing a variety of options gives you the best chance of making it comfortable for users. Merlyn Holkar of Money and Mental Health explained the benefits of this to me:

> *The option of having different ways of getting in touch can really help. Some people get really flustered on the phone, but if they can use a webchat to talk and send other information, they can have a break, they can read back over what's been said – you don't have to rely on your memory and you can take it at your own pace.*[55]

Most people with mental health problems understand that they "should" be more engaged consumers though. Research on essential services (e.g., water, energy, Internet, etc.) found that more than two thirds (69%) recognised that switching suppliers is the key to getting the best deal on essential services. However, the barriers faced when communicating with new prospective suppliers often deter such action.[56]

Therefore, it's important to offer alternative ways of communication for those unable or unwilling to interact via a specific medium. Amazon now offers phone, chat, and email as ways of finalising an account closure, and by doing the same, you follow The United Kingdom Home Office's recommendation – "give users the support they need to complete a service" and do not "make support or help hard to access."[57] As we mentioned in the chapter on Deafness and hard of hearing (Chapter 5), alternatives to phone such as email, live chat, or social integrations like Facebook Messenger allow you to communicate effectively with all of your customers. Giving users the freedom to choose provides some comfort - users can avoid communicating on channels they find difficult.

Familiar integrations

People experiencing anxiety can respond negatively when they're on unfamiliar sites, and so sometimes it's worth going to your prospective customers instead of relying on them coming to you. One solution to this is to integrate with the sites that users spend more time on and are more comfortable with – for example, social networks.

We tackled this particular problem at Octopus Energy by creating a chatbot that would allow someone to receive an energy quote based on their property and energy usage straight from Facebook (shown in Figure 7-13). It asks all of the same questions as our website's journey, but can be completed in a more familiar and informal setting. This familiarity makes users feel in control and means that they can dictate if and when they'd like to engage with us.

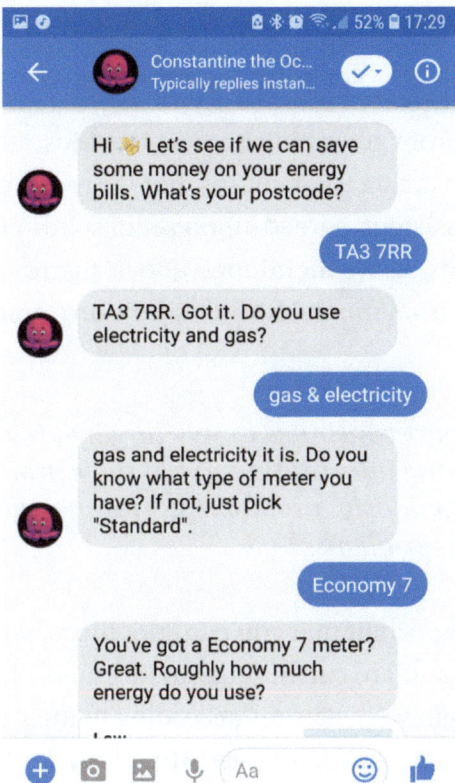

Figure 7-13. *A screenshot of the Octopus Energy Facebook chatbot "Constantine the Octopus"*

This addition means that users can investigate your company and its values on your Facebook page, and ask any follow-up questions they may have through Facebook Messenger. Having all of these options means that a customer can wait until the last possible moment before moving onto a less familiar site.

Conclusion

Mental health is still an area where the accessibility community is finding its feet. Comments from governing bodies, charities, and researchers are definitely helping to create a consensus, but we're not quite at the point where there is a consistent, agreed-upon set of solutions for fixing barriers to these access needs. As we mentioned above, figures differ regarding how many people suffer from mental health conditions, and one big reason is that:

> *Access to support continues to rely largely on vulnerable consumers disclosing information about their problems – a factor which is particularly problematic for people experiencing mental health problems.*[58]

It is therefore important that you can spot these barriers, as there's currently no test or audit to run in order to flag them. This is why I've continued to highlight web features according to the symptoms they amplify and not conditions themselves. Hopefully, in this chapter you have come across patterns that you can understand and clearly see are frustrating and damaging, especially for those with mental health impairments.

One problem that remains is that dark patterns are still profitable. The Dark Patterns website outlines this perfectly with the example of the airline Jetstar. They use misdirection when it comes to selecting seats by preselecting one that incurs a $5 charge. Now, you can choose another seat for the same price but, most importantly, you can skip this altogether and still receive a random seat for free. The way it's designed makes it look like an "opt-in" but it's done by default – if you don't change the random seat and instead hit "continue," you'll be charged for a seat you don't need to pay for. They estimate that Jetstar operate 208,000 flights a year (4,000 flights per week), so if even one person per flight ends up paying for a random seat, it'll equate to over $1million extra revenue per year.[59] As the Norwegian consumer council has said:

> *"When digital services employ dark patterns to nudge users... the financial incentive has taken precedence over respecting users' right to choose. The practice of misleading consumers into making certain choices, which may put their privacy at risk, is unethical and exploitative."*[60]

This is a choice that each business, and site, has to make. Everyone wants their site to be successful, but if you achieve this through deception, and do so in spite of (and often at the expense of) a user's mental health, then you risk damaging your reputation and long-term success.

Luckily, more and more is being done to highlight these patterns and the harmful effect that they have on people with mental health conditions. At the time of writing, there is an ongoing project between the Public Policy Lab and experience agency Snook to create a pattern library that improves online experiences for those with mental health issues.[61] Some of the points from their first phase have been mentioned in this chapter, but it's worth keeping an eye on the developments they make in the future. I'll add the library as a resource you can refer to in the "Tools and QA" chapter (Chapter 11).

For now, dark patterns are only becoming more obvious, and people will become more adept at spotting them. This means that their ability to extract profit from users will start to dwindle, making them less attractive. It's worth at least checking for the ones we covered in this chapter to ensure that you're not a culprit – nobody would want to be part of the "hall of shame" because of how badly they have misled customers.[62]

Notes

1. Harry Brignull, *Dark Patterns*, (2019),[accessed 05/07/2019].

2. Merlyn Holkar and Katie Evans, *Levelling the
    Playing Field*, Money and Mental Health, (12/2017),
    <www.moneyandmentalhealth.org/wp-content/
    uploads/2017/12/Levelling-the-playing-field-
    Regulators-report.pdf> [accessed 05/07/2019].

3. Money and Mental Health, *Fundamental facts about
    mental health,* (2016), <www.mentalhealth.org.uk/
    sites/default/files/fundamental-facts-about-
    mental-health-2016.pdf> [accessed 05/07/2019].

4. Merlyn Holkar, Senior Research Officer at Money
    and Mental Health, Interview with author,
    (14/05/2019).

5. Merlyn Holkar and Katie Evans, *Levelling the
    Playing Field*, Money and Mental Health, (12/2017),
    <www.moneyandmentalhealth.org/wp-content/
    uploads/2017/12/Levelling-the-playing-field-
    Regulators-report.pdf> [accessed 05/07/2019].

6. Forbruker Radet, *Deceived by Design*, (27/06/2018),
    <https://fil.forbrukerradet.no/wp-content/
    uploads/2018/06/2018-06-27-deceived-by-
    design-final.pdf> [accessed 05/07/2019].

7. Chris Fox, *Google hit with £44m GDPR fine over
    ads*, BBC, (21/01/2019), <www.bbc.co.uk/news/
    technology-46944696> [accessed 05/07/2019].

8. Harry Brignull, *Dark Patterns*, (2019),[accessed 05/07/2019].

9. Forbruker Radet, *Deceived by Design*, (2018),
    <https://fil.forbrukerradet.no/wp-content/
    uploads/2018/06/2018-06-27-deceived-by-
    design-final.pdf> [accessed 05/07/2019].

10. W3C, *Diverse Abilities and Barriers*, (15/05/2017),
    <www.w3.org/WAI/people-use-web/abilities-
    barriers/#visual> [accessed 05/07/2019].

11. W3C, *Cognitive Accessibility Roadmap and Gap
    Analysis*, (11/12/2018), <www.w3.org/TR/coga-gap-
    analysis/> [accessed 05/07/2019].

12. Harry Brignull, *Dark Patterns*, (2019),[accessed 05/07/2019].

13. Merlyn Holkar and Katie Evans, *Levelling the
    Playing Field, Money and Mental Health*, (12/2017),
    <www.moneyandmentalhealth.org/wp-content/
    uploads/2017/12/Levelling-the-playing-field-
    Regulators-report.pdf> [accessed 05/07/2019].

14. Harry Brignull, *Roach Motel*, (2019), <www.
    darkpatterns.org/types-of-dark-pattern/
    roach-motel> [accessed 05/07/2019].

15. Chris Fox, *Google hit with £44m GDPR fine
    over ads*, BBC, (2019), <www.bbc.co.uk/news/
    technology-46944696> [accessed 05/07/2019].

16. Andrei Lanovskii, Twitter, <https://twitter.com/
    gn0me/status/1129133677156458497> [accessed
    05/07/2019].

17.   Merlyn Holkar and Katie Evans, *Levelling the Playing Field, Money and Mental Health*, (12/2017), <www.moneyandmentalhealth.org/wp-content/uploads/2017/12/Levelling-the-playing-field-Regulators-report.pdf> [accessed 05/07/2019].

18.   Merlyn Holkar, Senior Research Officer at Money and Mental Health, Interview with author, (14/05/2019).

19.   Merlyn Holkar and Katie Evans, *Levelling the Playing Field, Money and Mental Health*, (12/2017) <www.moneyandmentalhealth.org/wp-content/uploads/2017/12/Levelling-the-playing-field-Regulators-report.pdf> [accessed 05/07/2019].

20.   W3C, *Diverse Abilities and Barriers*, (15/05/2017), <www.w3.org/WAI/people-use-web/abilities-barriers/#visual> [accessed 05/07/2019].

21.   Nielsen Norman Group, Flat vs. Deep Website Hierarchies, 2019, <www.nngroup.com/articles/flat-vs-deep-hierarchy/> [accessed 05/07/2019]

22.   Merlyn Holkar, Senior Research Officer at Money and Mental Health, Interview with author, (14/05/2019).

23.   Fineberg, N., Haddad, P., Carpenter, L., Gannon, B., Sharpe, R., Young, A., Joyce, E., Rowe, J., Wellsted, D., Nutt, D. and Sahakian, B. (2013). *The size, burden and cost of disorders of the brain in the UK. Journal of Psychopharmacology*, 27 (9), pp.761-770.

24. Merlyn Holkar, Senior Research Officer at Money and Mental Health, Interview with author, (14/05/2019).

25. BP Magazine, *How to Accomplish Tasks When Depressed: Motivation's Mystery*, (07/08/2017), <www.bphope.com/getting-things-done-when-youre-depressed-the-mystery-of-motivation/> [accessed 05/07/2019].

26. Karwai Pun, *Dos and don'ts on designing for accessibility*, Gov.UK, (02/09/2016), <https://accessibility.blog.gov.uk/2016/09/02/dos-and-donts-on-designing-for-accessibility/> [accessed 05/07/2019].

27. Íse Murphy, *Setting expectations: How to keep your queuing crowd happy*, (22/05/2019), <http://isemurphy.com/2019/05/22/setting-expectations-how-to-keep-your-queuing-crowd-happy/> [accessed 05/07/2019].

28. Sarah Drummond, *Positive Patterns for Designing Mental Health Services*, Medium, (05/10/2017), <https://medium.com/@sarahdrummond/positive-patterns-for-designing-mental-health-services-e2d323cdbdf8> [Accessed 05/07/2019].

29. Roman Cheplyaka, *How booking.com uses stress to rush your decisions*, TNW (21/09/2017), <https://thenextweb.com/contributors/2017/09/21/booking-com-uses-stress-rush-decisions/> [accessed 05/07/2019].

30. Merlyn Holkar and Katie Evans, *Levelling the Playing Field, Money and Mental Health*, (12/2017), <www.moneyandmentalhealth.org/wp-content/uploads/2017/12/Levelling-the-playing-field-Regulators-report.pdf> [accessed 05/07/2019].

31. Karwai Pun, *Dos and don'ts on designing for accessibility*, Gov.UK, (02/09/2016), <https://accessibility.blog.gov.uk/2016/09/02/dos-and-donts-on-designing-for-accessibility/> [accessed 05/07/2019].

32. Mind, *Paranoia*, (2013), <www.mind.org.uk/information-support/types-of-mental-health-problems/paranoia/about-paranoia/?gclid=EAIaIQobChMI4vH6_6T64gIVyrvtCh3KKwiUEAAYASAAEgKyH_D_BwE#.XQynEdNKjOQ> [accessed 05/07/2019].

33. NHS, *Borderline Personality Disorder*, (17/07/19), <www.nhs.uk/conditions/borderline-personality-disorder/> [accessed 18/07/2019] + Erin Johnson, *Managing Money with Borderline Personality Disorder,* Very Well Mind, (12/07/2019), <www.verywellmind.com/managing-money-issues-425362> [accessed 05/07/2019].

34. Roman Cheplyaka, *How* booking.com *uses stress to rush your decisions*, TNW (21/09/2017), <https://thenextweb.com/contributors/2017/09/21/booking-com-uses-stress-rush-decisions/> [accessed 05/07/2019].

35. Hacker News, *Blog Post by bogomipz,* (20/09/2017), <https://news.ycombinator.com/item?id=15297915> [accessed 05/07/2019].

36. Merlyn Holkar, Senior Research Officer at Money and Mental Health, Interview with author, (14/05/2019).

37. W3C, *Understanding Success Criterion 3.3.5: Help,* <www.w3.org/WAI/WCAG21/Understanding/help.html> [accessed 05/07/2019].

38. Harry Brignull, *Sneak-into-Basket,* (2019), <www.darkpatterns.org/types-of-dark-pattern/sneak-into-basket> [accessed 05/07/2019].

39. Zander Brade, *Designing a product with mental health issues in mind,* Monzo Blog, (27/01/2017), <https://monzo.com/blog/2017/01/27/designing-product-mental-health-mind/> [accessed 05/07/2019].

40. Confirm Shaming, Tumblr, <https://confirmshaming.tumblr.com/> [accessed 05/07/2019].

41. Confirm Shaming, Tumblr, <https://confirmshaming.tumblr.com/> [accessed 05/07/2019].

42. NHS, *Social Anxiety,* (09/03/2017), <www.nhs.uk/conditions/social-anxiety/> [accessed 05/07/2019].

43. NHS, *Generalised anxiety disorder in adults,* (19/12/2018), <www.nhs.uk/conditions/generalised-anxiety-disorder/> [accessed 05/07/2019].

44. Merlyn Holkar and Katie Evans, *Levelling the Playing Field, Money and Mental Health,* (12/2017),

<www.moneyandmentalhealth.org/wp-content/
uploads/2017/12/Levelling-the-playing-field-
Regulators-report.pdf> [accessed 05/07/2019].

45. Confirm Shaming, Tumblr, <https://
confirmshaming.tumblr.com/
image/179398684581> [accessed 05/07/2019].

46. Amherst College, *Safely Close a Malware Popup window*, <www.amherst.edu/offices/it/
knowledge_base/security/safely-close-a-
malware-pop-up-window/node/517308> [accessed
05/07/2019].

47. Harry Brignull, *Bait and Switch*, (2019), <www.
darkpatterns.org/types-of-dark-pattern/bait-
and-switch> [accessed 05/07/2019].

48. Bogdan Popa, *Microsoft Admits It 'Went Too
Far' with Aggressive Windows Updates*, (2016),
<https://news.softpedia.com/news/microsoft-
admits-it-went-too-far-with-aggressive-
windows-10-updates-511245.shtml> [accessed
05/07/2019].

49. Mental Health Foundation, *Stress,* (23/12/2016),
<www.mentalhealth.org.uk/a-to-z/s/stress>
[accessed 05/07/2019].

50. W3C, Consistent Identification, (2016), <www.
w3.org/TR/UNDERSTANDING-WCAG20/consistent-
behavior-consistent-functionality.html>
[accessed 05/07/2019].

51. Harry Brignull, *Dark Patterns*, (2019), <www.
darkpatterns.org/> [accessed 05/07/2019].

52. Merlyn Holkar and Katie Evans, *Levelling the Playing Field*, Money and Mental Health, (12/2017), <www.moneyandmentalhealth.org/wp-content/ uploads/2017/12/Levelling-the-playing-field-Regulators-report.pdf> [accessed 05/07/2019].

53. W3C, *Diverse Abilities and Barriers*, (15/05/2017), <www.w3.org/WAI/people-use-web/abilities-barriers/#visual> [accessed 05/07/2019].

54. Merlyn Holkar and Katie Evans, *Levelling the Playing Field*, Money and Mental Health, (12/2017), <www.moneyandmentalhealth.org/wp-content/ uploads/2017/12/Levelling-the-playing-field-Regulators-report.pdf> [accessed 05/07/2019].

55. Merlyn Holkar, Senior Research Officer at Money and Mental Health, Interview with author, (14/05/2019).

56. Merlyn Holkar and Katie Evans, *Levelling the Playing Field*, Money and Mental Health, (12/2017), <www.moneyandmentalhealth.org/wp-content/ uploads/2017/12/Levelling-the-playing-field-Regulators-report.pdf> [accessed 05/07/2019].

57. Karwai Pun, *Dos and don'ts on designing for accessibility*, Gov.UK, (02/09/2016), <https:// accessibility.blog.gov.uk/2016/09/02/dos-and-donts-on-designing-for-accessibility/> [accessed 05/07/2019].

58. Merlyn Holkar and Katie Evans, *Levelling the Playing Field*, Money and Mental Health, (12/2017), <https://www.moneyandmentalhealth.org/

wp-content/uploads/2017/12/Levelling-
the-playing-field-Regulators-report.pdf>
[accessed 05/07/2019].

59.   Harry Brignull, *Misdirection*, (2019), <www.
darkpatterns.org/types-of-dark-pattern/
misdirection> [accessed 05/07/2019].

60.   Forbruker Radet, *Deceived by Design*, (27/06/2018),
<https://fil.forbrukerradet.no/wp-content/
uploads/2018/06/2018-06-27-deceived-by-
design-final.pdf> [accessed 05/07/2019].

61.   Public Policy Lab & Snook, *Design
patterns for Mental Health*, (2019), <www.
designpatternsformentalhealth.org/pattern-
library> [accessed 05/07/2019].

62.   Harry Brignull, *Hall of Shame*, (2019), <www.
darkpatterns.org/hall-of-shame> [accessed
05/07/2019].

CHAPTER 8

Imagery

According to statistics from Amazon's data company Alexa Data Services, over 90% of the 10 million most popular websites on the Internet contain some form of imagery.[1] Images have become a near–unavoidable component of website design and development – used for everything from sharing experiences on social media to showcasing products. Mirroring their diverse range of uses, visual media can create barriers for an equally diverse range of users.

Starting with this chapter, we'll be shifting our focus from specific access needs to more general areas of online experience where a broad spectrum of users commonly encounter difficulties. Online imagery comes in a few different forms, but we'll start with images themselves – discussing content, colour, and several other things to keep in mind when using them.

These ideas are relevant when talking about video too. We've covered accessible captions for videos already, so this time we'll focus on how to implement video in a way that accommodates user needs and preferences, and how to safely use moving imagery as a form of backdrop.

We'll then look at the different ways in which icons have been added to sites over the past few years, and how to make each of these approaches accessible. This is largely for the sake of those of you who have been tasked with maintaining existing sites that rely on older icon implementations. This discussion will culminate in a brief overview of the advent of the Scalable Vector Graphics (SVG) image type, and how to ensure that this new and popular approach is as accessible (or even more so) than other formats.

© Ashley Firth 2019
A. Firth, *Practical Web Inclusion and Accessibility*,
https://doi.org/10.1007/978-1-4842-5452-3_8

Images

Let's start with standard images, which are by far the most common type of visual media seen online. In Chapter 2 ("Blindness"), we covered how images that are inserted into a web page's code (through HTML) require an alt tag in order to be accessible to screen reader users. This looked like so:

```
<img src="assets/cat.jpg" alt="A cat playing with a large blue
ball of yarn" />
```

It is always worth checking that the alt text has been properly added to each image on your site. This text should describe the image and any content in it. If you are maintaining a site's content, this is such a quick win because it doesn't require the image to be remade. It's also just as important to ensure that the alt attribute is actually filled – because even if it is left empty, it will still pass most accessibility audits:

```
<!-- The alt attribute exists, so it will still pass most
audits -->
<img src="assets/cat.jpg" alt="" />
```

This is because these auditing tools check for the presence of an alt tag, rather than whether it has a value. There are legitimate cases where a blank alt tag is a valid approach, such as when an image is being used purely for decorative purposes; however in the preceding example where the image provides relevant information, it should have a description.

For those using content management systems (CMS), most prompt you to add alt text when you add an image. Figure 8-1 is an example from WordPress, by far the most used CMS in the world.[2]

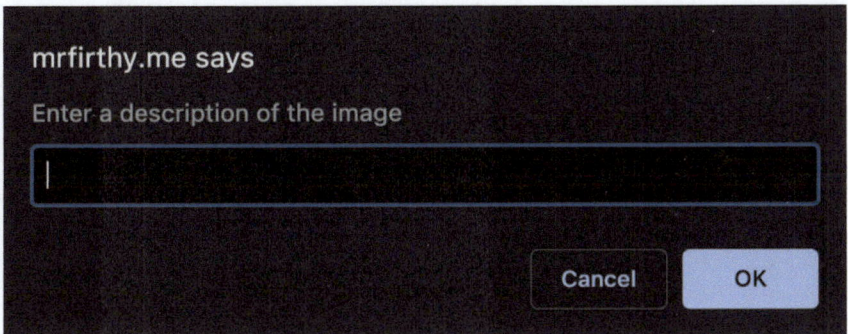

Figure 8-1. *A dialog window in WordPress prompts the user for a description of the image which will become the* alt *text content*

Background images

Adding an image in the way we've just mentioned will ensure that it displays directly on the page in the same way as any other content. However, there are many cases where images are displayed as the background of certain parts of sites. This could be as part of a banner (as shown in Figure 8-2) or a repeatable pattern. You can create background images using CSS instead of HTML:

```
<!-- HTML -->
<div class="banner">
    <h1>Welcome to my site</h1>
</div>

/* CSS */
.banner {
    background-image: url('assets/space.jpg');
}
```

Figure 8-2. *A site banner with a background image applied to it*

This is an entirely reasonable approach for displaying an image as a background, but if the image holds important information that a user would miss if they couldn't see it, then this impacts that image's accessibility. This is because the image itself isn't present in the page's code; you can't apply an alt tag to it and therefore can't provide a way of describing the image's contents to any visually impaired screen reader users.

It is therefore important to know when to use an image as a background and when instead to place it in a page and provide an alt tag. WCAG's 2.0 spec offers a neat distinction:

> *When an image is used for decoration, spacing or other purpose that is not part of the meaningful content in the page then the image has no meaning and should be ignored by assistive technologies.*[3]

The test is quick and easy – if your background image includes any important information, then move it into your page's HTML instead. If an image is purely decorative, then feel free to use it in CSS.

Text in images

Generally, you shouldn't have images with any text in them. However, this approach used to be quite popular, as it allowed designers to manipulate text in a way that wasn't possible otherwise. For example, they could use fonts that weren't supported by all browsers or to position text in ways that would be hard to achieve with CSS. This practice is still common when it comes to email, where the ability to use CSS is limited and less consistent.

The main problem with displaying text inside imagery is that it effectively hides that content for blind and visually impaired users. As we've mentioned above, screen reader software can recognise an `<img>` tag and read the contents of its `alt` text, but a background image is completely ignored – not purposefully, but simply because there's nothing in the code that shows the screen reader that anything is there.

For instance, if you were to display a banner image at the top of a page (as shown in Figure 8-3), and that page's title was part of the image, not the text on the page, that title wouldn't be read out by a screen reader.

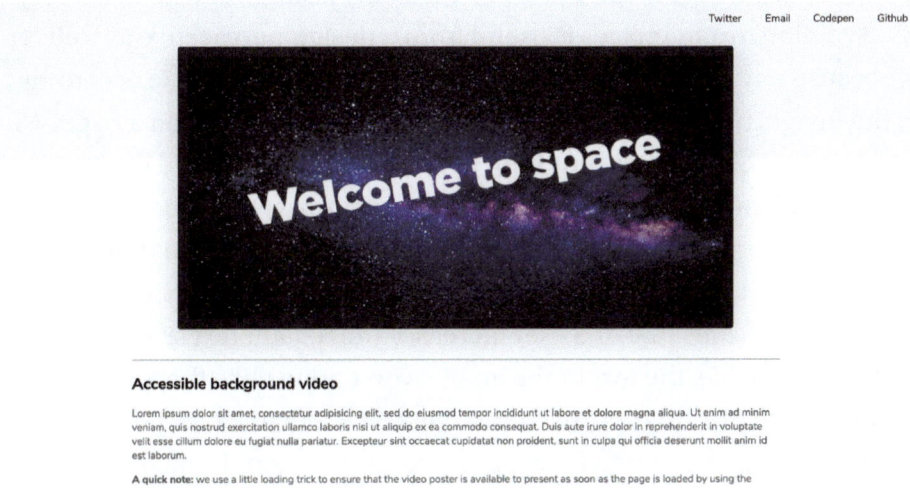

Figure 8-3. *A site banner with text as part of the actual image, rather than positioned over it*

As a result, the context behind an entire page could be lost. In this example, you could still use the image as a background without the text in it, and instead place the text in your site's HTML and then use CSS to position the text over or next to the image – this is immediately far more accessible. It is important to note though that when overlaying text over images, you must still check that there is a reasonable colour contrast between the background image and the foreground text, as we covered in Chapter 3 ("Low Vision and Colour Blindness").

You should try and keep decorative and meaningful content separate as much as possible – even if it's difficult to recreate the design you're hoping for consistently across browsers.

Text in responsive images

"But wait Ashley, couldn't I place an image with text inside it in the HTML and use the `alt` attribute to provide that same text for screen readers? Problem solved, right?!"

Smart thinking reader, but it's not the only issue with text in imagery.

Avoiding text in images is useful from a design perspective as well. This is because any text that is displayed inside an image will scale according to the image, but not in the same way as the rest of the text on a page. With so many responsive sites now built to adapt to different sized devices, you could be left in a position where the text in an image could be far bigger than any other text on the page (or worse, much smaller and therefore unreadable). Trapping content like this results in inconsistent content sizes. It also means that, if a user increases the default text size of their browser or device, the text in the image won't adjust like the text around it would. Therefore, this approach can create a real barrier for people with an impaired field of vision (like glaucoma), low vision (impaired visual acuity), or who prefer to zoom in on content. Figure 8-4 shows an example of a page containing a banner with text in it – both on a desktop computer screen and a mobile.

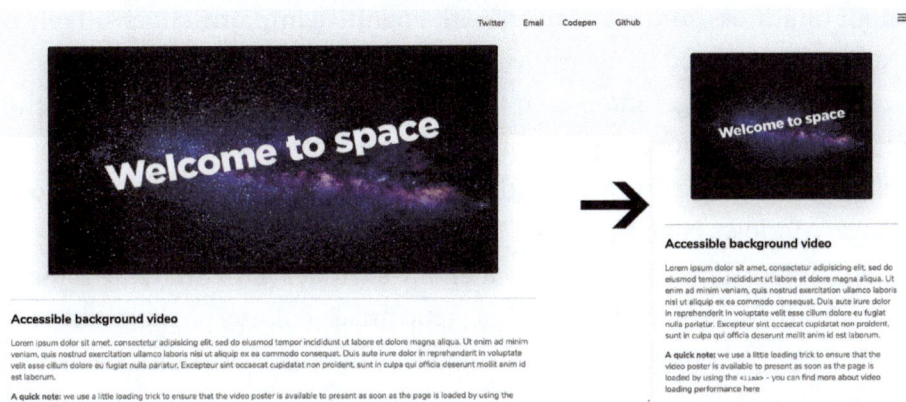

Figure 8-4. *A visual of how a banner with text inside it shrinks on a smaller device, making the text harder to read than the rest of the page's content*

As you can see, thanks to its sizing and style, the text looks like a page header when on a desktop. However, as the screen starts to shrink to fit a smaller device, the title ends up significantly smaller – becoming the same size or smaller than the text it's supposed to be introducing.

In addition, images will likely be pixelated on newer mobile devices due to the high pixel density (DPI) of their screens. This is also a big problem for visually impaired users who use screen magnifiers – as they zoom in, images could become unreadable due to low quality. With so many different sized screens on the market, you could either spend a lot of time ensuring that your banner text is readable in different scenarios or you could simply place the image on the page with code instead.

Colour in images

Finally, having text inside of images can also lead to inferior colour contrast – something that won't show up on the tests that you can perform on your website because, once again, these tests can't recognise text inside images. This, as we've covered, creates issues for those with low vision, colour blindness, and some users with cognitive impairments who rely on text being presented as clearly as possible (e.g., users with autism).

Moreover, images often aren't particularly responsive to users switching their browser or operating system colour scheme (which we covered in Chapter 3 – "Low Vision and Colour Blindness"), such as "dark mode" on Mac or Windows High Contrast Mode. The effects can be quite varied – sometimes images are ignored by a theme switcher (and therefore remain unchanged); alternatively, sometimes the image colours are inverted or it can disappear entirely (which is often true in Windows High Contrast Mode).

All of these factors create a situation where the imagery that has been added to a site to elevate its content can end up restricting or subverting it. Run the checks we've covered previously and, when in doubt, place the image in your page's HTML code.

Videos

Many websites now have moving images behind text. This in itself is an obstacle for someone trying to read the text. And it can mean that the text has no contrasting background to make it easier to read.[4]

Moving imagery, such as videos or animations, can pose just as much, if not more, trouble to users than static images. Not only can they have text in them, but because they can also contain sound that requires captioning, visual elements that need to be described in text, constant changes in lighting and colour, and movement that can affect users in a range of ways. Background videos are also becoming popular, especially at the time of writing – with some sites attributing conversion rate increases of up to 138% to their background videos.[5] Because of this, you may be asked to add one, or maintain a site that has one, so let's go through some of the pitfalls of foreground, and background videos, while learning to create accessible versions of both.

I've created an accessible background video for you in this chapter's practical example, which you can find in the "Chapter 8" folder of the Github repository or view live at `https://inclusive.guide/examples/imagery`

This practical example contains all of the following features in case you'd like to use it in a site (or just avoid the code examples). However, I'd still recommend reading the points below as they're important and it is always useful to know why they benefit users.

Pausing

First of all, users should always be able to easily stop any moving imagery that appears when they reach the page. Almost all background videos autoplay as soon as they've loaded, and this can have a negative effect on those sensitive to sharp movement or changes in light such as epilepsy, photosensitive visual impairments, or those with conditions that can lead to heightened sensory awareness, such as autism. For example, research in the *Autism in Adulthood* journal tells us to

> *Avoid textured backgrounds, moving images and decorative elements that do not convey information...these types of elements may make the site difficult or impossible to comprehend.*[6]

In many cases, the video displayed in the background of a home page or landing page doesn't necessarily contain information. This can be a good thing, as we've mentioned regarding text in images. However, it could be argued that when videos sit directly behind content (text or calls to action are often overlaid), they can interfere with a user's ability to comprehend information in the foreground.

Luckily WCAG's 2.1 spec has mentioned this exact issue in their section on 'Pause, Stop, Hide':

> *For any moving, blinking or scrolling information that (1) starts automatically, (2) lasts more than five seconds, and (3) is presented in parallel with other content, there [must be] a mechanism for the user to pause, stop, or hide it unless the movement, blinking, or scrolling is part of an activity where it is essential.*[7]

Because of this, the first challenge is creating a way for users to pause and play the video. This is quite easy to add when you're using the native HTML5 `<video>` tag. Firstly, there is a `controls` attribute that you can add that will give you a full range of controls for pausing, playing, moving between parts of the video, and going full screen (shown in Figure 8-5).

Figure 8-5. *How the default controls of the `<video>` element look in Google Chrome*

However, this often doesn't look particularly nice, and you usually end up compromising the effect you were trying to create by adding the video. To make it accessible, we're realistically only looking to be able to stop and start the video, and this can be accomplished with one button. You can add this to create your own custom controls and change their behavior through code depending on what the video is doing.

To achieve this, we add a single, small button that sits in the corner of the video, with a class of `js-video-button` so we can target it in code.

```
<button class="js-video-button">Pause</button>
```

The following code is run every time the button is interacted with by the user:

```
$('.js-video-button').on('click', function() {
    video.paused ? video.play() : video.pause();
    let buttonText = video.paused ? 'Play' : 'Pause';
    $('.js-video-button').text(buttonText);
});
```

This should hopefully be very easy to follow. If the video is paused, we ask it to play, and if isn't, we know that it's playing and so ask to pause it. We use the same check to alter the button text to reflect the current action that the user can perform on the video (so it displays "Pause" when the video is playing and "Play" when it's paused). We're using a `<button>` tag for this, as it'll mean that it can be tabbed to, and focused on, by default – a useful feature for keyboard-only users.

No sound

We also want to avoid sound coming from an autoplaying video as soon as a user reaches the site. It's often unexpected, can be very distracting, and excludes users that are deaf and hard of hearing or who are simply browsing on a muted device. You can handle this by ensuring that the video you use has no audio, but to be safe you can add an attribute called `muted` to the `<video>` tag to make sure:

```
<video muted>
    ...
</video>
```

Consider the colour scheme of the video

When using moving video as a background, problems often arise if the colours change quickly and frequently. This means that any text that you've overlaid can become unreadable. It's a tricky balance to strike, so I would consider one or more of the following when overlaying content on top of a video:

- Choose one main colour scheme for content in the video, so that text can work consistently over it.

- Provide a consistent background colour for your overlaid content. That way, your text remains readable even if the background video changes colour. This is the approach that W3C recommends, and Figure 8-6 shows an example of their approach.

Figure 8-6. *Content displayed over a background video, but with a semitransparent background to prevent problems with contrast between the background and foreground*

Note that background colours can be partially transparent, so that you can still see the video behind it to some extent. This is perhaps the safest approach to placing written content over a video.

- Limit the animation in the background video or restrict that animation to a particular part of the banner. This allows you to separate the animation from any important content and allows the user to focus their attention more on the latter.

- Blur the video slightly to reduce the chance of sharp clashes between it and the foreground content. Some users also argue that a softly blurred video requires less focus, as there are fewer details competing for attention.[8]

It's also worth mentioning that rapid changes in bright colour can seriously impact users who experience photosensitivity – like some users with low vision or epilepsy. WCAG found that having more than three flashes per second renders a page inaccessible (flashes are usually found in badly made banner images, optical illusions, background videos, and effects).[9]

Only play once the video has loaded

Even if you create a background video with minimal animation, your users could still experience unpleasant sharp movements if your video regularly starts and stops. This could happen when you attempt to display a video as soon as the page loads, but it hasn't downloaded completely.

Luckily you can tell a `<video>` tag to wait until that is no longer a problem:

```
video.addEventListener('canplaythrough', playVideo);
```

We can do this by "listening" for an "event" that happens on the video. Once this event occurs, we can run a piece of code. An "event" could be when the video has finished playing, or when it's paused, but in this case, we're interested in the `canplaythrough` event. Waiting for this event to occur ensures that a video is only played once the browser has downloaded enough of the video that it can play the whole thing without any additional buffering. This prevents a constant start/stop motion for users with a slower Internet connection – something that could confuse screen reader users or contribute to a complex experience that excludes those with cognitive impairments (as mentioned in Chapter 6 – "Cognitive Impairments").

Loading a poster first and then the video

If you use the preceding approach, you still need to handle what the user sees until the video has loaded enough to play. On a slow connection, this lasts for a few seconds, and then suddenly the page will go from displaying nothing to showing a moving video, which constitutes unexpected behavior. For these reasons, loading a temporary "poster" to display first is the best solution.

```
<video poster="assets/poster.jpg">
```

These are easily attached to the `<video>` tag itself and almost always take less time to load as images are a much smaller resource. If you don't include one, the `<video>` tag will sometimes try to use the first frame of the video instead, but this is often just a black screen. Adding one provides more freedom to specify the initial visual that the user sees.

Don't loop your video

This is our final slam dunk, particularly if the video doesn't have a play/ pause button. If the video on your site is constantly playing by looping, there is no way for users with access needs such as autism and epilepsy to avoid it, and they may well be forced to leave your site.

This time, instead of adding an attribute, you need to ensure that the following **isn't** present on your `<video>` tags:

```
<video loop>
    ...
</video>
```

A neat alternative is to transition your video to a static image or background colour once the video is finished. This lets the user know that the movement has finished and ensures that the decision not to loop the video feels deliberate.

This involves listening for another "event" just like we did so we knew when the video could be played. Here, we're grabbing the poster we displayed before – in case the video hadn't loaded – and setting it as the background image of the element that holds the video. Once this is done, we remove the video:

```
video.addEventListener("ended", function() {
    $(video).parent().css({
        'background-image' : 'url(' + video.getAttribute('data-
        poster') +      ')'
    });
    Video.remove();
});
```

Should you do it?

It is my personal opinion that videos can create a nice effect if they are included correctly. I would, however, generally avoid displaying any information over them, as it's usually too difficult to ensure that the content will be visible throughout the video. Again, it's also important to avoid sound entirely if the video is being autoplayed. This can contribute to an assault on the senses and exclude deaf users, especially if there is no clear way to turn it off.

Reducing movement

I'd also like to touch on the topic of animation inside and outside of videos and the potential effect that this can have on users. Val Head, a specialist web animation consultant explains that:

> *As animated interfaces increasingly become the norm, more people have begun to notice that large-scale motion on screen can cause them dizziness, nausea, headaches, or worse. For some, the symptoms can last long after the animation is over.*[10]

Users with visually triggered vestibular disorders (which usually involve problems with the inner ear that can cause dizziness and balance problems) feel an especially strong sensation of motion sickness when viewing animation with excessive movement.[11] Reports suggest that over 10% of adults experience chronic dizziness at least once in their lives.[12] The A11y Project describes the impact of these disorders as such:

> *'Your personal steady-cam is broken. Whatever you look at tends to move regardless of if you are moving.'*[13]

We've already talked about making sure sites can adapt to user preferences such as colour scheme or magnification. Thankfully there are also other checks that can be made to deal with common image-based barriers. This is accomplished using a feature called "media queries" – a way of including some styling or functional code but only if a certain condition is true.

Here are a few examples of checks that can be made in code and the user preferences that they represent:

- `prefers-reduced-motion`: The user prefers less motion, such as animation, on the page.

- `prefers-reduced-transparency`: The user prefers a reduced amount of transparent imagery or translucent layering of content.

- `prefers-contrast`: Detects if the user has requested the system increase or decrease the amount of contrast between adjacent colours.

- `prefers-color-scheme`: Detect if the user prefers a light or dark colour scheme.[14]

It's worth noting that these rules aren't supported in every major browser, but they can be used in Google Chrome, Firefox, Safari, and Opera, which represent most users online.[15]

All of these are worth looking into, but for our purposes the query that we're interested in here is `prefers-reduced-motion`. This preference can be set by a user on Windows 10 by going to

`Settings > Ease of Access > Display > Show animations.`

Or on macOS, by going to

`System Preferences > Accessibility > Display > Reduce motion.`

Once this is done, you can make changes in the functionality or styling of your sites to take this preference into account. Here is an example of how to remove autoplay and pause a background video in JavaScript when this setting is active:

```
if (window.matchMedia('(prefers-reduced-motion)').matches) {
    video.removeAttribute('autoplay');
    video.pause();
}
```

And here is an example of removing an animation in CSS using the same preference:

```
/* An animation that makes a button vibrate quickly */
.animation {
    animation: vibrate 0.3s linear infinite both;
}

@media (prefers-reduced-motion: reduce) {
    .animation {
        animation: none;
    }
}
```

I'm not suggesting that everyone should remove all animation or movement from their pages. Instead, we can be mindful of excessive movement on pages, and seek to reduce it – either through changing the original material shown to all users or by tapping into these preferences to tone down the level of animation. Try enabling this setting on your device and see if it has an effect on your typical browsing experience – the setting is part of the practical example for this chapter, so you can see it in action there!

Parallax

It's worth pointing out that it's not always images and videos that create movement on a web page. Parallax scrolling is a design effect, where the background of a web page moves at a slower rate to the foreground, creating a 3D effect as you scroll. It's currently a hugely popular feature of websites, as it creates a subtle effect of depth that can make a page stand out immediately.

Parallax takes content that is typically static (with scrolling usually being the only source of movement) and changes it in a way that users often don't expect. Additionally, seeing as scrolling is typically the only source of movement and is controlled by the user, altering the effect and speed in this way takes some of that control away.

Unlike a video or image, these effects typically apply to the entire page – and have therefore been known to cause bigger problems than "smaller" animations:

> *Animations that move an object across a large amount of space are most apt to trigger a negative response for someone suffering from a vestibular disorder. The physical size of screen matters less than the size of the motion relative to the screen space available—so a small button with a 3D rotation probably won't cause trouble, but a full-screen wipe transition covering the entire screen likely would.*[16]

Not only is parallax scrolling often a full-screen animation, but it also only stops when the user stops scrolling – if they want to engage with content that is currently off-screen, then the animation resumes the moment they move up or down the page.

Carrying on from our example – ensuring that your site responds to users `prefers-reduced motion` setting – it is also fairly easy to use this feature to reduce, or altogether remove, parallax for users who have specified that they have a problem with excessive motion. Then you can add a feature like this knowing that it won't create barriers for these users, and without altering your design or experience for your wider audience. This way, you create a feeling that your site's experience is unique while ensuring that it is not overwhelming either.

We are now going to turn our attention to another popular image-based feature that also suffers from overuse (and misuse) on the Web – iconography.

Iconography

Icons on the Web have evolved significantly over the last few years, and their ability to help keep a design looking clean has seen their popularity soar. In Chapter 6 ("Cognitive impairments") we spoke about the perils of creating your own icons. However, whether you're deciding on an approach for a new site or if you're trying to improve the accessibility of icons in a site you maintain, it's worth looking at a brief history of how icons have been implemented, and how to make sure each approach is as inclusive as possible.

`<img>` tag

This was the original way of adding an icon to a web page: creating an icon and then linking to it in an `<img>` tag allows you to provide `alt` text for it.

```
<img src="cat.jpg" alt="A cat playing with a large blue ball of yarn" />
```

A quick note: if you're adding a link around an icon, the `alt` text should describe the action that clicking the icon would perform, like so

```
<a href="cat-toys.html">
    <img src="cat.jpg" alt="View our cat toys" />
</a>
```

Sprites

Popular in the late 2000s, an "image sprite" is a large collection of images and icons stored in one single file. The thought process behind this was mostly performance-driven, as it would only require retrieving one file (as opposed to dozens) from a server to load all the images on a page. This led to quicker load times but meant that you had to use CSS (styling code) to display any one of the images by itself. You accomplished this by setting one "sprite" (containing lots of icons) as a background, and then using "background position" to position the background at the point on the X and Y-axis that matched your target image. As a quick example, let's try displaying the second icon in this sprite – shown in Figure 8-7.

Figure 8-7. *An image "sprite," containing multiple icons in one file*

What you'd do is work out how big the icon is by itself, then determine its position within the full sprite, and then create a rule in CSS for it. Figure 8-8 visualises how you would do this.

Figure 8-8. *A breakdown of how to work out how to display a particular icon inside a sprite. This takes the chosen icon's width and height into account, as well as the size of the sprite itself in order to determine the icon's X and Y position*

Here, the flame icon is 100 pixels wide and 200 pixels high, and it's positioned 100 pixels along the X-axis. Therefore, we would need to use CSS as follows:

```
.flame-icon {
    width: 100px;
    height: 200px;
    background-image: url('sprite.png');
    /* Negative number because a positive one would move it to
    the right instead */
    background-position: -100px 0;
    background-repeat: no-repeat;
}
```

This approach was very popular for a while but eventually abandoned by developers. It was found that it didn't really help with performance and had restrictions because it couldn't handle multiple image formats and, as you could probably tell, it was a nightmare to maintain. The minute you changed a sprite, perhaps by adding another icon, the position of the other icons could change too, and suddenly none of your code works anymore.[17]

However, you may well be maintaining a site that still uses image sprites and undoing that can take a fair amount of effort. In the meantime, sprites can be made accessible with little effort. As the sprite is only ever displayed via CSS, there is no "alt" attribute (like we have when using an `<img>` tag) to describe its contents. Therefore, the only way to achieve some form of accessibility is to use a solution we covered earlier in Chapter 2 ("Blindness"). This involved creating a small piece of HTML, hidden visually, to describe the icon for screen readers and other assistive technologies:

```
<div class="flame-icon">
    <span class="screen-reader-only">View your gas meter
    readings</span>
</div>
```

Windows High Contrast Mode

We've mentioned this setting briefly before, but High Contrast Mode (HCM) is an accessibility feature built into Windows that assists people with vision impairments by allowing them to change the colour scheme of content, at an operating system level, to make it more readable. This feature does a great job of automatically adjusting the colour scheme of most of your page's content in response to this user preference, but it does hold a couple of problems where imagery is concerned. Primarily, there have been issues with background images not displaying when High Contrast Mode is active – which affected image sprites as a result – and images with transparent backgrounds that seemed to "disappear" when the content in them matched the now-altered background colour. For example, if this image and text combo (Figure 8-9) was displayed on a page.

Figure 8-9. *An icon of a lightning bolt, as well as some text – both displayed as black on a light background*

Switching to High Contrast Mode would invert the background and text colour but the image, as a separate file, wouldn't update. This would often result in it appearing as though it's not there, as shown in Figure 8-10.

Figure 8-10. *The same image and text combination as above, but with the colour scheme inverted due to High Contrast Mode. The text has been inverted, but the image now appears to be invisible as it couldn't be inverted by High Contrast Mode*

Luckily for those maintaining sites that still use sprites, Windows 10 (with Microsoft Edge) High Contrast Mode no longer removes background images, and in fact there is now a CSS media query that can be used to explicitly enhance a design in High Contrast Mode and combat the issue above. You can set specific styles that will respond if High Contrast Mode is active, and even when a certain foreground/background colour scheme is active:

```
/* Change a style if High Contrast Mode is active */
@media (-ms-high-contrast: active) {
    img { display: none; }
}

/* Change a background if High Contrast Mode is set to black on
white */
@media screen and (-ms-high-contrast: black-on-white) {
    div { background-image: url('image-black.png'); }
}

/* Change a background if High Contrast Mode is set to white on
black */
@media screen and (-ms-high-contrast: white-on-black) {
    div { background-image: url('image-white.png'); }
}
```

With this information, you could load a different colour lightning bolt icon for the given example so that it always remained visible. As well as media queries, there is also a CSS rule that you can add to elements in order to dictate how they behave when High Contrast Mode is active:

```
/* Don't let High Contrast Mode change the display of
this div */
div {
```

```
    background-color: green;
    -ms-high-contrast-adjust: none;
}
```

Doing this would prevent any visual change to this part of the web page when High Contrast Mode is active. I would discourage this approach though, once again to ensure that your users have as much control as possible over their browsing experience.

Icon fonts

These arrived in earnest in 2012, namely, through a library called Font Awesome. This library was initially made for use with Twitter's Bootstrap framework but has since gained massive adoption throughout all types of websites. Icon fonts as an approach provide two key benefits over older icons. Firstly, they scaled better than regular images, meaning that they would stay sharp if they were made larger, while standard images would become grainy and pixelated. Secondly, an icon font is added into a page's code, not in its styles like a background image or sprite. This meant that you could adjust an icon's appearance such as size and colour using just CSS:

HTML
```
<i class="fas fa-pound-sign"></i>
```

CSS
```
i.fa-pound-sign {
    color: red;
    font-size: 24px;
}
```

Decorative vs. functional icons

Font Awesome have also done some good work on distinguishing between what are known as decorative and functional icons (as we discussed earlier regarding static images). Again, you must ensure that the ones not in a page's HTML code hold no value to the user that would be otherwise lost to screen reader users. Decorative icons hold no value or information beyond aesthetics, so for those you can use the ARIA attribute `aria-hidden` to ensure that they don't get in the way for people using assistive technology. Figure 8-11 shows an icon that holds no meaning or action whatsoever – an icon of some bacon.

Figure 8-11. *A completely decorative icon of some tasty bacon*

As the icon holds no meaning, we'd hide it from assistive technology using aria-hidden like so

```
<i class="fas bacon" aria-hidden="true"></i>
```

On the other hand, functional icons hold some form of information or meaning, and as a result, it's important that this same information can be shared in a way that doesn't rely on the icon. A solution for this involves a combination of the following:

- An `aria-hidden="true"` attribute added to the icon, so that screen readers will ignore the icon itself

- A text alternative inside an element that is invisible, but keeps the icon accessible to assistive technologies (this requires an appropriate CSS class to visually hide the element, which we discussed earlier in this chapter and before, in Chapter 2 – "Blindness")

- A `title` attribute on the icon, so that a tooltip will appear for sighted mouse users who may not understand the meaning of the icon

```
<i aria-hidden="true" class="fas fa-car" title="Time to
destination by car"></i>
<span class="screen-reader-only">Time to destination by car:</
span>
```

Providing context for icons

Accessibility for icons can currently provide improvements for a variety of users, but these improvements are still primarily aimed at those using assistive technology such as screen readers. These users will receive alternative text to help them understand what is being displayed and the action it holds. However, as we mentioned earlier, icons can be confusing even when you can interact with them visually, and this may not simply be because the icon is vague. An icon might accurately represent an action, but that action may still be confusing, or new to the user. If we think about the original rise of social networking sites, actions such as "liking," "retweeting," and "pinning" were completely alien without tutorials and practice.

As we've mentioned already, you can also always add text next to the icon to also help sighted users if you think the icon is somewhat ambiguous. In the case of icon fonts, we could look at displaying descriptions for the icons visually, when a user interacts with them (e.g., by focusing and hovering). Not only does this allow keyboard-only users to see a description of the icon's action, it means those using a mouse will be provided the same contextual information when they hover over it.

This is easy to add for the approaches above that already hide text visually that describes the icon inside the page. Here you could add some simple CSS styling to show that text when a user hovers or focuses on the icon:

```
i:hover + .sr-only,
i:focus + .sr-only {
    display: block;
}
```

This code will simply show the text as the next item in the page after the icon, and therefore it's position may not fit neatly with the design of your page. In this case, many people opt to position the icon in a tooltip that hovers above or below the icon.

SVG

The Scalable Vector Graphic (SVG) marks the latest development not only in imagery, but also in displaying accessible iconography online. These image files are supported by all modern web browsers and, as the name suggests, are capable of scaling in size while maintaining a higher level of quality than icon fonts (as shown in Figure 8-12).

Figure 8-12. *The same SVG icon displayed four times at four different sizes. Despite increasing in scale from its original size, it shows no change in the sharpness of the icon*

They also offer even more freedom for customisation – because they're made using code they can have multiple colours as part of the same icon (instead of just one like icon fonts), and they can be animated using CSS like any other part of a site. This is great news for both designers and developers as they can be altered without the designer needing to find the original design file and re-export it to allow the developer to implement and redeploy it.

They've therefore become particularly popular for creating icons. As an extra seal of approval for SVGs – the icon font "Font Awesome" actually converted their entire font library to SVG in their fifth version.[18]

Still, it's important to consider accessibility when a technology receives a surge in popularity, and SVGs do come with their own set of drawbacks. Their level of accessibility can be inconsistent, and there is a debate over the best delivery method. Here are a few possible approaches:

`<img>` tag

This is the simplest approach, but if you are displaying SVGs through the `<img>` tag, it's important to at least have the `alt` attribute describing the asset:

```
<img src="apple.svg" alt="Silhouette of an Apple" />
```

The main problem with this approach is that it makes customisation through code impossible. If the SVG code isn't actually in the page, which it wouldn't be here, you won't be able to style or animate parts of it. This takes away a lot of the benefits of SVGs, so I wouldn't advise it.

CSS background image

Much like any other image, you can set an SVG as a background image in CSS. You can scale and position it this way but, as with setting any background image, there is nothing in the code of the page to describe it or the content it might hold. Much like placing them in an `<img>` tag, I'd avoid this route.

Inline SVG

As SVG's are made using code, the most accessible way to use them is by placing them in your web page's code. This way you have full control over altering their appearance and behavior, without having to recreate different versions for different purposes. For example, Figure 8-13 shows the same SVG's shown in Figure 8-12, but altered in different ways using CSS:

Figure 8-13. *The same SVG used four times, with each of them being displayed in different sizes, colours, and positions through code*

There are, however, a few things that also need to be added to an SVG's code, to ensure that they're accessible:

role attribute

Firstly, an ARIA *role* attribute of "img" is required to make the asset's purpose clear to screen readers:

```
<svg role="img">
    ...
</svg>
```

aria-labelledby and aria-describedby

Another way to give your SVGs the same level of accessibility as images is to provide <title> and <desc> tags. As the names suggest, these provide a title for the image that can be read out, as well as a more detailed description of the image's contents. Doing this, you can actually provide more context to screen readers that a standard alt tag. To make sure that these tags can be recognised and read out by technology like screen readers, you then need to add labelledby and describedby attributes to the SVG, whose values match the ID's of the <title> and <desc> elements like so:

```
<svg aria-labelledby="logo-title" aria-describedby="logo-desc"
role="img">
    <title id="logo-title">Apple logo</title>
    <desc id="logo-desc">A silhouette of an apple with a bite
    taken out of it</desc>
    ...
</svg>
```

Hidden element

In the same way that we covered for icons in the previous section, some SVGs may well simply be decorative and so don't need to be described by screen readers. In this case, we can add the exact same ARIA attribute to the `<svg>` tag as we did there:

```
<div>
    <svg class="icon" aria-hidden="true">
        ...
    </svg>
</div>
```

Note   I've added these points as "Do's and don'ts" in this chapter's practical example for easy reference. Again, this is found in the "Chapter 8" folder of the Github repository, or by visiting `https://inclusive.guide/examples/imagery`

Font awesome

The latest version of the "Font Awesome" icon library actually handles a lot of these accessibility issues for you, as part of their "Auto-accessibility" feature when you use their SVG approach. If the icon you are using is for decorative purposes, it'll automatically hide it from screen readers and give it a `role` of "img" without any additional code being required. If the icon is functional, then all you need to do is add a `title` attribute like so

```
<i title="Magic is included!" class="fas fa-magic"></i>
```

They will then add the role attribute, a `<title>` tag, and an aria-labelledby attribute that it will link to the `<title>`.[19] If you're looking to use common icons in your site and not custom ones, I would recommend using Font Awesome to save time while ensuring accessibility.

High Contrast Mode

Returning quickly to High Contrast Mode, SVG's are great at adapting to changes in user preference. You can set an SVG's colour in CSS, using the `currentColor` rule, which means that as a colour scheme changes between contrast modes, the SVG will automatically update. Figure 8-14 shows an example from the United Kingdom Government website, with their SVG logo displaying well on both their standard colour scheme, and in High Contrast Mode.[20]

Figure 8-14. *The United Kingdom government logo as an SVG, responding to a change in High Contrast Mode, thanks to the* `currentColor` *attribute*

This will likely become even more useful in the future, as a new feature is currently being worked on where sites can be styled according to the ambient light-level in which a device is being used.[21] This is brilliant as it means that web pages can adapt quickly and seamlessly to avoid barriers – without users needing to constantly change their settings. It also means that the setting may change numerous times while a user is on a site. Having imagery that can adapt to these changes on the fly will improve long-term accessibility without requiring additional effort from designers and developers.

Conclusion

Having covered the three main areas of visual media that are commonly present on the Web – images, video, and iconography – hopefully you now feel confident in your ability to both add content that you know will be inclusive, and go back retrospectively to make content like this accessible.

The fact is, a lot of these issues can be solved by the inclusion of a couple of attributes, or even automatically by using libraries like Font Awesome. This means that you can see this area of accessibility as a quick and somewhat effortless win – for you and your users.

Finally, I hope that this chapter has also acted as an advert for the flexibility and accessibility of SVG as an image type. Being able to add attributes directly to them that make them accessible to screen readers, their ability to adjust automatically to circumstances like a user's colour settings, and their potential for animation, scaling, and styling through code, means that SVGs are a highly versatile form of online imagery.

Notes

1. W3Techs, *Usage of image file formats for websites,* (2019), <https://w3techs.com/technologies/overview/image_format/all> [accessed 19/07/2019].

2. Nick Schäferhoff, *Popular CMS by Market Share,* (2018), <https://websitesetup.org/popular-cms/> [accessed 19/07/2019].

3. W3C, *F39: Failure of Success Criterion 1.1.1,* (2016) <www.w3.org/WAI/GL/2016/WD-WCAG20-TECHS-20160105/F39> [accessed 19/07/2019].

4. Molly Watt, *Accessibility and Me, Gov.uk,* (09/01/2017), <https://accessibility.blog.gov.uk/2017/01/09/accessibility-and-me-molly-watt/> [accessed 19/07/2019].

5. Connie Wong, *How to Use Video Background On Your Website – The Right Way!,* in WebsiteBuilderExpert, (03/06/2019), <www.websitebuilderexpert.com/designing-websites/video-background-for-websites/> [accessed 03/06/2019].

6. Dora M. Raymaker, Steven K. Kapp, Katherine E. McDonald, Michael Weiner, Elesia Ashkenazy, and Christina Nicolaidis, *Development of the AASPIRE Web Accessibility Guidelines for Autistic Web Users,* in Autism in Adulthood, 1:2, (13/04/2019), <www.liebertpub.com/doi/abs/10.1089/aut.2018.0020?journalCode=aut> [accessed 19/07/2019].

7. W3C, *Understanding Success Criterion 2.2.2: Pause, Stop, Hide,* <www.w3.org/TR/WCAG21/#pause-stop-hide> [accessed 19/07/2019].

8. Punkchip, *Accessible HTML video as a background,* <www.punkchip.com/accessible-html-video-as-a-background/> [accessed 19/07/2019].

9. W3C, *Three Flashes or Below Threshold: Understanding SC 2.3.1,* (2016), <www.w3.org/TR/UNDERSTANDING-WCAG20/seizure-does-not-violate.html> [accessed 19/07/2019].

10. Val Head, *Designing Safer Web Animation For Motion Sensitivity,* in A List Apart, (08/09/2015), <https://alistapart.com/article/designing-safer-web-animation-for-motion-sensitivity/> [accessed 19/07/2019].

11. Val Head, *Designing Safer Web Animation For Motion Sensitivity*, in A List Apart, (08/09/2015), <https://alistapart.com/article/designing-safer-web-animation-for-motion-sensitivity/> [accessed 19/07/2019].

12. Ko C, Hoffman HJ, Sklare DA, *Chronic Imbalance or Dizziness and Falling: Results from the 1994 Disability Supplement to the National Health Interview Survey and the Second Supplement on Aging Study. Poster session of the Twenty-ninth Annual Midwinter Meeting of the Association for Research in Otolaryngology*, (2006).

13. Grey Ghost Visuals, *A primer to vestibular disorders*, in The A11y Project, (15/05/2013), <https://a11yproject.com/posts/understanding-vestibular-disorders/> [accessed 19/07/2019].

14. Mozilla, *Using media queries,* (03/09/2019), <https://developer.mozilla.org/en-US/docs/Web/CSS/Media_Queries/Using_media_queries#Media_features> [accessed 18/09/2019].

15. Can I Use, *CSS at-rule: @media: prefers-reduced-motion media feature*, (08/2019), <https://caniuse.com/#search=prefers-reduced-motion> [accessed 18/09/2019].

16. Val Head, *Designing Safer Web Animation For Motion Sensitivity*, in A List Apart, (08/09/2015), <https://alistapart.com/article/designing-safer-web-animation-for-motion-sensitivity/> [accessed 19/07/2019].

17.   Gery Teague, *Reasons You Shouldn't Use Sprite Sheets*, (04/05/2016), `<www.hbdesign.com/sprite-sheets-3-things-know/>` [accessed 19/07/2019].

18.   Font Awesome, *Home*, `<https://fontawesome.com>` [accessed 19/07/2019].

19.   Front Awesome, *Accessibility*, `<https://fontawesome.com/how-to-use/on-the-web/other-topics/accessibility>` [accessed 19/07/2019].

20.   Nick Colley, *Supporting users who change colours on GOV.UK*, Gov.uk's Accessibility in government blog, (01/08/2018), `<https://accessibility.blog.gov.uk/2018/08/01/supporting-users-who-change-colours-on-gov-uk/>` [accessed 19/07/2019].

21.   W3C, *Media Queries Level 5*, (21/05/2019), `<https://drafts.csswg.org/mediaqueries-5/#light-level>` [accessed 19/07/2019].

CHAPTER 9

Communication

Websites only form one part of a user's online journey. We've frequently talked about providing multiple ways for customers to access information and complete tasks online, but this concept equally applies to communication on the Web, and away from it as well.

We will start by talking about emails. Over 111 billion personal emails are sent and received each day.[1] Thanks to their sheer volume, and the fact that they are coded similarly to websites, they deserve special attention. However, it is also worth focusing on them because they can be extremely troublesome and inconsistent.

We'll look at what's behind these inconsistencies and how to ensure that your formats, content, and styling are all accessible – even if you rely on a third-party email service to handle yours. After that, we'll look into a feature that makes user actions both quicker to complete, and possible without even opening the email you send them.

From a feature that's designed to make interacting with email easier than ever, we'll turn our attention to a feature that makes interacting with emails extremely difficult: no-reply addresses. This tactic can affect your accessibility, your delivery rates, and your reputation, so it's worth exploring the benefits of removing them.

Finally, we'll take a look at the broader idea of best practice when communicating directly with users, on whatever platform that may be. It benefits you, and your users, if you are able to identify those in need, what their needs are, and how best to help.

© Ashley Firth 2019
A. Firth, *Practical Web Inclusion and Accessibility*,
https://doi.org/10.1007/978-1-4842-5452-3_9

Accessible email

Email is the most common way that sites and brands communicate with their users. Contrary to common belief, email is not a dying technology. According to one study by The Radicati Group, there will be nearly 3 billion email users worldwide by the time this book is released (late 2019) – over a third of the world's population.[2]

This popularity certainly isn't lost on brands, nor is the importance of making this form of communication accessible. In recent research, 77% of brands say that email accessibility is a priority for them. This is a comforting statistic, but it's marred by another more important figure: only 8% of these same brands rigidly follow best practices for email accessibility.[3] It might sound a little counterproductive, but part of me doesn't blame them entirely. While web accessibility is undoubtedly a significant undertaking, in my personal opinion, building an accessible email can be even harder.

The single biggest problem with building emails today is the massive variety of email clients, all of which require different methods to ensure accessibility. For reference here are the ten most popular email clients at the time of writing,[4] based on 800 million email "opens" in June 2019:

1) Gmail (29%)

2) Apple iPhone (27%)

3) Outlook (10%)

4) Apple iPad (8%)

5) Apple Mail (7%)

6) Yahoo! Mail (6%)

7) Google Android (3%)

8) Outlook.com (2%)

9) Samsung Mail (1%)

10) Thunderbird (> 1%)

Levels of user adoption vary from one provider to another, but irritatingly, most also have their own way of displaying an email (known as a rendering engine), and differing levels of support for things like styling through CSS, laying out content, and even displaying text.

Outlook is a particularly good (or bad) example. From 2000 to 2003, Outlook were using their then browser, Internet Explorer, as a rendering engine to display emails. Then in 2007 they switched to using Microsoft Word to render and display emails instead – yes seriously.[5] In Outlook 2011 (known as Outlook for Mac), they switched again to use the "WebKit" engine, and it provided great support and capabilities, but then they switched back to Word again in 2013. The result is three completely separate sets of rules and restrictions regarding how an email can be displayed, all under the same name. What's more, people don't upgrade their email platform very often – in fact, all three of these versions of Outlook are still actively used.

This situation extends to all email clients, devices, and operating systems, and causes havoc when it comes to creating emails that work consistently for everyone. Here are just a few examples of features that work well on the Web but are fundamentally unreliable in emails:

– Form elements like checkboxes or radio buttons work in Gmail but not Outlook 2007. In Outlook 2003 checkboxes render completely differently, with square brackets instead, but these aren't functional in any way.[6]

– You can play a video in Apple Mail on iOS10 and above, but not in iOS9. It works in Thunderbird mail but doesn't work in Gmail and works in Outlook for Mac but not Yahoo!.[7]

- The ability to make an email responsive using media queries is possible in Outlook 2000–2003 but not in Outlook 2007–2016 and is possible in the Gmail app but not in the Gmail mobile web mail.

- Using a custom font is possible in iOS mail but impossible in older Outlook versions, Gmail, Yahoo!, and Windows mail.

- The ability to add CSS animations for emails is impossible in every form of Gmail, Outlook, Windows mail, and Yahoo!.

- Adding rounded corners to part of an email works everywhere apart from in Outlook and Windows Mail (and it works in AOL web mail but not AOL desktop).

- Want to change the style of an element when a user hovers on it? You can't in any mobile Gmail client apart from for the Android app version.[8]

These inconsistencies might seem small in isolation, but any one of them could lead to broken layouts and features. Some (like broken form elements) can prevent users from completing actions, and this can be especially distressing for users with impaired mental health or cognitive function. Other inconsistencies (like animation and responsive design) can lead to confusing and exclusionary layouts and visuals, complicated experiences, and a lack of functionality.

Finding ways around these problems can take a large amount of time and, when it comes to solving issues with email clients that very few people use, your time and effort doesn't equate to helping many people. Instead, RebelMail raises the argument that your time could be spent more wisely:

People spend a lot of time worrying about email clients with 1% usage; accessibility is a much bigger issue[9]

This echoes a point I made at the start of the book about focusing on accessibility instead of out-of-date browsers – accessibility is often pushed aside, despite it being more useful to a wider range of people.

When it comes to email though, there are ways to "outsource" a lot of these problems. Due to the issues and time required to build and test emails properly, many people have turned to third-party platforms that can handle this for them. Email and marketing services such as MailChimp or SendGrid are designed to take the stress away from managing and sending email for brands and offer a range of templates that can render consistently across different email clients.

However, some templates may not be fully accessible to begin with, and not every email service has every accessible feature available from the offset. Moreover, an email service can build an accessible template, but this can then be rendered inaccessible by the content that's added to it. Therefore, whichever approach you have opted for or have to maintain, whether internal or external, must be reviewed and tested to ensure that it is accessible.

With that in mind, here are some common things to consider in order to ensure that everybody on your send list can readily access your emails. What's great is that many of the items on this list build on points that we've covered earlier in the book. Alongside each point, I have also discussed whether email services support this or a similar solution.

Include a link to view your email as a web page

First, you should provide users with a way to view your email outside of the email platform they typically receive mail in. Browsers are far more consistent and feature-rich than most email clients, so many issues involving emails displaying incorrectly in clients like Outlook or Gmail may simply disappear in Google Chrome or Firefox. This gives users another chance to interact with content they've been sent if it's not displaying correctly in their inbox or missing some accessible features (a reasonable possibility given the inconsistencies I raised earlier). What's useful in this case is that emails are actually written in HTML just like web pages are (although they use an older syntax that largely relies on frequent use of the `<table>` tag). I won't go into the details of how to code an email here, but what this similarity means is that a browser is fully capable of displaying the code for an email on a web page. Therefore, providing the backup of a link to the email that can be viewed in a browser is a useful feature that will allow users to take advantage of any software they typically use on browsers, such as screen readers, applications that magnify text, or ones that heighten colour contrast.

Does an email service handle this?

Most templates will come with a "view this email in your browser" link, which will open a copy of the email in their browser of choice. It's also a feature that many services recommend, such as MailChimp:

> *Most Mailchimp templates include a View this email in your browser link that goes to a browser-based copy of your campaign. This campaign page link helps contacts who aren't able to view your content in their email client.*[10]

Provide a plain-text version of your email

Given the diverse range of quirks and rendering issues across email clients, a plain text version of your email is, in comparison, far more likely to display consistently across all of them. As a result, many users opt for this level of simplicity, as opposed to the potential rendering issues and complex layouts that come with stylised HTML versions. This is easily handled in the settings of most email clients. Plain text emails are much easier for screen readers to read through (or anyone skimming content for that matter), they ensure acceptable contrast levels (which benefits those with low vision), and their layout is always consistent and linear (making them more accessible to users with cognitive impairments). To top it off, they also require very little additional effort to create – there are even programs that will convert your email's HTML code into a text version, which I'll add to the list of useful tools in Chapter 11 ("Tools and QA").

By ensuring that you have a text version of your email as well as a styled HTML one, you also help your campaigns, as it makes them more trustworthy in the eyes of spam filters.[11]

Does an email service handle this?

Most do. SendGrid handle sending both, so that the plain text version can be displayed as a fallback. The reason they do this is very important:

> *If you only send HTML emails and a recipient's server or mail client blocks HTML content, they will not see anything in your emails.*[12]

If a user opts to receive only plain text emails, an email without a text version of its contents accompanying it won't be seen at all. This, plus all of the above, caters for access needs and general user preference, and many users now opt for it. It's important to make sure that a plain text version accompanies the emails you send.

Content

It's good to offer multiple ways to access an email, but now let's turn our attention toward some choices you can make to ensure that the email's content is as accessible as possible.

alt tags

We've covered `alt` tags quite heavily in Chapter 2 ("Blindness") and Chapter 8 ("Imagery"), but images are also frequently used in emails, and blind users need to be able to perceive them here too. Images are often used to overcome an inability to create difficult layouts or consistent visuals across the wide variety of email clients, and so providing `alt` tags on images is just as important in emails as they are on websites. It's always worth remembering to provide alternative text for users with visual impairments and to ensure text and other meaningful content is not embedded in images.

It's also important to consider that many email clients now block images from displaying by default, and this is because images became a popular delivery method in spam emails. With many email clients incorporating spam filters to keep suspicious content out of user's inboxes, spammers turned to embedding content in images so it couldn't be picked up as easily.[13] Adding `alt` text therefore not only lets users know what's in an image in the event that it's not displayed immediately but also goes a long way to proving that your images aren't actually spam – thereby identifying you as a "trusted sender."[14]

Does an email service handle this?

All of the major email services offer a way to add `alt` text to an image – either through a form field, accessed when specifying details like the source of an image, or through the code itself. However, I've noticed that in many services these fields are mandatory, meaning that you can easily upload an image without providing `alt` text by mistake. This places the responsibility firmly on the person who creates the email content to make sure it's there.

role="presentation"

As we know, alt tags help screen reader users understand what they can't see. However, it is also just as important to hide superfluous features these users might hear, but don't need to.

As I mentioned briefly earlier, emails are typically built using a series of `<table>` tags. This is largely to account for older email clients that don't support new ways of rendering content (such as older versions of Outlook, unsurprisingly). In order to accomplish most layouts, a developer has to use quite a few `<table>` tags, nested within one another, which creates a lot of extra code. Furthermore, inside every table you will find table rows (`<tr>`), and inside those rows are columns (`<td>`), all used in emails to separate and lay out content. That's a lot of code. As we learnt in Chapter 2 ("Blindness"), screen readers will read out any tag that it finds and understands, in an attempt to provide as much information as possible to the user about the page. However, in this instance, a screen reader could end up reading out several `<table>`, `<tr>`, and `<td>` tags – all of which hold no meaningful information for the user – until it finally reaches a tag with content in it. There is, however, a way to avoid this with an attribute that we have used in other situations: `role`.

We've used this attribute before to ensure that SVG's are recognisable as images and that a piece of custom markup can behave like a button. Here, we want to tell screen reader users that certain code is being used purely for decorative purposes. The "presentation" value for the `role` attribute does just that:

```
<table role="presentation">
```

Adding this means that screen reader software won't read the tag out. We're basically telling it that this tag is purely for decoration – so ignore it. Ensuring that you add `role="presentation"` on tables that are only used to structure the layout of the email will save a lot of time (and frustration) for those listening to your emails.

Does an email service handle this?

This will be handled in most templates you select from an email service, so this point is only important for people developing their own emails. It's a big win for very little effort, so it's definitely worth adding.

Set the language

In Chapter 2 ("Blindness"), I mentioned the need to set the `lang` attribute in HTML so that assistive technologies could read out content with the correct dialect and pronunciation. This is just as important in email, because your send list could include people from multiple countries.

```
<html lang="en">
```

Does an email service handle this?

Translation in some form is offered by many email services, but its application largely comes down to the level of translation required.

Full localisation (adjusting the entire contents of an email based on the location of the recipient) can be done automatically. Mailchimp, for example, can hook up to Google translate to generate links to translated versions of text for users, as well as tap into the user's preferred language setting.[15]

However, while Google translate is always getting smarter, it is still less reliable for larger chunks of text. As you have control of the content of an email, both when you've built the email and when you've used an email service, you can always get the content translated by a professional translator. You could then create multiple campaigns for each language in your send list. I'd recommend assessing the amount of content in your email before deciding, and testing anything generated by Google translate before sending it to your full send list.

Too Long; Didn't Read (TL;DR)s

While we are on the topic of accessible content, it's worth briefly mentioning TL;DRs again. They can help those with cognitive impairments understand emails more easily and save time for everybody else. For particularly long emails, a box highlighting and summarising the main points helps get that information across quickly, particularly on mobile devices where the smaller screen size means that fewer words can be displayed per line (Figure 9-1).

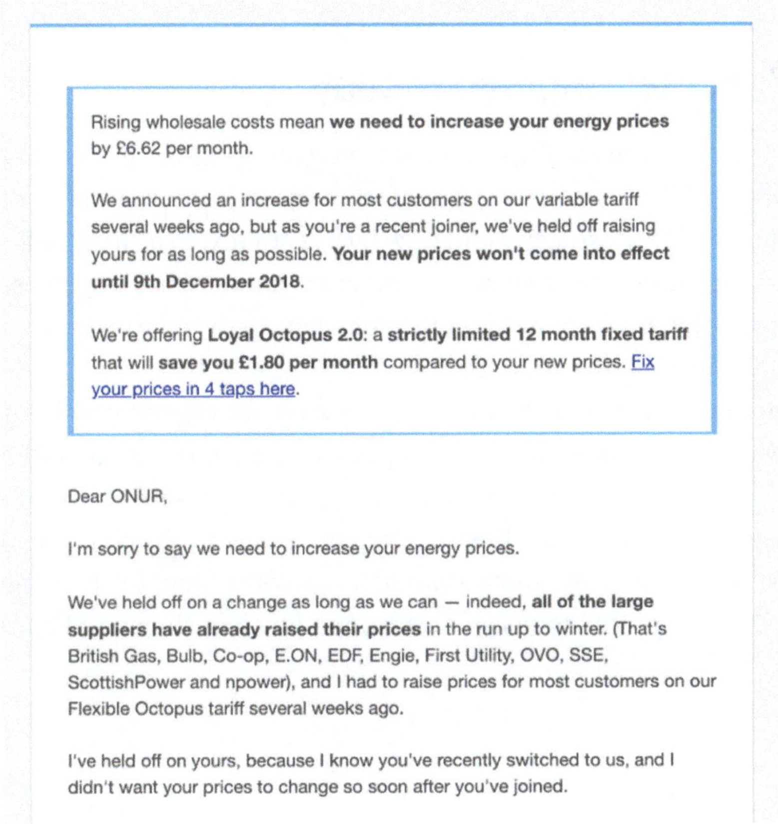

Rising wholesale costs mean **we need to increase your energy prices by £6.62 per month.**

We announced an increase for most customers on our variable tariff several weeks ago, but as you're a recent joiner, we've held off raising yours for as long as possible. **Your new prices won't come into effect until 9th December 2018.**

We're offering **Loyal Octopus 2.0: a strictly limited 12 month fixed tariff** that will **save you £1.80 per month** compared to your new prices. <u>Fix your prices in 4 taps here</u>.

Dear ONUR,

I'm sorry to say we need to increase your energy prices.

We've held off on a change as long as we can — indeed, **all of the large suppliers have already raised their prices** in the run up to winter. (That's British Gas, Bulb, Co-op, E.ON, EDF, Engie, First Utility, OVO, SSE, ScottishPower and npower), and I had to raise prices for most customers on our Flexible Octopus tariff several weeks ago.

I've held off on yours, because I know you've recently switched to us, and I didn't want your prices to change so soon after you've joined.

Figure 9-1. *A version of a TL;DR at the top of a long email*

Does an email service handle this?

As this technique concerns the content of an email, it is the responsibility of the person adding that content to include a TL;DR.

Styling

Now that we've thought about some ways in which an email's content can work harder for those with access needs, let's finally turn our attention to how we style and present that content.

Don't center align your copy

Accessible text is just as important when creating emails as it is online. In Chapter 3 ("Low Vision and Colour Blindness"), we spoke about the importance of letter spacing and how laying out text in a "justified" way (forcing each line to both start and end at the same point, regardless of the copy in that line) creates inconsistent gaps between words – thereby making it much harder to read.

The same can also be true of aligning your text centrally without justification. It can often look more appealing, but those with dyslexia and cognitive impairments that affect written comprehension, or those who experience adverse mental health, often have to work much harder to read this text. This is because, due to varied length of content in each line of text, you end up with inconsistent starting points, as shown in Figure 9-2.

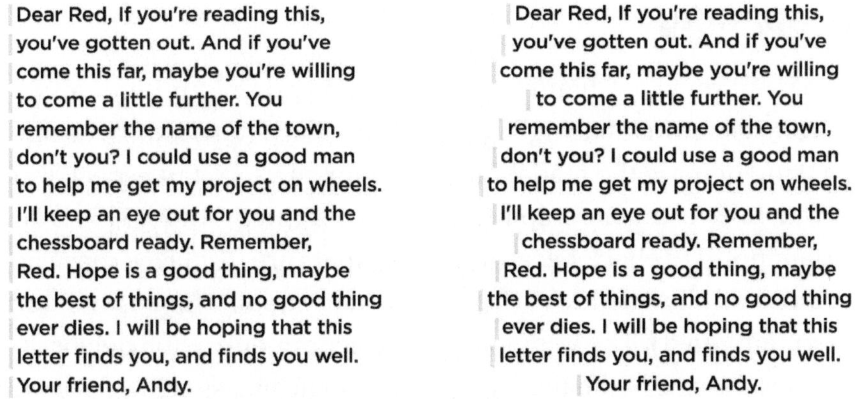

Dear Red, If you're reading this,
you've gotten out. And if you've
come this far, maybe you're willing
to come a little further. You
remember the name of the town,
don't you? I could use a good man
to help me get my project on wheels.
I'll keep an eye out for you and the
chessboard ready. Remember,
Red. Hope is a good thing, maybe
the best of things, and no good thing
ever dies. I will be hoping that this
letter finds you, and finds you well.
Your friend, Andy.

Dear Red, If you're reading this,
you've gotten out. And if you've
come this far, maybe you're willing
to come a little further. You
remember the name of the town,
don't you? I could use a good man
to help me get my project on wheels.
I'll keep an eye out for you and the
chessboard ready. Remember,
Red. Hope is a good thing, maybe
the best of things, and no good thing
ever dies. I will be hoping that this
letter finds you, and finds you well.
Your friend, Andy.

Figure 9-2. *A visual comparison of the starting points of sentences, in a block of left-aligned text vs. a block of center-aligned text*

As switching to the next line is the longest break a reader typically takes when going through a block of text, aligning text in this way increases the chance of readers losing their place.

Centered text *can* be used sparingly for small pieces of text like headlines that only cover 1–2 lines without causing problems for users and can even make your page feel more balanced and symmetrical. This is because, at this length, it's easy to scan quickly and doesn't require the repeated line-to-line eye movement that larger pieces of text do.[16] For anything longer though, aligning your text in this way creates a barrier.

Does an email service handle this?

You can handle the alignment of content in most email services, but enforcing it is the job of the person adding the content. It's worth double-checking you've done this.

Line spacing

We also mentioned in Chapter 3 ("Low Vision and Colour Blindness") that having generous spacing between lines of text (also known as line height) can increase the readability of text for all users, but especially for those with low vision and impaired written comprehension. This is an important point to check because the way fonts are displayed may vary between email clients (due to the inconsistent support for custom fonts that we mentioned). The W3C guidelines recommend a line height of 1.5–2 times the size of the text, rather than single line spacing.[17] It's worth noting that this rule is a requirement for AAA compliance (the highest and strictest form of compliance). Although this is best practice, for some text this amount of spacing may seem like overkill. I'd recommend starting with the lowest of that value range (1.5 times the size of text) and then using your best judgment to see how readable the text is. If you're unsure, ask others to read a few paragraphs in that style and see how comfortable they are with it.

Does an email service handle this?

Most templates have a consistent line height set by default, but that doesn't guarantee that it's an *accessible* one. You can check and override this setting for an entire email or on a case-by-case basis in every major email service. Figure 9-3 shows how it looks in SendGrid.

Figure 9-3. *A text editing panel in the email service SendGrid, which includes an option to adjust the line height value of a block of text*

This is more of a "check and make sure" tip.

Use semantic elements

This point is aimed more specifically at developers. You can highlight the most important pieces of text using "semantic" elements such as headers and paragraphs (e.g., <h1> and <p>) just as you do on a website, which helps assistive technologies to understand the hierarchy of your content. It sounds obvious (use the right tags for the right content), but developers are sometimes put off because these tags can render slightly differently between email clients. However, they give your subscribers the option to scan through an email more easily. Screen reader software also puts emphasis on specific headers, which makes navigating emails by headers and sections easier too.[18]

Highlight actions

You can also use styling to ensure that the most important actions in an email are clear. This is especially useful for users with impaired planning and executive function, who often have trouble completing step-by-step tasks.

The email testing program Litmus do this well by consistently applying hover styles to buttons in their emails.[19] What this does is help identify where the primary actions are by providing a visual change when the user hovers over them.

As with most email features, the ability to apply hover styles is inconsistent. Litmus state that they only work in AOL, Apple Mail, Gmail, and Yahoo! Mail.

What's important here though is that adding this feature doesn't negatively affect other users' experiences on clients that don't support it. These other users can still engage with the button, they simply won't see a change in style when they hover over it. This is known as progressive enhancement – you start with the core content and functionality and then add to that with features for services that can support it. The end result is a win for a good chunk of your audience, while everyone else is unaffected. The same idea could apply to other enhancements, such as adding animation or transitions into your email (while being mindful that this movement is not too erratic).

Does an email service handle this?

It's not something you're likely to see an email service offering, largely because it can't be consistently provided for all customers. However, these sites *will* allow you to add your own style rules to your email campaigns using CSS, so you could create a hover style and add it yourself (or get a developer to help you). Here's an example:

```
button:hover {
    background-color: red;
}
```

Testing

Because of the maddening inconsistencies surrounding email, testing
is essential to avoiding rendering issues that you can't take back once
your email has been sent. Litmus, which I mentioned previously in this
section, along with "Email on Acid" and "Mailgun," offer great platforms
to build and test emails. In Figure 9-4, you can see immediately how the
email you've built appears in every major email platform and almost every
widely used device. They are paid services, but they offer free trials to get
you started.

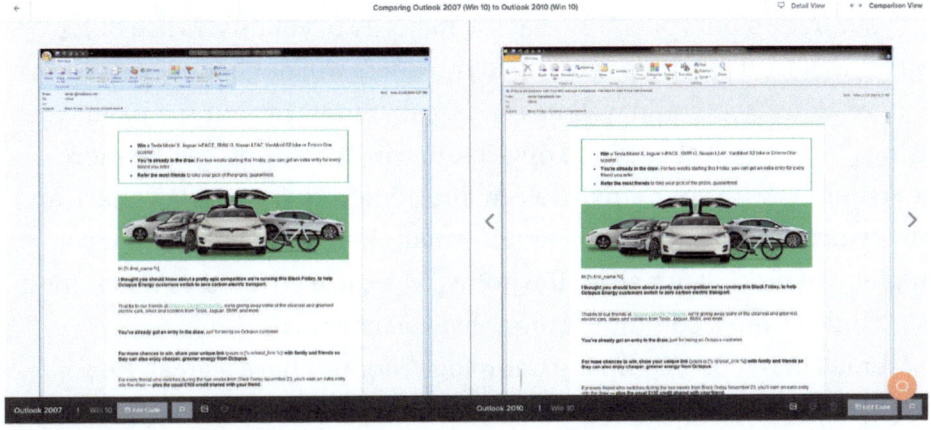

Figure 9-4. *A visual comparison of the same email in Outlook 2007
and Outlook 2010 using Litmus*

Understanding email support

With so many different email clients in circulation, it's really important to understand the percentage of your send list using each email platform. We posed the question in the book's introduction, but it applies here too – why not cut the time you spend trying to support your email on a platform that less than 1% of your recipients use and direct that energy to help all of those who are currently being excluded instead.

> *A lot of people think any email they design and build has to be perfect across all clients, when really, the work to do that is kind of wasted effort.*[20]

Understanding which clients your recipients use allows you to think about which features are functionally safe to build into emails aimed at your audience. For instance, if you want to add a hover style for your button but you know that the majority of your users use older versions of Outlook, then most of your readers will not benefit from that feature. Equally, it could well be the case that most of your recipients are using newer email clients and devices, in which case you can be more adventurous with your email design. Just remember: you must check and understand the drawbacks of certain email clients and ensure that you implement most, if not all, of the points we've just covered so that nobody is excluded from a communication that *you* have sent.

Email marketing company Campaign Monitor have a great, free resource that shows the level of support for CSS features and approaches in all major email clients. As this is always changing, it's an ever-useful tool. You can find it at `www.campaignmonitor.com/csrs/`, but I'll also add it to Chapter 11 ("Tools and QA"). Pairing this up with whatever analytics you use to understand your send list and their platform of choice, you can more accurately work out the type of improvements that you should think about adding to you emails.

Attachments

In many cases, emails can come with attachments – these could be bills, receipts, or even books. PDFs are one of the most common forms of attachment.

PDFs used to be extremely inaccessible but have made significant progress in recent years. That being said there are still huge issues with consistency – PDF accessibility varies depending on a user's operating system, browser, and assistive technology. (In fact, this process is so complicated that WCAG 2.0's guide to creating accessible PDFs is nearly half the size of this entire book.[21]) This can create issues for many users, especially those who use screen readers, or rely on custom browser settings (which PDFs often ignore). This topic is far too broad to discuss here, but with this in mind, where possible, I would recommend putting all information that you would send in PDFs into web pages and sending links to those instead. For the same reasons we talked about displaying emails in a browser as an option, publishing content online as opposed to in documents empowers the user to make the most of their custom tools and setups to interact with the content. You do of course have to be mindful of publishing sensitive, user-specific information on web pages, but in many cases these pages can simply be stored within a user's dashboard that only they can gain access to.

One-click action buttons

We just spoke about highlighting actions within your emails so that users can clearly understand what you're asking them to do. There are ways for you to optimise these actions for all users, without and without accessibility needs, by exposing them before they've even opened your email.

Google have pioneered "one-click action" buttons, which are a great way to reduce the amount of time that users spend interacting with regular emails from you, or emails where the action is clear. With a few lines of code, and verification from Google, you can add a button with a link that's visible right from the inbox of someone using Google mail, rather than forcing the user to open the email, scan (or listen to) the content, and then click the same link (Figure 9-5).

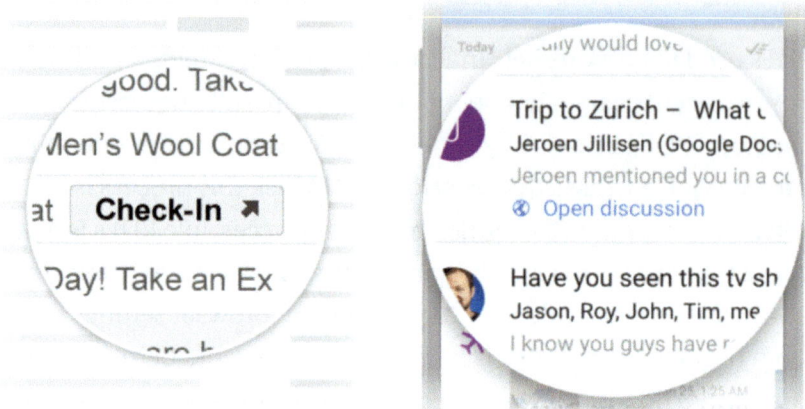

Figure 9-5. *Two examples of how a Google "one-click action" button looks, in both Gmail desktop and their mobile app. The first is a "Check-in" button for a flight confirmation email, and the second is an "Open discussion" button to view a Google doc that the user has been mentioned in*

There are a few different types of action button that Google offers, catering for a broad range of possible actions you may want a user to perform. Here are a few examples:

- Responding to an invitation

- Quickly viewing information for a flight they've booked

- Reviewing a restaurant they've been to recently

- Opening a Google Doc, Sheet, or Slide that's been shared with them

- Performing a single action, pre-defined in the email (i.e., verify your account, reset your password, or provide information in some form)[22]

Although useful for everyone, one-click action buttons have the potential to make a big difference to those with a range of access needs. Firstly, they can make an email-based journey much quicker and clearer for motor-impaired and assistive technology users who often take longer to complete actions. The fact that they don't have to open the email and find the action prevents extra, unnecessary steps. This also acts as a time-saver for users who are in a rush, especially for communications that you send users regularly and ask for the same action every time (e.g., asking for a meter reading as an energy supplier every month).

They also help *many* others: those with heightened sensory awareness, those who are easily overwhelmed by long, busy, pages, and many different users with cognitive impairments, including those who get "lost" in content (e.g., those with visual spatial disorders), people who have trouble focusing (like those with ADHD) or working out their next step (users with executive function and planning disorders), and those who experience difficulties remembering what they have to do next (e.g., as a result of Alzheimer's). Because the action button is always visible when the user views their Google Mail inbox, it also acts as a constant signpost to remind users what the purpose of the email was without reopening it.

Adding an action button

The code needed to add a button is fairly simple, and is similar for all different action types, with only an `itemprop` attribute to distinguish them. Here is an example for a "one-click" action, used to encourage users to submit their monthly meter reading for their energy account:

```
<div itemscope itemtype="https://schema.org/EmailMessage">
    <div itemprop="potentialAction" itemscope
    itemtype="https://schema.org/ViewAction">
        <link itemprop="target" href="meter_reading_link_goes_
        here"/>
```

```
        <meta itemprop="name" content="Submit meter reading"/>
    </div>
    <meta itemprop="description" content="Submit your monthly
    meter reading"/>
</div>
```

This simply requires the type of action you want to display, its name, a quick description, and a link that the button will take the user to when it's clicked. This code goes directly into the source code of an email (which is possible for anyone that uses a service like MailChimp or SendGrid to send their emails, as well as those who build them themselves).

This isn't an approach I would recommend for a one-off campaign email – as there are no "regular" actions – all of the content is new. Furthermore, there may be more than one action in the email, and you wouldn't want them to skip the process of opening the email and viewing the content. However, for emails that are sent regularly, action buttons have been shown to drive high engagement on regular communications. They're also useful in terms of metrics; a user hitting a one-click action button counts as both an open and a click through so it's great for email conversion rates.

Unfortunately, there is no equivalent to action buttons that works on all email clients. However, they do allow you to think about the main purpose of the emails that you send, and if you can distill that into one action for these customers, you can design your content to be just as direct for users that still have to open the email. This could entail promoting the key action(s) to the top of the email (similar to the TL;DRs we have covered).

Note   You will need to register and verify your own button with Google before it will appear. You can find out how to register yours here: `https://developers.google.com/gmail/markup/registering-with-google`

Information on how to test it can be found here:

```
https://developers.google.com/gmail/markup/testing-your-schema
```

I know it's quite annoying to type long web addresses from a book into a browser, so if you search for "Add a Google one-click action button," you should find the above links with relative ease.

No-reply email addresses

It's important to bear in mind that communication generally requires a two-way exchange. If you send an email, text message, or even mail something to your users, they should be able to reply to you with minimal effort.

One of my personal pet-peeves is "no-reply" email addresses (emails sent to users from an address that won't allow them to reply). Businesses use them to exercise a degree of control over how they receive customer communications. Instead of accepting queries from multiple places, such as in response to purchase receipts or reminders, no-reply emails ensure that queries only come through predetermined channels such as a dedicated email address for customer support.

No-reply emails remove the possibility of an immediate response – they're a one-way street. Even if you provide alternative methods of communication within the email (like a different dedicated support email), you still leave users in a position where, should they wish to contact you, they're forced to leave the email (and the conversation) and try to pick it up elsewhere. This can be infuriating because it's likely that their query will be centered on the particular email you sent them.

The following sections explore some other important things to keep in mind if you're currently using, or considering using, a "no-reply" email address.

You're far more likely to find a home in the junk folder

When someone receives an email, providers such as Yahoo! and Gmail will attempt to add the sender's email address to the user's contacts list. This is part of marking you as a trustworthy sender, and emails from someone in a user's contact list typically won't be sent to the "junk" folder. However, this is not possible with a no-reply address. If the user can't reply to your email address, providers are also likely to mark the communication as spam and send any future messages from that sender directly to the "junk" folder without the user ever seeing it.[23] Spam filters have also been known to auto-assign "no-reply" emails into junk folders by default.[24] Sifting through mounds of junk mail for your email is tiring and frustrating, and those who aren't tech literate may not even be aware that they can do this.

You're going to annoy your users

Auto-assign isn't the only way to make it to the "junk" folder. Users have been known to mark emails as spam (rather than going through the process of unsubscribing),[25] in frustration at not being able to respond.[26] This forever categorises all of your future communications, and so any information of value from that address is almost certainly lost.

Moreover, if the user tries to reply and receives an email telling them to get in touch through a different address or channel, they have to decide between going through these extra steps and simply giving up. If they choose the former, any message you receive from them will likely be less positive, thanks to that needlessly complicated journey; and if it's the latter, then you've lost out on some potentially valuable information or feedback.

What's more, if someone sends an email to a no-reply address and you don't have an auto-reply set up, the user may receive a standard "failed to send" email from their email provider. This could convince them that they are doing something wrong or that there's something wrong with their email (e.g., these anxieties can be amplified for users with panic disorders or who experience paranoia). If they don't receive that, they might assume that you chose to ignore the email – further damaging your relationship with them.

It can be useful (from an operational perspective) to restrict email responses to just one avenue, which is why no-reply email address are appealing, but you have to think about how this affects a user. No-reply emails put extra barriers between you and your users and hinder accessible communication. Alternatively, you could use different email addresses for different types of communication (offers, announcements, support, etc.) or send and receive everything from a single inbox and simply manage user expectations by acknowledging their message and letting them know when you'll be able to get back to them.

Good uses of email

We don't often think of email as a social media platform, yet it is. Any communication tool that facilitates two-way communications is, by its very nature, social.[27]

When you choose not to use a "no-reply" email address, you're not just avoiding all of the negative outcomes that we just covered – you're also opening yourself up to a range of positive benefits. Let's go through some of the good that can come from sending emails to customers from an address that they can actually respond to.

You receive more feedback

Having opened yourself up to replies from any communication you send, you might receive more complaints. However, replies could just as easily mention a typo they've spotted, a bug report, or even a healthy dose of praise. Most importantly from an accessibility perspective, users can quickly and easily let you know if they're having trouble, what they're having trouble with, and whether they need any assistance. The two-way communication promotes honesty, trust, and shows that you care what your users have to say, whenever or however they want to say it.

Your email reaches more users

Again, "no-reply" addresses are often marked as spam, so doing away with them improves the percentage of your emails that get successfully delivered. As a result, you have a higher possibility of users interacting with the email that you spent so long creating.

It can promote engagement

Because email is used so frequently, opening up this channel for users can drive engagement. Sites like Airbnb and Gumtree allow you to respond to messages from other users by simply replying to the email notification that you receive from the site, in your email inbox. These sites will then route the message back to the other user. This encourages quicker responses and results in a more active site overall. None of this would be possible with no-reply emails.

We've just discussed the importance of two-way communication, but this doesn't just apply to email – we are now going to look at ensuring that all forms of communication are responsive and accessible in a wider sense. This involves turning our attention to the places where the Web meets the outside world.

Communicating with users directly

Here, we are going to focus less on the content that we design, create, and send out into the world and more on the *way* that we communicate with users directly.

As we mentioned in Chapter 7 ("Mental Health"), customers have different preferences when it comes to communicating with businesses and services, and these vary based on their individual access needs. Accordingly, it is important to provide a range of communication options and not rely on a single channel.

It is therefore vital to establish how a customer prefers to be communicated with. Some users' preferences are obvious. For deaf and hard-of-hearing users this involves making sure that you don't provide a phone number as the only way of getting in touch. Similarly, some motor or visually impaired users might find it easier to talk on the phone than to email.[28] Other users' communication-based needs can be less obvious: three quarters of people who have experienced mental health problems have serious difficulties engaging with at least one common communication channel, but these channels can vary from user to user.[29]

Identifying access needs

When communicating, it is vitally important to be aware of a user's access needs so you can provide them greater support, and make sure that they can complete any necessary actions. Now, it can sometimes be difficult to ask directly about a user's access needs. Some users are perfectly happy to talk to you about their situation, but equally some users choose not to – they may not see it as relevant, may worry about what will be done with the information,[30] or they might simply not like to be seen as vulnerable:

A customer who doesn't think of themselves as vulnerable may be a little embarrassed or even offended if they feel that they are being singled out.[31]

This is a tricky topic that requires real care, but luckily others have already put real time and effort into tackling this challenge. Mental health charity Money and Mental Health use a system called "BRUCE" to help them work out whether a customer might have access needs that require attention.

They accomplish this by observing the user's **b**ehavior and speech and then weighing up whether they have problems with processes such as **r**emembering, **u**nderstanding, **c**ommunicating their thoughts, and **e**valuating different options – BRUCE. There is a lot of reading and many guides on this so I won't go into a lot of detail, but here is a fairly comprehensive list from *Call Centre Helper* magazine that can help you work out what to look out for:

- The customer asks unrelated questions and make irrelevant points.

- The customer constantly repeats themselves.

- The customer says "yes" in response to each of your questions, when it's clear that they haven't kept up with the conversation.

- The customer doesn't talk much and takes a long time to answer your questions.

- The customer becomes distressed during the contact.

- The customer sounds flustered.

- The customer says things like "My partner dealt with all these things for me."

- The customer complains about the way that they (currently) have to communicate.

- The customer makes a passing mention of illness, reference to contact with the health sector, and receipt of benefits.[32]

Even if you cannot identify exactly what users' needs are, you should make sure that you establish their communication preferences and look out for (and address) any specific difficulties they are having.

How to pass on information effectively

After you have established a user's needs, there are some key steps you can take to ensure sure that the *way* you communicate is as accessible as possible. These are all similar to points that we have touched upon elsewhere, but the real beauty here is that these solutions can be applied to all forms of communication and will help all users, regardless of their access needs.

Use plain language

Whether writing emails or letters, using live chat, or even talking on the phone, you can support vulnerable customers by writing and speaking plainly. We covered this in detail in Chapter 6 ("Cognitive Impairments"), so it's best to look there for more information, but plain English involves things like structuring your points and sentences well (with the most important information at the beginning) and avoiding idioms or technical jargon wherever possible.

This will help absolutely everyone, but especially those who face language-based barriers. For example, it will benefit those who experience cognitive impairments or learning difficulties that make comprehending information more difficult. Plain language is also useful to deaf users who do not speak English comfortably and those who do not speak or read English as their first language. Likewise, users with impaired mental health often find communication labor intensive or anxiety-inducing and will therefore be less able to concentrate. For example, to quote a user who took part in some research conducted by Money and Mental Health: "I have to force myself to contact the provider which takes a long time, then I have trouble making myself understood, and because I am panicking I forget what they tell me."[33]

Experiences like this are fairly common and can be amplified by the "communication anxiety" that we covered in Chapter 6 ("Cognitive Impairments"). If a user gets in contact with a company and finds the tone of the conversation to be formal and official, this can make matters even worse for users who experience paranoia and psychosis and more generally for any individual who does not have a lot of self-confidence, or is shy and may feel intimated.[34] Plain English is therefore useful for ensuring these users don't have to expend extra effort to understand confusing (and sometimes intimidating) language.

Set expectations

When communicating directly with a user, you should also let them know how long actions are going to take and what is needed in order to complete them. This is similar to how we dealt with long online journeys (like checkouts or multipage forms).

In Chapter 7 ("Mental Health"), we talked about how breadcrumbs let a user know how far they've come in an online journey, and similarly, you should prepare them by providing the same information via phone, email, or web chat. First, let them know what they'll need in order to complete the next steps (such as bank details or security information). You should then tell users how long the process is going to take, and keep them updated with regard to how far through the process they are. It's also important to clarify understanding throughout and at the end of each important piece of information. This is especially useful for some users with cognitive impairments or mental health issues, who are more likely to say "yes" in response to a question – even when they don't understand.[35]

Finally, just as a good review page lets you know what you've just completed and what comes next, at the end of an exchange via phone, email, or live chat, you should summarise the most important points from the conversation. You should also ask whether anything needs repeating, and ensure that both parties understand what is going to happen next. This is useful for those with issues with planning and executive functioning (who have trouble working things out in a step-by-step manner) or those with ADHD, for example, who might have struggled to pay attention. Finally, you should ensure that you ask if there is anything else that you can help them with. It takes a second to ask, shows that you care about more than simply finishing the interaction, and may well make someone feel comfortable enough to share that they need some extra support.

After communication

Once you've had an interaction with a user, you will have learned about them and their needs. As a result, you should make sure that the user encounters fewer barriers if they ever communicate with you again. You should have a way of saving and recording user's preferences. This could mean that communication with them only happens through a certain channel in the future, or involve setting preferences for them in other areas too. This could involve anything from adjusting colour, a need for higher contrast or reduced motion, an increase or decrease in font size, or whether they prefer their emails in plain text. Every potential takeaway is useful and shows that you're trying to support them long term.

Now, it's also worth noting that communication doesn't always go smoothly. Some users may be upset or confused – they may be getting in touch because they feel they have been excluded. In this case, you may have to de-escalate the situation and be exceptionally sensitive when resolving the issue. There are a plethora of resources out there that help you with these situations and provide more detailed information about communicating with vulnerable customers, and here are some of the best:

Vulnerability Matters podcasts from the Money Advice Trust

This podcast examines from a range of perspectives how firms are supporting consumers in vulnerable situations, such as those with a gambling addiction, suicidal tendencies, and mental health relating to financial services. You can find all the podcasts at `https://mailchi.mp/moneyadvicetrust/vulnerability-podcasts`.

Vulnerability, decision-making, and mental capacity webinar

An online seminar that looked at the importance of identifying customers with mental capacity limitations, and the practical tools and strategies to use to support them. You can watch it at `www.youtube.com/watch?v=hRo6qqsAM4M`.

The University of Bristol's personal finance research center

This research group has created a range of research papers on vulnerability that center around both the challenges and opportunities for supporting users in vulnerable situations. These are all free online and you can view an overview of their research at `www.bristol.ac.uk/geography/research/pfrc/themes/vulnerability/`.

Accessibility champions

If possible, it's good to have a few "accessibility champions" on board who are more experienced in facilitating accessible communication. In the introduction, we mentioned that a project manager is well positioned to help here, because they typically have oversight of an entire project or feature, and are best placed to make sure further issues don't happen in the future. Eventually, it would be good to be in a position where we don't need these champions and everyone is aware of these needs.

Ultimately, finding out where and why users need help can be invaluable for understanding what you're doing right and wrong. We've spoken about some of the pitfalls that can occur when situations aren't handled well, but on the other hand, there is no better feeling than getting it right.

Conclusion

We've now looked at how you can make your communication channels more accessible for your users. We examined the inconsistencies of email and, given our deep dive into these points, you should now be able to decide whether using third-party services instead of building your own emails might better suit your circumstances.

This is an important consideration, as nearly all of the points we covered aren't actually about how emails are built, and more about the content you provide within them. Factors such as content layout, language choice, and even sizing and spacing seem small in isolation, but together they significantly improve the experience of all users who interact with your emails.

Many emails often require a user to act in some form, so I have encouraged you to reflect upon the clarity of your actions and look at whether implementing features like Google's "one-click" action buttons could reduce the stress associated with common email-based tasks.

Of course, many of these actions rely on user's ability to communicate with you too, and hopefully the many arguments I've raised against using "no-reply" email addresses will encourage you to examine how easy it is for your users to get in touch. Whether they choose to do this directly over the phone, through email, or on web chat, you can use the suggestions mentioned in this chapter to pass information to them clearly, set their expectations, and identify any access needs that you may be able to cater for – ensuring that communication will be easier in the future.

Our main aim here is to provide ease of use to the greatest number of people, and I believe this can be achieved by focusing on accessibility instead of trying to support every email client and version that exists. The points we've covered will provide some form of improvement for every user and, as a result, you'll be able to use your time far more effectively.

Notes

1. Campaign Monitor, *The Shocking Truth about How Many Emails Are Sent*, (21/05/2019), <https://www.campaignmonitor.com/blog/email-marketing/2019/05/shocking-truth-about-how-many-emails-sent/> [accessed 01/08/2019].

2. The Radicati Group, *Email Statistics Report: 2015-2019*, (2015), <www.radicati.com/wp/wp-content/uploads/2015/02/Email-Statistics-Report-2015-2019-Executive-Summary.pdf> [accessed 01/08/2019].

3. Jaina Mistry, *The Ultimate Guide to Accessible Emails*, Litmus, (27/02/2017), <https://litmus.com/blog/ultimate-guide-accessible-emails>

4. Litmus Email Analytics, *Email Client Market Share*, (06/2019), <https://emailclientmarketshare.com/> [Accessed 23/07/2019].

5. Lauren Smith, *A Guide to Rendering Differences in Microsoft Outlook Clients*, Litmus, (19/03/2014), <https://litmus.com/blog/a-guide-to-rendering-differences-in-microsoft-outlook-clients> [accessed 01/08/2019].

6. Ros Hodgekiss, *Do Forms Work in HTML Emails?,* Campaign Monitor, (07/11/2007), <www.campaignmonitor.com/blog/email-marketing/2007/11/how-forms-perform-in-html-emai/> [accessed 01/08/2019].

7. Email on Acid, *A How-To Guide on Embedding HTML5 Video in Email,* (24/08/2018), <www.emailonacid.com/blog/article/email-development/a_how_to_guide_to_embedding_html5_video_in_email/> [accessed 01/08/2019].

8. Campaign Monitor, *The Ultimate Guide to CSS,* (14/11/2017), <www.campaignmonitor.com/css/> [accessed 01/08/2019].

9. Campaign Monitor, *Accessibility and Email Campaigns,* (2019), <www.campaignmonitor.com/resources/guides/accessibility/> [accessed 01/08/2019].

10. Mailchimp, *Add a Campaign Page Link to Your Email Campaign,* (2019), <https://mailchimp.com/help/add-a-campaign-page-link-to-your-email-campaign/> [accessed 01/08/2019].

11. Campaign Monitor, *HTML vs. Plain Text Emails: Everything You Need to Know,* (05/05/2019), <www.campaignmonitor.com/blog/email-marketing/2019/03/html-vs-plain-text-emails-everything-you-need-to-know/> [accessed 01/08/2019].

12. Sendgrid, *HTML Formatting Issues*, (2019), <https://sendgrid.com/docs/ui/sending-email/formatting-html/> [accessed 01/08/2019].

13. Gary Eckstein, *Image spam and how it affects your email campaigns*, (25/07/2017), <https://organicweb.com.au/marketing/image-spam/> [accessed 01/08/2019].

14. Gmail, and Today's Popular Email Clients, Campaign Monitor, (2018), <www.campaignmonitor.com/resources/guides/most-popular-email-clients/> [accessed 01/08/2019].

15. Mailchimp, *Translate Content in a Campaign*, (2019), <https://mailchimp.com/help/translate-content-in-a-campaign/> [accessed 01/08/2019].

16. Anthony Thomas, *Why You Should Never Center Align Paragraph Text*, UX Movement, (19/01/2011), <https://uxmovement.com/content/why-you-should-never-center-align-paragraph-text/> [accessed 01/08/2019].

17. W3C, *Specifying line spacing in CSS*, (2016), <www.w3.org/TR/WCAG20-TECHS/C21.html> [accessed 01/08/2019].

18. Alice Li, *Accessibility in Email Marketing: 7 Simple Tricks to Make Your Code More Accessible*, Litmus, (16/04/2019), <https://litmus.com/blog/7-simple-tricks-to-make-your-email-code-more-accessible?utm_campaign=newsletter&utm_source=email&utm_medium=marketing&utm_content=comm> [accessed 01/08/2019].

19. Alice LI, *Accessibility in Email Marketing: 7 Simple Tricks to Make Your Code More Accessible*, Litmus, (16/04/2019), <https:// litmus.com/blog/7-simple-tricks-to-make-your-email-code-more-accessible?utm_ campaign=newsletter&utm_source=email&utm_ medium=marketing&utm_content=comm> [accessed 01/08/2019].

20. Emily Ryan, *Why Clients Render Email Differently*, (30/09/2016), <https://mailchimp.com/ resources/why-clients-render-email-differently/> [accessed 01/08/2019].

21. W3C, *PDF Techniques for WCAG 2.0*, (2012) <www. w3.org/TR/WCAG20-TECHS/pdf#pdf_notes> [accessed 01/08/2019].

22. Gmail, *What Are Actions?*, (23/04/2019), <https:// developers.google.com/gmail/markup/actions/ actions-overview> [accessed 01/08/2019].

23. Carly Brandtz, *Do Not Reply Email Best Practices*, SendGrid, (08/08/2018), <https://sendgrid.com/ blog/why-you-should-not-use-noreplydomain-com-in-your-emails/> [accessed 01/08/2019].

24. Chris Arrendale, *The NoReply Dilemma: Best Practices For Your Email Strategy*, Mailjet, (07/06/2018), <https://www.mailjet.com/blog/ news/the-noreply-dilemma-going-from-no-to-yes/> [accessed 01/08/2019].

25. Chris Arrendale, *The NoReply Dilemma: Best Practices For Your Email Strategy*, (07/06/2018), <https://www.mailjet.com/blog/news/the-noreply-dilemma-going-from-no-to-yes/> [accessed 01/08/2019].

26. *Raelene Morey, Never Use a "No-Reply" Email Address (and What to Do Instead)*, MailPoet, (31/01/2019), <https://www.mailpoet.com/blog/never-use-not-reply-email-address/> [accessed 01/08/2019].

27. Carly Brandtz, *Do Not Reply Email Best Practices*, SendGrid, (08/08/2018), <https://sendgrid.com/blog/why-you-should-not-use-noreplydomain-com-in-your-emails/> [accessed 01/08/2019].

28. Merlyn Holkar and Katie Evans, *Levelling the Playing Field, Money and Mental Health*, (2017) <www.moneyandmentalhealth.org/wp-content/uploads/2017/12/Levelling-the-playing-field-Regulators-report.pdf> [accessed 05/07/2019].

29. Merlyn Holkar, Katie Evans and Kate Langston, *Access Essentials, Money and Mental Health*, (04/07/2018), <www.moneyandmentalhealth.org/wp-content/uploads/2018/06/Money-and-Mental-Health-Access-Essentials-report.pdf> [accessed 01/08/2019].

30. Jamie Evans, Chris Fitch, Sharon Collard, *Vulnerability: the experience of debt advisers*, Money and Mental Health, (11/2018), <https://www.moneyandmentalhealth.org/wp-content/uploads/2018/11/Vulnerability-the-experience-of-debt-advisers.pdf> [accessed 01/08/2019].

31. Callcentrehelper, *Dealing With Vulnerable Customers*, (16/01/2019), <https://www.callcentrehelper.com/dealing-vulnerable-customers-135486.htm> [accessed 01/08/2019].

32. Callcentrehelper, *Dealing With Vulnerable Customers*, (16/01/2019), <www.callcentrehelper.com/dealing-vulnerable-customers-135486.htm> [accessed 01/08/2019].

33. Merlyn Holkar, Katie Evans and Kate Langston, *Access Essentials, Money and Mental Health*, (04/07/2018), <www.moneyandmentalhealth.org/wp-content/uploads/2018/06/Money-and-Mental-Health-Access-Essentials-report.pdf> [accessed 01/08/2019].

34. Mind, *About Paranoia*, (2013), <www.mind.org.uk/information-support/types-of-mental-health-problems/paranoia/about-paranoia/?o=6292#.XRD1WYhKg2w> [accessed 01/08/2019].

35. Callcentrehelper, *Dealing With Vulnerable Customers*, (16/01/2019), <www.callcentrehelper.com/dealing-vulnerable-customers-135486.htm> [accessed 01/08/2019].

CHAPTER 10

New Technologies

Technologies with the potential to make the Web a more inclusive place are constantly being created. Many of these developments can be considered "assistive technologies." These are tools – from machines to pieces of software – that help people with a wide range of impairments (and resulting access needs) overcome barriers in their lives.

Now of course, not all technology has to be designed to solve one specific problem, nor do they have to help everyone in the same way. Think about automatic doors for example: they might help people with motor impairments or those speaking sign language who do not want to stop their conversations to open the door, but they are also equally useful for anybody who has their hands full. Here, the same technology helps different people for different reasons. This is an example of "universal design" at work. This concept aims to ensure that everything we make can be "accessed, understood and used to the greatest extent possible by all people regardless of their age, size, ability or disability."[1]

With this in mind, in this chapter we'll be looking at new technologies, from those already in the marketplace to those that are still being developed and the (sometimes unexpected) ways in which they can empower users who have previously been excluded. Many of these technologies aren't strictly confined to the Web, but extend it, or have the potential to change the way that people interact with it. For example, as the number of "smart devices" in our homes continues to rise, we'll start by looking at voice assistants – understanding how they work, how they

© Ashley Firth 2019
A. Firth, *Practical Web Inclusion and Accessibility*,
https://doi.org/10.1007/978-1-4842-5452-3_10

are already improving the lives of those with disabilities, and some of the unique applications people have invented to leverage that technology. We'll then look at some other devices that are being used to level the playing field in the name of accessibility – making interaction with the world of gaming, apps, and entertainment more inclusive too.

Now, "new" tech isn't necessary always on the cutting edge. It doesn't always manifest itself as a shiny new device – sometimes a technological breakthrough can happen when old tech is used in a new way. For example, natural language processing (NLP) has been around for decades but has recently been applied in a whole host of exciting new ways. We'll focus on how this technology can assist users, even when they don't have an Internet connection – thereby allowing those that are offline and disconnected from tech to still benefit from recent developments.

Finally, we'll look to the future, into the world of artificial intelligence. With a multitude of imaginative applications for AI being brought to market, we'll examine a range of interesting new devices and software that have the potential to solve a whole host of accessibility issues.

Smart devices

Over the past few years, a new wave of "smart" products have appeared on the market. These technologies use the Web to provide greater connectivity between the devices in our lives and encompass everything from virtual assistants to appliances that can be controlled remotely.

There's an ease of use that comes from integrating all these devices in a way that allows for consistent control. Consequently, smart devices are becoming extremely popular. According to Statista, 17.5 billion are currently in use.[2] As a result, great strides have also been made regarding what you can achieve with smart devices, and this has created a massive potential to empower users with disabilities.

This is because, at their core, smart devices offer many new ways to engage with information – at a time when a lack of viable channels still excludes many potential web users. For instance, we've spoken previously about the immense power of screen readers and the doors they've been able to open for blind users, but they're still currently the only real way these users can interact with the Web. Meanwhile, not every blind customer has access to a screen reader or knows how to use one. Here, a voice-controlled smart device can offer an alternative, more intuitive way of engaging. What's really exciting is that smart devices have the potential to open up new channels for users with a vast array of different access needs.

So far, this book has focused largely on the nuances and challenges of catering for these users on the Web itself. However, here, I'd like to explore the potential for smart devices to both extend the progress we've made on our websites and to allow users to interact with the Web in new ways. Let's start by discussing the merits of one of the biggest and most popular pieces of smart technology in recent years: voice assistants.

Voice assistants

Whilst these in-built AI agents are hard at work making life easier for all smartphone users, the disabled community is benefitting from the escalating efforts of the tech giants more than any other.[3]

—Robin Christoperson, Founding member of AbilityNet

The introduction of voice assistant software – like Amazon Alexa, Apple's Siri, and Google Assistant – has meant that assistive technologies have effectively gone mainstream (Figure 10-1). According to industry tracker Voicebot.ai, voice assistant users rose to 66.4 million in the United States alone in 2018, a 40% increase from 2017.[4] In fact, research firm Juniper predicts that voice assistants will be used in 275 million homes worldwide by 2023.[5] They are already built into every major mobile device, and also live in homes as standalone devices, ready to provide anything from music to weather and news information. You do this by saying a predefined "wake" word (e.g., "Alexa," "Siri," or "Ok, Google") and then tell the voice assistant what you'd like it to do.

Figure 10-1. *A picture of four voice-activated virtual assistant devices. (Left to right) Alexa in Amazon Echo and Echo Dot, Siri in Apple HomePod, Google Assistant in Google Home, and Cortana in the Harman Kardon Invoke*

How do they understand us?

> *The complexity and diversity of human language is so vast that even humans themselves cannot comprehend it all. Given this, modern machines and computer systems are tasked with the labor of understanding text and speech while interpreting it and making sense of intent.*[6]

Voice assistants are able to understand voice commands through a technology called natural language processing (NLP). Now, this isn't exactly a new technology. It's development dates back to the 1950s, when the Georgetown–IBM experiment used machine translation to automatically translate over 60 Russian sentences into English.[7] This was the first stepping-stone toward NLP; however, it's only really been applied to web applications in the last few years.

Combining expertise from computer science, machine learning, and linguistics (with roots in artificial intelligence), NLP is capable of "understanding" words, interpreting them, and then acting upon them in real time. For example, every time you say a "wake" word to an in-home device or smartphone, natural language processing is being used in this way. Equally, the same technology is applied when you type a question to a chatbot and it understands what you're asking. This technology allows "computers to communicate with humans in their own language by pulling meaningful data from loosely-structured text or speech."[8] This can improve customer service by allowing customers to speak to bots more naturally, rather than offering them predefined choices.

How do smart devices help accessibility?

Although the various applications of this technology are clear, it's perhaps not quite as clear how these current uses can benefit those with a range of disabilities. Let's run through some of the main reasons why NLP is capable of helping users overcome their access needs.

They don't require sight

This is one of the most obvious benefits – issuing commands and receiving information through voice alone removes a lot of barriers for those with blindness and low vision. The Royal National Institute of Blind People (RNIB) has written about the benefit of devices like this, calling them an "enormous benefit to many people – in particular, people who have a vision impairment."[9] In fact Ellie Southwood, the chair of the RNIB, said the following about her Amazon Echo dot at the AI and Disability conference TechShare Pro:

> *The Echo Dot makes me feel included...I spend far less time searching for things online; I can multitask while online and be more productive.*[10]

They don't require lots of extra equipment

"Remember when you had to buy a computer for £500, then pay another £600 for special software?" This was said by Robin Spinks, senior strategy manager at RNIB Solutions – an arm of the RNIB that advises technology companies about accessibility. Although the Internet previously required third-party software or custom setups to enable access, voice assistants are now built in. Technology like this sets a great precedent, both technically and financially: "You fundamentally change the economics by building accessibility in."[11]

They avoid potentially complex and damaging experiences

You don't have to visit news sites with endless modals and popups, nor do you risk being asked to join a site's mailing list 12 times over. You simply ask a voice assistant a question and receive the answer. One potential downside that's worth considering though, is that this can limit or impact the quality of the information that they receive:

> The Echo uses Google or another search engine to source the answer and often, the first few results are bought by companies who pay to have their websites displayed at the top of the results page. In reality, expensive goods or services or "fake news" may be relayed at the top, thus relayed to the Echo user as fact or as the best commercial option available and users may not ask hear the second or third result from Google to compare it to.[12]

However, for simple, fact-based questions such as "What is the time?" and "How much is £100 in dollars?" this is not much of an issue.

They don't require a physical input to retrieve information

This is great for those with motor disabilities, or cognitive impairments that affect coordination. Like many accessible features we've mentioned, this will benefit all users: studies have suggested that 55% of people use digital voice assistants because it allows them to keep their hands free.[13]

These capabilities could well remove the need for physical input in other aspects of a user's life in the future as well. One user has even adapted an Amazon echo (along with a small computer called a Raspberry Pi) to move a wheelchair purely through voice commands.[14]

They combat low tech literacy

You now don't need to understand how to use a computer in order to receive information, or how to navigate Spotify to play a song. Therefore, anyone who struggles with technology will benefit. Someone can now say to a device in their home, "Play me some country music," and that's all there is to it (why they'd ask it to do that is beyond me, but each to their own).

They allow users to focus on speech alone

The fact that users communicate with voice assistants through speech alone can help those that have trouble handling the other aspects involved in typical interpersonal communication (e.g., social cues or body language).

For this reason, smart devices can be useful to those with certain cognitive impairments, like autism. Users with autism often struggle with the wider social aspects of communication but can find it much easier to communicate with voice assistants. This is because, "They don't have to contend with trying to understand nuanced body language, facial expressions, moods or the million-and-one other things that can be happening every time we talk to someone."[15] Some users with autism have even been able to form in-depth relationships with applications like Siri. American writer Judith Newman documented her son's in-depth experience with Siri for the New York Times back in 2014, explaining how it helped him to satisfy his constant curiosity about any subject, and even improve his communication with other people:

> *For most of us, Siri is merely a momentary diversion. But for some, it's more. My son's practice conversation with Siri is translating into more facility with actual humans. Yesterday I had the longest conversation with him that I've ever had. Admittedly, it was about different species of turtles and whether I preferred the red-eared slider to the diamond-backed terrapin. This might not have been my choice of topic, but it was back and forth, and it followed a logical trajectory. I can promise you that for most of my beautiful son's 13 years of existence, that has not been the case.*[16]

How much can you interact with the Web on them?

Considering how liberating devices like these can be already, the more feature-rich they become, the more useful they stand to be. Luckily companies are always expanding the capabilities of this technology. At the time of writing, there are more than 80,000 Alexa "skills" available to install – you can even do this through Alexa itself if you know the name of the skill you want. These allow you to extend the functionality of Alexa to perform more complicated actions than asking simple questions. Whenever someone uses a skill, Alexa will retrieve information from the company or developer's tech through the Internet. This is a bit of extra effort to set up, but if you decide to go the extra mile and build your own Alexa product, you will have given your users another new and extremely accessible way to retrieve information and complete actions.[17]

Anyone can make a skill for Alexa and Google Assistant, so the degree to which you can allow your users to retrieve information, perform actions, and add to the feature set of these devices more generally, is entirely up to you. There are whole books on how to do it, but the following sections showcase just a few of the many possibilities that are already available.

Read your email

Google and Microsoft email accounts now allow Alexa to read your email for you, as well as delete or reply to one through voice commands.[18] This means that users can avoid a web interface altogether for one of the most commonly used functions on the Web.

Control your home

There are now a plethora of smart products that aim to create a "connected home." These range from adaptors to turn on appliances manually, to smart-enabled light bulbs, radiators, kettles, and many more. At the time of writing, over 28,000 devices on the market are "Alexa compatible."[19]

Of course, this functionality requires the purchase of smart-enabled devices but, once installed, these can help those who may have trouble interacting with standard devices and appliances physically due to a disability and allows them to do so in an intuitive, consistent way. For example, if someone is already used to asking Google Assistant a question, or to play a song, then it requires no extra effort to ask it to turn the lights off.

Monitor your health

There are also some other interesting devices being made with built-in voice assistants. A company called TruSense have developed an Alexa-powered Personal Emergency Response pendant that will allow those in need of care to be monitored remotely:

> *Customized alerts can notify caretakers when the wearer has arrived at frequently visited locations or has travelled outside a defined safe zone. The GPS Smart Pendant also has a two-way help button and can identify when a potential fall has occurred, triggering a notification to family members and the 24/7 emergency response center.*[20]

It's not just third-party devices either – Siri is available in the Apple Watch, and the newest version is capable of generating a medical-quality ECG, as well as detecting when the user has fallen over and may be in need of help.[21] Meanwhile, assistance can also be as simple as regularly reminding those with memory issues to complete tasks or take medication. Whatever the type of assistance, these technologies protect those in need, but in a way that allows them to live a more independent life.

Perform conditional actions

Because voice assistants can hook up to various sets of data, they can perform an action when certain criteria are met. For example, a skill can take in information about the weather and inform the user of when it is about to rain, or turn on a fan when it gets too hot. Creating conditional actions is something I've been working on myself recently with Octopus Energy. We created a tariff that changes price every half an hour to reflect the cost of energy at the time and let people play with the data for it at a hack day. One of the results was a voice assistant that told appliances like washing machines to run when it was cheapest to do so, or when it created the smallest carbon footprint.[22]

Disability-driven design

Although some smart devices are able to cater for users both with and without disabilities, there are some areas of tech where people with certain access needs require a little more attention. Two good examples are smartphones and gaming, which still cause particular issues for those who can't physically hold a device. As we've previously mentioned, being able to tilt or rotate a device can be impossible if it is mounted to a wheelchair, and the acts of tapping and scrolling become barriers for users who experience tremors or have had amputations. There have been two particularly amazing advancements in this area. I would still consider these "smart" devices, but they are smart in a slightly different way.

Sesame smartphone

Sesame is the world's first completely touch-free smartphone, designed by and for people with disabilities.[23] Its core navigation technique is a camera that can track users' head movements, however subtle, to carry out tasks. This makes almost every aspect of using a smartphone possible for many motor-impaired users, and Sesame provides much easier access to applications than existing switch devices. They recommend it for any user with access needs that involve a loss of mobility in their hands and/or fingers – ranging from cerebral palsy and ALS to those who have experienced strokes or amputations.[24]

Importantly, it's also affordable – the full kit costs roughly the same price as an iPhone. The app itself has won numerous awards and has fostered an active community, full of people with heartwarming stories about how this technology has changed their lives.

Microsoft adaptive controller

According to research for the Entertainment Software Association, over 166 million adults in the United States play video games, and three-quarters of all Americans have at least one gamer in their household.[25] In the United Kingdom, the number is smaller, yet still staggering, coming in at 37.3 million.[26] Although not considered "essential" for daily life, playing games can provide a great source of entertainment. They also allow you to connect socially with other people through online gameplay, and gaming has even been found to help combat depression and other mental health problems.[27] For all of these reasons and more, helping previously excluded users play games can be massively important. Microsoft have recently tried to make that as easy and affordable as possible.

Released in 2018, Microsoft's adaptive controller (shown in Figure 10-2) is their way of trying to make gaming accessible and inclusive, primarily for those with limited mobility. It was built alongside charities such as the AbleGamers Foundation, Cerebral Palsy Foundation and SpecialEffect, along with many members of their community.[28]

Figure 10-2. *A picture of Microsoft's adaptive controller*

It can be used with Microsoft's Xbox console and their Windows computers (for PC gamers). It can complete all of the same actions as their standard Xbox controller, but with a large surface area to make actions easier. Most importantly though, a user can connect any assistive devices that they already use, such as buttons, switches, joysticks, and others using standard USB or 3.5mm connectors. The device can be easily mounted to a wheelchair or any other setup, can be customised to alter which inputs correspond to which actions, and can work alongside standard controllers so users can play with friends. Importantly, its retail price is also only slightly higher than that of their standard controllers. Microsoft launched their "inclusive design" movement many years ago, with the aim of making their products as accessible as possible, and this controller will open up the world of gaming to many people in the future.

Hopefully devices like this could soon hold the potential to benefit those using the Web. For example, the adaptive controller could provide a model to improve devices like single switches or head wands that are still very time consuming to use.

In my opinion, the "smart device" industry is a mainstream extension of what is, most importantly, an assistive technology industry. You can save time in a hurry with voice assistants, smart lights, and smart locks, but they also make actions possible for those who were previously unable to carry them out – and in the process, provide new, accessible ways to interact with the Web. As forms of entertainment like gaming become more and more mainstream, harnessing technology to create accessible devices can make those activities more inclusive too.

Microsoft's motto for their adaptive controller is "When everyone plays, we all win," and I couldn't have said it better myself.

Support for offline customers

The smart devices we covered earlier do have one drawback. Fundamentally, all voice assistants require an Internet connection to function properly.

In 2016, the UN published a nonbinding resolution that condemns the removal of someone's Internet access as a human rights violation.[29] However, many people have still never been online in the first place. The Office for National Statistics (ONS) reported in 2018 that 5.3 million people in the United Kingdom have either never been online or have not used the Internet in the last three months.[30] Of that figure, 79% were aged 65 or over, and 23.3% had a disability. I've spoken to many customers that don't have Internet access, and reasons include a lack of interest, confidence, understanding, or capacity. Therefore, we have to consider the inability to reach your website (or Alexa skill or chatbot) to retrieve information as a barrier.

Since the ONS's last report in 2011, the amount of people that had never been online shrank from 8.7 million, so the numbers are improving, but it does still leave many (and arguably those who would benefit most) in a position where their means of retrieving support or information are limited.

You'd be forgiven for thinking that our hands are tied when we reach this point, but all is not lost – again, we simply have to shift our focus to a different medium.

Telephony software

The telephone and the Internet have long been intertwined – one of the first forms of Internet access required a direct link to a phone line (known as dial-up Internet). It's funny to think that one of the Web's first forms leveraged telephone technology, because recently, there have been great developments in telephone technology that leverages the Internet.

Twilio (`www.twilio.com/`) is a great example of a company that applies Internet smarts to telephony software. Twilio lets you make, manage, and route calls to a browser, an app, your phone, or anywhere else you can take a call. You can create a team of customer service agents who can communicate with users without a phone line in site.

When a user rings a number run by Twilio (no different to any other number), it hooks up to a web application that routes the call through the Internet and the user is completely unaware of this; they can have a normal phone conversation without ever knowing that it's happening through the Web. This platform also enables companies to write code that will perform actions such as sending a text message when certain things happen, such as their parcel being dispatched.

This technology provides immense integration with websites and web applications and importantly, doesn't require the user to have an Internet connection. Here are a few ways that a system like Twilio can improve a customer's telephone experience (regardless of their access needs):

- Twilio can route a call from the nearest data center in the world to the user, providing better call quality than a regular phone.

- You can write simple code to route calls to (and between) teams instantly, based on the type of query the user has.

- You can quickly change and add phone numbers without any change to your code, and scale it far more rapidly – anyone with a laptop and a headset can use it in the way they would use any other website.

- A Twilio application can recognise the phone number that is calling and load account-specific information about the user associated with that number, so customer service have that information on hand by the time they've answered the call.

- You can cater content to a user based on the information you have associated with their phone number. For example, at Octopus Energy, if we recognise the number of someone calling in, we actually play them the most popular song from when they were 14 years old (according to scientific research, this is when we first begin to properly form our "musical identity").[31]

These are just a few examples of internet-based telephony software's many potential applications. In terms of access needs, it helps enhance the phone – ensuring that, as a communication channel, it's as robust as it can be. This, of course, helps blind users to receive information in a nonvisual format and those with written comprehension issues to quickly get in touch and speak to someone if they don't understand something that has been sent to them. Moreover, actions like loading customer information as they ring you will reduce average call lengths and, as a result, wait times. This helps manage any potential phone anxiety by limiting the length of the experience. It also removes the need to retrieve as much information from the user (phone number, address, etc.) which helps those who have trouble communicating or retaining information. Even the idea of playing a song from when the user was 14 can create a pleasant element of unexpected nostalgia and can prevent the anxiety that other types of hold music (such as repeating melodies) can cause:

Short, repeating melodies or messages will drive anyone crazy; you anticipate that a message or small piece of music is going to repeat over and over—and it does. This is highly likely to produce anxiety for the caller, resulting in 'wearout.'[32]

These advancements are useful; however, they do require a representative from your organisation to be at the other end of the phone to answer. This raises two large issues for those who are both offline and have certain access needs. Firstly, regardless of the impressive technology behind it, many people, such as those with communication anxiety or certain cognitive impairments, don't like using the phone. Secondly, phone lines can't run every hour of every day – people need a rest! This is an issue because many people with mental health issues (such as depression) often have disrupted sleep patterns, and so may have trouble getting in touch during normal office hours:

For me sleep problems are a tell-tale sign of declining mental health. The worse I sleep, the less I feel able to cope during the day. The less I am coping, the worse I seem to sleep.[33]

Then there's also the issue of catering for users that need to get in contact frequently, and handling any resulting stigma they might feel as a result – especially if calling you is the only way they can contact you and retrieve information. Those with learning difficulties or problems with short-term memory may also have trouble here, due to problems retaining the information you provide them. This is a challenge I've been trying to solve recently. I was in touch with a customer who has no vision, no computer with assistive technology, no Internet access, and no smartphone. Her only method of contacting us was by telephone. Her main concern was not that she was disconnected but that she didn't want to be treated as a vulnerable customer. Equally, she expressed that she didn't want to "waste" our customer support team's time by phoning constantly.

But what if we could allow users to call in at all hours, prevent them from feeling like they're being a nuisance, and still help them? After all, chatbots can run 24/7. This is where natural language processing (NLP) might once again be able to help.

Natural language processing

We touched upon natural language processing earlier in the chapter, regarding its use in smart voice assistants, but it's also increasingly being used for telephone support. This technology builds upon previous IVR (interactive voice response) applications, which listen to verbal requests and commands over the phone to guide people to the correct customer service department. Several such technologies are being developed by companies like Zendesk and Twilio, and the latter has a new piece of technology, currently in beta (the stage before full release) called Autopilot. The aim is to leverage the power of both natural language processing and chatbots to create a technology that can not only hold a conversation with a user but retain what they have said and provide information specific to them.

Continuing to use Twilio as an example, you could use Autopilot to recognise the number of the customer calling and then use natural language processing to interpret questions that they would normally only ask a human. In the case of an energy company, for example, this could include questions like "When will my next payment be taken?" "What tariff am I on?" and "How much am I paying each month?" Each one of these questions is classed as an action, and the number of these that you can create is limited only by your imagination.

What's even more exciting here is that, hypothetically, NLP-based telephony software could be used to do more than simply return information:

With Autopilot actions, your virtual assistants can say something to the user, show something to the user if the device has a visual display, remember something for context, collect data, or redirect so you can control the flow of your dialogue.[34]

It can also help users perform or initiate actions in the same way as smart devices allow you to do, such as submitting information you've asked them to provide, requesting actions be taken on their behalf, or choosing a good time for you to call them back in person. Twilio themselves advertise that you can use the same set of prompts and actions you've set up for your telephony software in a chatbot, or an Alexa skill, for example.

Fallbacks

Autopilot breaks conversations down into digestible pieces to support natural conversations. Take action automatically based on input and handoff interactions to agents while maintaining conversational context.[35]

When I say that actions are limited by imagination, that does imply a limit. However, here, hitting that limit needn't result in a dead end for the user. If they happen to ask a question that the technology isn't set up to answer, integration with Twilio's regular telephony software allows software like Autopilot to transfer users to an available customer service agent. For companies that are often burdened with large numbers of calls and long wait times leading to customer dissatisfaction, this offers the opportunity for users to potentially self-serve while they wait and resolve their query before even reaching the top of the queue. If they are able to solve their query before this happens, then they feel empowered, and if they don't, then a customer service expert can then help them.

Impact on accessibility

This technology is another awesome example of accessibility impacting everyone for the better. This is largely because software like Autopilot can provide a similar level of support for those offline that those online currently enjoy. This logic has been reflected in the recent rise in popularity for chatbots. Notably, talking to an automated bot has also been known to help those with a range of needs, such as those with communication anxiety, who need a variety of communication channels, and users with attention deficit or learning difficulties who may need to ask the same question multiple times.

There are three main reasons why chatbots have become so common. The 2018 "State of Chatbots" report listed those benefits as 24-hour service (64%), instant responses to enquiries (55%), and answers to simple questions (55%).[36] It's worth noting, given what we've covered, that all of these benefits are also available through telephony software – without the user needing an Internet connection:

- **24-hour service**: There is no reason that Autopilot couldn't run 24/7. Users can try and self-serve while waiting in a queue during office hours but also use it as a first port of call outside of those hours.

- **Instant responses to enquiries**: If a user's query matches a prompt, then the subsequent action will occur instantly – be that returning information from, or initiating an action on, the customer's account.

- **Answers to simple questions**: You can build predefined responses to as many questions as you'd like, perhaps based on the most common queries you typically receive. This can always be added to and will naturally grow, becoming smarter and more accurate over time.

This means that customers with a wide range of access needs can now retrieve unique, account-specific information without access to the Internet: blind and low-vision customers can receive information without reading braille or using assistive technologies, users with motor disabilities can receive information using their voice, and those on the autism spectrum or with anxiety can receive information without the potentially daunting prospect of talking to another person.

Finally, it is also worth noting that for returning customer-specific information, security is a reasonable concern. In this case, a PIN or security question could be added as a form of authentication (again, this can also be spoken and interpreted by Autopilot).

We've now looked at some of the newer technologies that have reached the marketplace and gained mainstream popularity, and in the process improved accessibility for those with a wide range of access needs. Now let's turn to an emerging technology that has influenced the development of NLP and smart devices more widely, and has the potential to revolutionise several areas of accessibility: artificial intelligence.

Artificial Intelligence

The term artificial intelligence (AI) has become virtually synonymous with the idea of new and emerging technology, and yet, if you ask people what is actually is, you'd be hard-pressed to get a clear answer – it's usually much easier to describe the sort of things that AI can do. Here are two of the most succinct definitions I've found:

> *The theory and development of computer systems able to perform tasks normally requiring human intelligence, such as visual perception, speech recognition, decision-making, and translation between languages.*[37]

the term "artificial intelligence" is often used to describe machines (or computers) that mimic "cognitive" functions that humans associate with the human mind, such as "learning" and "problem solving.[38]

It's probably best to emphasise the word "mimic" in the last quote and not get too distracted by the word "intelligence." Outside of science fiction, it is currently much more realistic to think of AI as a set of sophisticated tools as opposed to nearly conscious robots. As a tool, AI has countless possible applications and use cases, and the tech industry is currently riding a wave of breakthroughs – 78% of brands have already, or are planning to, implement some form of AI by 2020.[39] Many of these approaches are capable of opening new avenues for companies and users that were previously considered impossible. However, we're only interested in one area in this book! So, let's look at some advancements that artificial intelligence is making in the world of accessibility.

Providing automatic video captioning

As we mentioned in "Deafness and Hard of Hearing" (Chapter 5), YouTube has been developing speech-recognition technology, using machine-learning algorithms to automatically generate captions for its videos.[40] They have stated that "the quality of the captions may vary" at this point but, as with any machine learning, the longer it is running, the smarter it'll get. Importantly, as mentioned, any generated captions can easily be edited by the person that uploaded the video should they contain any incorrectly translated speech. This also improves the system's accuracy for future captions, as it helps the AI to understand where it went wrong. This technology holds the potential to provide nearly immediate accessibility for one of the most popular websites, and mediums, on the Internet – helping those who are deaf, have hearing loss, or encounter a language barrier engage with content freely, and eventually, without having to wait for captions to be added or edited manually.

A recent update to Microsoft PowerPoint added AI-generated captions, so that while you are giving a presentation, PowerPoint transcribes the words you say and displays them on-screen as captions for your audience. It can also translate those words into another language, all in real time. When they released this update, Microsoft specifically mentioned that this use of AI in their software "can help accommodate individuals in the audience who may be deaf or hard of hearing, or more familiar with another language."[41]

Google's DeepMind division has also been using AI to generate closed captions based on lip reading. In a 2016 joint study with the University of Oxford, DeepMind's algorithm watched over 5,000 hours of television and analysed 17,500 unique words. It then went head-to-head with a professional lip reader over 200 random video clips and won clearly – achieving 46.8% of translated words without error, compared to the lip reader's 12.4%.[42]

Providing human-level language translation

In April 2018, Microsoft announced its free translator app, where audio is translated into other languages and into text for captions. It showed for the first time "a Machine Translation system that could perform as well as human translators (in a specific scenario – Chinese-English news translation)."[43] This was a major breakthrough and, in the year since, they've managed to make huge strides in the system's ability to provide accurate translations for other languages (shown in Figure 10-3).[44]

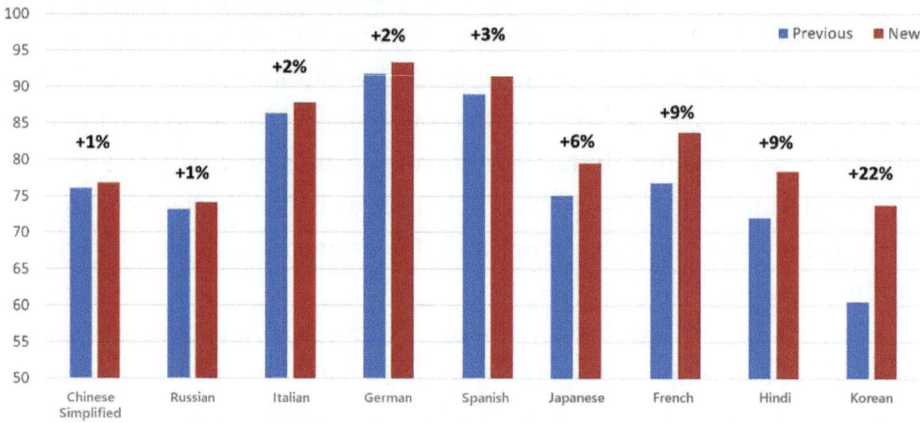

Translation quality improvements

Human evaluation results for news translation

Source: Translator FY19 human parity evaluations, data collected in June 2019

Figure 10-3. A graph displaying the improvement in Microsoft's AI translation app, between June 2018 and June 2019. Every language shown has improved in some form, with Korean improving by 22%

It now comes as a mobile app, on all major platforms, that can provide real-time translation even when the device is offline.[45] This is really useful for people who have to regularly interact with content that isn't in their first language, but also to people heading on a holiday.[46]

Providing information about images

One of the most common issues with accessibility is the lack of alternative text for images, which, as we know, means people who are blind or have sight loss could be missing important information. There have been a host of success stories recently, with large companies using new technology to address this problem. Google's Cloud Vision API has been using a neural network to classify images, but also to extract text embedded in them.[47] This is achieved through optical character recognition (OCR) technology, that can "read" the text and display it alongside the image.

In a slightly different use case, Facebook has been working for the past few years on automatically adding `alt` text to images that are uploaded to its platforms. Every day, people share more than 2 billion photos across Facebook, Instagram, Messenger, and WhatsApp,[48] so they set about creating a neural network that could understand what is going on in an image and make that information available to screen readers. At the time of writing, it can detect "objects, scenes, actions, places of interest, and whether an image/video contains objectionable content." Right now, they start every alt text entry with "Image may contain" as they try to perfect its ability to analyse an image, but this is a brilliant piece of work from the world's most used social network that will help anyone using a screen reader.

Providing information about a user's surroundings

One of my personal favorite uses of artificial intelligence is Microsoft's Seeing AI application, that has "changed the lives of the blind and low vision community."[49] Here, a user can use their device's camera as a form of sight in a range of situations, and the app will then interpret what it can see using artificial intelligence and inform the user audibly. At the time of writing, it's available in 35 countries and can do things like read out short pieces of written text, identify currency, describe products by reading their barcode, understand documents, and even describe people around you and their emotions.[50]

Making speech recognition even more inclusive

As we've covered, voice assistants, along with other voice-recognition-based software like Dragon Naturally Speaking, are very important tools, used by a lot of disabled users (e.g., those who are blind or have motor impairments) to interact with the Web through voice commands. However, many have run into issues with it not comprehending nonstandard speech

(speech that differs from the usual accepted, easily recognisable speech of native adult members of a speech community).[51] This is a common problem for people who have strong accents but is also a barrier for many with disabilities.[52] Each year, millions of people experience impaired speech, as a result of strokes and aneurysms or conditions such as cerebral palsy and Parkinson's. People with access needs such as these are left in a situation where they could potentially benefit from software like this but currently cannot access it.

Thankfully, a start-up called Voiceitt is working on this problem – using a hybrid of statistical modeling and machine learning to create voice recognition software for those with nonstandard speech. Voiceitt's first product was a mobile app that can accurately convert nonstandard language into readily understood speech. They're currently in beta testing but are working on integrating their work with smart devices such as Amazon Echo or Google Assistant.[53] Given the massive popularity of these devices, and everything that can connect to them, getting this technology to work could open up a whole new world for those with nonstandard speech.

Providing catered content for users

Services that are capable of adapting to a user's needs and preferences often have the potential to become immensely popular. According to Business Insider, Netflix made $1 billion in 2018 alone as a result of its machine learning algorithm which recommends personalised TV shows and movies to subscribers.[54] This same concept is also being applied to making the process of searching for something on a website easier, such as offering related products based on previous purchases. It can also help highlight certain actions based on users' previous behavior. Machine learning applied in this way could make a site much easier to navigate, thereby preventing stress for those with cognitive impairments or low-tech literacy.

It can protect against spam

Spam detection has existed in email for a while, but spam campaigns are getting both more damaging and more convincing. For example, the National Fraud Intelligence Bureau (NFIB) noticed a large amount of fake TV licensing emails being sent out in September 2018, asking for user's personal and financial information. They estimated that those involved lost over £830,000 through this campaign alone.[55]

To combat this, artificial intelligence is now being used to help determine whether an email is spam with much greater accuracy. Over the past couple of years, Google's spam filter, for example, has been learning how to identify spam through observing user's use of the "mark as spam" and "report spam" buttons.[56] On top of that, they've recently added a new machine learning program called TensorFlow that has helped them block an **additional** 100 million spam messages every day, through identifying and blocking:

> *image-based messages, emails with hidden embedded content, and messages from newly created domains that try to hide a low volume of spammy messages within legitimate traffic*[57]

All of this helps to protect vulnerable customers from being taken advantage of.

Providing automatic summaries of text

The Internet is full of an ever-growing amount of information, and distilling that information is a challenge that machine learning is working toward. We mentioned TensorFlow a moment ago, and it's being used again, this time by the Google Brain team in an effort to be able to generate single line summaries of news articles.[58]

Software company Salesforce took this one step further in 2017 by using a type of machine learning called "reinforcement learning" to create a summarised paragraph of long emails or documents that a user has received.[59] People with attention deficit disorders, those who are easily overwhelmed by information, or those with low literacy and learning difficulties stand to benefit from this greatly – as well as anyone in a rush or has to digest large amounts of information. They're basically making automatic Too long; Didn't Read (TL;DR) summaries!

It can make what you build more profitable

As we've mentioned before, profitability shouldn't be the primary motivator for accessibility, but it is often a well-deserved outcome for doing the right thing. Accountants Deloitte have concluded that 83% of early AI adopters have already achieved substantial (30%) or moderate (53%) economic benefits.

Conclusion

In this chapter, we have seen that there is a wealth of progress being made in the emerging AI sector. We're also at a stage where technology such as voice assistants have reached worldwide appeal, and the underlying technology of natural language processing has the capability of creating inclusive experiences for even the most disconnected of users.

We've also seen that some of the world's largest companies are simultaneously investing heavy amounts of time and resources to develop solutions specifically for those with disabilities. The resulting developments make for an exciting time in accessibility – with the potential to radically alter (and improve) how those with a wide array of access needs interact with technology, and indeed the wider world around them.

Ability.net speculate that one day artificial intelligence might be so clever it can automatically make web pages entirely accessible automatically.[60] As great as that might sound, we are still a long way off, and they don't really back up their claim. In the meantime, you'll just have to settle for books like this one!

Notes

1. The Centre for Excellence in Universal Design, What is Universal Design, (2014), <http://universaldesign.ie/What-is-Universal-Design/> [Accessed 16/08/2019].

2. Shanhong Liu, Smart home – Statistics & Facts, Statista, (18/04/2019), <www.statista.com/topics/2430/smart-homes/> [Accessed 16/08/2019].

3. Robin Christopherson, What virtual assistants mean for accessibility, Creative Bloq, (06/03/2015), <www.creativebloq.com/web-design/what-virtual-assistants-mean-accessibility-31514357> [Accessed 16/08/2019].

4. Bret Kinsella, U.S. Smart Speaker Ownership Rises 40% in 2018 to 66.4 Million and Amazon Echo Maintains Market Share Lead Says New Report from Voicebot, Voicebot, (07/03/2019), <https://voicebot.ai/2019/03/07/u-s-smart-speaker-ownership-rises-40-in-2018-to-66-4-million-and-amazon-echo-maintains-market-share-lead-says-new-report-from-voicebot/> [Accessed 16/08/2019].

5.   Imogen Hargreaves, Voice Assistant use to grow
     1000% to reach 275 million by 2023, Juniper says,
     PC World, (26/06/2018), <www.pcworld.idg.com.
     au/article/642969/voice-assistants-use-grow-
     1000-reach-275-million-by-2023-juniper-
     says/> [Accessed 16/08/2019].

6.   Rebecca Reynoso, What Is NLP (Natural Language
     Processing)?, G2 Learning Hub, (31/05/2019),
     <https://learn.g2.com/natural-language-
     processing#JL-3> [Accessed 16/08/2019].

7.   Rebecca Reynoso, What Is NLP (Natural Language
     Processing)?, G2 Learning Hub, (31/05/2019),
     <https://learn.g2.com/natural-language-
     processing#JL-3> [Accessed 16/08/2019].

8.   Kat King, Natural Language Processing (NLP),
     Twilio, (2019), <www.twilio.com/docs/glossary/
     what-natural-language-processing-nlp>
     [Accessed 16/08/2019].

9.   RNIB, How does the Amazon Echo help people with
     a vision impairment?, (06/04/2017), <www.rnib.
     org.uk/nb-online/how-does-amazon-echo-help-
     disabled-people> [Accessed 16/08/2019].

10. Ability.net, Techshare Pro, (2019), <www.
     abilitynet.org.uk/techsharepro> [Accessed
     16/08/2019].

11. Andrew Jack, Disability tech goes mainstream,
     Financial Times, (26/10/2017), <www.ft.com/
     content/ae91d600-8caf-11e7-9580-
     c651950d3672> [Accessed 16/08/2019].

12.   RNIB, How does the Amazon Echo help people with a vision impairment?, (06/04/2017), <https://www.rnib.org.uk/nb-online/how-does-amazon-echo-help-disabled-people> [Accessed 16/08/2019].

13.   Go-Gulf, The Rise of Virtual Digital Assistants Usage – Statistics and Trends, (27/04/2018), <www.go-gulf.com/blog/virtual-digital-assistants/> [Accessed 16/08/2019].

14.   Bob Paradiso, Amazon Echo Controlled Wheelchair, Youtube, (12/07/2015), <www.youtube.com/watch?v=K89sE2RXwuI> [Accessed 16/08/2019].

15.   Mark Walker, How Artificial Intelligence is empowering people on the autism spectrum, Ability.net, (30/10/2017), <www.abilitynet.org.uk/news-blogs/how-artificial-intelligence-empowering-people-autism-spectrum> [Accessed 16/08/2019].

16.   Judith Newman, To Siri, With Love, The New York Times, (19/10/2014), <www.nytimes.com/2014/10/19/fashion/how-apples-siri-became-one-autistic-boys-bff.html> [Accessed 16/08/2019].

17.   Bret Kinsella, Amazon Announces 80,000 Alexa Skills Worldwide and Jeff Bezos Earnings Release Quote Focuses Solely on Alexa Momentum, Voicebot.ai, (31/012019), <https://voicebot.ai/2019/01/31/amazon-announces-80000-alexa-skills-worldwide-and-jeff-bezos-earnings-release-quote-focuses-solely-on-alexa-momentum/> [Accessed 16/08/2019].

18. Todd Haselton, You can now ask Amazon Alexa to read your email messages and respond by voice — here's how, CNBC, (10/12/2018), <www.cnbc.com/2018/12/10/how-to-check-your-email-with-amazon-alexa.html> [Accessed 16/08/2019].

19. Bret Kinsella, Amazon Announces 80,000 Alexa Skills Worldwide and Jeff Bezos Earnings Release Quote Focuses Solely on Alexa Momentum, Voicebot.ai, (31/01/2019), <https://voicebot.ai/2019/01/31/amazon-announces-80000-alexa-skills-worldwide-and-jeff-bezos-earnings-release-quote-focuses-solely-on-alexa-momentum/> [Accessed 16/08/2019].

20. Jasmine Pennic, TruSense Releases Amazon Alexa Integrated 'Smart' Personal Emergency Response Pendant, Hit Consultant, (06/04/2018), <https://hitconsultant.net/2018/04/06/trusense-smart-per-pendant/#.XU1XaZNKjOQ> [Accessed 16/08/2019].

21. Apple, Apple Watch Series 4, (2019), <www.apple.com/uk/apple-watch-series-4/health/> [Accessed 16/08/2019].

22. Ecopush, Ecopush, (2019), <https://ecopush.co> [Accessed 16/08/2019].

23. Sesame, Touch Free Control for All Your Devices, (2017), <https://sesame-enable.com/> [Accessed 16/08/2019].

24. Sesame, Touch Free Control for All Your Devices, (2017), <https://sesame-enable.com/> [Accessed 16/08/2019].

25. Entertainment Software Association, 2019 Essential Facts About the Computer and Video Game Industry, (2019), <www.theesa.com/esa-research/2019-essential-facts-about-the-computer-and-video-game-industry/> [Accessed 16/08/2019].

26. UK Interactive Entertainment, The games industry in numbers, (2017), <https://ukie.org.uk/research> [Accessed 16/08/2019].

27. Jane McGonigal, How Video Games Can Teach Your Brain to Fight Depression, Slate, (09/11/2019), <https://slate.com/technology/2015/11/how-video-games-can-teach-your-brain-to-fight-depression.html> [Accessed 16/08/2019].

28. Microsoft, Xbox Adaptive Controller, (2019), <www.microsoft.com/en-gb/p/xbox-adaptive-controller/8nsdbhz1n3d8> [Accessed 16/08/2019].

29. United Nations, The promotion, protection and enjoyment of human rights on the Internet, (27/06/2016), <www.article19.org/data/files/Internet_Statement_Adopted.pdf> [Accessed 16/08/2019].

30. Office for National Statistics, Home internet and social media usage Internet access – households and individuals, Great Britain: 2018, (07/08/2019), <www.ons.gov.uk/peoplepopulationandcommunity/householdcharacteristics/homeinternetandsocialmediausage/bulletins/internetaccesshouseholdsandindividuals/2018> [Accessed 16/08/2019].

31. Seth Stephens-Davidowitz, The Songs That Bind, The New York Times, (02/10/2018), <www.nytimes. com/2018/02/10/opinion/sunday/favorite-songs.html> [Accessed 16/08/2019].

32. Patrick Foster, On Hold Music and the Psychology of Waiting, Talk Route, (2019), <https://talkroute. com/on-hold-music-and-the-psychology-of-waiting/> [Accessed 16/08/2019].

33. Mind, How to cope with sleep problems, (2013), <www.mind.org.uk/information-support/types-of-mental-health-problems/sleep-problems/#. XUhSgJNKjUo> [Accessed 16/08/2019].

34. Nupur Vilas Bhade, Introducing Twilio Autopilot — A conversational AI platform to build bots that work, Twilio, (17/10/2018), <www.twilio.com/ blog/introducing-twilio-autopilot-a-conversational-ai-platform-to-build-bots-that-work> [Accessed 16/08/2019].

35. Twilio, Twilio Autopilot, (2019), <www.twilio.com/ autopilot> [Accessed 16/08/2019].

36. Drift, The 2018 State of Chatbots Report, (01/2018), <https://www.drift.com/wp-content/ uploads/2018/01/2018-state-of-chatbots-report.pdf> [Accessed 16/08/2019].

37. Lexico (English Oxford Living Dictionary), 'Artificial Intelligence', (2019), <www.lexico.com/en/ definition/artificial_intelligence> [Accessed 16/08/2019].

38. Wikipedia, 'Artificial Intelligence', (2019), <https://en.wikipedia.org/wiki/Artificial_ intelligence> [Accessed 16/08/2019].

39. Finances Online, 50+ Vital Artificial Intelligence Statistics: 2019 Data Analysis & Market Share, (2019), <https://financesonline. com/artificial-intelligence- statistics/#benefits> [Accessed 16/08/2019].

40. Google Support, Use automatic captioning, (2019), <https://support.google.com/ youtube/answer/6373554?hl=en-GB#> [Accessed 16/08/2019].

41. Microsoft, Present with real-time, automatic captions or subtitles in PowerPoint, (2019), <https://support.office.com/en-us/article/ present-with-real-time-automatic-captions- or-subtitles-in-powerpoint-68d20e49-aec3- 456a-939d-34a79e8ddd5f> [Accessed 16/08/2019].

42. Hal Hodson, Google's DeepMind AI can lip- read TV shows better than a pro, New Scientist, (21/11/2016), <www.newscientist.com/ article/2113299-googles-deepmind-ai-can-lip- read-tv-shows-better-than-a-pro/> [Accessed 16/08/2019].

43. Microsoft Translator, Neural Machine Translation Enabling Human Parity Innovations In the Cloud, (17/06/2019), <www.microsoft.com/en-us/ translator/blog/2019/06/17/neural-machine- translation-enabling-human-parity-innovations- in-the-cloud/> [Accessed 16/08/2019].

44.   Microsoft Translator, Neural Machine Translation Enabling Human Parity Innovations In the Cloud, (17/06/2019), <www.microsoft.com/ en-us/translator/blog/2019/06/17/neural- machine-translation-enabling-human- parity-innovations-in-the-cloud/> [Accessed 16/08/2019].

45.   Microsoft Translator, Microsoft brings AI- powered translation to end users and developers, whether you're online or offline, (18/04/2019), <www.microsoft.com/en-us/translator/ blog/2018/04/18/microsoft-brings-ai-powered- translation-to-end-users-and-developers- whether-youre-online-or-offline/> [Accessed 16/08/2019].

46.   Joe Chidzik, 5 ways AI could transform digital accessibility, Ability,net, (26/03/2019), <www. abilitynet.org.uk/news-blogs/5-ways-ai- could-transform-digital-accessibility> [Accessed 16/08/2019].

47.   Google Cloud, Vision AI, (2019), <https://cloud. google.com/vision/> [Accessed 16/08/2019].

48.   Darío García, Manohar Paluri, Shaomei Wu, Under the hood: Building accessibility tools for the visually impaired on Facebook, Facebook Engineering, (04/04/2018), <https://code.fb.com/ios/under- the-hood-building-accessibility-tools-for- the-visually-impaired-on-facebook/> [Accessed 16/08/2019].

49. Pradeep Viswav, Microsoft Seeing AI app updated with new battery saver mode, MSPU, (08/07/2019), `<https://mspoweruser.com/microsoft-seeing-ai-app-updated-with-new-battery-saver-mode/>` [Accessed 16/08/2019].

50. Microsoft, Seeing AI, (2019), `<www.microsoft.com/en-us/ai/seeing-ai>` [Accessed 16/08/2019].

51. Quote from, Vocabulary.com, Non-Standard Speech, (2013), `<www.vocabulary.com/dictionary/non-standard%20speech>` [Accessed 16/08/2019].

52. Alan Cantor, "Dragon doesn't understand me:" Why people give up on speech recognition, LinkedIn, (15/02/2018), `<www.linkedin.com/pulse/dragon-doesnt-understand-me-why-people-give-up-speech-alan-cantor/>` [Accessed 16/08/2019].

53. Voiceitt, Why are we developing Voiceitt? (2019), `<www.voiceitt.com/why-voiceitt.html>` [Accessed 16/08/2019].

54. Nathan Mcalone, Why Netflix thinks its personalized recommendation engine is worth $1 billion per year, Business Insider, (14/07/2016), `<www.businessinsider.com/netflix-recommendation-engine-worth-1-billion-per-year-2016-6?r=US&IR=T>` [Accessed 16/08/2019].

55. Barnet AgeUK, Latest scams, (2019), `<www.ageuk.org.uk/barnet/our-services/latest-scams/>` [Accessed 16/08/2019].

56. Your ICT Magazine, Google's spam filters to use Artificial Intelligence (AI) to curb those annoying spam emails, (2019), < www.yourictmagazine.com/apps-software/467-google-s-spam-filters-to-use-artificial-intelligence-ai-to-curb-those-annoying-spam-emails.html> [Accessed 16/08/2019].

57. Google Cloud, Spam does not bring us joy—ridding Gmail of 100 million more spam messages with TensorFlow, (2019), <https://cloud.google.com/blog/products/g-suite/ridding-gmail-of-100-million-more-spam-messages-with-tensorflow> [Accessed 16/08/2019].

58. Peter Liu, Xin Pan, Text summarization with TensorFlow, Google AI Blog, (24/08/2016), <https://ai.googleblog.com/2016/08/text-summarization-with-tensorflow.html> [Accessed 16/08/2019].

59. Romain Paulus, New AI Breakthrough from Salesforce Research Boosts Productivity with Text Summarization, Salesforce, (11/05/2019), <www.salesforce.com/blog/2017/05/ai-salesforce-research-text-summarization.html> [Accessed 16/08/2019].

60. Joe Chidzik, 5 ways AI could transform digital accessibility, Ability,net, (26/03/2019), <www.abilitynet.org.uk/news-blogs/5-ways-ai-could-transform-digital-accessibility> [Accessed 16/08/2019]

CHAPTER 11

Tools and QA

After everything we've covered so far, you must be itching to start testing and improving your sites! Quality assurance (or QA) is a vital part of the process of building any website – the more bugs and problems you and those you work with can find and fix yourselves, the lower the chance is that a user will encounter them instead. Perfecting this process is key to enabling all customers to complete online journeys, reducing complaints, and ensuring all users have a positive experience on your site.

However, this task takes on added importance when it comes to accessibility. During conventional browsing, a bug or design issue can lead to confusion or frustration, but for those with visual, aural, motor, cognitive, or mental health impairments, these issues can prevent access altogether. Think back to the introduction, and our example of Beyoncé's website – things as simple as a lack of `alt` and ARIA attributes prevented interaction entirely.

Even once you've learned about how to make a website accessible and managed to build an inclusive site, websites tend to change frequently. This means that there is always the danger that new features can accidentally undo your hard work – becoming accessible is great, but staying there is paramount.

Now that you're (hopefully) ready to take the lessons we've covered back to your workplace and get started on upping your accessibility game, I'd like to make it even easier! In this chapter, we'll cover some of the best

© Ashley Firth 2019
A. Firth, *Practical Web Inclusion and Accessibility*,
https://doi.org/10.1007/978-1-4842-5452-3_11

tools available for testing and improving accessibility, looking at both specific access needs and accessibility more broadly.

We'll also discuss how automation can make testing easier and is especially useful for convincing groups of developers to embrace accessibility. We'll look at how this makes testing more likely to be used consistently moving forward – thereby ensuring that your hard work implementing accessible standards isn't undone over time. Finally, we'll look at a specific framework I've developed to act as a starting point for auditing an existing website. It focuses on identifying some of the most common accessibility issues and will allow you to make some big strides forward right away. Please note that this is only a *starter guide* though – if you rely solely on checklists, more obscure accessibility issues will slip through the net.

Tools

When it comes to accessibility, you can run into problems with both identifying issues and fixing them. Luckily, I've compiled a list of the most useful tools I have come across during my time in development, along with explanations of why they're so useful and where you can find them, so that you can claim the credit! I've broken these down into two areas: The first consists of tools and resources that are useful for a number of different reasons, and the second are tools that are useful for solving issues for a particular group of access needs (based on those mentioned throughout this book). It's worth remembering that the reasons these tools are useful will be less clear if you haven't read the previous chapters, so if you've skipped here then I'd recommend heading back to page 1, but welcome to the book all the same!

To save you the time and effort of typing out website addresses from this book, and to use as a handy reference, I have added a link to every resource in this chapter's practical example. You can find the code for this in the 'Chapter 11' folder of the Github repository or view it live by visiting `https://inclusive.guide/examples/tools`

General

I've listed the following as "general" tools because they have the capacity to benefit a range of access needs. As a result, they're a great first stop when you begin attempting to make your sites accessible to everyone.

The A11y Project

The A11y Project (`https://a11yproject.com`) works tirelessly to provide clear advice on web accessibility. The A11y Project actually came up with the numeronym A11y, as there are eleven letters between the "A" and "y" in accessibility! It was part of a campaign to raise more awareness around accessibility and at the time freed up more characters for posting content on social media when there was a 140-character limit on Twitter.

Their website contains its own list of resources and recommended reading, and an accessible widget and pattern library which many developers frequently contribute to. They also have sections dedicated to debunking myths about accessibility (like "Accessibility is for blind people"), offer quick guides and checklists for testing specific parts of a site,[1] and have how-to's for creating accessible components that are also open source (and so free to use in your own projects). If I had to recommend one site to keep an eye on regularly, it'd be this one.

Browser developer tools

Web browsers are a tool that you work with every day when building and maintaining a website, so it stands to reason that they are amongst the best places to test accessibility too. Luckily most modern browsers come complete with tools that help you do just that.

Google Chrome dev tools

To open the Chrome developer tools, go to View ➤ Developer ➤ Developer Tools (or by right-clicking and selecting "Inspect Element"). You can then click on elements within a page to understand and view their properties under the "Accessibility" panel (as shown in Figure 11-1).

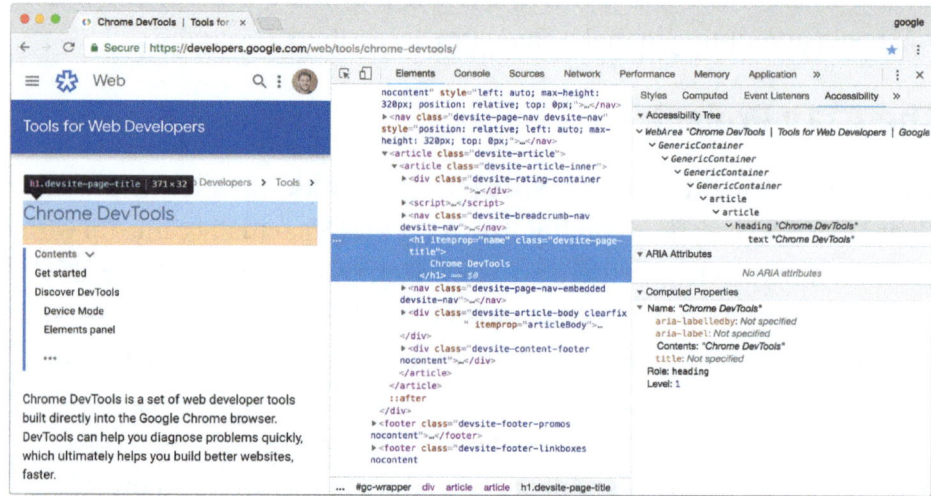

Figure 11-1. *An image of the accessibility panel inside Google Chrome dev tools*

When an element is selected, it displays the "tree" that describes where a selected element sits within the context of page, as well as any ARIA attributes present on the element, and also any "computed" properties (ones that the element has applied it by default, such as its role). All of this helps ensure that content is correctly labelled and described for those using screen readers, or only a keyboard, for example.

Furthermore, a recent update has meant that you can now check the contrast levels between two colours from within the Chrome developer tools too – simply by clicking on the colour of the element. This is really useful, because if your site is failing contrast ratio checks, you could end up trying quite a few different foreground/background colour combinations before finding one that passes. To make this process easier, Google Chrome's dev tools has an interactive colour picker (shown in Figure 11-2) that, as you move it, will automatically update to display the new contrast level. It also displays whether it passes AA and/or AAA compliance for contrast levels based on WCAG.

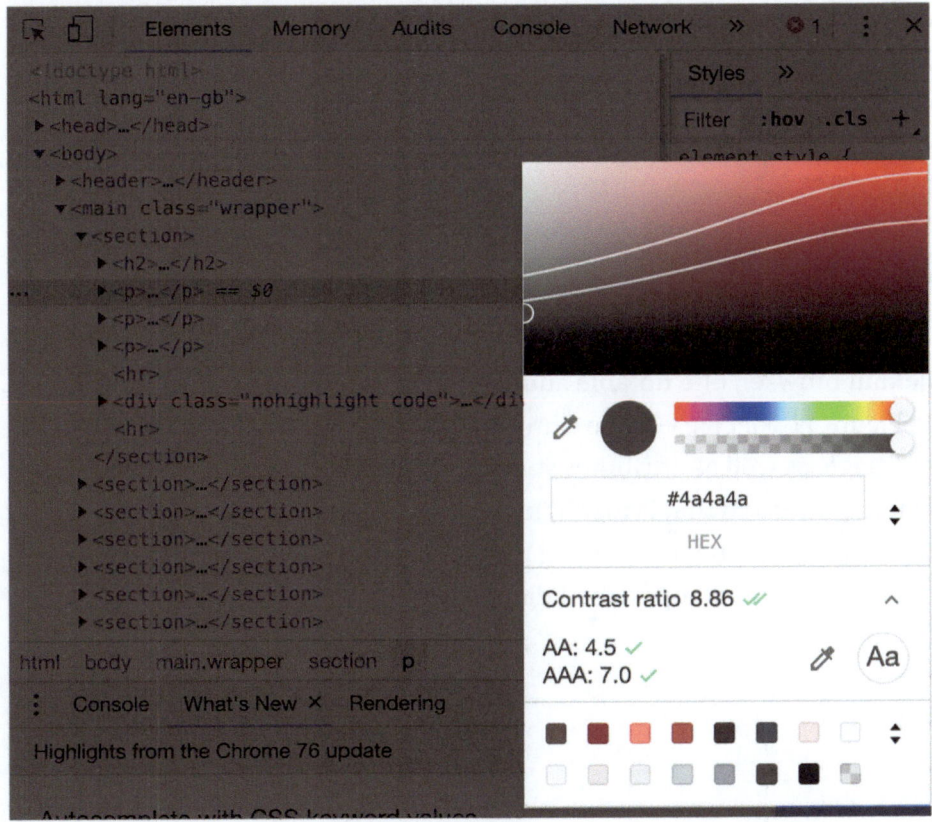

Figure 11-2. *The Google Chrome colour picker, displaying the current contrast ratio of the colour selected, along with lines for WCAG AA and AAA level contrast compliance*

My favorite part of this feature is the two lines displayed by the colour picker – representing the minimum point of compliance for AA and AAA, respectively. This takes a lot of the guesswork out of the process – you just drag the colour picker to below both lines and copy the new colour code it provides, and suddenly you're AAA compliant! This is especially useful as it's another tool that everyone using Google Chrome has access to, even if they're not a developer. Hypothetically a project manager, tester, or anyone else for that matter could run this accessibility audit on a site using their browser, identify a contrast ratio issue, and use the colour picker to find a colour that is compliant. Suddenly you've spotted a problem, found a solution, and can give it to a designer or developer, all within a matter of moments.

Microsoft Edge

There has been a wealth of improvements since Edge became Windows' default browser, one notable addition is an accessibility panel (as shown in Figure 11-3). Like Google Chrome, it can display the accessibility tree of a page, as well as attributes such as its role. What's more, you can see whether the item that is highlighted in the inspector has keyboard focus, which really helps when testing how an experience works for keyboard-only users. You can open the Edge developer tools by simply pressing F12.[2]

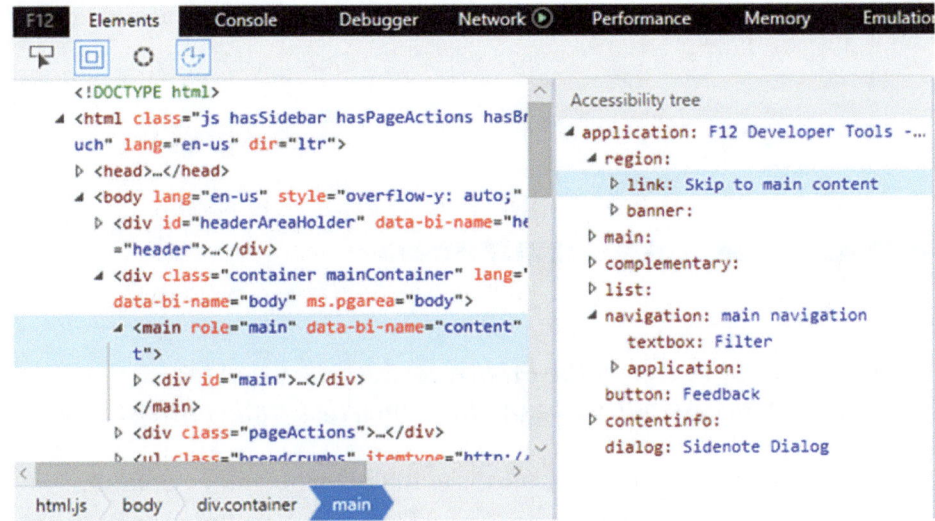

Figure 11-3. An image of Microsoft Edge's web inspector, displaying the accessibility tree of an element

Firefox

Mozilla's browser Firefox's dev tools can be opened by going to Tools ➤ Web Developer ➤ Toggle Tools. It contains the same features as the two mentioned above, and can display the contrast ratio of a selected element when compared to its background, and describe whether the contrast is high enough to pass WCAG's AA or AAA level contrast requirements, like Google Chrome. Now, it doesn't have the same visual lines as Google Chrome's colour picker, but it does show the contrast level automatically, saving you having to click on a colour picker to see it. Figure 11-4 displays the layout of this.[3]

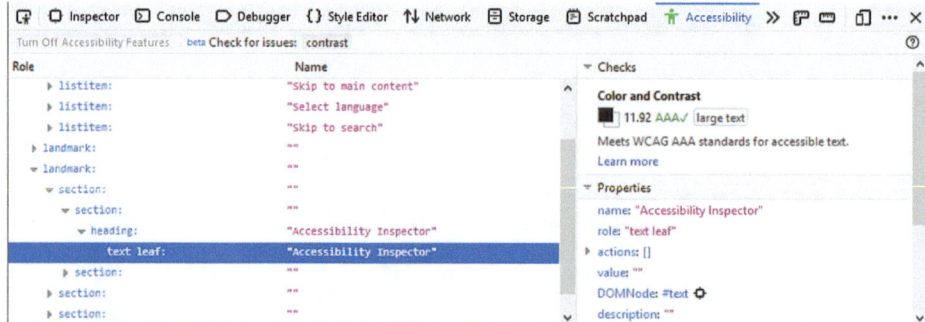

Figure 11-4. *An image of the Firefox accessibility dev tools, displaying an accessibility tree, ARIA properties, and contrast levels*

The accessibility panel in Firefox is actually turned off by default, but all you'll need to do is open the panel (`Tools ➤ Web Developer ➤ Accessibility`) and click "Turn On Accessibility Features", as Figure 11-5 shows.

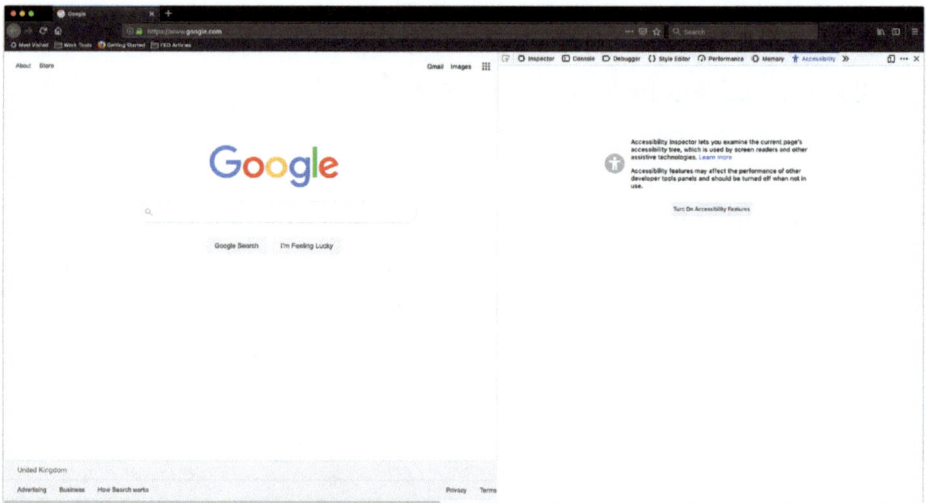

Figure 11-5. *An image of the Firefox developer tools' "Accessibility" panel, displaying a message that accessibility features are currently turned off and a button to turn them on*

Lighthouse

Lighthouse (`https://developers.google.com/web/tools/lighthouse/`) is an open-source tool that can audit the accessibility, performance, best practice, and progressive web app standards of any web page. It can also be run via the command line or as a "module" on your code but, most importantly, it's built into Google Chrome's web browser – you can find it in their "audit" panel of their web inspector – meaning that many of you already have immediate access to it. Figure 11-6 shows you how to find this panel.

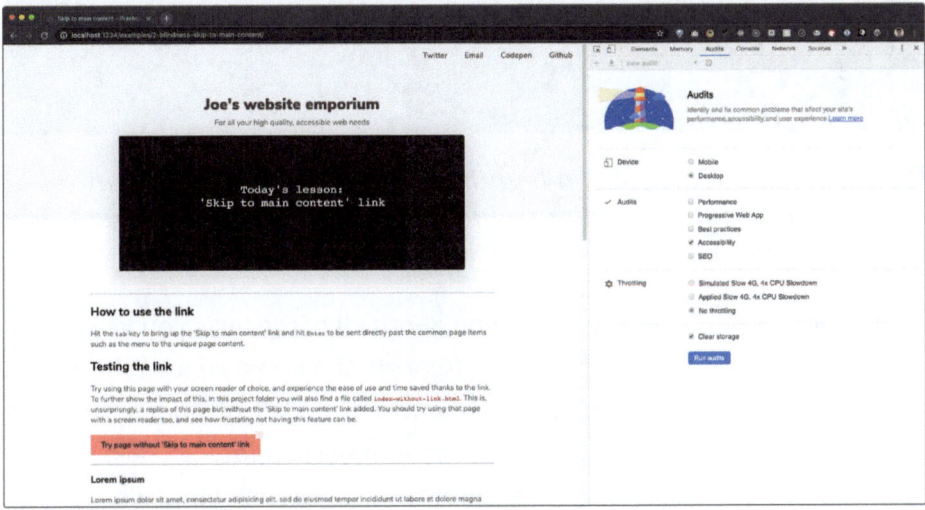

Figure 11-6. *A web page in Google Chrome, with the developer tools open on the "Audit" panel*

The tool itself is brilliantly detailed, providing a full report on everything from correct ARIA use, valid HTML, foreground/background contrast ratio, and much more.[4] Figure 11-7 shows the result of an audit like this, along with suggestions for ways that it found to improve the page.

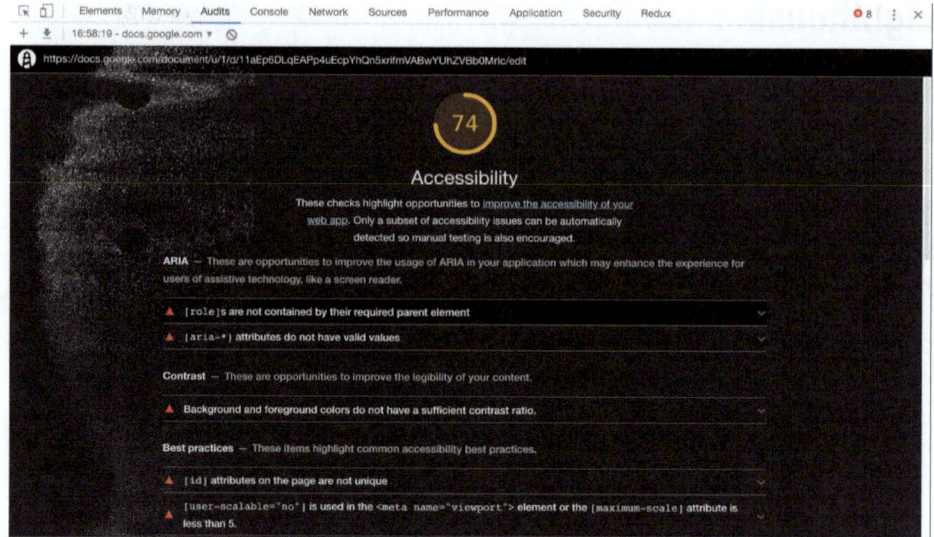

Figure 11-7. *An image of a Lighthouse accessibility audit from within Google Chrome, along with suggestions on improvements for the page it has audited*

Furthermore, Lighthouse tells you about all of the tests you've passed, as well as the ones that you've failed. Reports can be saved and shared with others easily, meaning that anyone with Google Chrome installed can perform basic accessibility testing in a matter of seconds.

Tools like this exist for other major browsers as well. Firefox's "WAVE accessibility" browser add-on (`https://wave.webaim.org/extension/`), for example, is also free to add. WAVE provides a feature, like Lighthouse, that will directly identify the offending code behind any failed test, and it follows the full WCAG guidelines. For Safari, there is a feature-rich extension called a11y tools (`http://pauljadam.com/extension.html`), but unfortunately it isn't free.

With tools like Lighthouse being built directly into popular browsers, the Web itself becomes a great place to carry out a lot of your accessibility testing.

tota11y

The Khan Academy, a nonprofit with the mission of providing free education to everyone, created an accessibility visualisation toolkit that provides a more interactive way of debugging and visualising your site's accessibility. Tota11y requires you to add a small piece of code to your website, after which every page will contain a small popup with some options (shown in Figure 11-8).

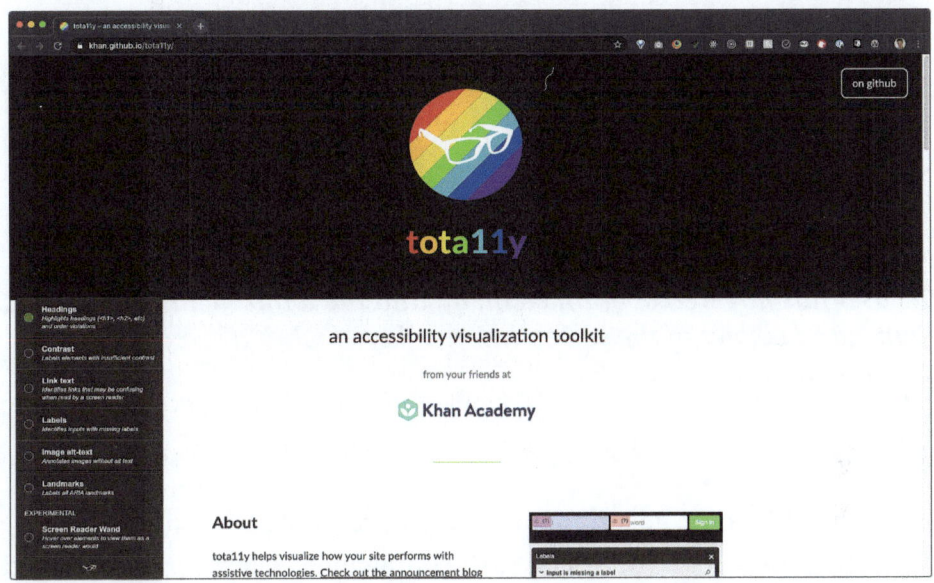

Figure 11-8. *A screenshot of the tota11y home page, with the tool running and displaying the various options in the bottom left-hand corner*

Many of tota11y's features actually come straight from Google Chrome's Accessibility Developer Tools. It can visualise errors with your heading structure, ARIA attributes, contrast ratio, alt text, and labels (among others). A particularly good feature is the screen reader wand that allows you to hover over an element to view the contents as a screen reader would (Figure 11-9).

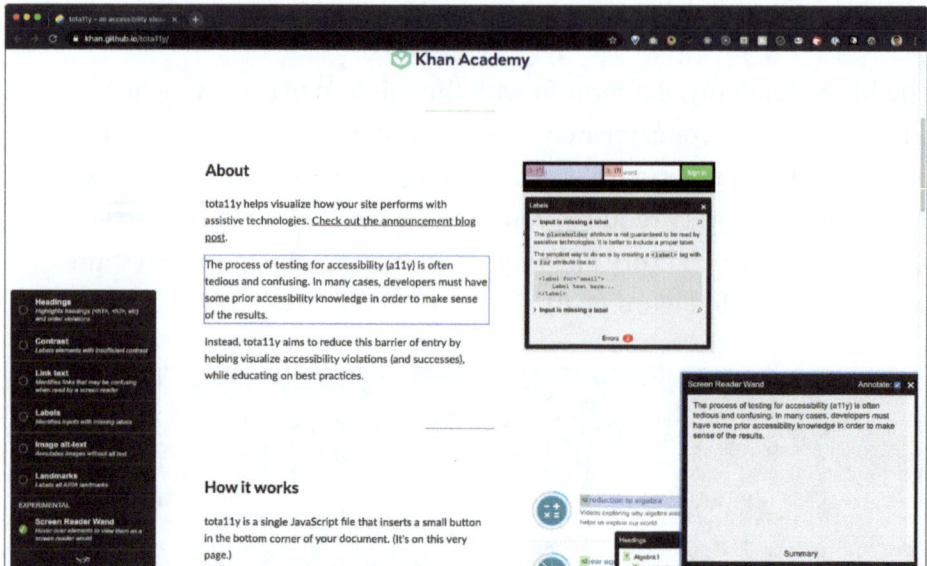

Figure 11-9. *An example of* tota11y's *screen reader wand feature – the user has hovered over an element, and the window in the bottom right-hand corner of the screen has displayed what a screen reader would read out*

Gov UK

The United Kingdom government are legally required to ensure that all of their sites pass at least AA level WCAG compliance.[5] However, Gov UK and more specifically the Government Digital Service have been responsible for creating and championing a range of tools to test and identify accessibility issues. Let's take a look at a few of their projects.

Designing for accessibility posters

In 2017, the United Kingdom home office released some posters (`https://github.com/UKHomeOffice/posters`) offering guidance on how designers and developers can make sites accessible to users with specific sets of access needs. They outline rules to help those with low vision, deafness, dyslexia, users on the autism spectrum, or those using screen readers. These posters have been updated several times – a few months after their initial release they added one about designing for users with anxiety. Figure 11-10 shows an example of one of these posters.

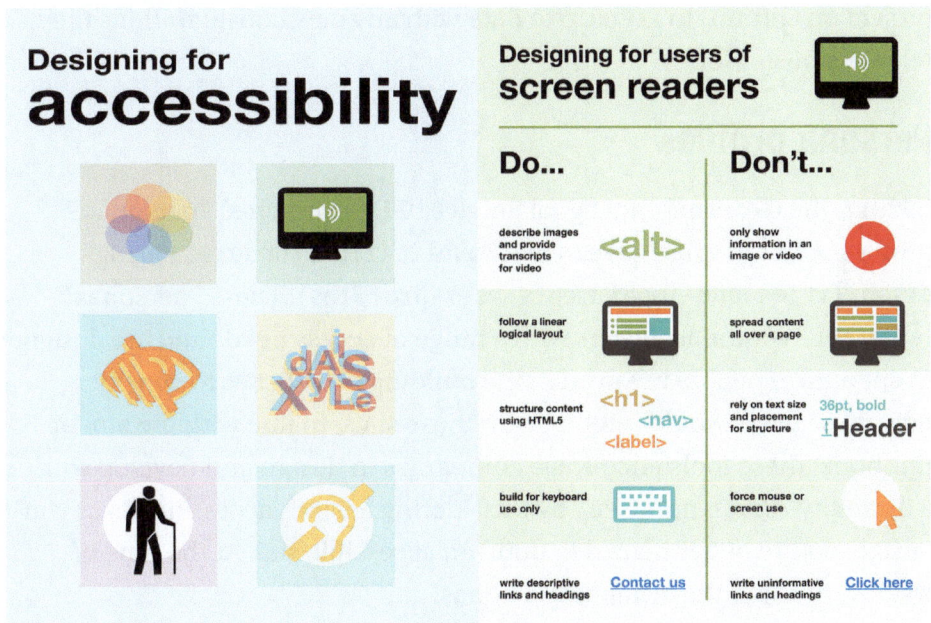

Figure 11-10. *The cover image for GOV UK's "designing for accessibility" posters, as well as the poster centered on designing for users of screen readers*

Each poster has around five simple do's and don'ts that range from design decisions around choice of colour and contrast to functional improvements such as accounting for misspelt user-submitted information. As they're just small sentences, they require further reading, but they also offer a clear set of starting points in a format that everyone can engage with and can act as a good memory aid to keep these needs and solutions in mind – I have them up on a wall by my desk! These posters actually formed the basis of my initial research and accessibility development when I first started work at Octopus Energy. If you've taken the time to read this book, they won't provide you with a lot of new information, but they are certainly worth circulating with colleagues and clients to act as an easy starting point for a discussion on accessibility. You can also subscribe (through their newsletter or by "starring" their poster project on Github) to keep up to date with any new considerations they release a poster for.

Persona profiles

In 2017, the Government Digital Service (GDS) launched "persona profiles" (`www.gov.uk/government/publications/understanding-disabilities-and-impairments-user-profiles`). These "personas" represent hypothetical users with a range of access needs and are designed to encourage people involved in the building of websites to consider how these users would interact with those sites. In line with the aim of this book, these tools encourage companies to design and develop with a disability-driven mindset – by considering a user's access needs as you design, you're better placed to build an accessible site. At the time of writing, here are the available personas:

- Ashleigh: partially sighted screen reader user

- Christopher: user with rheumatoid arthritis

- Claudia: partially sighted screen magnifier user

- Pawel: user with Asperger's

- Ron: older user with multiple conditions

- Saleem: profoundly deaf user

- Simone: dyslexic user

Each persona is free to download and comes with a list of devices that they have access to, the goals that they hope to achieve online, and frustrations that they typically encounter when trying to complete those goals. Internally, the GDS use these personas regularly, where they have their designers and developers attempt to complete certain actions within an hour using a personas devices and tools of choice.[6] The aim is to not only discover bugs in what they've developed (the absence of bugs is, of course, also a win) but appreciate the effort often required to complete routine tasks, and hopefully find ways to reduce that. In my opinion, it's an extremely useful task that everyone should try – it will help you keep access needs in mind, and nothing motivates you to make an experience more accessible than learning more about the struggles people face.

The GDS blog (`https://gds.blog.gov.uk/`) is generally a great resource to keep bookmarked as they continuously research accessibility, and draw a lot of conclusions from rigorous user testing. They also have a free newsletter so you can stay up to date with no effort. Furthermore James Buller (who's featured in this book) is a frequent contributor, so what more reason do you need to check it out!

Empathy lab

An empathy lab is a space designed to help people involved with website design and development understand the barriers faced by users with certain access needs. They usually contain a range of technologies, from specialist software to devices whose settings mirror those used by people with certain disabilities. The GDS set up a lab just like this, and it is open to anyone from the public sector – they also regularly get people to come in and test the technologies for free.[7] The idea behind this is that every time it's used, awareness is raised. This particular lab even has devices that attempt to mirror access needs themselves, such as goggles that simulate different visual impairments and noise-cancelling headphones to simulate partial hearing loss. Figure 11-11 shows someone using the lab.

Figure 11-11. *An image of GDS's Accessibility Empathy Lab, with someone using a website in Windows High Contrast Mode*

Here is a list of things present in the GDS empathy lab, in case you're interested in attempting to create a similar setup:

– Windows 7 and Windows 10 laptops with JAWS and
  NVDA screen readers, Dragon Naturally Speaking
  (voice recognition and activation), and ZoomText
  (screen magnification)

– iPhone and iPad (for using the VoiceOver screen reader
  and other accessibility settings)

– Android phone and tablet (for using the Talkback
  screen reader)

– Mac (for using VoiceOver and other accessibility
  settings)

- Two switch devices (for demonstrating switch access on both an iPhone/iPad and Mac)

- A set of goggles that simulate different visual impairments

- Magnifying glass

- Two sound defender headphones to simulate loss of hearing

- Television screen playing a film about visual impairments[8]

An empathy lab is a potentially costly investment, but they provide the opportunity to expose a lot of people to the circumstances that many face every day. If creating one for your own company (or personal) use is out of the question, GDS is just one example of an empathy lab that can be booked out,[9] giving you access to some great facilities, while at least some of the software can be tried at home.

Now, let's take a look at some tools and resources that are ideal for testing on behalf of specific disabilities.

Blindness

We've spoken a lot about screen readers in this book, but very little on the options available to users and how to use them. Here is a quick overview of some of the main screen readers on the market, along with some complimentary tools that can help you operate them and make content easier for those using them.

Screen readers

First and foremost, we need to speak about the screen readers that you can test your sites with. As someone who works on building and maintaining websites, I can safely say that first-hand experience with a screen reader is the easiest way to familiarise yourself with the barriers that those with blindness and significant sight loss face online.

Apple devices – VoiceOver

VoiceOver is built into every major Apple operating software (MacOS, iOS, tvOS, watchOS) and provides audible assistance for blind and visually impaired users on everything from personal computers to wearable technology. VoiceOver is also completely free, giving you easy access. Enabling VoiceOver is a little different on every device, but generally easy to do. You can learn more about this technology via the Apple website: (`www.apple.com/voiceover/info/guide/_1121.html`)

Google devices – TalkBack

The android equivalent to VoiceOver, Google TalkBack is an accessibility service that handles user interactions with the entire operating system and not just the Web. It is fully capable of acting as a screen reader inside the default Chrome app or any other downloadable browser from the Google Play store. Google have a full overview of TalkBack, its features, and how to enable it in their Android Accessibility section: (`https://support.google.com/accessibility/android/answer/6283677`)

Windows – JAWS

JAWS (Job Access with Speech) is the world's most popular screen reader. It can be installed to read the screen with text-to-speech, but also has a wide array of features (such as refreshable braille display compatibility).

It's an application that you pay for on a subscription basis, ranging from $90 per year for students to an eye-watering $1000 per year.[10]

Windows – NVDA

NVDA (Non-Visual Desktop Access) is a free screen reader that was initially developed due to the large cost of other options. It was once considered a "last resort" because it lacked several key features present in screen readers like JAWS, but it has now been fleshed out to include a comparative list of capabilities. It's also the first Windows-based screen reader that works with touch screens.[11] It doesn't have a support network that mirrors that of JAWS, but it does represent a free, popular option.

Windows – Narrator

It's worth noting that Windows does have a screen reader built into its operating system. Narrator has been part of Windows since Windows 2000 but was only originally designed as a way to help users install a fully featured screen reader. In Windows 10 it is available in multiple languages and is also included on all Windows phones – you can learn more about it in Windows' "Complete guide to Narrator": (`https://support.microsoft.com/en-gb/help/22798/windows-10-complete-guide-to-narrator`).

Linus – Linux screen reader and Orca

There are two popular Linux-based screen readers that are also open source efforts. The Linux screen reader was launched in 2006 by IBM and uses speech, braille, and screen magnification to aid users, and Orca is GNOME's default screen reader (a popular operating system that you can install on Linux – like MacOS for Mac).

Learning how to use a screen reader

After choosing a screen reader to test with, it can take a little time to get used to navigating with one. Luckily, the Paciello Group has created a cheat sheet (`https://developer.paciellogroup.com/blog/2015/01/basic-screen-reader-commands-for-accessibility-testing/`), full of the most useful shortcuts for JAWS, Narrator, NVDA, and VoiceOver to help you get started.

Headings map

Another tiny tool that's always part of my checklist, the headings map extension (`http://bit.ly/2ER31Nf`) generates a "tree" based on the headings on your page (Figure 11-12) and highlights any that are out of place in terms of hierarchy, or have been skipped entirely.

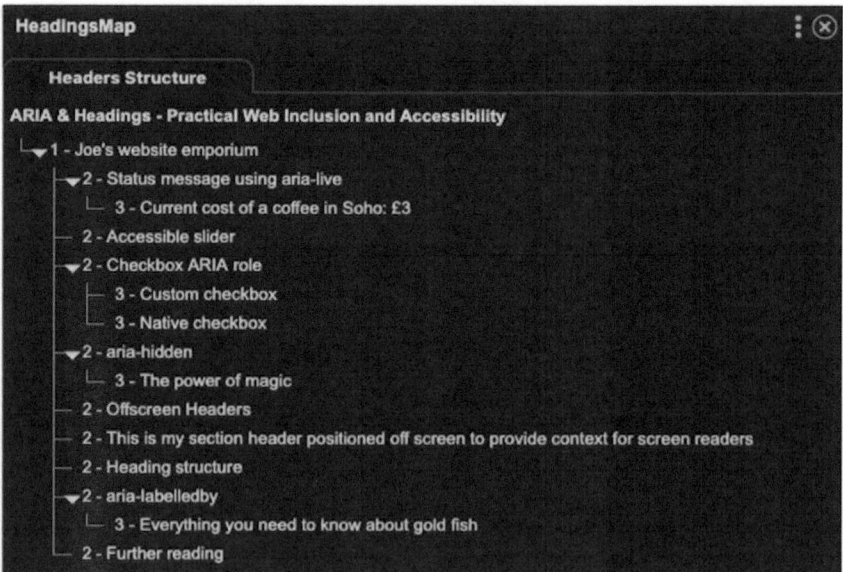

Figure 11-12. *An example of the output from the Heading Maps browser extension, showing the heading hierarchy of the page*

It's important for both screen reader users and for SEO, and so worth one click to check! This extension is also available in Firefox (extensions in Firefox are known as add-ons).

Validity

This is a nice and simple extension to perform inline HTML validation checks on your pages (`http://bit.ly/2BLqlx3`), with the results being outputted to the browser console (yellow for warning, red for error). This extension is available in most modern browsers. Figure 11-13 shows an example of how page validation errors are displayed.

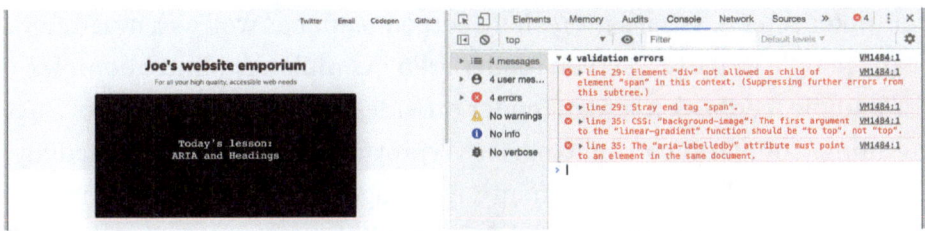

Figure 11-13. *The output of the Validity browser extension, shown in the browser's console, displaying issues with invalid and non-semantic HTML*

There are a wide range of other browser extensions built by the development community that can help you test for and identify accessibility issues. The ones mentioned earlier are good examples and are also available in all other modern browsers. In fact, the libraries for extensions or add-ons in all browsers is a good area to visit semi-regularly, as you never know when someone might release a handy new extension.

Low vision

Two major takeaways from Chapter 3 (Low vision and Colour blindness) were the need to magnify content and for it to be presented with a high enough contrast between the foreground and background colours to be usable. Here are a few tools that will help you test both of those points.

ZoomText

We've seen that many of the challenges that people with low vision face are related to content that is too small to interact with. ZoomText is a popular solution, as it can quickly enlarge and enhance everything on your computer screen. What's more, it's a screen reader as well as a magnifier! Many people that use a screen reader aren't completely blind but prefer the audible feedback a screen reader provides instead of the effort of zooming. ZoomText can echo a user's typing and other computer activity and automatically reads documents, web pages, and email. What's more, ZoomText has recently combined the capabilities of ZoomText with JAWS – creating ZoomText Fusion.[12]

Contrast ratio checkers

Want to test a combination of two colours before using them throughout a design? WebAIM have created a very comprehensive Contrast Checker (`https://webaim.org/resources/contrastchecker/`) that shows whether your foreground and background colours pass AA and/or AAA WCAG contrast compliance. It also shows how the contrast level changes based on different text sizes, and whether the contrast is good enough to be used in "interface" components such as text inputs. On top of this, it gives you the option to use a slider to tweak your noncompliant colours to be lighter or darker until they pass. This is all shown in Figure 11-14.

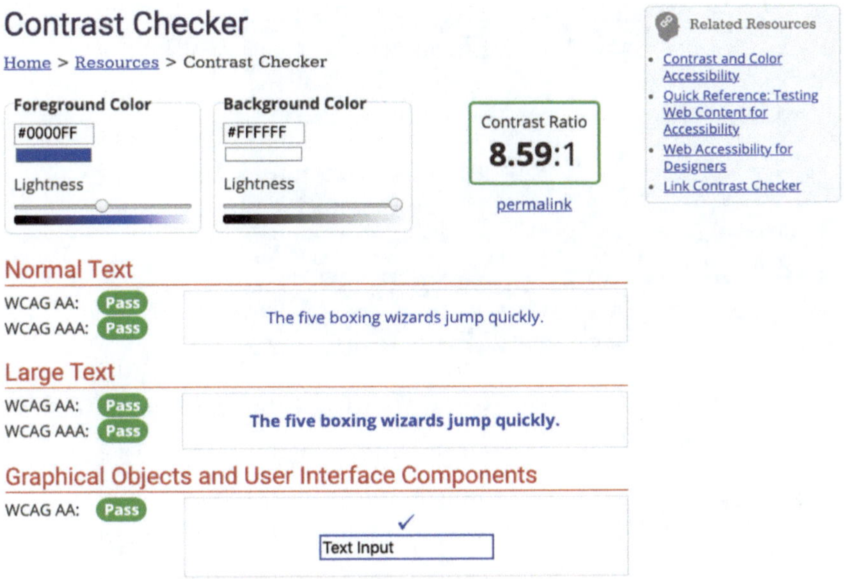

Contrast Checker

Home > Resources > Contrast Checker

Foreground Color

#0000FF

Lightness

Background Color

#FFFFFF

Lightness

Contrast Ratio

8.59:1

permalink

Related Resources

- Contrast and Color Accessibility
- Quick Reference: Testing Web Content for Accessibility
- Web Accessibility for Designers
- Link Contrast Checker

Normal Text

WCAG AA: **Pass**
WCAG AAA: **Pass**

The five boxing wizards jump quickly.

Large Text

WCAG AA: **Pass**
WCAG AAA: **Pass**

The five boxing wizards jump quickly.

Graphical Objects and User Interface Components

WCAG AA: **Pass**

✓

Text Input

Figure 11-14. *The WebAIM contrast ratio website, showing the contrast level between two colours for normal text, large text, and user interface components*

They also have a separate tool dedicated to checking the contrast levels of links on websites that you can find at `https://webaim.org/resources/linkcontrastchecker/`.

If you're looking for a simpler (and more visual) checker, Lea Verou has made a neat online checker (`http://leaverou.github.io/contrast-ratio/`) that, after inputting your two colours, will show you an example of how they look, display the contrast ratio, and tell you whether it is WCAG compliant (as shown in Figure 11-15).

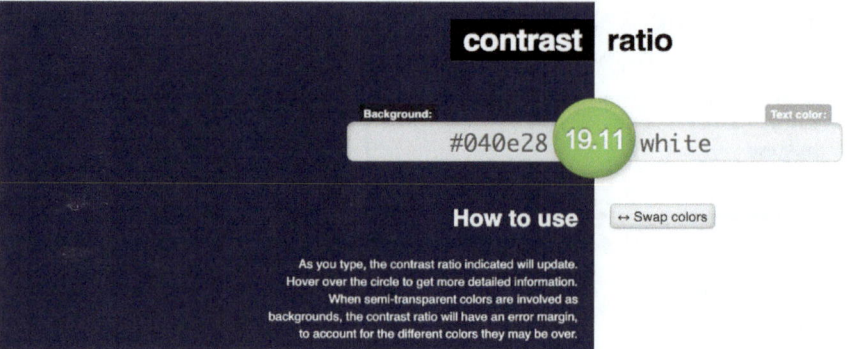

Figure 11-15. *The contrast ratio website, showing the contrast level between two colours*

Colour blindness

We talked previously about ensuring that you use more than just colour to convey meaning. There are some great tools to test if your site is accessible for those with red–green confusion (deuteranopia, protanopia), yellow–blue confusion (tritanopia), or monochromacy.

Colourblind web page filter

This is an online tool (`www.toptal.com/designers/colorfilter`) that allows you to input a URL and then select from any of the strains of colour blindness mentioned earlier to test against. It will then provide you a side-by-side comparison of the original page and the filtered page and copy the output to share with others. One slight drawback is that you're a little restricted in what you can test. For instance, it won't be possible to test pages that sit behind any form of authentication or any sites that you're working on locally. Figure 11-16 displays how a site would look for users with and without monochromacy.

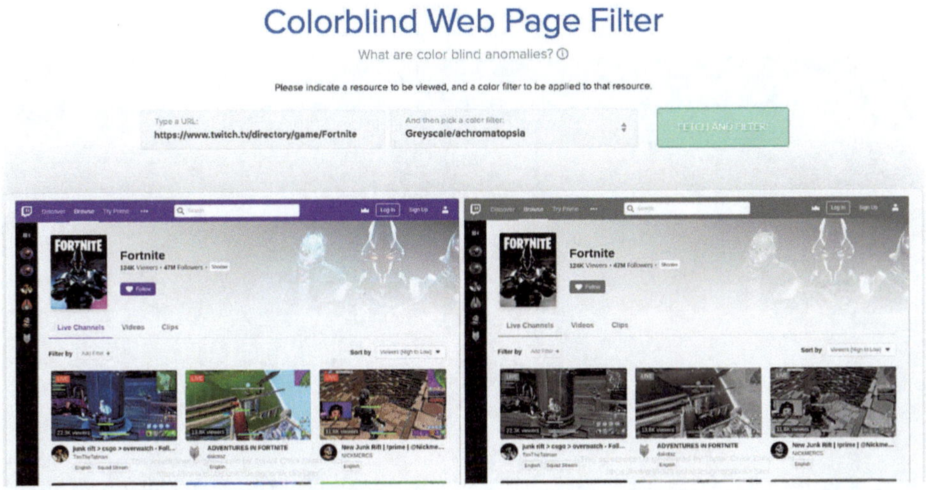

Figure 11-16. *A screenshot of the colourblind web page filter, showing side-by-side how the same URL would be viewed by users with and without monochromacy*

Sim Daltonism

This great app by Michael Fortin (`https://michelf.ca/projects/sim-daltonism/`) provides a way around the problems associated with the tool above (if you're using MacOS). It allows you to overlay a window directly over anything you're viewing on a computer (as shown in Figure 11-17) and see a live preview of what it looks like for each form of colour blindness – it even offers a quick way to switch between them. You can resize the window to any size and you aren't restricted like you are with the previous tool – it will sit on top of any browser, app, or document on your computer in order to greater understand what those with colour blindness see. This app also has an iOS version, where you can use the devices camera to achieve the same result with any surroundings.

417

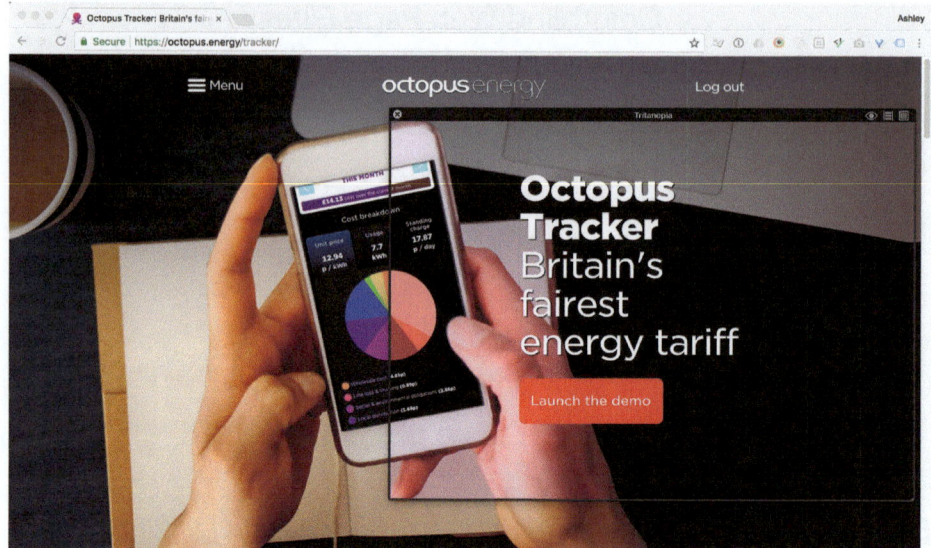

Figure 11-17. *A screenshot of the Sim Daltonism application overlaid on a browser, displaying everything within that window as a person with Tritanopia would see it*

Deaf and hard of hearing

In the chapter for "Deaf and Hard of Hearing" (Chapter 5), we spoke a lot about the importance of providing subtitles and captions for your content. This approach was centered around creating your own using WebVTT. Here are two useful tools to ensure that you both create these files correctly and can make use of them in more than one way.

WebVTT validator

Firstly, you need to ensure that your .vtt files have been made correctly. You may encounter unexpected errors when trying to upload them to sites such as YouTube and Vimeo to accompany your videos and, despite these errors appearing vague and somewhat ominous, they can often be caused by simple problems with syntax. Checking that they follow valid syntax will make sure that your good work won't go to waste. Anne van Kesteren has created a simple, free tool (`https://quuz.org/webvtt/`) where you paste in the contents of your WebVTT file, and it will assess whether it's valid. More importantly though, if there is a problem it will let you know what you need to do in order to get it in working order.

Converting a WebVTT file into a transcript

Now that you have working, valid WebVTT files, it'd be good if you could get them to work even harder for you. There are quite a few sites online (`https://subtitletools.com/convert-subtitles-to-plain-text-online`) that allow you to convert multiple types of caption file into a text file or transcript. This would allow you to provide them as a supplementary download, or publish them alongside your audio and video content for those that don't want to interact with it directly.

A developer called Ian Devlin has even created a way to convert these files programmatically, so that you don't have to convert your WebVTT files manually for every piece of content in your code. If this is more useful to you, then you can check it out here: `https://github.com/iandevlin/webvtt-transcript`

Note   For understanding the difference between captions and subtitles, try watching a show on Netflix. It may sound surprising, but turning on both in a movie will show you what adding nonspeech information does to improving the comprehension of what is going on on-screen. This simple practice could help you understand what you need to add to your videos in order to help your users.

Cognitive impairments

In Chapter 6 ("Cognitive Impairments") we spent a lot of time talking about the problems faced by users with language comprehension impairments. Ensuring that your content is readable goes a long way toward improving their experience, and luckily there's an easy way to test how well you've done this.

Readable's online Flesch-Kincaid Reading Ease test

When writing copy that is fit for websites and emails, it's always worth making sure that your text is easy to read. One interesting way to test this – the Flesch-Kincaid readability test – was developed under contract for the US Navy in 1975. It was first used by the Army for assessing the difficulty of technical manuals in 1978.[13]

Tech company Readable have created a free online tool (`https://app.readable.com/text/?demo`) using this test, which allows you to paste in text you've written and it will score it from 0 to 100 (with 0 being the most difficult to read and 100 being the easiest). Anything over 60 is considered a good score. This tool will also let you know where your content is letting you down with a scoring system based on factors like sentences with more than 30 syllables, words with more than 4 syllables, and even the amount adverbs and clichés you include. You also have the opportunity to edit your text within the website, and it will update as soon as you make any changes, so you can instantly see if your score has improved or not.

Mental health

There are a lot of great resources, available for free, around how to effectively communicate with, and about, those who suffer from mental health issues. Here are a couple of the most informative examples in this area that I've found.

How to report on mental health (for content creators)

Media reporting can have a huge influence on public attitudes towards mental health. When dealing with a topic already entrenched with stigma and misunderstanding, fair and accurate journalism is essential.[14]

Mental health charity Mind has done a lot of great work regarding how content creators should refer to, and report on, mental health issues. They have worked with charity Rethink Mental Illness to create "Time to Change" – an anti-stigma campaign (www.mind.org.uk/news-campaigns/minds-media-office/how-to-report-on-mental-health/) centered on how to cover mental health sensitively and responsibly. Their focus is around how these disabilities are portrayed in television shows and the news, but this applies as much to content written and published online. Problems like representing those with mental health issues with images of people holding their heads, for example, can be quite offensive. This work contains the correct terms to use for a range of topics, easy-to-follow A–Z guides, and even offers alternative images that are free to use and are more sensitive to those suffering from mental health disorders.

This resource links quite nicely to our work on using plain language, ensuring that your content can be both sensitive and easy to follow. The last thing you want to do is take the time to make your site and experiences accessible and then exclude people by using misleading, false, and potentially offensive language and imagery.

Design patterns for mental health

We've mentioned how the agency, Snook, and the Public Policy Lab have been working together on a pattern library to support policymakers, service providers, and designers in building better digital mental-health products and services. This includes providing information about changes of services to customers in a positive way and allowing them to leave a service without "strings attached." At the time of writing, they have only released the first phase of the library (`www.designpatternsformentalhealth.org/`) and have mentioned that the second phase will be released soon. With this in mind, it's well worth checking back periodically to gain some more insight and stay informed about designing with mental health in mind.

Communication

Being able to provide consistent emails to users is a key component in communicating clearly with them, and the secret to that is working within the bounds of the email platform, and format, that they choose to receive them. Here are a couple of tools that make that job fundamentally easier to do.

Email CSS Support – Campaign Monitor

This is another endlessly useful tool. Campaign Monitor (a product designed to manage and send email campaigns, much like MailChimp and Sendgrid) has created a reference page (`www.campaignmonitor.com/css/`) that allows you to quickly check which email platforms support certain CSS styling rules. For example, say you're thinking about adding an animation to your email, you can visit this page and see a breakdown of the email platforms that support the `animation` CSS rule (Figure 11-18).

Animations   SEE ALL 9 >

| animation | ^ | animation-delay | v |

Desktop	Mobile	Webmail
✗ AOL Desktop	✓ Android 4.2.2 Mail Supported with `-webkit` prefix.	✓ AOL Mail
✓ Apple Mail 10	✓ Android 4.4.4 Mail Supported with `-webkit` prefix.	✗ G Suite
✗ IBM Notes 9	✓ AOL Alto Android app	✗ Gmail
✗ Outlook 2000–03	✓ AOL Alto iOS app	✗ Google Inbox
✗ Outlook 2007–16	✓ BlackBerry Supported with `-webkit` prefix.	✗ Outlook.com
✗ Outlook Express		✗ Yahoo! Mail
✓ Outlook for Mac	✗ Gmail Android app	
✗ Postbox	✓ iOS 10 Mail	
✓ Thunderbird	✓ iOS 11 Mail	
✗ Windows 10 Mail	✓ Outlook Android app	
✗ Windows Live Mail	✗ Outlook iOS app	

Figure 11-18. *A screenshot from the Campaign Monitor email CSS support page, showing the support for the CSS "animation" property across various email platforms*

Based on this information, you can make a quick judgment call about whether your recipients would benefit from you taking the time to add a particular feature or rule. It covers dozens of email platforms spanning desktop, mobile, and web mail, and even lets you know if there is partial support in a platform for a particular CSS rule (and what that is).

Finally, it has an especially handy "Version history" section at the bottom of the page that lets you know any changes to CSS support in email platforms – allowing you to take advantage of any new functionality in your emails as quickly as possible.

HTML to TXT email converter – Mailchimp

In the "Communication" chapter (Chapter 10), we described why it's always a good idea to provide users with a plain text (known as TXT) version of your email to accompany your styled HTML version. Again, it allows recipients to interact with your content if the HTML email doesn't display correctly in their email platform, or if they've specified that they only want to receive text emails (perhaps for the sake of using a screen reader, for instance).

To make the process of generating this alternative version of your email as simple as possible, MailChimp have created a tool that will handle it for you! You simply visit `https://templates.mailchimp.com/resources/html-to-text/` and paste in your raw HTML email code, and it will strip out all of the unnecessary tags and formatting – leaving you with a simple, ready-to-send text version of your email.

Now, we've just covered a wide range of tools that can put you in a great position to test and improve a whole host of common accessibility issues. They do, however, all share one downside: each one requires manual effort in order to be used, be that by a developer, a tester, or anyone else attempting to maintain accessibility standards. Let's delve into how you can automate some aspects of your accessibility testing.

Automating your accessibility testing

Manual testing is not necessarily always a bad thing – manually performing actions can help make them routine, so that eventually they can be done with relatively little effort, and it can also help you understand needs and barriers. However, considering how many people are sometimes involved in building a website, you can often end up in a situation where not everyone remembers to (or wants to) expend the effort to maintain accessible standards.

This is obviously something that needs to be solved – but you don't want to go to the effort of learning how to test and improve a site's accessibility, and then the additional effort of teaching everyone else in your team/department/company, only for accessibility to gradually fade away over time. As we said in the introduction, many people involved in building websites work under very tight schedules and deadlines – if those running one project decide that they don't have the time to check accessibility, these issues can snowball. To combat this, it's important to keep talking about accessibility, but it can also be useful to automate, or at least streamline as much of the testing and quality assurance process as you can.

Automation is commonly used to run tests on code and make sure everything is working as expected, and the same concept applies here. You can do the same thing to ensure that any changes that have been made to a website don't create new accessibility issues (or bring back old ones). Here are a few good examples of ways you can automate your accessibility testing:

AccessLint

Use AccessLint to hold on to the hard-earned progress you've made with accessibility, or to inspire your team to start chipping away at issues. That frees you from costly bug-fixes and remediation, and socializes accessibility to your team.[15]

AccessLint (www.accesslint.com/) is an accessibility bot that can be added to a Github project (like the one that contains all of the practical examples for this book) and reviews any potential changes to code to ensure that it doesn't contain any accessibility issues.

When someone wants to make a change to a website in Github, they open what is known as a "pull request." This request shows the difference between the current site code and what has been added, altered, or deleted. What AccessLint does is it automatically casts an eye over any pull request made and, using WCAG 2.0 guidelines, checks for any problems that could cause problems for those with a range of disabilities. For example, in Figure 11-19 below, a developer has tried to add an image as part of a "pull request," but it doesn't have any alt text, so AccessLint comments on that line of code to raise the issue.

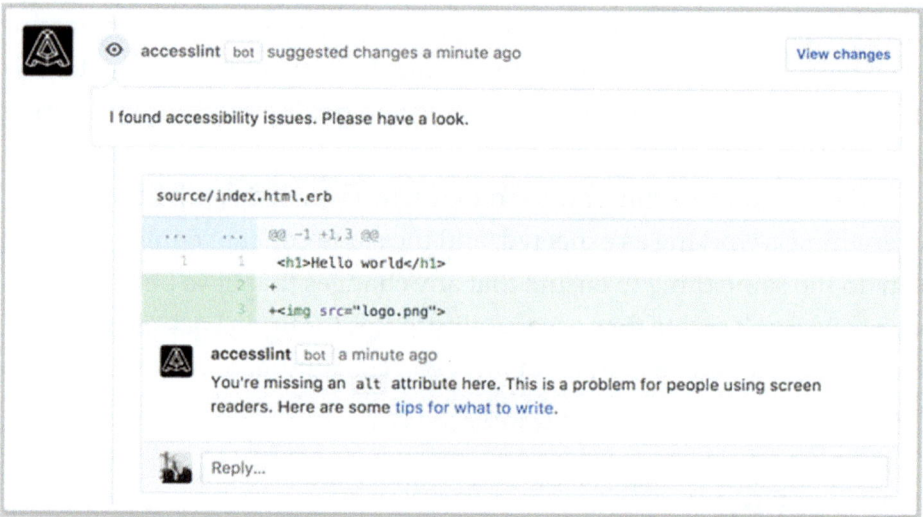

Figure 11-19. *A screenshot of some advice that AccessLint has left on a Github pull request, suggesting that the new <img> tag that's been added needs alt text*

It even offers a link for how (and why) you need to solve the issue to help those making changes to understand the importance, and in this case even offers tips on how to write good alt text – neat!

What's also great is that when an issue has been raised, and the person changing the code goes back and makes the recommended alterations, AccessLint will check the code again and let them know if the problem is now fixed. In Figure 11-20, a user has fixed an AccessLint suggestion.

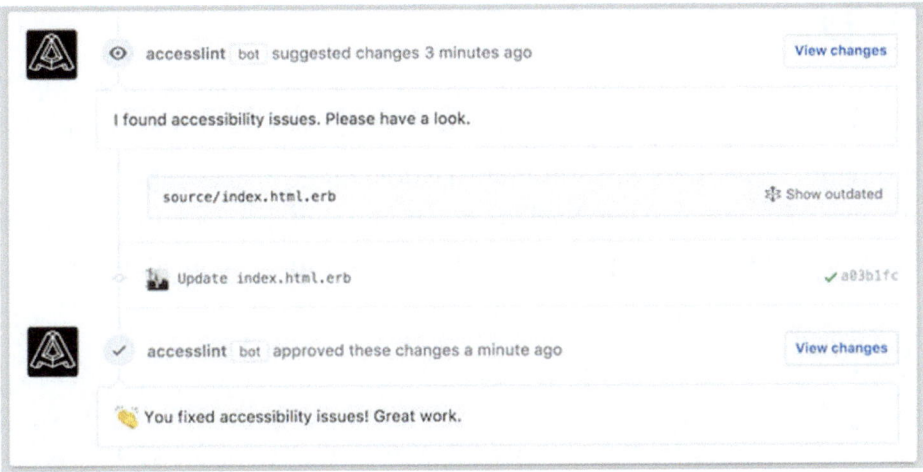

Figure 11-20. *A screenshot of AccessLint congratulating someone on fixing an accessibility issue that it had spotted*

AccessLint is built on a great accessibility testing system called Axe.[16] Axe's 'core rules' engine is actually part of the technology used behind the scenes in Lighthouse's accessibility audits.[17] They even have their own browser extensions that you might want to try (available at `www.deque.com/axe`) that allows you to specify which areas of your code to test, and which rules you'd like to follow. As for AccessLint, it only adds comments on pull requests rather than stopping new code from being used until the issues it finds are fixed. This is useful because adding something incredibly strict could cause frustration for developers and would likely be removed. However, it still provides consistent advice, visible to all developers, in a way that prevents them from having to search around to discover how to solve the problem. Implemented in this nonintrusive way, using AccessLint can quickly become second nature when submitting new code.

AccessLint is free for all open source projects and for projects for educational purposes. They also offer a free trial for any other project so you can try it out.[18]

Pa11y

If AccessLint becomes a developer's friend after they've submitted code, then Pa11y (https://pa11y.org/) is their friend as they write it. With one command, developers can automate a whole range of accessibility tests and receive immediate feedback on any issues that they can then fix before submitting their code. Figure 11-21 shows this command in action.

```
 ⌐  pa11y git:(master) ✗ npm run test:accessibility

> pa11y@1.0.0 test:accessibility
> pa11y-ci —config ./screenshots-output/.pa11yci.json

Running Pa11y on 2 URLs:
 > http://pa11y.org – 0 errors
 > http://pa11y.org/ – 1 errors

Errors in http://pa11y.org/:

 · This element has insufficient contrast at this conformance level. Expected a contrast ratio of
   at least 4.5:1, but text in this element has a contrast ratio of 2.94:1. Recommendation: change
   background to #1276b9.

   (html > body > div > header > nav > ul > li:nth-child(4) > button)

   <button class="site-nav__link site-nav__link--button " aria-haspopup="true"
   aria-expanded="true"> Contributing </button>

✗ 1/2 URLs passed
```

Figure 11-21. *A terminal output, showing Pa11y running on two URLs and displaying the accessibility issue for the one that failed*

It can even be set up to run every time a developer saves a file they're working on![19] The main benefit to using Pa11y is how configurable it is – you can specifically choose which rules from the large number available to follow. This is a big win as it allows you to gradually adopt more accessible standards in stages (or even one rule at a time), rather than all at once (which can cause a lot of pushback). For example, you can set it to any three of the W3C compliance levels (A, AA, or AAA). This sort of consistent exposure, and granular control, to accessibility rules makes it easier than ever to make it a common part of a development process.

One of my favorite parts of Pa11y is that it comes with a set of available "actions." These mimic the sort of behavior that a user would make on a page, such as clicking a button or inputting form information. This means that rather than just testing the page as it appears, Pa11y can also see if any accessibility issues occur at different stages in a user's journey through your website.[20] You can also get Pa11y to capture a picture of the page that it's tested for you, so that you can understand exactly what it is testing for. If you set up both Pa11y and AccessLint with the same rules, you can create an environment where developers have immediate, hassle-free access to accessibility rules and solutions, plus a noninvasive reminder of those same rules when they submit code.

A11y machine

This tool (`https://github.com/liip/TheA11yMachine`) can generate a consolidated report (shown in Figure 11-22) based on multiple web links to check for accessibility issues – which are broken down into errors, warnings, and notices. It validates against all three levels of WCAG compliance, and the W3C's HTML5 recommendations.[21]

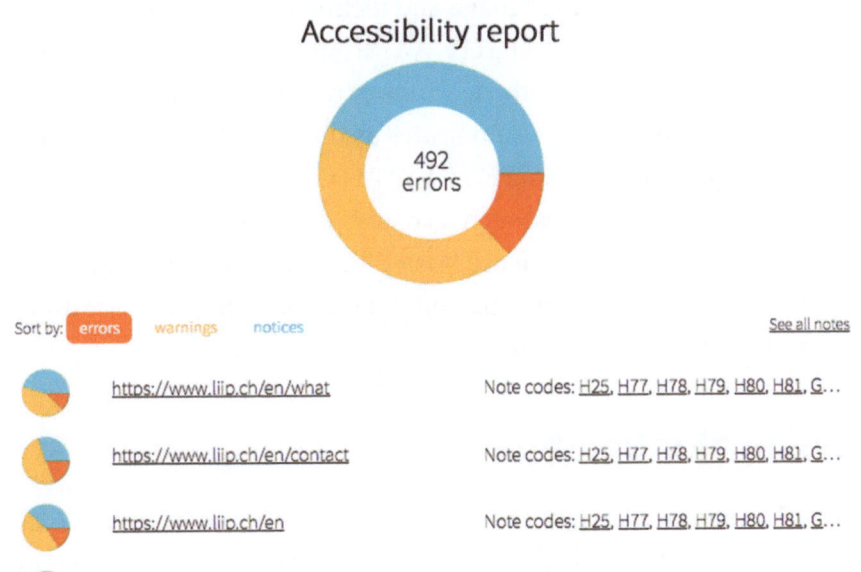

Figure 11-22. *An accessibility report generated by A11y machine, showing a breakdown of errors, warnings, and notices for multiple pages*

The A11y Machine lets you know which one of the guidelines each point corresponds to, so you can decide whether it falls under a framework you've chosen to support (e.g., WCAG AA compliance). This tool is especially useful if you maintain multiple sites and want a consistent way to monitor them all, or provide a report for nondevelopers that clearly shows the current status of an organisation's websites. It could also prove handy for consistently mapping progress if you're in the process of making your sites more accessible or conducting competitor analysis to see who in a particular sector is the most accessible!

AATT

Automated Accessibility Testing Tool (AATT) is a tool created by online payment company Paypal and comes complete with an API (`https://github.com/paypal/AATT`). This means that it can integrate nicely with nearly every programming language and technology that a company uses.[22]

Much like AccessLint and Pa11y, AATT makes use of the Axe testing system but also incorporates the features of popular HTML checker "HTML CodeSniffer," and the same rules as the Google Chrome developer tools.[23] One of the big advantages of AATT is that it can handle the testing of password-protected pages, such as dashboards that a user has to log into, or websites and tools that are hosted behind basic authentication (a username and password is required to even view the site). For user-focused sites, this is a big bonus.

WAVE evaluation tool

The WAVE evaluation tool (`https://chrome.google.com/webstore/detail/wave-evaluation-tool/jbbplnpkjmmeebjpijfedlgcdilocofh`) is a browser extension powered by WebAIM that is available for both Google Chrome and Firefox, and is handy for automatically reviewing the accessibility of any site you visit. It takes a more visual and interactive approach to accessibility.

You can visit any website and after activating the extension, WAVE will automatically inject a series of icons and indicators into the page (shown in Figure 11-23) to display not only errors and warnings but also accessibility features that are currently working, like HTML tags, and ARIA attributes.[24]

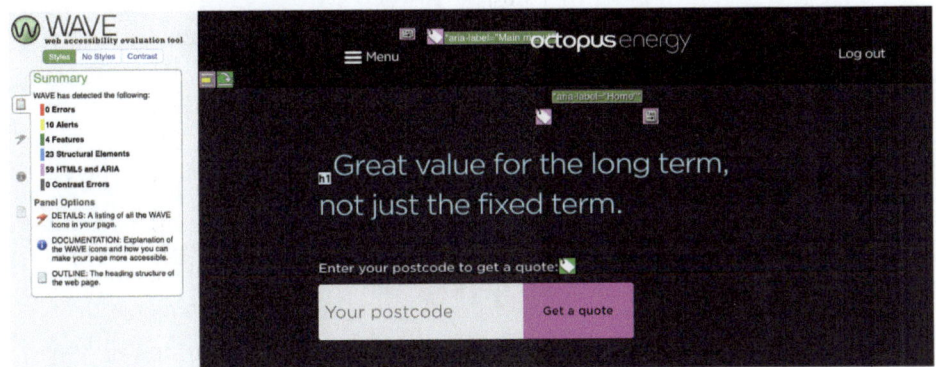

Figure 11-23. *A visual of the way in which the WAVE evaluation tool displays parts of a web page such as HTML5 tags and ARIA attributes*

This is a nice mixture of displaying what has been optimised alongside what could do with a bit more work – making the testing process a little less negative.

Auditing an existing site

Now that we've covered all of my favorite tools, and the ways in which they can help you (with little effort on your part), you're fully equipped to put them and your new knowledge into action. The following is a small list, based on some of the points raised throughout this book. You can use it to start an audit of a site you've built, or one that you've been tasked with maintaining or improving.

Please note that this section is not in any way designed to be all-encompassing, and many of the things you've learned in this book are not in this list – otherwise it'd be as long as the book itself! That being said, I've included this section simply because knowing where to start can sometimes be the hardest challenge, particularly when a site is fairly large. The idea is that once you've completed the points on this list, you can then gradually implement your newfound knowledge of access needs, barriers, and solutions to extend and evolve this plan.

There are six key areas that I have outlined, that can be easily referred to as **ACCESS** – clever, huh!

Aesthetics

- Does the text and content of the site pass a standard WCAG colour contrast check?

- Does anything on the site rely on colour alone to convey meaning (e.g., a status message or graphs with coloured segments)?

- Imagery:
    - Do all images assets being displayed have `alt` tags?

    - Do purely decorative images have no alt text set, so that they are ignored by screen readers?

    - Do any images or text rely on each other for contextual meaning?

    - Are there any images with text embedded in them? (Check any content management systems for uploaded images too.)

    - Is there an overreliance on icons, and are the meanings of these clear?

- Do you have any animations on your site? If so, are they potentially excessive, too fast, distracting, and/or potentially harmful to users?

- Do any videos autoplay?

- Do any videos loop unnecessarily?

- Does the design provide users with feedback when actions occur or changes are made?

- Does the site's design respond to a range of different devices/screen dimensions?

Content

- Is your heading structure logical and linear, starting with an <h1> and moving down without skipping levels?

- Are there long bodies of text that can be condensed and moved into other formats?

- Is the content written in plain language? Is it accessible for hearing impaired users, cognitive-impaired users, and users who experience mental health issues?

- Are there large pieces of text that are center-aligned when they should be left aligned?

- Are there videos being served outside of sites like YouTube and Vimeo and if so, do they handle closed captioning?

Communication

- Do users have several ways to get in touch with you?

- Can users respond to the communications you send them?

- Can users specify the format in which they receive messages? (e.g., plain text instead of HTML).

Ease of use

This step comes in the form of tasks that you can set yourself, and you'll be interested in the results.

- How long does a user have to wait to hear the unique or main parts of the page I'm on (if they're on a screen reader)?

- Do you provide a "skip to main content" link on every page that allows users to skip common content?

- Have you used the correct tags within your page (e.g., a `<button>` tag for a button instead of an `<a>` link tag styled to look like a button)?

- Does every form element have a label that is associated with it, that is, both visible and screen reader accessible?

- Are there any areas where you could make a journey easier for the user (e.g., by using autocomplete on certain form inputs, breadcrumbs, and setting expectations)?

- Can your core journey be completed with just a keyboard? Is it clear where the user's focus is as they move through content via a keyboard?

- Do links and actions make sense by themselves, or are there a lot of examples of "Next" and "Click here"?

Settings

Here we ensure that users can change or adapt parts of their experience with you to cater for their needs or preferences.

- Does the site work well in when using applications like Windows High Contrast Mode?

- For those without applications like this, do you offer a way to invert or alter colour schemes?

- Does the site respond well to changes in a user's font setting? If not, consider using relative units such as em or rem for your sizing and not pixels (px).

- Does the web page allow for zooming in general? And does it adapt to prevent the need for horizontal scrolling?

- Does content use the lang attribute so that it can change based on a user's language of choice?

- Does the site adapt to other user preferences such as prefer-reduced-motion?

Specifics

At this point you've covered the main bases of not only how your site and content can be accessed by people with a range of disabilities, but you've also thought about your core journeys, and about how your site can adapt to its users. You're now ready to go into individual use cases and start testing. Think hard about what you've learned over the course of this book – what is unique about my site's layout and content? Is there anything that could pose an accessibility issue? If so, how do I solve it?

Conclusion

While tools (both automated and manual) can pick up a lot of critical issues related to accessibility, there are many other issues that need human analysis. A test can determine whether there is `alt` text on an image, but a human can determine whether the `alt` text makes sense. A test can determine if HTML is valid, but a human can determine whether its order and semantics can be understood by a user. This is why both are required, and the good news is that while you're using tools to ensure the quality of your sites, you're also invariably getting into the right mindset to spot, and solve, other, more site-specific accessibility issues. Hopefully this means that you can make the most of the resources in this chapter, and what you've learned in the rest of this book at the same time.

Notes

1. A11y Project, *Checklist*, (2019), <https://a11yproject.com/checklist/> [accessed 30/08/2019].

2. Microsoft, *Accessibility*, (03/28/2018), <https://docs.microsoft.com/en-us/microsoft-edge/devtools-guide/elements/accessibility> [accessed 30/08/2019].

3. Mozilla, *Accessibility Inspector,* (2019), `<https://developer.mozilla.org/en-US/docs/Tools/Accessibility_inspector>` [accessed 30/08/2019].

4. Google, *Tools for Web Developers: Lighthouse,* (2019), `<https://developers.google.com/web/tools/lighthouse/>` [accessed 30/08/2019].

5. *Making your service accessible: an introduction,* (15/07/2019), `<www.gov.uk/service-manual/helping-people-to-use-your-service/making-your-service-accessible-an-introduction>` [accessed 30/08/2019] + W3C, *United Kingdom,* (04/05/2017), `<www.w3.org/WAI/policies/united-kingdom/>` [accessed 30/08/2019].

6. Anika Henke, *Using persona profiles to test accessibility,* Accessibility in government blog, (11/02/2019) `<https://accessibility.blog.gov.uk/2019/02/11/using-persona-profiles-to-test-accessibility/>` [accessed 30/08/2019].

7. Anika Henke, *Assistive technology tools you can test with at no cost, Accessibility in government,* (27/09/2018), `<https://accessibility.blog.gov.uk/2018/09/27/assistive-technology-tools-you-can-use-at-no-cost/>` [accessed 30/08/2019].

8. Government Digital Service, *Creating the UK government's accessibility empathy lab,* (20/06/2018), `<https://gds.blog.gov.uk/2018/06/20/creating-the-uk-governments-accessibility-empathy-lab/>` [accessed 30/08/2019].

9. Government Digital Service, *Book the GDS user research lab,* (16/08/2018), <www.gov.uk/guidance/book-the-gds-user-research-lab> [accessed 30/08/2019].

10. Freedom Scientific, *Jaws,* (2019), <www.freedomscientific.com/products/software/jaws/> [accessed 30/08/2019].

11. RNIB, *Top screen readers for Windows,* (14/11/2017), <www.rnib.org.uk/rnibconnect/screen-reader-windows-review?gclid=EAIaIQobChMIt-Xp9Z6W5A IV1obVChO8WQZjEAAYASAAEgIkSvD_BwE> [accessed 30/08/2019].

12. ZoomText, *Fusion Professional,* (2019), <www.zoomtext.com/products/zoomtext-fusion/> [accessed 30/08/2019].

13. Wikipedia, *Flesch–Kincaid readability tests,* <https://en.wikipedia.org/wiki/Flesch-Kincaid_readability_tests> [accessed 30/08/2019].

14. Mind, *How to report on mental health,* (2013) <www.mind.org.uk/news-campaigns/minds-media-office/how-to-report-on-mental-health/> [accessed 30/08/2019].

15. Github, *AccessLint,* (2019), <https://github.com/marketplace/accesslint> [accessed 30/08/2019].

16. Deque, *axe: Accessibility for Development Teams,* (2019), <www.deque.com/axe/> [accessed 30/08/2019].

17. Deque, *Google Selects Deque's axe for Chrome DevTools*, (2019), < www.deque.com/blog/google-selects-deques-axe-chrome-devtools/> [accessed 30/08/2019].

18. Github, *AcessLint*, (2019) <https://github.com/marketplace/accesslint> [accessed 30/08/2019].

19. Github, *pa11y*, (2019) <https://github.com/pa11y/pa11y#javascript-interface> [accessed 30/08/2019].

20. Github, *pa11y*, (2019) <https://github.com/pa11y/pa11y#javascript-interface> [accessed 30/08/2019].

21. Github, *TheA11yMachine*, (2019) <https://github.com/liip/TheA11yMachine> [accessed 30/08/2019].

22. Github, *AATT*, (2019), <https://github.com/paypal/AATT#integration-with-aatt-api> [accessed 30/08/2019].

23. Github, *AATT*, (2019), <https://github.com/paypal/AATT#integration-with-aatt-api> [accessed 30/08/2019].

24. Webaim, *WAVE Evaluation Tool*, (2019), <https://chrome.google.com/webstore/detail/wave-evaluation-tool/jbbplnpkjmmeebjpijfedlgcdilocofh> [accessed 30/08/2019].

CHAPTER 12

Conclusion

Congratulations on making it to the last chapter! I appreciate you sticking with me, and this topic, and I hope that you've enjoyed the book. Web accessibility is a deep well of information, encompassing so many different needs, requirements, and solutions, but I hope that the level of detail we've gone into has shown just how important it is to take this subject seriously. Before we bring things to close, there are just a few more things to cover.

First, we'll go through some practical questions that you should ask yourself as you go about building (or auditing) an accessible website or digital service. It would have been tough to appreciate the importance of these questions before you had read the previous chapters, but they should stand you in good stead as you evaluate when, and how, to approach a site's accessibility.

We'll then take a look at the legal landscape surrounding accessibility since the high-profile case against Beyoncé and why it has never been more important to fight for accessibility. We'll end with some final thoughts about the most important themes that have run through this book. Let's get started.

Questions you should ask yourself

Now that you're in a good position to work with accessibility in mind, it's worth addressing some of the questions that might arise as you start to think about accessibility specifically in relation to your own sites. Here are a few things that you should ask yourself.

© Ashley Firth 2019
A. Firth, *Practical Web Inclusion and Accessibility*,
https://doi.org/10.1007/978-1-4842-5452-3_12

How can I engage more with users with different access needs?

In the last chapter, we finished by emphasising the importance of human involvement when testing a site. We have seen that tools like persona profiles and empathy labs are great at allowing you to understand various access needs and experiences and for getting you into the right mindset. However, the best thing you can do is get users with a variety of access needs involved in the testing and development of your sites.

> *Who better to test for accessibility than the people who need it most? They have practical life experience using assistive technologies...and they know where their pain points are. They are the real experts in disability access to the web, because they live it.*[1]

I think this is one of the most important questions to ask yourself. I have spoken to a lot of charities, experts, and developers over the course of writing this book, and all agree that when fixing a specific problem, nothing matches the honest feedback of someone that lives with a disability every day. It's the cornerstone of all accessibility testing I conduct at Octopus Energy.

There are several ways in which you can engage more with these users. The first, and most obvious one, is to reach out to your own users. They're the ones that will be the primary recipients (and beneficiaries) of your site changes, and whatever changes you make will impact them deeply. Asking for feedback not only provides a group of willing testers but also shows that you care about them and their experiences online.

Alternatively, you could also run your own testing session. The United Kingdom government have created a document that explains how to run a testing session with users that have disabilities, so this could act as a great starting point.[2]

If you choose to run a session yourself, it's highly important that you first go about trying to make your site accessible and *then* work with people with a range of disabilities. This may sound obvious, but to receive genuinely useful feedback you don't want the focus to be on changes that could have been provided by a simple accessibility audit. With some baseline accessibility in place, the spotlight should instead be on the intricacies of completing tasks and journeys on the site – working to ensure that what you've added empowers users and makes their experience on your site easier and more enjoyable.

> *To get the most out of this research, it is best if the participants are not discovering basic accessibility issues that should have been discovered during an accessibility review and/or testing.*[3]

This is from Peter McNally, UX Consultant at the User Experience Center at Bentley University. He has run a large number of testing sessions with users who have a range of disabilities. His opinion on the usefulness of testing with users mirrors mine, and he also echoes another claim that we've made throughout the book – being compliant isn't the same as ensuring that what you've built is usable:

> *Typically, in order to ensure that disabled people can use their digital products and services, companies aim for compliance with accessibility guidelines such as the Web Content Accessibility Guidelines (WCAG 2.0). While this is critical, it is also important to have users with disabilities try to accomplish real tasks on the site in usability testing. There may be gaps in the overall user experience...*[4]

Peter has also raised some useful points for anyone looking to involve users with disabilities in their testing for the first time. These include starting with participants that are used to the environment and

443

requirements of user testing (a point that is true for anyone conducting user testing for the first time with any users), and starting with a small number of participants to ensure you get the most out of your session – starting with too many participants can make it difficult to provide adequate support or learn from everyone involved.

A key point that he raised is that you should ensure that your first testing session consists of people that are highly proficient with their assistive tools of choice, so that the focus of the session can be on gathering feedback for your site rather than delving into how they use their tools. This is because, even though users with disabilities often require certain assistive technology or applications to aid their use of the Web, you shouldn't make the assumption that all of them are experts with those tools.

Now, user sessions also raise other questions, such as "how often should I run them?" and "at what stage in a project should I run one?" and these are fair points. This is because, as we mentioned earlier, accessibility is a never-ending process – sites change and grow, and even the strictest of testing processes might not catch everything.

Paul Bohman, Director of Training at Deque University, actually suggests an alternative to these constant user testing sessions – hire people with disabilities for quality assurance (QA) testing full-time. He describes standalone, ad-hoc testing sessions as "piecemeal" because users with disabilities would only be present for the specific things that you've asked them to test, and not throughout the entire process. In his mind, the result of this approach "gives the whole company the impression that web accessibility is a checklist item, when it really should be a way of thinking at every stage of development."[5]

It may seem like hiring testers full-time might require more of a financial commitment, but it could actually end up being more cost-effective. If they provide feedback throughout the whole process of building a site, it's far less likely that large issues will make it into production that require costly redesigns. However, moving beyond the financial perspective (we know that money should not be the primary motivation), having testers with disabilities around full-time also highlights the importance of accessibility to the whole company, and allows for a constant sharing of awareness and knowledge:

> *Working alongside people with disabilities also educates fellow developers and testers, making them more intimately aware of the needs of people with disabilities. You change the company's culture, and that's kind of a big deal.*[6]

Personally, I think any of the options above are worth doing, if possible. They also work as a series of steps that you can complete one after the other, allowing you to build up your approach to accessibility in line with what you or your organisation can manage. First, you can start by implementing what you've learned in this book, then test using the tools we mentioned in the last chapter, and then start to involve experienced testers with disabilities. Finally, if possible, you can bring someone in regularly to allow for a constant focus on accessibility.

Should I ask for help?

Although this book has introduced you to many access needs, barriers, and solutions, it is simply not big enough to cover them all – or provide an expert level of detail on every topic. Truthfully, a book could be dedicated to every one of the chapters we've covered. The suggestions we've covered will drastically improve the accessibility of any site you're working on, but the scope of a project can sometimes be so large that it is difficult for one person to implement accessibility correctly, or to convince others to maintain it moving forward.

In these cases, I would advise you to not be afraid to call in help; nothing bad can come from seeking another opinion. There are consultants out there if you ever need advice on something that is especially important. The A11y Project has compiled a list of trusted professional help here:

```
https://a11yproject.com/resources/#professional-help
```

Should I build everything myself?

Remember, you don't always have to come up with your own solutions either – there is a huge development community out there who are doing a lot of great work for technology, and accessibility. For example, Font Awesome allows you to add fully accessible icons to your site for free without extra work (covered in Chapter 8). The two libraries for adding autocomplete functionality that we covered in the chapter on "Cognitive Impairments" (Chapter 6) are both feature-rich and actively maintained – available for free. In situations like this, it's worth thinking about taking some work off your hands, particularly in cases where you're essentially trying to recreate the same functionality yourself.

What can I do to engage others in accessibility?

I suppose the first and obvious thing is to share this book, and what you've learned in it! In all seriousness, sharing anything, from some of the tricks we've covered, to an interesting stat or a small tip, is enough to start a conversation about accessibility. Any of this, plus all of the current mainstream coverage around accessibility means that it's an important time to talk about and understand the topic.

You could take it one step further and encourage people to experience what it is like to browse with certain disabilities – using the empathy labs that we discussed earlier, for example. Anything that exposes people to a world of access needs they may not have known about previously, and encourages them to actively engage in some use cases (such as putting on glasses to simulate low vision or using a screen readers), can really help educate people. In their blog, the Government Digital Service (GDS) talked about the effect that creating their empathy lab had on other parts of government. Alastair Duggin, former head of accessibility at the GDS, mentioned that:

> *Many internal and several external teams have used the lab so far including...the Cabinet Office. [the] team adapted Register to Vote as a result of the accessibility empathy lab.*[7]

This is exactly the tangible benefit that can come out of exposing people to a disability-driven approach to accessibility; rather than simply testing as they normally would, those involved with the building of websites get a chance to replicate the same access needs that their users face. Here, a completely different entity within government became more inclusive because somebody took the time to introduce accessibility to them.

Asking yourself these questions will change how you build and test your sites for the better – it's another thing to consider that perhaps you weren't before, but it's the right thing to do.

We've just seen how useful it can be to enlist your colleagues and people with disabilities in the building of accessible sites. All of these things can save you time in the long term but also make it far less likely that you will exclude your users. In doing so, you will decrease the risk of lengthy site rebuilds and complaints from your users that damage your reputation. As we know though, it can get even more serious than that – let's turn our attention to the legal sphere, where some vital decisions about accessibility are being made.

Takeaways

I'd like to turn briefly to the state of mainstream accessibility today. At the start of this book, I mentioned the case brought against Beyoncé, where she was sued for her inaccessible website. Since the case was initially filed, it looks as though work has been done in order to make the site accessible.

This is positive news, although we don't want every site to have to be sued before they're made accessible of course. Given that it seems to be a particularly decisive time for web accessibility, I'd like to quickly talk about the most recent case to impact the world of web accessibility and the wide-ranging implications it will have.

Robles vs. Domino's Pizza

In 2016 Guillermo Robles, who is blind, filed a lawsuit against Domino's pizza in the United States. As a screen reader user, Mr. Robles tried on multiple occasions to order food through their website but wasn't able to because the site was inaccessible.[8]

The reaction was mixed. The 9th district court, who oversaw the case, ruled that Domino's had indeed violated the American Disabilities Act (the US equivalent of the United Kingdom Equality Act) by creating a site that was inaccessible to those who are blind or visually impaired. However, the sting here was that, because there were technically no specific guidelines in the United States on *how* to make a site that was compliant, the case was dismissed.[9] Unlike countries like Australia, America hadn't officially adopted WCAG (or any other set of rules) as their guideline or benchmark test (American courts had been using WCAG to check accessibility since a case in 2017, but it has not been enshrined in law), so the 9th district court decided there was nothing that could be legally enforced. The Department of Justice had actually planned to publish regulations for site accessibility as far back as 2010, but in 2017 announced that they wouldn't be doing so.[10] This was a frustrating decision seeing as the district court actually sided with Mr. Robles.

However, in 2019, a federal appeals court reversed the decision of the district court, ruling in favor of Mr. Robles.[11] They argued that the company's website and mobile app are critical avenues for the public to order online and find a nearby Domino's restaurant. More importantly, they made it clear that just because there are no specific rules to legally adhere to in order to be accessible, that doesn't mean that it's fine not to be. In his 25-page opinion, Circuit Judge Owens stated that the American Disabilities Act has been clear on equal access for those with disabilities since 1990:

> *full and equal enjoyment of the goods, services, facilities, privileges, advantages, or accommodations" to people with disabilities.*[12]

Furthermore, despite there being no official regulation, the Department of Justice have shown in cases since 1996 that this act applies to websites as well as physical stores:

> *While we understand why Domino's wants... specific guidelines for website and app accessibility, the Constitution only requires that Domino's receive fair notice of its legal duties, not a blueprint for compliance with its statutory obligations*[13]

Ironically this ruling further entrenches the guidelines that Domino's and other companies had been arguing didn't officially exist. WCAG is now an even more tenable part of case law – reinforcing a precedent for its use as a guideline and providing a clear (but not exhaustive) set of rules to ensure that websites are inclusive. If sites are not compliant to the lowest level (A), they're open to penalties under the American Disabilities Act.

Mr. Robles' lawyer, Jacob Manning, summed up the importance of this very neatly:

> *We're very happy with this opinion because we think it will eliminate many of the common objections to accessibility and encourage companies to just start the process of making sites accessible instead of quibbling over the precise standard...In the case of Domino's, you can't order a pizza. Isn't that the test? We aren't arguing over a comma here.*[14]

The saga didn't stop there though. Instead of accepting the ruling and making their website accessible, Domino's decided, in what experts called an unprecedented move, to petition the supreme court to get the decision reversed.[15]

What makes Domino's recent actions even more ridiculous is that, in an affidavit from the original lawsuit, they claimed that it would cost $38,000 to sort the original issue that Mr. Robles opened the case over.[16] Dominos turnover in 2018 was $3.43 billion.[17] Instead of the minor investment (in the grand scheme of things) to make the experience more accessible for blind users, the company decided instead to spend much more than this on legal fees to fight it (I'm purely speculating here, but the legal proceedings have lasted for well over 3 years and they're asking now for it to be reopened – it's likely that it will have cost them far more than $38,000).

This makes neither moral nor financial sense. Mr. Robles (and I'm sure others) want Domino's to have an accessible website so that they can buy their products. Chances are the improvements would also return much more in revenue than the $38,000 required to solve the initial accessibility issue.[18] Christopher Danielson said it best:

> *"There is a ton of space for innovation in this area. Rather than refusing to take the money of those of us with disabilities, why not innovate and take our money?"*[19]

The result of this case, more than any other before it, held immense consequences for the world of web accessibility. If the ruling was upheld, it would send a clear message to all businesses – they must take the needs of people with disabilities online into account – along with clear, approved guidelines, in the form of WCAG, on how to do so.

The alternative was dire. The US government would lose its teeth when it comes to enforcing accessibility –making it easier for companies to avoid their responsibility to these users. Christopher Danielsen of the National Federation of the Blind commented:

> *If businesses are allowed to say, 'We do not have to make our websites accessible to blind people,' that would be shutting blind people out of the economy in the 21st century.*[20]

With charities and disability foundations lining up behind Mr. Robles, and business groups like the Chamber of Commerce and the National Retail Federation lining up behind Domino's, the ruling was a big moment for accessibility.

I am pleased to say that the Supreme Court eventually decided to reject Dominos' appeal. This is, without a doubt, a massive win for accessibility, and the ruling was described as "the right call on every level" and "a credit to our society". However, this *still* doesn't firmly close the case – with the original ruling still in place, Domino's can fight Mr. Roble's claims in court and, when asked for comment, said that "we look forward to presenting our case at the trial court." [21]

It's clear that, despite this victory, a lot more needs to be done to ensure the equal treatment of those with a wide variety of access needs. We spoke at the start of the book about an "onslaught" of accessibility-related lawsuits in the last 2 years alone, and the harsh fact is that those who rely most on accessibility and inclusivity online are currently the ones who have to fight for it. If we are to create a more inclusive world, this needs to be a fight we all engage in, not just in courtrooms but in the workplace, and whenever we build anything online. If Domino's had won, this fight would have only become more important, and the fact that they lost doesn't mean that we can take a step back. In this corner of the accessibility movement, we still have the ability to ensure that the right things get done on each site we touch, without it ever having to reach the news, or a courtroom.

Final words

I want you to make your site accessible. Throughout this book, I've been trying to convince you why you should and show you how to do so. Having gotten this far, it's now time for you to take these ideas and move forward with them.

How you move forward now relies on not only understanding these points but, crucially, whether you decide to implement them – not just for a few weeks but every day. As you do that, I would hope that you keep several themes from this book in mind.

First, in every chapter we have seen countless examples of how, if you design with accessibility in mind, it will make your websites easier for everybody to use. Remember: **Access needs are user needs**, regardless of what form they take.

The material that we have covered allows you to think about the accessibility of wider parts of your site, such as its imagery, content, and how it communicates with users. However, and this is important, you're now also capable of drilling down into the specific needs of users with certain disabilities, from specific types of colour blindness to individual forms of cognitive and motor impairment – **you haven't just picked up a vague knowledge of these areas, you've engaged in great detail** with them.

We have also seen that **if you design with one access need in mind, you end up removing barriers for other users** (sometimes unexpectedly). In every chapter there has been many opportunities to say "this is also useful for users who experience this." Therefore, even if it isn't possible to hit every access need in this book, learning to understand as many needs as you can, spotting barriers, and implementing these suggestions will allow you to cater for a whole host of other unexpected needs.

Given this wide array of needs, there has also been a consistent theme of not following just one ruleset or group of guidelines when it comes to ensuring accessibility, because it's not as simple as "ticking boxes." **Being "compliant" to rules and frameworks like WCAG doesn't guarantee**

accessibility. This should be underlined and in capitals. Instead, you need to approach accessibility from the perspective of users, and the challenges and barriers they face, to ensure that your websites are inclusive.

When you design and build for a disability, you are trying to remove barriers to content and help empower users. We've covered a wealth of examples, but the common thread has always been the **mindset** you need to get into in order to both identify them and then solve/improve them.

I've also aimed to provide value for everyone involved in the building or maintaining of a website. Beyond the practical coding examples for developers, we've looked at this topic from the perspective of design, user experience, content creation, and testing. Hopefully having read the book, even if you don't code, you now feel as though you've learned enough to think about access needs on your sites and other projects, and hopefully you could explain why it's so important to others. This alone will have a massive impact on the awareness and advancement of web accessibility. This is because **when everyone gets into an accessibility-driven mindset it starts, slowly, to become a part of our culture**, and eventually, it should become second nature.

Tackling inclusivity from a few different professional perspectives is especially useful, because it helps ensure that **accessibility is considered throughout a site's lifecycle, not retrospectively**. I've covered all of these areas because, of course, it would be great for every area of a site's build and maintenance to have been carried out with accessibility in mind. Hopefully one day awareness will be good enough that we won't need "accessibility champions." For now, you can act as the accessibility champion in your team or company, to start spreading your new-found knowledge and awareness.

It's simply the right thing to do. So, let's go and make a truly inclusive Web together, for those we care for and those we've never met.

Notes

1. Paul Bohmon, *Hire Real People with Disabilities for QA Testing,* Deque University, (2019), <https://dequeuniversity.com/tips/hire-people-with-disabilities> [accessed 13/09/2019].

2. Gov.uk, *Running research sessions with people with disabilities,* (03/10/2017), <www.gov.uk/service-manual/user-research/running-research-sessions-with-people-with-disabilities> [accessed 13/09/2019].

3. Peter McNally, *Tips For Conducting Usability Studies With Participants With Disabilities,* (12/03/2018), <www.smashingmagazine.com/2018/03/tips-conducting-usability-studies-participants-disabilities/> [accessed 13/09/2019].

4. Peter McNally, *Tips For Conducting Usability Studies With Participants With Disabilities,* (12/03/2018), <www.smashingmagazine.com/2018/03/tips-conducting-usability-studies-participants-disabilities/> [accessed 13/09/2019].

5. Paul Bohmon, *Hire Real People with Disabilities for QA Testing,* Deque University, (2019), <https://dequeuniversity.com/tips/hire-people-with-disabilities> [accessed 13/09/2019].

6. Paul Bohmon, *Hire Real People with Disabilities for QA Testing,* Deque University, (2019), <https://dequeuniversity.com/tips/hire-people-with-disabilities> [accessed 13/09/2019].

7. Alistair Duggin, *Creating the UK government's accessibility empathy lab,* Gov.uk, (20/06/2018), <https://gds.blog.gov.uk/2018/06/20/creating-the-uk-governments-accessibility-empathy-lab/> [accessed 13/09/2019].

8. Tucker Higgins, *A blind man couldn't order pizza from Domino's. The company wants the Supreme Court to say websites don't have to be accessible,* CNBC, (25/06/2019), <www.cnbc.com/2019/07/25/dominos-asks-supreme-court-to-say-disability-protections-dont-apply-online.html> [accessed 13/09/2019].

9. Courtlistener, *Guillermo Robles v. Domino's Pizza LLC, 17-55504 (9th Cir. 2019),* (15/01/2019), <www.courtlistener.com/opinion/4581582/guillermo-robles-v-dominos-pizza-llc/> [accessed 13/09/2019].

10. Amanda Robert, *ADA questions remain over web accessibility cases and the lack of DOJ regulations,* (01/07/2019), <www.abajournal.com/magazine/article/ada-web-accessibility-doj-regulations> [accessed 13/09/2019].

11. United States Court of Appeals for the Ninth Circuit, Robles v. Domino's Pizza, (15/01/2019), <http://cdn.ca9.uscourts.gov/datastore/opinions/2019/01/15/17-55504.pdf> [accessed 13/09/2019].

12. Liebert Cassidy Whitmore, *Website Accessibility Under The ADA: A Tale As Old As 1996*, (30/08/2019), <www.courthousenews.com/wp-content/uploads/2019/01/Dominos-Ruling.pdf> [accessed 13/09/2019].

13. Liebert Cassidy Whitmore, *Website Accessibility Under The ADA: A Tale As Old As 1996*, (30/08/2019), <www.courthousenews.com/wp-content/uploads/2019/01/Dominos-Ruling.pdf> [accessed 13/09/2019].

14. Karina Brown, *Court Says Domino's Pizza Website Must Be Accessible to the Blind,* (15/01/2019), <www.courthousenews.com/court-says-dominos-pizza-website-must-be-accessible-to-the-blind/> [accessed 13/09/2019].

15. The Supreme Court of the United States, *Domino's Pizza v. Guillermo Robles – Petition for a writ of certIiorari*, (03/06/2019), <www.supremecourt.gov/DocketPDF/18/18-1539/102950/20190613153319483_DominosPetition.pdf> [accessed 13/09/2019].

16. Jared Spool, *Twitter*, (01/08/2019), <https://twitter.com/jmspool/status/1157021965020016640> [accessed 13/09/2019].

17. S. Lock, *Revenue of Domino's Pizza 2006-2018*, Statista, (09/08/2019), <www.statista.com/statistics/207133/revenue-of-dominos-pizza-2017/> [accessed 13/09/2019].

18. These numerous sources have cited this figure
    from the court documents: Jared Spool, *Twitter*,
    (04/09/2019), <https://twitter.com/jmspool/
    status/1169255821735342080> [accessed 13/09/2019]
    + Daniel S. Levine, *Domino's Fights Website
    Accessibility Ruling in Supreme Court, Social Media
    Weighs In*, (02/08/2019), <https://popculture.
    com/trending/2019/08/02/dominos-fights-
    accessibility-ruling-supreme-court-social-media-
    weighs-in/> [accessed 13/09/2019] + Amanda Rush,
    Domino's is evil, (02/08/2019),[accessed 13/09/2019].

19. Tucker Higgins, *A blind man couldn't order pizza
    from Domino's. The company wants the Supreme
    Court to say websites don't have to be accessible*,
    CNBC, (25/06/2019), <www.cnbc.com/2019/07/25/
    dominos-asks-supreme-court-to-say-
    disability-protections-dont-apply-online.
    html> [accessed 13/09/2019].

20. Tucker Higgins, *A blind man couldn't order pizza
    from Domino's. The company wants the Supreme
    Court to say websites don't have to be accessible*,
    CNBC, (25/06/2019), <www.cnbc.com/2019/07/25/
    dominos-asks-supreme-court-to-say-
    disability-protections-dont-apply-online.
    html> [accessed 13/09/2019].

21. Tucker Higgins, *Supreme Court hands victory to
    blind man who sued Domino's over site accessibility*,
    CNBC, (07/10/2019), < https://www.cnbc.
    com/2019/10/07/dominos-supreme-court.html>
    [accessed 16/10/2019].

Index

A

A11y project, 292, 395
Accessibility, 1
    access users, 442
    Cerf, Vinton, 1
    competitive advantages, 9, 10
    disability-driven
        approach, 1, 10
    Duggin, Alastair, 447
    help option, 445
    legal action, 8
    mainstream attention, 7, 8
    meaning, 446, 447
    QA testing, 444
    state of
        approaches, 5
        Buller, James, 4
        definition, 6
        disability-driven
          accessibility, 5
        WCAG, 3
        W3C, 3
Accessibility testing, 424
    A11y machine, 429, 430
    AATT, 430
    AccessLint, 425–427
    automation, 425

Pa11y, 428–430
    WAVE evaluation tool, 430, 431
Accessible overlays
    content, focus, 104, 105
    features, 103
    feedback modal overlaid, 104
    keyboard trap, 105
    login modal window, 106
    overlaid content, 109–111
    return option, 111
    tab focus, 107–109
    third-party software, 112
Accessible Rich Internet
        Applications (ARIA)
    aria-hidden, 26
    aria-label, 26
    aria-live, 25, 26
    attributes, 23, 24
    benefit of, 22
    components, 24, 25
    HTML attributes, 20
    HTML5 implicit mapping, 27, 28
    labels, 26
    reCAPTCHA verification, 23
    roles, 21, 22
    states and properties, 21
    support, 27
    websites, 20

© Ashley Firth 2019
A. Firth, *Practical Web Inclusion and Accessibility*,
https://doi.org/10.1007/978-1-4842-5452-3